Advancements in Applied Metaheuristic Computing

Nilanjan Dey
Techno India College of Technology, India

A volume in the Advances in Data
Mining and Database Management
(ADMDM) Book Series

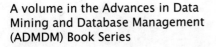

Published in the United States of America by
   IGI Global
   Engineering Science Reference (an imprint of IGI Global)
   701 E. Chocolate Avenue
   Hershey PA, USA 17033
   Tel: 717-533-8845
   Fax: 717-533-8661
   E-mail: cust@igi-global.com
   Web site: http://www.igi-global.com

Library of Congress Cataloging-in-Publication Data

Names: Dey, Nilanjan, 1984- editor.
Title: Advancements in applied metaheuristic computing / Nilanjan Dey, editor.
Description: Hershey, PA : Engineering Science Reference, [2018] | Includes
   bibliographical references and index.
Identifiers: LCCN 2017028945| ISBN 9781522541516 (hardcover) | ISBN
   9781522541523 (ebook)
Subjects: LCSH: Systems engineering--Data processing. | Heuristic algorithms.
   | Mathematical optimization. | Artificial intelligence.
Classification: LCC TA168 .A286 2018 | DDC 006.3--dc23 LC record available at https://lccn.loc.
gov/2017028945

This book is published in the IGI Global book series Advances in Data Mining and Database Management (ADMDM) (ISSN: 2327-1981; eISSN: 2327-199X)

British Cataloguing in Publication Data
A Cataloguing in Publication record for this book is available from the British Library.

All work contributed to this book is new, previously-unpublished material.
The views expressed in this book are those of the authors, but not necessarily of the publisher.

For electronic access to this publication, please contact: eresources@igi-global.com.

Advances in Data Mining and Database Management (ADMDM) Book Series

ISSN:2327-1981
EISSN:2327-199X

Editor-in-Chief: David Taniar, Monash University, Australia

MISSION

With the large amounts of information available to organizations in today's digital world, there is a need for continual research surrounding emerging methods and tools for collecting, analyzing, and storing data.

The **Advances in Data Mining & Database Management (ADMDM)** series aims to bring together research in information retrieval, data analysis, data warehousing, and related areas in order to become an ideal resource for those working and studying in these fields. IT professionals, software engineers, academicians and upper-level students will find titles within the ADMDM book series particularly useful for staying up-to-date on emerging research, theories, and applications in the fields of data mining and database management.

COVERAGE

- Database Testing
- Association Rule Learning
- Enterprise systems
- Quantitative Structure–Activity Relationship
- Profiling Practices
- Decision Support Systems
- Sequence analysis
- Data warehousing
- Database Security
- Customer Analytics

IGI Global is currently accepting manuscripts for publication within this series. To submit a proposal for a volume in this series, please contact our Acquisition Editors at Acquisitions@igi-global.com or visit: http://www.igi-global.com/publish/.

Titles in this Series

For a list of additional titles in this series, please visit:
https://www.igi-global.com/book-series/advances-data-mining-database-management/37146

Deep Learning Innovations and Their Convergence Wih Big Data
S. Karthik (SNS College of Technology, Anna University, India) Anand Paul (Kyungpook National University, South Korea) and N. Karthikeyan (Mizan-Tepi University, Ethiopia)
Information Science Reference • ©2018 • 265pp • H/C (ISBN: 9781522530152) • US $205.00

Modern Technologies for Big Data Classification and Clustering
Hari Seetha (Vellore Institute of Technology-Andhra Pradesh, India) M. Narasimha Murty (Indian Institute of Science, India) and B. K. Tripathy (VIT University, India)
Information Science Reference • ©2018 • 360pp • H/C (ISBN: 9781522528050) • US $215.00

Data Visualization and Statistical Literacy for Open and Big Data
Theodosia Prodromou (University of New England, Australia)
Information Science Reference • ©2017 • 365pp • H/C (ISBN: 9781522525127) • US $205.00

Web Semantics for Textual and Visual Information Retrieval
Aarti Singh (Guru Nanak Girls College, Yamuna Nagar, India) Nilanjan Dey (Techno India College of Technology, India) Amira S. Ashour (Tanta University, Egypt & Taif University, Saudi Arabia) and V. Santhi (VIT University, India)
Information Science Reference • ©2017 • 290pp • H/C (ISBN: 9781522524830) • US $185.00

Advancing Cloud Database Systems and Capacity Planning With Dynamic Applications
Narendra Kumar Kamila (C.V. Raman College of Engineering, India)
Information Science Reference • ©2017 • 430pp • H/C (ISBN: 9781522520139) • US $210.00

Web Data Mining and the Development of Knowledge-Based Decision Support Systems
G. Sreedhar (Rashtriya Sanskrit Vidyapeetha (Deemed University), India)
Information Science Reference • ©2017 • 409pp • H/C (ISBN: 9781522518778) • US $165.00

Intelligent Multidimensional Data Clustering and Analysis
Siddhartha Bhattacharyya (RCC Institute of Information Technology, India) Sourav De (Cooch Behar Government Engineering College, India) Indrajit Pan (RCC Institute of Information Technology, India) and Paramartha Dutta (Visva-Bharati University, India)
Information Science Reference • ©2017 • 450pp • H/C (ISBN: 9781522517764) • US $210.00

For an enitre list of titles in this series, please visit:
https://www.igi-global.com/book-series/advances-data-mining-database-management/37146

701 East Chocolate Avenue, Hershey, PA 17033, USA
Tel: 717-533-8845 x100 • Fax: 717-533-8661
E-Mail: cust@igi-global.com • www.igi-global.com

Table of Contents

Section 2
Genetic Algorithm Applications

Detailed Table of Contents

Section 1
Meta-Heuristic Optimization-Algorithms-Based Advanced Applications

    G. V. Nagesh Kumar, Vignans Institute of Information Technology
        (Autonomous), India
    B. Venkateswara Rao, V. R. Siddhartha Engineering College
        (Autonomous), India
    D. Deepak Chowdary, Dr. L. Bullayya College of Engineering, India
    Polamraju V. S. Sobhan, Vignan's Foundation for Science, Technology,
        and Research University, India

In this chapter a multi objective optimal power flow (OPF) is obtained by using latest Metaheuristic optimization techniques BAT search algorithm (BAT), cuckoo search algorithm (CSA) and firefly algorithm (FA) with Unified power flow controller (UPFC). UPFC is a voltage source converter type Flexible Alternating Current Transmission System (FACTS) device. It is able to control the voltage magnitudes, voltage angles and line impedances individually or simultaneously. To enhance the power system performance, the optimal power flow has been incorporated UPFC along with BAT algorithm, cuckoo search algorithm and firefly algorithm based multi objective function comprising of two objectives those are total real power loss and the fuel cost of total real power generation. The BAT algorithm, cuckoo search algorithm and firefly algorithm based OPF has been examined and tested on a 5 bus test system and modified IEEE 30 bus system without and with UPFC. The results obtained with BAT algorithm, cuckoo search algorithm and firefly algorithms are compared with Differential Evaluation (DE).

J. Sangeetha, PES University, India
Keerthiraj Nagaraj, University of Florida, USA
K. N. Balasubramanya Murthy, PES University, India
Ram P. Rustagi, PES University, India

The WiMAX network provides an efficient QoS to the large number of users. The real time and non-real time multimedia applications are gaining importance in the WiMAX network. To support such applications, there is a need to propose an efficient QoS of traffic prediction mechanism for the WiMAX networks. To address this, the authors have applied Gene Expression Programming technique for CBR based traffic and file transfer applications in the WiMAX network. The main focus of this chapter is to develop the mathematical expressions for throughput of the network by considering bandwidth, average end-to-end delay and average jitter as inputs for CBR based traffic and file transfer applications. This expression helps to analyze and predict the QoS of traffic of a given network. The simulation results show that the model values and the target values match with better approximation. Experimentally GEP performs better than other existing algorithms. Furthermore, sensitivity analysis has been carried out for both the applications

Krishna Gopal Dhal, Midnapore College (Autonomous), India
Sanjoy Das, University of Kalyani, India

This study concentrates to develop one novel parameterized Bi-Histogram Fuzzy Contrast Stretching (BHFCS) method for enhancing the contrast of the grey level as well as color images properly. The parameters of this method have been optimized by employing one modified Chaotic Differential Evolution (CDE) with the combined assistance of Fractal Dimension (FD) and Quality Index based on Local Variance (QILV) as objective function. Experimental results prove that the modified DE gives better result than particle swarm optimization (PSO), genetic algorithm (GA) and traditional DE in this enhancement domain and the used objective function is also very useful to preserve the image's original brightness which is the one of the main criterion of the consumer electronics field.

    R. Gowri, Periyar University, India
    R. Rathipriya, Periyar University, India

In this scientific world, the evolution of the disease is predominantly higher than the medicines. The diagnosis and prognosis of such diseases will differ from patient to patient. In this scenario, the protein motifs are very useful for understanding the functionality and lethality of the disease. Most of the existing techniques are supervised approaches which require prior knowledge of the data. As the protein sequences are unsupervised data, the unsupervised data mining techniques like Clustering and 2-way Clustering are chosen to mine the homologous protein motifs. The quality of the results is refined further using the bio-inspired computing models like Particle Swarm Optimization, Genetic Algorithm and Venus Flytrap Optimization in this research work. The existing approaches can mine homologous patterns with structure similarity of 75 percent which is increased in this proposed approach. The results from these three different approaches show that the bio-inspired based 2-way Clustering approaches can mine more homologous motifs than the clustering approaches.

    Mohammad Zadshakoyan, University of Tabriz, Iran
    Vahid Pourmostaghimi, University of Tabriz, Iran

The state of a cutting tool is an important factor in any metal cutting process as additional costs in terms of scrapped components, machine tool breakage and unscheduled downtime result from worn tool usage. Therefore, tool wear prediction plays an important role in industry automation for higher productivity and acceptable product quality. Therefore, in order to increase the productivity of turning process, various researches have been made recently for tool wear estimation and classification in turning process. Chip form is one of the most important factors commonly considered in evaluating the performance of machining process. On account of the effect of the progressive tool wear on the shape and geometrical features of produced chip, it is possible to predict some measurable machining outputs such as crater wear. According to experimentally performed researches, cutting speed and cutting time are two extremely effective parameters which contribute to the development of the crater wear on the tool rake face. As a result, these parameters will change the chip radius and geometry. This chapter presents the development of the genetic equation for the tool wear using occurred changes in chip radius in turning process.

The development of the equation combines different methods and technologies like evolutionary methods, manufacturing technology, measuring and control technology with the adequate hardware and software support. The results obtained from genetic equation and experiments showed that obtained genetic equations are correlated well with the experimental data. Furthermore, it can be used for tool wear estimation during cutting process and because of its parametric form, genetic equation enables us to analyze the effect of input parameters on the crater wear parameters.

Chapter 6

    Shouvik Chakraborty, University of Kalyani, India
    Sankhadeep Chatterjee, University of Calcutta, India
    Amira S. Ashour, Tanta University, Egypt
    Kalyani Mali, University of Kalyani, India
    Nilanjan Dey, Techno India College of Technology, India

Biomedical imaging is considered main procedure to acquire valuable physical information about the human body and some other biological species. It produces specialized images of different parts of the biological species for clinical analysis. It assimilates various specialized domains including nuclear medicine, radiological imaging, Positron emission tomography (PET), and microscopy. From the early discovery of X-rays, progress in biomedical imaging continued resulting in highly sophisticated medical imaging modalities, such as magnetic resonance imaging (MRI), ultrasound, Computed Tomography (CT), and lungs monitoring. These biomedical imaging techniques assist physicians for faster and accurate analysis and treatment. The present chapter discussed the impact of intelligent computing methods for biomedical image analysis and healthcare. Different Artificial Intelligence (AI) based automated biomedical image analysis are considered. Different approaches are discussed including the AI ability to resolve various medical imaging problems. It also introduced the popular AI procedures that employed to solve some special problems in medicine. Artificial Neural Network (ANN) and support vector machine (SVM) are active to classify different types of images from various imaging modalities. Different diagnostic analysis, such as mammogram analysis, MRI brain image analysis, CT images, PET images, and bone/retinal analysis using ANN, feed-forward back propagation ANN, probabilistic ANN, and extreme learning machine continuously. Various optimization techniques of ant colony optimization (ACO), genetic algorithm (GA), particle swarm optimization (PSO) and other bio-inspired procedures are also frequently conducted for feature extraction/selection and classification. The advantages and disadvantages of some AI approaches are discussed in the present chapter along with some suggested future research perspectives.

Chapter 7

Load changes in any one of interconnected power system that influence the system response from their nominal values. The Proportional–Integral- Derivative (PID) controller is employed to mitigate this issue as a secondary controller in addition to the Superconducting Magnetic Energy Storage (SMES) unit. In Automatic Generation Control (AGC), the current work proposed an Ant Colony Optimization (ACO) technique to tune PID controller gain values of multi-area interconnected thermal power system. The gain value of PID controller is tuned by using the ACO techniques. The system response is compared with and without considering SMES unit in the system. The comparative results clearly established that the system response with SMES unit improve the performance of system during sudden load disturbance.

Artificial intelligence is the outlet of computer science apprehensive with creating computers that perform as humans. It compromises expert systems, playing games, natural language, and robotics. However, soft computing (SC) varies from the hard (conventional) computing in its tolerant of partial truth, uncertainty, imprecision, and approximation, thus, it models the human mind. The most common SC techniques include neural networks, fuzzy systems, machine learning, and the meta-heuristic stochastic algorithms (e.g., Cellular automata, ant colony optimization, Memetic algorithms, particle swarms, Tabu search, evolutionary computation and simulated annealing. Due to the required accurate diseases analysis, magnetic resonance imaging, computed tomography images and images of other modalities segmentation remains a challenging problem. Over the past years, soft computing approaches attract attention of several researchers for problems solving in medical data applications. Image segmentation is the process that partitioned an image into some groups based on similarity measures. This process is employed for abnormalities volumetric analysis in medical images to identify the disease nature. Recently, meta-heuristic algorithms are conducted to support the segmentation techniques. In the current chapter, different segmentation procedures are addressed. Several meta-heuristic approaches are reported with highlights on their procedures. Finally, several medical applications using meta-heuristic based-approaches for segmentation are discussed.

Section 2
Genetic Algorithm Applications

Chapter 9

Hicham El Hassani, ENSEM Casablanca, Morocco
Said Benkachcha, ENSEM Casablanca, Morocco
Jamal Benhra, ENSEM Casablanca, Morocco

Inspired by nature, genetic algorithms (GA) are among the greatest meta-heuristics optimization methods that have proved their effectiveness to conventional NP-hard problems, especially the traveling salesman problem (TSP) which is one of the most studied Supply chain management problems. This paper proposes a new crossover operator called Jump Crossover (JMPX) for solving the travelling salesmen problem using a genetic algorithm (GA) for near-optimal solutions, to conclude on its efficiency compared to solutions quality given by other conventional operators to the same problem, namely, Partially matched crossover (PMX), Edge recombination Crossover (ERX) and r-opt heuristic with consideration of computational overload. We adopt the path representation technique for our chromosome which is the most direct representation and a low mutation rate to isolate the search space exploration ability of each crossover. The experimental results show that in most cases JMPX can remarkably improve the solution quality of the GA compared to the two existing classic crossover approaches and the r-opt heuristic.

Chapter 10

Sarat Chandra Nayak, Kommuri Pratap Reddy Institute of Technology,
India
Bijan Bihari Misra, Silicon Institute of Technology, India
Himansu Sekhar Behera, Veer Surendra Sai University of Technology,
India

Financial time series forecasting has been regarded as a challenging issue because of successful prediction could yield significant profit, hence require an efficient prediction system. Conventional ANN based models are not competent systems. Higher order neural networks have several advantages over traditional neural networks such as stronger approximation, higher fault tolerance capacity and faster convergence. With the aim of achieving improved forecasting accuracy, this article develops and evaluates the performance of an adaptive single layer second order neural network with GA based training (ASONN-GA). The global search ability of GA has been incorporated with the better generalization ability of a second order neural network and the model is found quite capable in handling the uncertainties and nonlinearities associated with the financial time series. The model takes minimal input data and considered the partially optimized weight set from previous training, hence a significant reduction in training time. The efficiency of the model has been evaluated by forecasting one-step-ahead closing prices and exchange rates of five real stock markets and it is revealed that the ASONN-GA model achieves better forecasting accuracy over other state of the art models.

Chapter 11
  Sankhadeep Chatterjee, University of Calcutta, India
  Sarbartha Sarkar, Indian Institute of Technology Dhanbad, India
  Nilanjan Dey, Techno India College of Technology, India
  Amira S. Ashour, Tanta University, Egypt
  Soumya Sen, University of Calcutta, India

Water pollution due to industrial and domestic reasons is highly affecting the water quality. In undeveloped and developed countries, it has become a major reason behind a number of water borne diseases. Poor public health is putting an extra economic liability in order to deploy precautionary measures against these diseases. Recent research works have been directed toward more sustainable solutions to this problem. It has been revealed that good quality of water supply can not only improve the public health, it also accelerates economic growth of a geographical location as well. Water quality prediction using machine learning methods is still at its primitive stage. Besides, most of the studies did not follow any national or international standard for water quality prediction. In the current work, both the problems have been addressed. First, advanced machine learning methods, namely Artificial Neural Networks (ANNs) supported by a well-known multi-objective optimization algorithm called the Non-dominated Sorting Genetic Algorithm-II (NSGA-II) has been used to classify the water samples into two different classes. Secondly, Indian national standard for water quality (IS 10500:2012) has been utilized for this classification task. The hybrid NN-NSGA-II model is compared with another two well-known meta-heuristic supported ANN classifiers, namely ANN trained by Genetic Algorithm (NN-GA) and by Particle Swarm Optimization (NN-PSO).

Apart from that, the support vector machine (SVM) has also been included in the comparative study. Besides analysing the performance based on several performance measuring methods, the statistical significance of the results obtained by NN-NSGA-II has been judged by performing Wilcoxon rank sum test with 5% confidence level. Results have indicated the ingenuity of the proposed NN-NSGA-II model over the other classifiers under current study.

Preface

INTRODUCTION

Recently, researchers have attracted to study the nature laws as a good source for inspiration of effective meta-heuristic algorithms to provide optimal solutions to develop intelligent systems and complicated problems. Meta-heuristic algorithms have long history back to evolutionary computing and genetic algorithms. Natural phenomena as well as animal behaviors inspired nature-inspired algorithms, such as genetic algorithms, particle swarm optimization algorithms, artificial bee colony algorithms, ant colony optimization algorithms and differential evolution algorithms that have been widely applied in various domains. The living creatures' ways, such as interaction, movement, and adaption to their environments offer ideas for meta-heuristic designs. Due to their established competence and merits in realizing novel and optimal solutions for complex problems, nature-inspired algorithms have fascinated engineers' and researchers' attention in numerous engineering fields.

The meta-heuristic algorithms prevalence is established in several applications for different domains, such as financial optimisation, engineering design, computer network routing and scheduling. These applications are carried out to solve several types of problems, including large-scaled, continuous/discrete/ mixed, combinatorial, multimodal optimisation problems. Different concepts and components in different meta-heuristics algorithms in order to analyze their similarities and differences are considered in this book. In addition, this book includes up-to-date approaches in the domain of nature-inspired algorithms and their engineering applications. It intends a set of high-quality and leading contributions on proposed algorithms, technologies and concepts that use meta-heuristic algorithm algorithms in several research areas. The book focuses on exploring different applications for the meta-heuristics optimization algorithms in several applications.

OBJECTIVE OF THE BOOK

This book considers the foremost optimization algorithms in several applications. It deals primarily with methods and approaches that include meta-heuristics for further systems improvements. This book grants substantial frameworks and the most contemporary empirical research outcomes in employing optimization algorithms. It is edited for researchers, academicians, advanced-level students, and technology developers and professionals working in various disciplines.

ORGANIZATION OF THE BOOK

The book contains 11 chapters that are organized in two sections as shown below. The first eight chapters outline the various meta-heuristic optimization algorithms in different applications. The second section includes three chapters focusing on the genetic algorithms concept and applications in several domains.

Section 1: Meta-Heuristic Optimization-Algorithms-Based Advanced Applications (Chapters 1-8)

This section elaborated different meta-heuristic algorithms for solving multi-objective problems. Another context is introduced related to predicting the traffic quality of services in WiMAX network supported by optimization algorithms. Contrast enhancement is also proposed using modified Chaotic Differential Evolution along with Fractal Dimension and Quality Index based on Local Variance objective function. In the medical domain, the role of the intelligent computing and the optimization algorithms is also covered.

Chapter 1

This chapter included meta-heuristic optimization algorithms have been conducted to solve multi- objective optimal power flow problem in the presence of Unified power flow controller. The results demonstrated the proposed approach robustness with the Unified power flow controller. Firefly algorithm, BAT algorithm, and cuckoo search algorithm provided less total generation cost compared to differential evaluation algorithm based optimal power flow.

Chapter 2

The real and non-real time multimedia applications have a significant role in the WiMAX network. This chapter is carried out to develop a mathematical expression for the network throughput by considering average end-to-end delay, bandwidth, and average jitter. An efficient traffic QoS prediction mechanism for the WiMAX networks is proposed based on Gene Expression Programming technique.

Chapter 3

This current chapter introduced parameterized Bi-histogram fuzzy contrast stretching method to enhance the image crucially by preserving its original brightness based on associated three parameters with diverse ranges.

Chapter 4

In biological systems, protein motifs have a significant role to study their characteristics. For the unsupervised protein sequences data, clustering approaches are proposed for protein motif prediction in this chapter. The bio-inspired computing models, such as the particle swarm optimization and genetic algorithms based k-means are proposed.

Chapter 5

In industry automation, tool wear prediction is imperative to achieve higher productivity and acceptable product quality. This chapter developed the genetic equation in machining process, where the variation of chip radius at different stages of progressive tool wear for the inter-relationships is measured. The chip radius reduction with tool wear progression shows a consistent pattern for the flat faced tool under all used cutting conditions.

Chapter 6

Intelligent computing methods have great impact in the biomedical image analysis and healthcare. In this chapter, different artificial intelligence based automated biomedical image analysis. Different diagnostic analysis using feed-forward back propagation neural network are considered. Various optimization techniques, such as ant colony optimization, genetic algorithm, particle swarm optimization and other bio-inspired procedures are also frequently conducted for feature extraction/ selection and classification.

Chapter 7

The Proportional-Integral-Derivative (PID) controller is used as a secondary controller in addition to the Superconducting Magnetic Energy Storage (SMES) unit. This chapter proposed an Ant Colony Optimization (ACO) algorithm to tune PID controller gain values of multi-interconnected thermal power system. A comparative study is conducted to compare the system response with and without considering SMES unit in the system.

Chapter 8

Artificial intelligence is the core of computer science apprehensive with creating computers that perform as humans. Accurate diseases analysis, magnetic resonance imaging, computed tomography images and images of other modalities segmentation remains a challenging problem. Image segmentation is employed for abnormalities volumetric analysis in medical images to identify the disease nature. Recently, meta-heuristic algorithms are conducted to support the segmentation techniques. This chapter addresses different segmentation procedures. Several meta-heuristic approaches are reported with highlights on their procedures. Finally, several medical applications using meta-heuristic based-approaches for segmentation are discussed.

Section 2: Genetic Algorithm Applications (Chapters 9-11)

Genetic algorithms have various applications in several domains. This section reports the Genetic algorithms fundamental algorithm as applied in several real-life applications. It highlights the use of multi-objective genetic algorithm as well for water quality prediction. In addition, this section discussed the financial time series prediction using the genetic algorithm to support the adaptive second order neural network.

Chapter 9

This chapter proposed a new crossover operator called Jump Crossover (JMPX) to solve the travelling salesmen problem using a genetic algorithm for near-optimal solutions. The path representation technique for the chromosome which is the most direct representation and a low mutation rate to isolate the search space exploration ability of each crossover is adopted.

Chapter 10

Financial time series forecasting is a challenging issue that requires efficient prediction system. In this chapter, the performance of an adaptive single layer second order neural network based on the genetic algorithm is evaluated. The efficiency of the propose model is evaluated by forecasting one-step-ahead closing prices.

Chapter 11

Polluted water is a major reason behind several community diseases, mainly in undeveloped and developing countries. Measuring and detecting the drinking water quality can prevent such scenarios prior to the critical stage. In this chapter, a multi-objective genetic algorithm is used to train the artificial neural network to improve its performance over its traditional counterparts. The proposed model gradually minimizes two different objective functions; namely root mean square error and maximum error in order for finding the optimal weight vector for the neural network.

Nilanjan Dey
Techno India College of Technology, India

Acknowledgment

I am prominently grateful to my parents, to my daughter, to my wife and to my family for their boundless support, and love. I commit this book to all of them as well as to all peoples who read, support, share and offered comments through the book journey. Furthermore, I am obliged to all the authors who offer in time seamless knowledge and skills.

Special thanks to Prof. Peng-Yeng Yin the Editor-in-Chief of the *International Journal of Applied Metaheuristic Computing* for recommending my name as a book editor under the large volume summation project.

Lastly, I appreciate the IGI Global team for their continuous support. My gratitude is extended to the readers, who gave me their trust, and I hope this work guides and inspires them.

Nilanjan Dey
Techno India College of Technology, India

Section 1
Meta–Heuristic Optimization–Algorithms–Based Advanced Applications

Chapter 1

Multi-Objective Optimal Power Flow Using Metaheuristic Optimization Algorithms With Unified Power Flow Controller to Enhance the Power System Performance

G. V. Nagesh Kumar
Vignans Institute of Information Technology (Autonomous), India

B. Venkateswara Rao
V. R. Siddhartha Engineering College (Autonomous), India

D. Deepak Chowdary
Dr. L. Bullayya College of Engineering, India

Polamraju V. S. Sobhan
Vignan's Foundation for Science, Technology, and Research University, India

ABSTRACT

In this chapter a multi objective optimal power flow (OPF) is obtained by using latest Metaheuristic optimization techniques BAT search algorithm (BAT), cuckoo search algorithm (CSA) and firefly algorithm (FA) with Unified power flow controller (UPFC). UPFC is a voltage source converter type Flexible Alternating Current Transmission System (FACTS) device. It is able to control the voltage magnitudes, voltage angles and line impedances individually or simultaneously. To enhance the power system performance, the optimal power flow has been incorporated UPFC

DOI: 10.4018/978-1-5225-4151-6.ch001

along with BAT algorithm, cuckoo search algorithm and firefly algorithm based multi objective function comprising of two objectives those are total real power loss and the fuel cost of total real power generation. The BAT algorithm, cuckoo search algorithm and firefly algorithm based OPF has been examined and tested on a 5 bus test system and modified IEEE 30 bus system without and with UPFC. The results obtained with BAT algorithm, cuckoo search algorithm and firefly algorithms are compared with Differential Evaluation (DE).

INTRODUCTION

Due to economic growth the demand of electric power has been increased drastically which needs optimal operation in Power systems. Optimal power flow is the one strategy for minimizing the real power generation cost and losses in transmission lines. The transmission line losses can be further reduced by installing FACTS controllers. The variables and parameter of the transmission line, which include line reactance, voltage magnitude, and phase angle are able to be controlled using FACTS controllers in a fast and effective way. Controlling power flows is the main function of FACTS controllers (Acha et al., 2004; Jirapong, 2013). According to the IEEE definition, FACTS is defined as "The Flexible AC Transmission System(FACTS) is a new technology based on power electronic devices which offers an opportunity to enhance controllability, stability and power transfer capability of AC Transmission Systems" (Hingorani, 2000; Edris, 2000).

The Flexible AC Transmission System (FACTS) is a transmission system which use reliable high-speed thyristor based controllable elements such as SVC, TCSC, and UPFC etc. are designed based on state of the art developments in power semiconductor devices. Issues include increased utilization of existing facilities such as secure system operation at higher power transfers across existing transmission lines which are limited by stability constraints, the development of control designs for FACTS devices, and determination of functional performance requirements for FACTS components. The reactive power compensation of AC transmission systems using fixed series or shunt capacitors can solve some of the problems associated with AC networks. However the slow nature of control using mechanical switches (circuit breaker) and limits on the frequency of switching imply that faster dynamic controls are required to overcome the above mentioned problems. (Hammons and Lim, 1997) presented a review literature, which addresses the application of FACTS, concepts for the improvement of power system utilization and performance. Recent developments involving deregulation and restructuring of the power industry is feasible only if the operation of AC transmission systems is made flexible by introducing

FACTS devices. In view of increased power demand, power engineers are looking for ways to better utilize their existing transmission systems. The system loadability and stability margins also need to be improved. In recent years, advances in the power electronic devices, have led to the development of controllers that provide controllability and flexibility for power transmission. Flexible AC Transmission System controllers have been developed and their usage in controlling power transmission is seen to be increasing now a days. Among FACTS controllers, UPFC is a versatile device that plays the vital function of controlling all power system parameters simultaneously. The primary function of the UPFC device is to control the load flow of the power system.

Optimal power flow (OPF) is an important tool for power system operation, control and planning. It was first introduced by (Dommel and Tinney, 1968). The main purpose of an OPF program is calculating the optimal operating point of a power system and setting the variables that optimize a certain objective function while satisfying power flow equations, inequality and equality constraints. The optimal power flow (OPF) is a power flow problem in which certain variables are adjusted to minimize an objective function such as cost of the active power generation and the real power losses explained in (Tinney, 1968). Over the last three decades, many successful OPF techniques have been developed such as, the generalized reduced gradient method (Stagg, 1968), linear programming solution, quadratic programming, the Newton method (Carpentier, 1979), the Interior Point Method (IPM), Genetic Algorithm (GA), Evolutionary Programming, Differential Evolutionary algorithm etc. After obtaining the OPF solution (Sun, 1984 ; Kumar Roy, 2013), the implementation of the optimal control variables will bring the system to the "optimum" state (Kundur P,1993 ; Chung, T. S., & Li, Y. Z, 2001).

In recent past so many authors use the meta heuristic algorithms for various applications like medical, image processing, wireless sensor networks to optimize their parameters. In this (Dey, N., Samanta, S., Chakraborty, S., Das, A., Chaudhuri, S. S., & Suri, J. S., 2014) presents, the use of firefly algorithm in medical applications, it is one of the modern nature-inspired meta-heuristic algorithm. This algorithm is used to find the best possible scaling factors for embedding of manifold medical information. In this (Dey, N., Samanta, S., Yang, X. S., Das, A., & Chaudhuri, S. S., 2013), propose a new approach to design a robust biomedical content authentication system by embedding logo of the hospital within the electrocardiogram signal by means of both discrete wavelet transformation and cuckoo search (CS). An adaptive meta-heuristic cuckoo search is used to find the optimal scaling factor settings for logo embedding. For the purpose of overcome the difficulties in Wireless Sensor Networks (Binh, H. T. T., Hanh, N. T., & Dey, N.,2016) proposed two nature-based algorithms, namely Improved Cuckoo Search (ICS) and Chaotic Flower Pollination algorithm (CFPA). Those two algorithms are able to improve their performance of

3

the Wireless Sensor Network . In this (Samantaa, S., Dey, N., Das, P., Acharjee, S., & Chaudhuri, S. S., 2013) proposed, multilevel thresholding technique has been used for image segmentation. A new approach of Cuckoo Search (CS) is used for selection of optimal threshold value. In 2015 (Ashour, A. S., Samanta, S., Dey, N., Kausar, N., Abdessalemkaraa, W. B., & Hassanien, A. E., 2015) says to achieve accurate diagnosis, medical image enhancement is a must for noise removal and sharp/clear images. In this work, a well-known meta-heuristic algorithm, namely: Cuckoo search (CS) algorithm is used to determine the optimal parameter settings for log transform. (Dey, N., Chakraborty, S., & Samanta, S., 2014) The author has used embedding of watermark within biomedical signal as the optimization problem, which is solved using Particle Swarm Optimization and Genetic Algorithm based techniques. (Hore, S., Chatterjee, S., Santhi, V., Dey, N., Ashour, A. S., Balas, V. E., & Shi, F., 2017) recently use three novel methods to solve the problem of recognition of ISL gestures effectively by combining Neural Network (NN) with Genetic Algorithm (GA), Evolutionary algorithm (EA) and Particle Swarm Optimization (PSO) separately to attain novel NN-GA, NN-EA and NN-PSO methods; respectively. In 2015, the authors (Dey, N., Ashour, A. S., Beagum, S., Pistola, D. S., Gospodinov, M., Gospodinova, E. P., & Tavares, J. M. R., 2015) proposed a novel technique for parameter optimization of LPA-ICI filter using genetic algorithm (GA) for brain MR images de-noising. From the above literature it is indicate that cuckoo search algorithm and firefly algorithm are used for various applications effectively as compared to other algorithms like PSO and genetic algorithm. .

In (H. Am briz-Perez E.Acha C.R. Fuerte-Esquivel A.De la Torre, 1998), has been showed the issue of UPFC modeling within the context of OPF solutions. The nonlinear optimization problem is solved by newton's method leading to highly robust iterative solutions even for cases of large scale power networks, where hundreds of variables are to be optimized is presented in literature. It is presented the literature that networks modified to include several UPFCs are solved with equal reliability. The UPFC model itself is very flexible; it allows the control of active and reactive powers and voltage magnitude simultaneously. It can also be set to control one or more of these parameters in any combination or to control none of them. Considerable progress has been achieved in UPFC modeling intended for conventional load flow studies but this is the first time that the more complex issue of UPFC modeling intended for OPF solutions has been addressed in literature. (RR Aparna, 2016), explains the use of swarm intelligence techniques for different applications. In 2016 (Dung A. Le & Dieu N. Vo, 2016), uses a cuckoo search algorithm (CSA) to solve the optimal reactive power dispatch (ORPD) problem in power system operation considering the power loss and voltage deviation. The advantages of the CSA method are few control parameters and high optimal solution quality. The objective of the ORPD problem is to minimize real power losses or bus voltage deviation satisfying equality and inequality constraints of real and reactive power balance. In this the authors use the single objective function for solving ORPD problem. Static synchronous series compensator (SSSC) is one of the most effective flexible AC transmission systems (FACTS) devices used for enhancing power system security. Optimal location and sizing of SSSC are investigated for solving the optimal reactive power dispatch (ORPD) problem in order to minimize the active power loss in the transmission networks. Optimal reactive power dispatch (ORPD), a sub problem of optimal power flow (OPF), has significant influence on the economic and secure operation of power systems. (Susanta Dutta, Provas Kumar Roy & Debashis Nandi, 2016) use chemical reaction optimization (CRO) to solve the above problem with minimization of single objective function.

(Aparajita Mukherjee, Sourav Paul & Provas Kumar Roy, 2015) solve the Transient stability constrained optimal power flow (TSC-OPF) is a non-linear optimization problem which is not easy to deal directly because of its huge dimension. In order to solve the TSC-OPF problem efficiently, a relatively new optimization technique named teaching learning based optimization (TLBO) is proposed. TLBO algorithm simulates the teaching–learning phenomenon of a classroom to solve multi-dimensional, linear and nonlinear problems with appreciable efficiency. In 2014 the authors (Samiksha Goel, Arpita Sharma and V. K. Panchal, 2014), use Anticipatory Multi objective Cuckoo Search (AMOCS) algorithm to identify the best probable location for deployment of enemy forces. For the second phase a hybrid CS-ACO algorithm is developed for obtaining the most suitable path to the location identified in the first phase. Results demonstrate that the system makes accurate predictions with multi objective cuckoo search algorithm.

The UPFC is an advanced power systems device capable of providing simultaneous control of voltage magnitude and active and reactive power flows, all this in adaptive fashion. Owing to its almost instantaneous speed of response and unrivalled functionality, it is well placed to solve most issues relating to power flow control while enhancing considerably transient and dynamic stability.Multi-objective Evolutionary Algorithms (MOEAs) have started receiving attention from researchers to handle Multi-objective Problems (MOPs). Although the first MOEA was published in the mid-eighties (Schaffer, 1985), a substantial progress has been observed in the past decade. In case of a multi-objective optimization problem with conflicting objective, instead of a single optimal solution that satisfies all the objectives, a number of solutions, which indicate the trade-off between the multiple objectives, exist. (Rahul Khandelwal, J. Senthilnath, S. N. Omkar and Narendra Shivanath, 2016). So this indicates that the multi objective function give better results than single objective function. Nature inspired algorithms are used over the past decade that provide efficient methods to resolve optimization problem that were not possible with the conventional methods. The main advantage with these algorithms is that they perform iterative searches efficiently in this context present comparative analysis of three metaheuristic algorithms namely –Firefly, Bat, and Cuckoo search are presented in this chapter. Out of these algorithms firefly algorithm has High convergences rate, robust rate. Finds good optimum solutions in less number of iterations, Bat algorithm is accurate and efficient and cuckoo search algorithm is simpler in implementation.

In this chapter Meta heuristic optimization algorithm has been used for solving multi objective OPF problem incorporating UPFC. The aims of this chapter choose the best values for all the generator buses and the impact of UPFC on generation reallocation. To minimize the real power generation cost and active power losses in the system, multi objective function is considered and it is minimized subject to power balance constraint, active and reactive power generation limits, voltage limits, transmission line limits and UPFC parameter limits. A comprehensive UPFC model suitable for Meta heuristic optimization algorithm based OPF solutions is presented and analyzed in this chapter. Computer simulations using MATLAB were done for 5 bus test system and modified IEEE 30 bus system. The obtained results are compared with Differential Evolution (DE).

The remaining organization of the chapter is as follows. Section 2 presents the UPFC; Section 3 presents multi objective OPF problem formulation. The implementation of Meta heuristic optimization algorithms to the problem is given in Section 4. Numerical results and discussion are followed in Section 5. Section 6 presents' future research directions finally, the conclusion is given in section 7.

UNIFIED POWER FLOW CONTROLLER

Gyugyi proposed the unified power flow controller (UPFC) concept in 1991 (Gyugi L, 1991; Lashkar Ara, 2012). UPFC device is used for the real time control and dynamic compensation of ac transmission system, providing multifunctional flexibility required solving many of the problems facing the delivery industry. UPFC provides multifunctional control to solve reactive power compensation and voltage stability enhancement problems in the power system. The UPFC is capable of controlling multiple aspects of the power systems, viz., voltage magnitude, line impedance and phase angle either individually or in combination thus improving the performance of the systems. Hence the term 'unified' has been designated. The device is an amalgamation of a shunt connected Static Synchronous Compensator (STATCOM) and a series connected Static Synchronous Series Compensator (SSSC). The combination of above two devices is UPFC. In UPFC exchange of real and reactive has been obtained through shared DC linkage. It is also capable of generation or absorption of controlled reactive power, thus providing autonomous shunt reactive

Figure 1. Block diagram of FACTS controllers

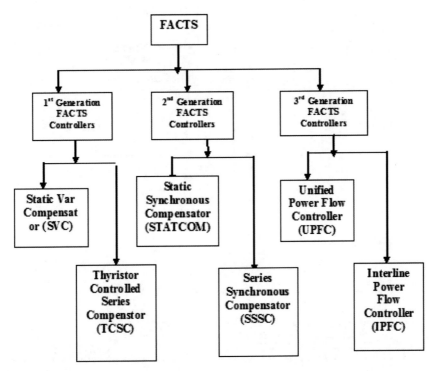

compensation. The UPFC not only performs the functions of STATCOM, SSSC, and the phase angle regulator but also provides additional flexibility by combining some of the functions of these controllers (Tiwari, 2012; Gyugyi, 1995).

The main components of the UPFC are two voltage source inverters (VSIs) sharing a common dc storage capacitor, and connected to the power system through coupling transformers. One VSI is connected in shunt to the transmission system via a shunt transformer and it is used for voltage regulation at the point of connection injecting required reactive power flow into the line and to balance the real power flow exchanged between the series inverter and the transmission line, while the other one is connected in series through a series transformer and it can be used to control the real and reactive line power flow inserting required voltage with controllable magnitude and phase in series with the transmission line (Padiyar., 1998; Padiyar K.R et.al 1999). Thereby, the UPFC can fulfill functions of reactive shunt compensation, series compensation and phase shifting. This arrangement functions as an ideal ac to ac power converter in which the real power can freely flow in either direction between the ac terminals of two converters and each converter can independently generate or absorb reactive power at its own ac output terminals.

Figure 2. Basic circuit arrangement of Unified Power Flow controller

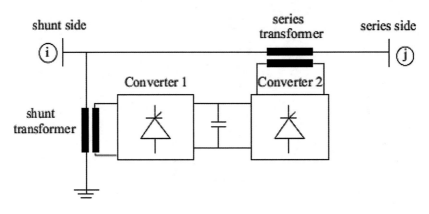

Figure 3. Basic scheme of UPFC

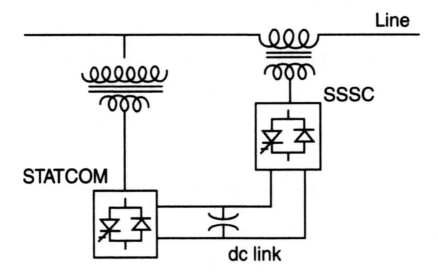

The concept of UPFC makes it possible to handle practically all the power flow control and transmission lines compensation problems using solid-state controllers that provide functional flexibility which are generally not obtained by thyristor-controlled controllers (Sanbao Zheng, 2000).

UPFC voltage sources are written in equations 1 & 2

$$V_{vR}(\cos\delta_{vR} + j\sin\delta_{vR}) \tag{1}$$

Figure 4. Equivalent circuit of the Unified Power Flow Controller

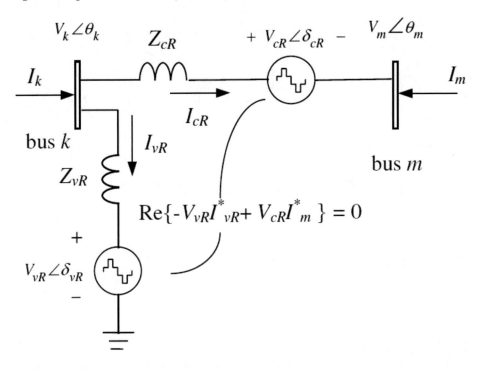

$$V_{cR}(\cos\delta_{cR} + j\sin\delta_{cR}) \qquad (2)$$

Where V_{vR} and δ_{vR} are the controllable voltage magnitude and phase angle of the voltage source representing the shunt converter. Similarly, V_{cR} and δ_{cR} are the controllable voltage magnitude and phase angle of the voltage source representing the series converter. The source impedance is considered to be resistance less.

The active and reactive power equations are

At bus k

$$P_k = [V_k V_m B_{km}\sin(\theta_k - \theta_m)] + [V_k V_{cR} B_{km}\sin(\theta_k - \delta_{cR})] + [V_k V_{vR} B_{vR}\sin(\theta_k - \delta_{vR})] \qquad (3)$$

$$Q_k = -V_k^2 B_{kk} - [V_k V_m B_{km}\cos(\theta_k - \theta_m)] - [V_k V_{cR} B_{km}\cos(\theta_k - \delta_{cR})] - [V_k V_{vR} B_{vR}\cos(\theta_k - \delta_{vR})] \qquad (4)$$

At bus m

$$P_m = [V_m V_k B_{mk} \sin(\theta_m - \theta_k)] + [V_m V_{cR} B_{mm} \sin(\theta_m - \delta_{cR})] \tag{5}$$

$$Q_m = -V_m {}^\wedge 2 \, B_{mm} - [V_m V_k B_{mk} \cos(\theta_m - \theta_k)] - [V_m V_{cR} B_{mm} \cos(\theta_m - \delta_{cR})] \tag{6}$$

At Series converter:

$$P_{cR} = [V_{cR} V_k B_{km} \sin(\delta_{cR} - \theta_k)] + [V_m V_{cR} B_{mm} \sin(\delta_{cR} - \theta_m)] \tag{7}$$

$$Q_{cR} = -V_{cR} {}^\wedge 2 \, B_{mm} - [V_k V_{cR} B_{km} \cos(\theta_k - \delta_{cR})] - [V_m V_{cR} B_{mm} \cos(\theta_m - \delta_{cR})] \tag{8}$$

At Shunt converter:

$$P_{vR} = [V_{vR} V_k B_{vR} \sin(\delta_{nR} - \theta_k)] \tag{9}$$

$$Q_{vR} = V_{vR} {}^\wedge 2 \, B_{vR} - [V_{vR} V_k B_{vR} \cos(\delta_{vR} - \theta_k)] \tag{10}$$

The starting values of the UPFC voltage sources are taken to be $V_{cr} = 0.06$ p.u, $\delta_{cr} = 90^0$, $V_{vr} = 1$ p.u. and $\delta_{vr} = 0^0$. The source impedances are taken as $Z_{cr} = Z_{vr} = 0.1$ p.u.

PROBLEM FORMULATION

Objective Function

For a given system load, find the best configuration of UPFC device and real power generation of the generating stations based on the minimizing the multi objective function consisting of total real power generation fuel cost and total real power losses. The objective function that is used in OPF problem formulation consists of minimization of real power generation cost and minimization of real power losses. Mathematically, the objective function can be written as:

$$\text{Min } F = \text{Min}\left(W_1 {}^* FC + W_2 {}^* F_{\text{PLoss}}\right) \tag{11}$$

Where w_1, w_2 are the weighting factors,

$$W_1 + W_2 = 1 \tag{12}$$

W1=W2= 0.5

- **Fuel cost of Total Real Power Generation:**

The objective function considering the minimization of total real power generation cost can be represented by following quadratic equation

$$FC = \min(\sum_{i=1}^{ng} a_i P_{Gi}^2 + b_i P_{Gi} + c_i) \tag{13}$$

Where ng= no of generator busesa, b, c are the fuel cost coefficients of a generator unit

- **Total Real Power Loss:**

This objective consists of minimizing the real power losses in the transmission lines. It can be expressed as

$$F_{\text{PLoss}} = \min\left(P_{\text{Loss}}\right) = \min\left[\sum_{k=1}^{ntl} \text{real}(S_{ij}^k + S_{ji}^k)\right] \tag{14}$$

Where ntl=no. Of transmission lines
S_{ij} is the total complex power flow from bus i to bus j in line k.

- **Equality constraints:**

$$\sum_{i=1}^{N} P_{Gi} = \sum_{i=1}^{N} P_{Di} + P_L \tag{15}$$

- **Inequality constraints:**

$$V_{Gi}^{\min} \leq V_{Gi} \leq V_{Gi}^{\max} \tag{16}$$

$$P_{Gi}^{\min} \leq P_{Gi} \leq P_{Gi}^{\max} \tag{17}$$

$$Q_{Gi}^{\min} \leq Q_{Gi} \leq Q_{Gi}^{\max} \tag{18}$$

- **UPFC device limits:**

$$V_{vr}^{\min} \leq V_{vr} \leq V_{vr}^{\max} \tag{19}$$

V_{vr} is the shunt converter voltage magnitude (p.u)

$$V_{cr}^{\min} \leq V_{cr} \leq V_{cr}^{\max} \tag{20}$$

V_{cr} is the series converter voltage magnitude (p.u)

Where P_L is the real power loss in the system, P_{Gi} is the real power generation at bus i, P_{Di} is the power demand at bus i, N and Ng are the number of buses and number of generator buses in the system respectively.

META HEURISTIC OPTIMIZATION ALGORITHMS

Bat Algorithm

In this paper we use a nature inspired metaheuristic method based on the echolocation behavior of bats. That is called BAT algorithm which is developed by Xin-She Yang in 2010. Bats are fascinating animals. They are the only mammals with wings and they also have advanced capability of echolocation. Most of bats use echolocation to a certain degree; the capability of echolocation of micro bats is fascinating as these bats can find their prey and discriminate different types of insects even in complete darkness. Among all the species, micro bats are famous example as micro bats use echolocation extensively, while mega bats do not. Micro bats use a type of sonar, called echolocation, avoid obstacles, to detect prey, and locate their roosting crevices in the dark. We will first formulate The BAT algorithm by idealizing the echolocation behavior of bats. These bats emit a very loud sound pulse and listen for the echo that bounces back from surrounding objects. Bat algorithm is developed by idealizing some of the characteristics of micro bats. The approximated or idealized rules are (Yang, 2008):

1. All bats use echolocation to sense distance and they also know the difference between food/prey and barriers in some magical way.
2. Bats fly randomly with velocity vi at position xi with a fixed frequency fmin, varying wavelength λ and loudness A0 to search for prey. They can automatically adjust the wavelength (or frequency) of their emitted pulses and the rate of pulse emission r ∈ [0,1] depending on the proximity of the target.
3. Loudness varies from a large positive A0 to a minimum constant value Amin.

Population

The initial population i.e., number of virtual bats for BAT algorithm is generated randomly. The number of bats can be anywhere between 10 and 40. After finding the initial fitness of the population for given objective function, the values are updated based on movement, loudness and pulse rate.

Movement of Virtual Bats

The rules for updating the positions xi and velocities vi of the virtual bats are given as (22)

$$f_i = f_{\min} + (f_{\max} - f_{\min})\beta \tag{21}$$

$$v_i^t = v_i^{t-1} + (x_i^t - x_*)f_i \tag{22}$$

$$x_i^t = x_i^{t-1} + v_i^t \tag{23}$$

Where, $\beta \in [0, 1]$ is a random vector drawn from a uniform distribution. Here x* is the current global best location (solution) which is located after comparing all the solutions among all the n bats. A new solution for each bat is generated locally using random walk given by equation (24)

$$x_{new} = x_{old} + \varepsilon A^t \tag{24}$$

Where $\varepsilon \in [-1, 1]$ is a random number, while At $=<$Ait$>$ is the average loudness of all the bats at this time step. Based on these approximations and idealization, the basic steps of the Bat Algorithm can be summarized as the pseudo code shown here. (Venkateswara Rao B et.al, 2014; Yang, X.-S, 2010)

Bat Algorithm

Objective function f(x), x = (x1,x2, ..., xd)T
Initialize the bat population xii (ii = 1, 2, ..., n) and vii
Define pulse frequency fii at xii
Initialize pulse rates rii and the loudness Aii
while (t <Max number of iterations)
Generate a new solution by changing frequency,
And modifying velocities and solutions
if (rand > rii)
Select a best solution in the available solutions
Create a local solution around the selected best solution
end if
Create a new solution by flying randomly
if (rand < Aii & f(xii) < f(xo))
Accept the new solutions
Increase rii and reduce Aii
end if
Rank the bats and find the current best xo
End while
Post process results and visualization
Pseudo code of the BAT algorithm.
Loudness and Pulse Emission

The loudness Ai and the rate of pulse emission ri are updated accordingly as the iterations proceed. The loudness decreases and rate of pulse emission increases as the bat closes on its prey i.e., the equations for convergence can be taken as (25)

$$A_i^{t+1} = \alpha A_i^t \tag{25}$$

$$R_i^{t+1} = r_i^0[1 - \exp(-\gamma t)] \qquad (26)$$

Where α and γ are constants.

The initial loudness A0 can typically be (1, 2), while the initial emission rate r_i^0 can be (0, 1).

Firefly Algorithm

The Firefly algorithm was developed by Dr Xin-She Yang at Cambridge University in 2007. FA is based on natural behaviour of the firefly, developed for solving the multimodal optimization problem [Yang, 2009; X. S. Yang, 2010]. Fireflies called as lighting bugs, are one of the most special and fascinating creatures in nature. For simplicity, the following three ideal rules are introduced in FA development those are 1) All the fireflies are gender-free that is every firefly will attract the other firefly substantive of their sex, 2) Attractiveness depend on their brightness. The less bright one will move towards the brighter one, 3) the landscape of the objective function affects the firefly brightness [Dey, N., Samanta, S., Chakraborty, S., Das, A., Chaudhuri, S. S., & Suri, J. S. (2014)]. Let us consider the continuous constrained optimization problem where the task is to minimize multi objective function f(x). Firefly algorithm is a dynamic converging algorithm. The solution for the algorithm depends on the selection of swarm size, maximum attractiveness value, the absorption coefficient value and the iteration limit. The basic steps of the FA can be summarized by the pseudo code [Lukasik S and Zak, 2009].

Firefly Algorithm

Objective function f(x), x = (x1,...,xd)T
Generate initial population of fireflies xii (i=1, 2..., n)
Light intensity Iii at xii is determined by f(xii)
Define light absorption coefficient γ
while (t < MaxGeneration)
for ii = 1: n all n fireflies
for jj = 1: ii all n fireflies
if (Ijj > Iii), More firefly ii towards jj in d-dimension; end if
Attractiveness varies with distance r
Evaluate new solutions and modify the light intensity
end for jj
end for ii
Rank all the fireflies and find the current best firefly

end while

Post process results and visualization

Pseudo code of the FA.

Cuckoo Search Algorithm

Yang and Deb developed a population-based optimization algorithm, based on the brood parasitism of some cuckoo species in nature and named as a Cuckoo search algorithm. This method simulates the actions of the female Cuckoo bird to lay her egg into the neighbour's nest. This method also considers the probability that the host bird finds out and abandons the Cuckoo egg. A recent study says that Cuckoo search algorithm gives better results as compared to other meta heuristics methods (Dey, N., Samanta, S., Yang, X. S., Das, A., & Chaudhuri, S. S., 2013).

The pseudo code of the cuckoo search algorithm is presented in (Dung A. Le & Dieu N. Vo, 2016) based on three main stages as below:

- **Initialization:** There is a population of Np host nests generated. This stage is corresponding to the phenomenon that cuckoo bird lays its eggs in nests of other species.
- **The First New Solution Generation:** This stage is to generate the first new solutions via Levy Flights corresponding to the case that host birds do not discover alien eggs in their nest and Cuckoo eggs will be hatched and carried over to the next generation.
- **The Second New Solution Generation:** This stage aims to generate the second new solutions corresponding to the case that the host birds discover Cuckoo eggs as alien ones in their nest and host bird will throw Cuckoo eggs away the nest or forsake both Cuckoo eggs and their nest.

A random set of solution is generated using Levy flight algorithm:

$$x_i^{t+1} = x_i^t + \alpha \oplus Levy(y) \tag{27}$$

Above equation is the stochastic equation of a random walk whose next step depends on current location (the first term) and the transition probability (the second term). α is the step size, the product means entry wise multiplications. Levy flight provides a random walk whose random step length is drawn from Levy distribution:

$$Levy \neq t^{-\lambda}, (1 < \lambda < 3) \tag{28}$$

Steps form a random walk process with a power-law step length distribution with a heavy tail. Objective function with this new set is also evaluated. If new objective function is better than old one, a portion Pa of new set is replaces an equivalent random set of the initial solution. The process is repeated until the maximum number of epochs is reached. Initial set of nests (n nests) may vary from 15 to 40 and Pa of 0.25 are suitable values for most optimization problems [Samantaa, S., Dey, N., Das, P., Acharjee, S., & Chaudhuri, S. S. (2013)].

Overall Procedure

The overall procedure of the CSA for solving the optimization problem is described in detail as follows.

Step 1: Read the power system bus data and line data for power flow calculations.
Step 2: Select the real power generation of all the PV buses and UPFC parameters as a control variables also select the number of nests Np, the maximum number of iterations $Iter_{max}$ and probability pa. Initialize a population of host nests.
Step 3: Get a cuckoo randomly/ generate solution by Levy flights algorithm and evaluate its objective function.
Step 4: Perform bound by best solution mechanism as described in algorithm to repair solutions violating upper or lower limitation.
Step 5: Generate the new solutions thank to the action of alien eggs to be abandoned and replace the old solution by the new one.
Step 6: Get the best nest Gbest for the current iteration.
Step 7: If the best nest Gbest at the current iteration is not better than that of the previous iteration, obtain the new value of the one rank ratio. Otherwise, retain the old value.
Step 8: If Iter < Itermax, Iter = Iter + 1 and return to Step 3. Otherwise, stop the procedure.
Step 9: If termination criterion is satisfied, then find the best solution in the search space.

RESULTS AND DISCUSSION

In this chapter, a 5-bus test system and modified IEEE 30 bus system have been considered to demonstrate the effectiveness and robustness of BAT algorithm, cuckoo search algorithm and firefly algorithm without and with UPFC.

For 5-Bus System

In 5-bus test system, bus 1 is considered as slack bus, bus 2 is taken as PV bus and buses 3, 4, 5 are PQ buses. To include a unified power flow controller an additional bus 6 placed in between buses 3 and 4 in the network. It maintains the active and reactive powers leaving the UPFC towards the bus 4. The UPFC shunt converter is set to regulate bus 3 nodal voltage magnitude at 1 p.u. A MATLAB program is implemented for the test system. Twenty runs have been performed for the test system. The optimal solution results over these twenty runs have been tabulated. The input parameters of BAT algorithm, cuckoo search algorithm and firefly algorithm are given in Table 1, Table 2 and Table 3 respectively and the input parameters of Differential evaluation are given in Table 4.

Table 1. Input parameters of BAT algorithm

S.No	Parameters	Quantity
1	Population size	20
2	Number of generations	50
3	Loudness	0.5
4	Pulse rate	0.5

Table 2. Input parameters of CSA

S.No	Variable	Value
1	Number of nests	20
2	Iterations Count	50
3	Discovery rate of alien eggs/solutions	0.5

Table 3. Input parameters of Firefly Algorithm

S.No	Parameters	Quantity
1	Number of fireflies	20
2	Max Generation	50
3	Alpha	0.5
4	Beta	0.5
5	Gama	1

Table 4. Input parameters of differential evaluation

S.No	Parameters	Quantity
1	Population size	20
2	Number of generations	50
3	DE-step size	0.8
4	Crossover probability constant	0.8

Initially, the optimal power flow solution i.e. active power generation cost and power loss for 5-bus system are calculated using proposed BAT algorithm, cuckoo search algorithm and firefly algorithm method without UPFC. Next, for the same system the optimal power flow solution is obtained using proposed BAT algorithm, cuckoo search algorithm and firefly algorithm method with UPFC. The results obtained with BAT algorithm, cuckoo search algorithm and firefly algorithm are compared with Differential evaluation. The active power generation cost and power loss for 5 bus test system without UPFC is shown in Table 5 and Table 6 represents the same as above with UPFC. From Table 5 and 6, it can be seen that total active power generation required is reduced to 150.0192 MW from 151.3557 MW and power loss has been reduced to 5.0192 MW from 6.3557 MW because of UPFC. Further, it is observed that there is a significant reduction in the cost because of UPFC. From Table 7, it is clear that the voltage profiles has been improved for most of buses because of UPFC and The UPFC shunt converter is set to regulate bus 3 nodal voltage magnitude at 1 p.u.

From the Figure 5 it is observed that by incorporating UPFC in Power flow calculations voltage profile has been improved. By placing the UPFC between bus no 3 and bus no 4 its voltage at bus no 3 has been increased from 0.9519 to 1 p.u. From the Table 8 it is observed that the active power losses are 5.0192 MW when the UPFC is placed between bus no 3 and bus no 4 which is the less as compared

Table 5. Comparison in case of OPF without UPFC

Variables	DE-OPF	BAT-OPF	CSA-OPF	FA-OPF
PG1(MW)	139.0764	109.1800	91.0192	57.5634
PG2(MW)	12.8518	42.1757	60.00	93.4171
Total real power generation(MW)	151.9282	151.3557	151.0192	150.9805
Total real power generation cost ($/hr)	1893.3	1726.4	1769.3	1689.8
Total real power Loss (MW)	6.9282	6.3557	6.0192	5.9805

Table 6. Comparison in case of OPF with UPFC

Variables	DE-OPF	BAT-OPF	CSA-OPF	FA-OPF
PG1(MW)	133.8120	90.0192	60.456	62.5170
PG2(MW)	16.8338	60.0000	89.6312	88.3601
UPFC(p.u.) VcR VvR	0.0400 1.0759	0.0370 1.0436	0.038 1.042	0.029 1.012
UPFC θcr (angle in degrees) θvr	-87.1236 -15.2311	-86.1393 -12.3421	-86.9576 -13.1258	-85.456 -10.632
Total real power generation(MW)	150.6458	150.0192	150.0872	149.8771
Total real power generation cost ($/hr)	1814.804	1684.3	1688.71	1672.56
Total real power Loss (MW)	5.6458	5.0192	5.0872	4.8771

Table 7. Comparison of bus voltages and its angles for 5 bus system using Bat OPF without and with UPFC

Bus No.	DE-OPF with UPFC		BAT-OPF with UPFC		CSA-OPF with UPFC		FA-OPF with UPFC	
	Voltage magnitude (volts)	Voltage angle (rad)	Voltage magnitude (volts)	Voltage angle (rad)	Voltage magnitude (volts)	Voltage angle (rad)	Voltage magnitude (volts)	Voltage angle (rad)
1	1.06	0	1.06	0	1.0600	0	1.0600	0
2	1	-0.83	1	-0.74	1.0000	-2.0356	1.0000	-1.0356
3	1	-3.32	1	-4.21	1.0000	-4.6213	1	-3.6213
4	0.9536	-3.67	0.9753	-3.59	0.9720	-3.3370	0.9863	-4.3370
5	0.9622	-4.52	0.9806	-4.37	0.9786	-5.6541	0.9929	-4.2555
UPFC Node	0.9785	-4.567	0.9806	-3.17	0.9689	-4.5254	0.995	-3.0524

to UPFC placed in other locations. Figure 6 indicates that real power losses are less when the UPFC placed between bus no. 3 and bus no.4. Comparison of real power generation cost after incorporation of UPFC at different locations in BAT algorithm based optimal power flow shown in Fig.7.

For 30 Bus System

In modified IEEE 30 bus system bus no 1 is consider as a slack bus and bus no's 2,5,8,11,13 are consider as a PV buses all other buses are consider as PQ buses.

Figure 5. Comparision of voltage profile with and without UPFC

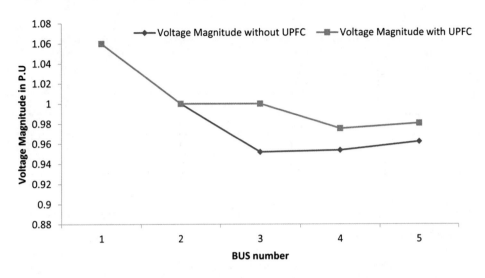

Table 8. Incorporation of UPFC in OPF with bat Algorithm in 5 different locations

UPFC Placed Between Bus No	Total Real Power Generation (MW)	Total Load (MW)	Total Real Power Loss (MW)
2-3	150.663	145	5.663
2-4	150.9119	145	5.9119
2-5	151.3845	145	6.3845
3-4	150.0192	145	5.0192
4-5	150.8784	145	5.8784

Table 9. Incorporation of UPFC in OPF with cuckoo search Algorithm in 5 different locations

UPFC Placed Between Bus No	Total Real Power Generation (MW)	Total Load (MW)	Total Real Power Loss (MW)
2-3	150.7829	145	5. 7829
2-4	150.9829	145	5. 9829
2-5	151.8653	145	6. 8653
3-4	150.0872	145	5.0872
4-5	150.9489	145	5. 9489

Table 10. Incorporation of UPFC in OPF with firefly Algorithm in 5 Different Locations

UPFC placed between Bus No	Total real power generation (MW)	Total load (MW)	Total real power loss (MW)
2-3	150.4531	145	5. 4531
2-4	150.0123	145	5. 0123
2-5	150.8562	145	5.8562
3-4	149.8771	145	4.8771
4-5	150.4854	145	5. 4854

Figure 6. Incorporation of UPFC at different locations in Optimal Power Flow with BAT Algorithm

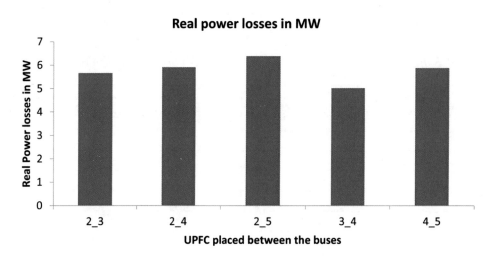

This system has 24 load buses with 41 interconnected lines. By simulating the optimal power flow with BAT algorithm in MATLAB it is observed that voltage magnitude at bus no 26 is 0.8159p.u which is less as compared to other buses. So for the purpose of improve the voltage profile at that bus it is required to place the UPFC between bus no 25 and bus no 26. To include a unified power flow controller an additional node 31 placed in between bus no 25 and bus no 26 in the network. It maintains the active and reactive powers leaving the UPFC towards the bus 25. The UPFC shunt converter is set to regulate bus 26 nodal voltage magnitude at 1 p.u. similarly simulating the optimal power flow with cuckoo search algorithm and firefly algorithm in MATLAB it is observed that voltage magnitude at bus no 26 is less as compared to other buses. So for the purpose of improve the voltage

Figure 7. Comparison of real power generation cost after incorporation of UPFC at different locations in BAT-OPF.

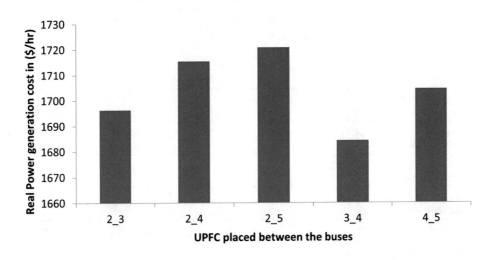

Real power generation cost in ($/h)

Table 11. Comparison in case of OPF without UPFC

Variables	DE-OPF	BAT-OPF	CSA-OPF	FA-OPF
PG1(MW)	169	170.1571	170.6130	173.8325
PG2(MW)	48.2537	50	50.3422	49.8952
PG5(MW)	19	25.2113	21.960	22.6231
PG8(MW)	30.5948	19.1717	24.1619	22.0648
PG11(MW)	15.4692	16	13.8316	11.5357
PG13(MW)	12	12.0396	13.1734	12.0871
Total real power generation(MW)	294.3177	292.5795	294.0821	292.0384
Total real power generation cost ($/hr)	810.5345	804.0134	808.4652	800.0942
Total real power Loss (MW)	10.9177	9.1795	10.6821	8.64

profile at that bus it is required to place the shunt converter of UPFC at that bus. A MATLAB program is implemented for the test system. Twenty runs have been performed for the test system. The optimal solution results over these twenty runs have been tabulated.

Table 12. Comparison in case of OPF with UPFC

Variables	DE-OPF	BAT-OPF	CSA-OPF	FA-OPF
PG1(MW)	166.722	175.4891	174.6537	205.7251
PG2(MW)	50.2537	46.9756	49.9251	31.8026
PG5(MW)	16	21.2113	22.0305	17.0127
PG8(MW)	28.7395	20.1717	21.6118	11.8741
PG11(MW)	17.4692	13.5542	11.8879	10.2405
PG13(MW)	12	12.0396	12.0	12.7050
UPFC(p.u.) VcR VvR	0.0540 1.0545	0.0410 1.0368	0.11 1.0176	0.0945 1.0176
UPFC θcr (angle in degrees) θvr	-92.4571 -14.3387	-104.178 -10.3848	-98.5673 -12.856	-87.515 -11.649
Total real power generation(MW)	291.1849	289.4415	292.109	289.36
Total real power generation cost ($/hr)	801.7493	794.5704	799.9800	793.162
Total real power Loss (MW)	7.7849	6.0415	8.7090	5.96

The total real power generation, total real power generation cost and real power loss for modified IEEE 30 bus system are obtained with BAT algorithm, cuckoo search algorithm, firefly algorithm and differential evaluation considering without and with UPFC are shown in Table 11 and Table 12. From Table 11 and 12, it can be seen that total active power generation required is reduced to 289.4415 MW from 292.5795 MW and power loss has been reduced to 6.0415 MW from 9.1795 MW because of UPFC with BAT algorithm. By incorporating UPFC in cuckoo search algorithm losses has been reduced to 8.709MW from 10.68MW, in firefly algorithm losses are reduced to 5.96MW from 8.64MW, which indicates that latest firefly algorithm gives better results compared to all other optimization algorithms.

Further, it is observed that there is a significant reduction in the cost because of UPFC. From the Figure 8 it is observed that active power losses are reduced to 6.0415 MW from 10.9177MW by placing the UPFC in BAT algorithm based optimal power flow. Figure 9 indicates the real power generation cost is less in BAT-OPF as compared to DE-OPF. From Table 12 it can be observed that Firefly algorithm gives better results when compare to other optimization algorithms in OPF problem with UPFC on the modified IEEE 30 bus test system.

Table 13 represents the bus voltage of the network without UPFC and with UPFC. From Table 13, it is clear that the voltage profiles has been improved for most of buses because of UPFC and The UPFC shunt converter is set to regulate

Figure 8. Comparison of Active power losses for different conditions

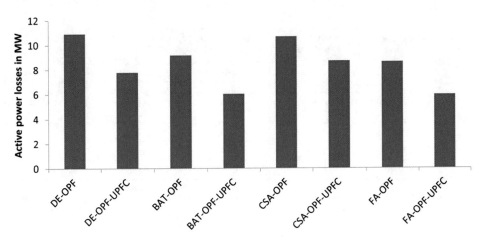

Figure 9. Comparison of real power generation cost for different conditions

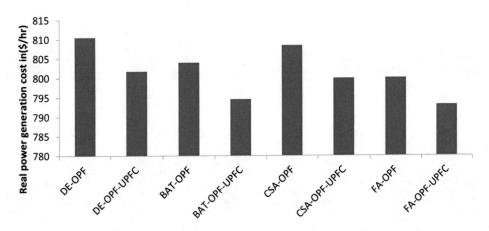

bus 26 nodal voltage magnitude at 1 p.u. From the Figure 10 it is observed that by incorporating UPFC in BAT algorithm based optimal Power flow calculations voltage profile has been improved. By placing the UPFC between bus no 25 and bus no 26 its voltage at bus no 26 has been increased from 0.8159 p.u to 1 p.u. Table 14 represents the total Active power losses when the bus no26 is loaded. From the table it is observed that losses are increased by increasing load. From the Figure 11 it is observed that by placing the UPFC in BAT algorithm based optimal power flow the losses are less. Similarly from Figure 12 it is observed that by placing the UPFC in BAT algorithm based optimal power flow real power generation cost is less and by increasing the load at particular bus real power generation cost is also increased.

Table 13. Comparison of bus VOLTAGES FOR 30bus system using Bat OPF without and with UPFC

Bus No.	Newton Raphson Method	DE-OPF with UPFC(UPFC placed between bus 25 and bus26)	BAT-OPF with UPFC(UPFC placed between bus 25 and bus26)	CSA-OPF with UPFC(UPFC placed between bus 25 and bus26)	FA-OPF with UPFC(UPFC placed between bus 25 and bus26)
	Voltage magnitude(volts)	Voltage magnitude (volts)	Voltage magnitude (volts)	Voltage magnitude (volts)	Voltage magnitude (volts)
1	1.0600	1.06	1.06	1.06	1.06
2	1.0430	1.0430	1.0430	1.0430	1.0430
3	0.9568	0.9641	0.9660	0.95660	0.9710
4	0.9756	0.9836	0.9869	0.9989	0.9962
5	1.01	1.0100	1.0100	1.0100	1.01
6	1.008	1.0118	1.0142	1.012	1.01
7	0.9967	0.9985	0.9997	0.997	0.999
8	1.01	1.0100	1.0100	1.0100	1.0100
9	0.9536	0.9637	0.9697	0.9978	0.9789
10	0.893	0.9045	0.9199	0.9099	0.9389
11	1.082	1.0820	1.0820	1.0820	1.0820
12	0.9179	0.9288	0.9396	0.9299	0.9468
13	1.071	1.0710	1.0710	1.0710	1.0710
14	0.8588	0.8707	0.8872	0.8842	0.8986
15	0.8521	0.8641	0.8851	0.8765	0.8982
16	0.8803	0.8920	0.9049	0.9095	0.9493
17	0.87	0.8821	0.8966	0.8912	0.8999
18	0.8207	0.8335	0.8544	0.8444	0.8964
19	0.8136	0.8267	0.8468	0.8348	0.8685
20	0.8374	0.8501	0.8682	0.8620	0.8827
21	0.8599	0.8717	0.8943	0.8848	0.8993
22	0.8529	0.8644	0.8933	0.8736	0.8993
23	0.8298	0.8415	0.8764	0.8664	0.8974
24	0.8349	0.8455	0.8927	0.8887	0.8978
25	0.8532	0.8610	0.9360	0.9160	0.9603
26	0.8075	1.0000	1.0000	1.0000	1.0000
27	0.9449	0.9480	0.9720	0.9567	0.9956
28	0.9824	0.9847	0.9934	0.9899	0.9974
29	0.9617	0.9633	0.9755	0.9711	0.9877
30	0.95	0.963	0.972	0.9700	0.9889
31	-----	0.9562	0.9678	0.9469	0.9789

Figure 10. Comparison of Voltage Profile with and without UPFC

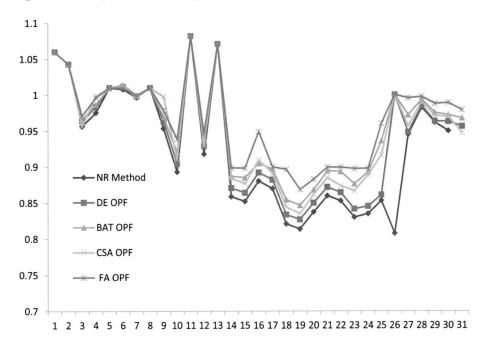

Table 14. Total Active Power Losses comparison with bus 26 loaded

S No	Bus 26 Loaded (Load in MW)	Active Power losses in MW (DE OPF with UPFC placed between bus 25 and bus26)	Active Power losses in MW (BAT OPF with UPFC placed between bus 25 and bus26)	Active Power losses in MW (CSA OPF with UPFC placed between bus 25 and bus26)	Active Power losses in MW (FA OPF with UPFC placed between bus 25 and bus26)
1	10	22.123	20.9837	21.0972	20.3217
2	20	24.692	22.2221	23.234	21.6546
3	30	28.654	27.4585	28.4298	26.9856
4	40	32.996	31.6879	32.8691	30.8978
5	50	39.578	37.6059	38.9562	36.9746

FUTURE RESEARCH DIRECTIONS

A combination of these optimization techniques as hybrid optimization techniques can be implemented for future work and better results. In this chapter power system performance has been enhanced by using single FACTS device that is UPFC only

Figure 11. Total Losses comparison with bus 26 loaded

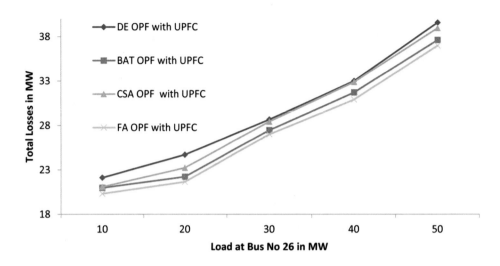

Figure 12. Total real power generation cost comparison with bus 26 loaded

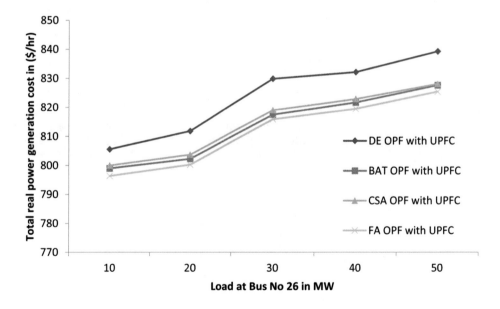

it can be implemented with multi type FACTS devices for future work and better performance. Here optimization planning is done for static environment. For future work this can be a challenging topic for planning for dynamic environment.

CONCLUSION

In this chapter, Meta heuristic optimization algorithms have been implemented to solve multi objective optimal power flow problem in the presence of Unified power flow controller. The results demonstrate the effectiveness and robustness of the proposed methods with Unified power flow controller. The results obtained for 5 bus test system and modified IEEE 30 bus system using the proposed methods without and with UPFC are compared and observations reveal that the losses are less with UPFC. In 5 bus test system UPFC is placed between bus 3 and bus 4 and in modified IEEE 30 bus system UPFC is placed between bus 25 and bus 26 the simulation results were taken and it was observed that the active power losses has been decreased because of generation reallocation. Simulation results show that UPFC device in the test systems can further minimize total real power generation cost and real power loss. BAT algorithm, CSA and firefly algorithm based optimal power flow with UPFC gives less total generation cost and real power losses as compared to differential evaluation algorithm based optimal power flow. While comparing BAT algorithm, cuckoo search algorithm and firefly algorithm, cuckoo search algorithm is simple in implementation, BAT algorithm gives accurate and efficient results, fire fly algorithm has robust, high convergence rate and gives best optimal solution in less number of iterations.

REFERENCES

Acha, E., Fuerte-Esquivel, C., Ambriz-Perez, H., & Angeles, C. (2004). *FACTS: Modelling and Simulation in Power Networks*. John Wiley & Sons; doi:10.1002/0470020164

Ambriz-Perez, Acha, Fuerte-Esquivel, & De la Torre. (1998). Incorporation of a UPFC model in an Optimal Power Flow Using Newton's method. *IEE Proc.-Generation Transmission Distribution, 145*(3).

Aparna, R. R. (2016). Swarm Intelligence for Automatic Video Image Contrast Adjustment. *International Journal of Rough Sets and Data Analysis, 3*(3), 21–37. doi:10.4018/IJRSDA.2016070102

Ashour, A. S., Samanta, S., Dey, N., Kausar, N., Abdessalemkaraa, W. B., & Hassanien, A. E. (2015). Computed tomography image enhancement using cuckoo search: A log transform based approach. *Journal of Signal and Information Processing, 6*(03), 244–257. doi:10.4236/jsip.2015.63023

Binh, H. T. T., Hanh, N. T., & Dey, N. (2016). Improved Cuckoo Search and Chaotic Flower Pollination optimization algorithm for maximizing area coverage in Wireless Sensor Networks. *Neural Computing & Applications*, 1–13.

Carpentier. (1979). Optimal Power Flows. *Electrical Power and Energy Systems, 1*, 959-972.

Chung, T. S., & Li, Y. Z. (2001). A hybrid CA approach for OPF with consideration of FACTS devices. *IEEE Power Engineering Review, 21*(2), 47–50. doi:10.1109/39.896822

Dey, N., Ashour, A. S., Beagum, S., Pistola, D. S., Gospodinov, M., Gospodinova, E. P., & Tavares, J. M. R. (2015). Parameter optimization for local polynomial approximation based intersection confidence interval filter using genetic algorithm: An application for brain MRI image de-noising. *Journal of Imaging, 1*(1), 60–84. doi:10.3390/jimaging1010060

Dey, N., Chakraborty, S., & Samanta, S. (2014). Optimization of watermarking in biomedical signal. *Lambert Publication. Heinrich-Böcking-Straße, 6*, 66121.

Dey, N., Samanta, S., Chakraborty, S., Das, A., Chaudhuri, S. S., & Suri, J. S. (2014). Firefly algorithm for optimization of scaling factors during embedding of manifold medical information: An application in ophthalmology imaging. *Journal of Medical Imaging and Health Informatics, 4*(3), 384–394. doi:10.1166/jmihi.2014.1265

Dey, N., Samanta, S., Yang, X. S., Das, A., & Chaudhuri, S. S. (2013). Optimisation of scaling factors in electrocardiogram signal watermarking using cuckoo search. *International Journal of Bio-inspired Computation, 5*(5), 315–326. doi:10.1504/IJBIC.2013.057193

Dutta, S. (2016). Optimal Allocation of Static Synchronous. Academic Press.

Dutta, S., Roy, P. K., & Nandi, D. (2016). Series Compensator Controllers using Chemical Reaction Optimization for Reactive Power Dispatch. *International Journal of Energy Optimization and Engineering, 5*(3), 43–62. doi:10.4018/IJEOE.2016070103

Edris, A. (2000, March). FACTS Technology Development: An Update. *IEEE Power Engineering Review*.

Goel, S., Sharma, A., & Panchal, V. K. (2014). Multiobjective Cuckoo Search for Anticipating the Enemys Movements in the Battleground. *International Journal of Applied Metaheuristic Computing, 5*(4), 26–46. doi:10.4018/ijamc.2014100102

Gyugi, L. (1992, July). A Unified Power Control Concept for Flexible AC Transmission Systems. *IEE Procedings-C, 139*(4), 323–332.

Gyugyi, Schauder, Williams, Rictman, Torgerson, & Edris. (1995). The Unified Power Flow Controller: A New Approach to Power Transmission Control. *IEEE Trans. on Power Delivery, 10*(2), 1085-1097.

Hingorani, N. G., & Gyugyi, L. (2000). *Understanding FACTS: Concepts and Technology of Flexible AC Transmission System.* IEEE Press.

Hore, S., Chatterjee, S., Santhi, V., Dey, N., Ashour, A. S., Balas, V. E., & Shi, F. (2017). Indian Sign Language Recognition Using Optimized Neural Networks. In *Information Technology and Intelligent Transportation Systems* (pp. 553–563). Springer International Publishing. doi:10.1007/978-3-319-38771-0_54

Hsmmns, T. J., & Lim, S. K. (1997). Flexible AC Transmission System (FACTS). *Electric Machines & Power System, 25,* 73–85.

Jirapong, P. (2013, April-June). FACTS Devices Allocation for Power Transfer Capability Enhancement and Power System Losses Reduction. *International Journal of Energy Optimization and Engineering, 2*(2), 1–14. doi:10.4018/ijeoe.2013040101

Kaur, P., & Kaur, T. (2014). A Comparative Study of Various Metaheuristic Algorithms. *International Journal of Computer Science and Information Technologies, 5*(5), 6701–6704.

Kumar Roy, P. (2013, July-September). Hybridization of Biogeography Based Optimization with Differential Evolution for solving Optimal Power Flow Problems. *International Journal of Energy Optimization and Engineering, 2*(3), 86–101. doi:10.4018/ijeoe.2013070106

Kundur, P. (1993). *Power System Stability and Control.* New York: McGraw-Hill, Inc.

Lashkar Ara, Kazemi, & Nabavi Niaki. (2012). Multi objective Optimal Location of FACTS Shunt-Series Controllers for Power System Operation Planning. *IEEE Transactions on Power Delivery, 27*(2), 481-490.

Le, D. A., & Vo, D. N. (2016, January-March). Cuckoo Search Algorithm for Minimization of Power Loss and Voltage Deviation. *International Journal of Energy Optimization and Engineering, 5*(1), 23–34. doi:10.4018/IJEOE.2016010102

Mukherjee, A., Paul, S., & Roy, P. K. (2015). Transient Stability Constrained Optimal Power Flow Using Teaching Learning Based Optimization. *International Journal of Energy Optimization and Engineering, 4*(1), 18–35. doi:10.4018/ijeoe.2015010102

Padiyar & Uma Rao. (1999). Modeling and Control of Unified Power Flow Controller For Transient Stability. *Electrical Power and Energy Systems, 21.*

Padiyar, K. R., & Kulakarni, A. M. (1998). Control Design and Simulation of Unified Power Flow Controller. *IEEE Trans. on Power Delivery, 13*(4), 1348-1354.

Rahul Khandelwal, J. (2016). A Novel Multiobjective Optimization for Cement Stabilized Soft Soil based on Artificial Bee Colony. *International Journal of Applied Metaheuristic Computing, 7*(4), 1–17. doi:10.4018/IJAMC.2016100101

Samantaa, S., Dey, N., Das, P., Acharjee, S., & Chaudhuri, S. S. (2013). *Multilevel threshold based gray scale image segmentation using cuckoo search.* arXiv preprint arXiv:1307.0277

Stagg, G. W., & El-Abid, A. H. (1968). *Computer Methods in Power System Analysis.* McGraw-Hill Book Co.

Sun, D. I., Ashley, B., Brewer, B., Hughes, A., & Tinney, W. F. (1984). Optimal Power Flow by Newton Approach. *IEEE Transactions on Power Apparatus and Systems, 103*(10), pp2864–pp2880. doi:10.1109/TPAS.1984.318284

Tinney, W. F., & Hart, C. E. (1967, November). Power Flow-Solution by Newton's Method. *IEEE Transactions, 86,* 1449.

Tiwari, P. K., & Sood, Y. R. (2012). Efficient and optimal approach for location and parameter setting of multiple unified power flow controllers for a deregulated power sector. *IET Gener. Transm. Distrib, 6*(10), 958–967. doi:10.1049/iet-gtd.2011.0722

Venkateswara Rao, B., & Nagesh Kumar, G. V. (2014). Optimal Location of Thyristor Controlled Series Capacitor for reduction of Transmission Line losses using BAT Search Algorithm. *WSEAS Transactions on Power Systems, 9,* 459–470.

Yang, X.-S. (2008). *Nature-Inspired Metaheuristic Algorithms.* Luniver Press.

Yang, X.-S. (2010). A new metaheuristic bat-inspired algorithm. In Nature Inspired Cooperative Strategies for Optimization. Springer Berlin. doi:10.1007/978-3-642-12538-6_6

Zheng & Tan. (2000). *Dynamic Character Study of UPFC Based on Detailed Simulation Model.* IEEE Power Conference 2000.

KEY TERMS AND DEFINITIONS

BAT Algorithm: BAT algorithm was developed by X S Yang in 2010, which works based on echo location behavior of micro bats.

CSA: Cuckoo search algorithm was developed by X S Yang and Suash Deb in 2009, which works based on obligate brood parasitism of cuckoo.

DE: Differential Evolution (DE) is a method that optimizes a problem by iteratively trying to improve a candidate solution with regard to a given measure of quality.

FA: Firefly algorithm was developed by X S Yang in 2008, which works based on flashing behavior of fire fly.

FACTS: Alternating current transmission systems incorporating power electronic-based and other static controllers to enhance controllability and increase power transfer capability.

FACTS Devices or FACTS Controllers: A power electronic-based system and other static equipment that provide control of one or more AC transmission system parameters.

OPF: Optimal power flow (OPF) is an important tool for power system operation, control and planning. It was first introduced by (Dommel and Tinney, 1968). The main purpose of an OPF program is calculating the optimal operating point of a power system and setting the variables that optimize a certain objective function while satisfying power flow equations, equality and inequality constraints.

Optimization: It is the action of making the best or most effective use of a situation or resource.

UPFC: A combination of static synchronous compensator (STATCOM) and a static series compensator (SSSC) which are coupled via a common dc link, to allow bidirectional flow of real power between the series output terminals of the SSSC and the shunt output terminals of the STATCOM, and are controlled to provide concurrent real and reactive series line compensation without an external electric energy source.

Chapter 2
Analyzing and Predicting the QoS of Traffic in WiMAX Network Using Gene Expression Programming

J. Sangeetha
PES University, India

Keerthiraj Nagaraj
University of Florida, USA

K. N. Balasubramanya Murthy
PES University, India

Ram P. Rustagi
PES University, India

ABSTRACT

The WiMAX network provides an efficient QoS to the large number of users. The real time and non-real time multimedia applications are gaining importance in the WiMAX network. To support such applications, there is a need to propose an efficient QoS of traffic prediction mechanism for the WiMAX networks. To address this, the authors have applied Gene Expression Programming technique for CBR based traffic and file transfer applications in the WiMAX network. The main focus of this chapter is to develop the mathematical expressions for throughput of the network by considering bandwidth, average end-to-end delay and average jitter as inputs for CBR based traffic and file transfer applications. This expression helps to analyze and predict the QoS of traffic of a given network. The simulation results show that the model values and the target values match with better approximation. Experimentally GEP performs better than other existing algorithms. Furthermore, sensitivity analysis has been carried out for both the applications

DOI: 10.4018/978-1-5225-4151-6.ch002

INTRODUCTION

IEEE 802.16 air interface standard (Jeffrey et al., 2007) provides the details of physical layer and Media Access Control (MAC) layer of wireless communication system, which aims to build a multi-service network with Worldwide Interoperability for Microwave Access (WiMAX) technology. The different standards of WiMAX networks are IEEE 802.16a, IEEE 802.16d, IEEE 802.16e and IEEE 802.16j. There is a constant evolution of different standards, along with the demand for real-time multimedia applications such as Constant Bit Rate (CBR) based traffic, video stream and Voice over Internet Protocol (VoIP) and non-real-time multimedia applications such as file transfer, web browsing and email. To support these multimedia applications, the standards must be sensitive to the need for bandwidth with high speed access, large network coverage and the provision of good Quality of Services (QoS) to a large number of users.

The basic topology of a WiMAX network consists of two participating entities, called Base Station (BS) and Subscriber Station (SS). The BS is the central node, responsible for coordinating all the communication and providing connectivity to the SSs. The BS is the station that provides access to the public network. This network can be categorized into two operating modes: a mandatory Point-to-Multipoint (PMP) mode and an optional mesh mode. In PMP mode (Akashdeep et al., 2014; Ali et al., 2009), all SSs are only one-hop away from the BS and communicate to the BS directly in a centralized manner and not through other neighboring SSs. Akashdeep et al. (2014) have investigated on design issues for the development of schedulers and also ensured QoS support in WiMAX networks.I n optional mesh mode (Akyildiz et al., 2005; Kas et al., 2010), all SSs are one hop or more than one hop away from the BS and so the SSs communicates with the BS directly or indirectly (i.e. with other SSs) in a distributed manner. In literature (Sharma et al., 2014; Sharma et al., 2017), many researchers have worked on wireless mesh network. Due to the dynamic behavior of the wireless mesh network, handling routing is a critical issue. Sharma et al. (2017) have applied a nature inspired technique called Termite Colony Optimization (TCO) on this network. The TCO algorithm is used to find an optimal route based on the link cost. In this chapter, the researchers focus on a centralized PMP mode, which provides better QoS performance compared to distributed mesh mode (Ni et al., 2007).

There are two ways of providing QoS (Sekercioglu et al., 2009), they are user-centric QoS and network-centric QoS. The user-centric QoS comprises the degree of satisfaction of a user for the service. The network-centric QoS comprises the ability to control the mix of bandwidth, average end-to-end delay and average jitter in the network in order to deliver a network service such as CBR based traffic, file transfer application and VoIP. This chapter is primarily concerned with the network-centric QoS. The QoS parameters such as bandwidth, packet delivery ratio, average end-to-end delay, average jitter and throughput are generally used to measure the effect of multimedia streams on the level of QoS. These QoS parameters are considered only for the network-centric QoS, but not on the user-centric QoS. The WiMAX network (Carvalho et al., 2013) mainly depends on parameters such as bandwidth, delay, jitter, and throughput for efficient communication. This influences the QoS with a certain level of end-to-end quality for multimedia applications through the management of MAC and network layer for the provision of better QoS services.

QoS (Cicconetti et al., 2006; Grewal et al., 2010; Liu et al., 2006) plays a major role in IEEE 802.16 MAC layer. The MAC layer uses connection oriented approach. For performing the data transmissions over the particular link, the downlink (from BS to SS) and uplink (from SS to BS) connections are controlled by the particular BS. Each connection is identified by a connection identifier (CID) and the connection in the network is associated with a Service Flow Identifier (SFID) that is composed of a set of QoS parameters namely bandwidth, average end-to-end delay, average jitter and throughput. The BS performs the functionality of issuing the SFID and mapping it to unique CIDs and sending the packet to the appropriate SS.

To support real-time and non-real-time multimedia applications, WiMAX network defines five scheduling service classes (Kuran et al., 2007; Li et al., 2007; Sekercioglu et al., 2009). The five scheduling service classes are Unsolicited Grant Service (UGS), Real Time Polling Service (rtPS), Non-Real Time Polling Service (nrtPS), Best Effort (BE) and Extended Real Time Polling Service (ertPS). These scheduling service classes define the nature of the data service supported and the following are its detail description:

- The UGS scheduling service class supports real-time service flow that generate a fixed-size data packets on a periodic basis and hence it is used to carry Constant Bit Rate (CBR) based traffic such as VoIP without silence suppression.
- The rtPS scheduling service class supports real-time service flow that generate variable-size data packets on a periodic basis and hence it is used to carry real-time Variable Bit Rate (VBR) traffic such as streaming audio and video.
- The nrtPS scheduling service class supports non-real-time service flow that generates variable-size data packets on a periodic basis and hence it is used to carry non-real-time Variable Bit Rate (VBR) traffic such as file transfer. This service class is the most appropriate for the delay tolerant applications.
- The BE scheduling service class supports non-real-time service flow that generate average-size data packets on a periodic basis and hence it is used

to carry non-real-time Average Bit Rate (ABR) traffic such as Data transfer, Web browsing and Email. This service class is applicable only for services that do not have strict QoS requirements.

- The ertPS scheduling service class (introduced by IEEE 802.16e) supports real-time service flow that generate variable size data packets on a periodic basis and hence it is used to carry real-time Variable Bit Rate (VBR) traffic such as VoIP with silence suppression.

These scheduling service classes can only be used in the PMP mode. The performance of these scheduling services is evaluated in the work of Cicconetti et al. (2006). Application layer services use the most appropriate of these five scheduling service classes for the given service. Hence, QoS provisioning is not devoted to single layer functionality, but requires the joint effort of all the layers. Hence, there is a need for network engineers using the existing resources to implement a network that can provide efficient QoS.

The objective of this chapter is to analyze and predict the QoS of traffic prediction mechanism for the WiMAX network. This is important and challenging problem and thus it requires trustable tools. In this chapter, the authors provide nature inspired techniques as one such alternative for efficient analysis. Here, the authors have used GEP techniques. They have also considered some of the conventional methods such as Artificial Neural Network.

BACKGROUND

Recently, many researchers are focusing on various nature inspired techniques (Binh et al., 2016; Dey et. al., 2014; Hore et. al., 2017) to solve the problems in different fields. One such nature inspired technique called Gene Expression Programming (GEP) developed by Ferreira (2001) is applied to solve the function approximation problem. The GEP technique (Ferreira, 2001; Ferreira, 2002) brings out the relationship between the future and the historical data directly. This technique is the computational model; it discovers knowledge from data and expresses as a mathematical expression. The nature of the populations of the individuals is encoded as linear strings of fixed length called chromosomes which are afterwards expressed as nonlinear entities of different sizes and shapes called expression trees. Senthilnath et al. (2014) has proposed an approach for river mapping and flood evaluation to aid multi-temporal time series analysis of satellite images using GEP technique. In their study, the results show that the use of image classification and region-based segmentation is an accurate and reliable for the extraction of water-covered region. Finally, the performance of the Artificial Neural Network (ANN) and GEP techniques are evaluated and compared. Omkar et al. (2013) has proposed a precise classification of agricultural crops that provides vital information on the crop type and its extent cultivated in a particular area. In their study, the results show that the GEP technique is used to classify the crop data obtained from the satellite images. This technique provides an efficient method for obtaining classification rules in the form of a mathematical expression for a given data set containing input and output variables. Kubusada et al. (2013) has proposed an efficient QoS aware routing protocol for Mobile Ad hoc Network (MANET) network based on GEP technique. Lee et al. (2013) has proposed a prediction approach called GEP prediction to tackle the queue variation during waiting times as well as to reduce the high-priority packet delay in Ethernet Passive Optical Network (EPON). In their study, the results show that the GEP prediction in dynamic bandwidth allocation can reduce the packet delay, shorten the queue length, enhance the quality of services and maintain the fairness among the optical network units. Xu et al. (2017) has introduced an effective function mining algorithm, Gene Expression Programming algorithm. They have improved the efficiency of GEP in big data for processing large-scale classification tasks. Sabar et al. (2015) has employed GEP to design a framework for hyper-heuristic in order to solve the combinatorial optimization problems. Their result shows that the proposed work solves the combinatorial optimization problems. For the risk assessment of cyber physical power system, Deng et al. (2015) has proposed GEP algorithm. Their study shows that the security risk levels of cyber physical power system are predicted and analyzed by using the proposed algorithm.

From the literature (Nayak et al., 2016; Chatterjee et al., 2016; Bag et al., 2017; Manogaran et al., 2017; Acharjya et al., 2017), it has been revealed that many researchers from diverse fields are working on prediction based system. An efficient prediction based system is required in the stock market world to generate significant profit. Hence, Nayak et al. (2016) has proposed an adaptive single layer second order neural network with genetic algorithm (ASONN-GA) and also compared the result with recurrent neural network (RNN) and a Multilayer Perceptron Neural Network (MLP-NN). Prediction based system is also applied in the structural failure of the multistory reinforced concrete (RC) buildings. Chatterjee et al. (2016) has proposed Neural Network-Particle Swarm Optimization (NN-PSO) classifier to tackle the problem of predicting and detecting the failure possibility of the multistoried RC building structure in the future. The NN-PSO model was compared with NN (Neural Network) and Multi Layer Perceptron Feed Forward Neural Network (MLP-FFN) classifier to find its ingenuity.

In this chapter, the authors propose an efficient QoS of traffic prediction mechanism for the WiMAX network using the GEP technique. Also, the authors are analyzing the throughput of the WiMAX network with respect to real time services such as CBR based traffic and non-real-time services such as file transfer. To perform this study, the authors have generated two datasets using QUALNET 7.1 network simulator one for CBR based traffic and other for file transfer applications. From the literature (Kubusada et al., 2013; Lee et al., 2013), it is observed that GEP technique is more efficient in predicting the future values of QoS parameters when compared to other nature inspired techniques by generating mathematical expression.

The GEP technique is applied to the CBR based traffic and file transfer application datasets obtained from the network simulator to formulate the mathematical expressions for throughput in terms of bandwidth, average end-to-end delay and average jitter. The performance evaluation of the obtained results from the CBR based traffic and file transfer applications are compared with the conventional method Multi-Layer Perceptron Neural Network (MLP-NN) (Marchant et al., 2003).

Further, in this chapter the author also focuses on sensitivity analysis. The sensitivity analysis is carried out for checking whether the throughput is sensitive to considered input parameters in both CBR based traffic and file transfer applications. This study helps researchers and network engineers to analyze the performance of the network.

Wimax Network Topology

The authors have considered a WiMAX network scenario, using QUALNET® 7.1 network simulator. Here, 100 mobile nodes are randomly distributed in an area of 1500m x 1500m as shown in Figure 1. The list of parameters used during the simulation is shown in Table 1. In this chapter, the researchers have considered two scheduling service classes such as Unsolicited Grant Service (UGS) and Non-Real Time Polling Service (nrtPS) (Kuran et al., 2007; Li, et al., 2007). The UGS service class supports real time services such as CBR based traffic, which generates a fixed-size data packet on a periodic basis. The nrtPS scheduling service class supports non-real-time services such as file transfer applications, which generate variable-size data packets on a periodic basis. Here, the authors have considered two applications namely, CBR based traffic and file transfer.

In (Carvalho et al., 2013; Kubusada et al., 2013; Lee et al., 2013), researchers have focused on analyzing the performance of the network. To provide better performance, the selection of QoS parameters plays a major role. To the best of the authors' knowledge, the QoS parameters often used in the literature are bandwidth, average end-to-end delay, average jitter and throughput. These QoS parameters are generally used to measure the effect of multimedia streams on the level of QoS. The WiMAX network (Jeffrey et al., 2007; Carvalho et al., 2013) mainly depends on these parameters for efficient communication and providing the good QoS to a large number of users. Hence, the authors have analyzed the performance of the

Figure 1. WiMAX network scenario

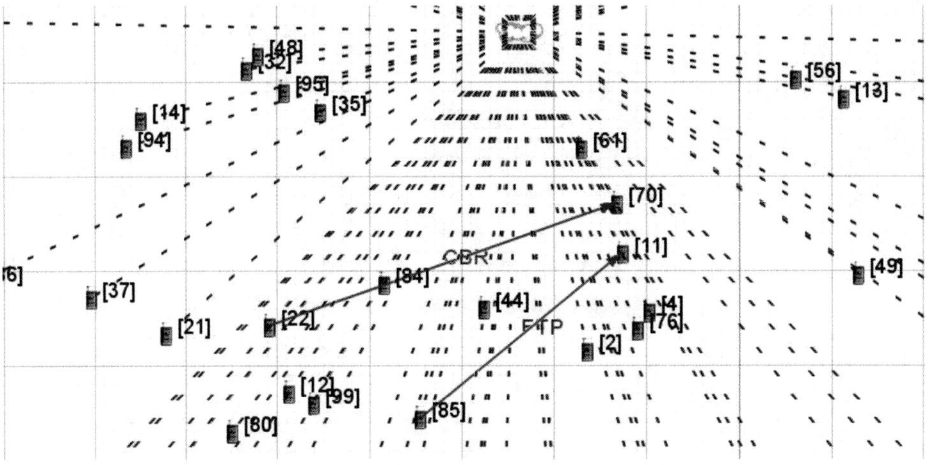

Table 1. Parameters used in the network simulator

Simulation Area	1500m x 1500m
Number of Mobile Nodes	100
Transmission Power	20dB
Simulation Time	150 seconds
Scheduling Service Class	UGS, nrtPS

WiMAX network by considering the dependent/output parameter such as throughput and the independent/input parameters such as bandwidth, average end-to-end delay and average jitter. The effects of these parameters are as follows:

1. **Throughput:** It is the rate of successful data delivery over a communication channel. Throughput is usually measured in bits per second (bit/s or bps).
2. **Bandwidth:** It is the measure of dataflow rate in a given network. This is usually measured in MHz.
3. **Average end-to-end delay**: It refers to the average time taken for data to be transmitted across a network from source to destination. This is usually measured in seconds.
4. **Average jitter:** It is the average of the all the time differences between transmission delay of a packet and transmission delay of its previous packet. Jitter can be calculated only if at least two packets have been received. This is usually measured in seconds.

Initially, the researchers have generated two datasets (i.e. training and testing datasets) using network simulator for CBR based traffic and file transfer applications. In both these applications, the datasets have been generated by considering three input parameters (i.e. bandwidth, average end-to-end delay and average jitter) and one output parameter (i.e. throughput). The training dataset is subjected to symbolic regression technique using the Gene Expression Programming (GEP) technique. The authors employ this technique to analyze and predict the QoS of traffic in both CBR based traffic and file transfer applications.

Gene Expression Programming

Gene Expression Programming (GEP) is a population based method, which was introduced and developed by Candida Ferreira (2001). The GEP is a nature inspired technique as the likes of Genetic Algorithm (GA) (Goldberg, 1989; Hamdan et al., 2016; El Hassani et al., 2017; Hore et. al., 2017; Dey et. al., 2015) and Genetic Programming (GP) (Koza, 1994; Zadshakoyan et al., 2015), which is used for the creation of computer programs to solve the problems such as symbolic regression (Kubusada et al., 2013), sequence induction, block stacking and density classification (Omkar et al., 2013; Omkar et al., 2012; Omkar et al., 2015), function mining (Xu et al., 2017), combinatorial optimization (Sabar et al., 2015), security risks (Deng et al., 2015).

The GEP technique is different from other adaptive techniques in the terms that it considers the individuals to be linear strings of fixed length at first but then encodes them to non-linear entities of different length and structure. The fixed length linear strings are considered as chromosomes or genomes and variable length non-linear strings are considered as Expression Trees (ETs) or phenotype. The GEP technique (Hu et al., 2007; Song et al., 2010) ensures modification in the individuals in successive generations by modifying its rate of mutation, transposition and recombination.

One of the most useful applications of GEP technique (Bakhshaii et al., 2009; Zuo et al., 2002) is symbolic regression or function finding. Symbolic regression mainly deals with formulating a new symbolic expression for an output variable that satisfies the fitness values for a given set of input variables. Different parameters like fitness function, function set {+, -, *, /, Q, sin, cos…}, population size, number of generations, linking function, number of genes, mutation rate, transposition rate and recombination rate has to be fixed to carry out this problem. The general steps of the GEP algorithm are explained below:

Step 1: Initial populations are randomly distributed.
Step 2: At each generation, the fitness value of each individual is evaluated.

Step 3: Individual with best fitness value is selected along with other individuals in the defined range of fitness value.

Step 4: The selected individuals are then subjected to the effects like mutation, transposition and recombination to give rise to the individuals for next generation.

In this chapter, the authors apply GEP technique to generate an expression tree for the QoS parameter throughput in terms of bandwidth, average end-to-end delay and average jitter in the WiMAX network. The steps involved in GEP implementation for prediction of QoS of traffic in the WiMAX network are as follows:

Step 1: For the training dataset, chromosomes of initial population that represent three input parameters (i.e. bandwidth, average end-to-end delay and average jitter) are randomly distributed.

Step 2: At each generation, fitness values of all these chromosomes are evaluated and are compared to the target throughput values.

Step 3: Evaluate the chromosomes of input parameters that are mapped to their respective output parameter to obtain best fitness value (i.e. minimum relative Mean Squared Error value).

Step 4: In successive generations, apply the genetic operators such as mutation, recombination and transposition to alter the characters of chromosomes to yield the throughput values that have better approximation to target values. The ways in which the different genetic operators in our problem are carried out are as follows:

- **Mutation:** The authors considered this genetic operator to account for sudden and drastic changes in values of bandwidth, average end-to-end delay and average jitter in the network.

- **Recombination:** This genetic operator was considered to account for random changes in individual input parameters while building the model for throughput of the network.

- **Transposition:** This operator plays a major role in maintaining genetic variation and evolvability as they induce necessary modifications in successive iterations. This iterative process results in better models for throughput in all the iterations than its previous one.

Step 5: The above-mentioned steps are repeated for considerably large number of generations and the chromosomes of bandwidth, average end-to-end delay and average jitter at the final generation are considered for finding the values of throughput of the network.

Illustrative Example for Symbolic Regression

To understand, let us consider a very simple training and testing datasets as shown in Table 2 and 3. The researchers have applied the symbolic regression problem for this dataset to obtain the expression for output (Y) in terms of input (d_0) using the GEP technique.

The GEP parameters such as mutation rate, recombination rate, transposition rate, number of generations, linking function, population size (i.e. number of chromosomes), number of genes per chromosome and fitness function have to be

Table 2. Training dataset for an illustrative example

d_0	Y
1	2
3	12
5	30
7	56
9	90
11	132
13	182
15	240
17	306
19	380

Table 3. Testing dataset for an illustrative example

d_0	Y
2	6
4	20
6	42
8	72
10	110
12	156
14	210
16	272
18	342
20	420

fixed to carry out the symbolic regression. The authors have empirically analyzed the values of these parameters after executing the GEP for different runs. The most favorable values of genetic operators after different runs is as shown in Table 4, by considering least rMSE values for a given dataset.

For the considered datasets, the researchers have assumed two genes per chromosome and one constant per gene; hence two sub-Expression Trees (i.e. two genes) are obtained and it is as shown in Figure 2 and two numerical constants as shown in Table 5.

In this example, the authors have considered 30 chromosomes and 2 genes per chromosome. Hence, there are 60 genes. The 60 genes gets evolved (i.e. undergoes mutation, recombination and transposition) over 1000 generations and best 2 genes (i.e. model values matching with the target values) are selected. The best 2 genes result in the following equations:

Table 4. GEP parameters for an illustrative example

GEP parameter	Value
Number of generations	1000
Population size	30
Mutation rate	0.044
Recombination rate	0.1
Transposition rate	0.1
Linking function	+
Number of genes	2
Fitness function	relative Mean Squared Error (rMSE)
Function set	+,-,*,/

Figure 2. Sub expression trees for an illustrative example

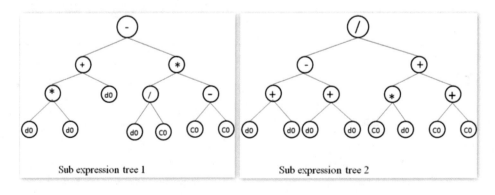

Table 5. Values of constants used in expression

Constant	Value	Explanation of the Constant
G_1C_0	-1.640137	1st constant of Gene 1
G_2C_0	-1.640137	1st constant of Gene 2

$$Y_1 = \left(\left(d_0 \times d_0 \right) + d_0 \right) - \left(\frac{d_0}{C_0} \times \left(G_1C_0 - G_1C_0 \right) \right) \qquad (1)$$

$$Y_2 = \left(\frac{\left(d_0 + d_0 \right) - \left(d_0 + d_0 \right)}{\left(\left(G_2C_0 \times d_0 \right) + \left(G_2C_0 + G_2C_0 \right) \right)} \right) \qquad (2)$$

where d_0 is the input parameter, G_1C_0 is the first constant of Gene 1 and G_2C_0 is the first constant of Gene 2. Y_1 and Y_2 are Gene 1 and Gene 2 respectively.

The authors have assumed 'addition' as the linking function for the two genes. Hence the expression for Y (i.e. chromosome) in terms of d_0 is obtained by adding Y_1 (i.e. Gene 1) with Y_2 (i.e. Gene 2) as shown in Figure 3.

$$Y = Y_1 + Y_2$$

Figure 3. Expression tree for an illustrative example

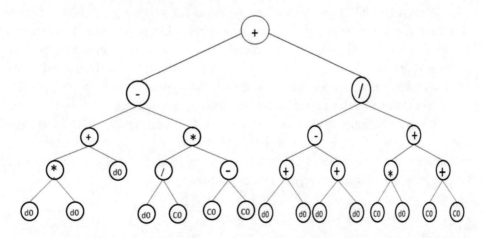

$$Y = \left(\left(d_0 \times d_0 \right) + d_0 \right) \qquad (3)$$

The Equation 3 (i.e. chromosome) is validated using the testing dataset as given in Table 3; the values obtained using this Equation proved to be matching exactly with the target values.

Artificial Neural Network

The Artificial Neural Networks (ANN) (Anderson, 1972; Bashiri et al., 2011; Hore et. al., 2017) technique is mainly used in the problems such as function approximation where the function depends on large number of inputs (Marchant et al., 2003). This technique is also used to solve the prediction based problems. For better approximation ANN needs training data to map the input data with their respective output by generating optimal weights. The ANN is interconnected by a group of artificial neurons.

In most cases an ANN adapts non-linear function approximation (i.e. learns to perform a function from data). This neural network is trained by adjusting the values of the weights between processing elements (i.e. input with their respective output sample). After training the neural network, when a particular input is given the expected output is achieved. ANN parameters such as the number of hidden layers and the learning rate are selected empirically (Bashiri et al., 2011). The optimal weight obtained during training phase can be used for the testing phase.

The ANN method used in this chapter is Multi-Layer Perceptron Neural Network (MLPNN) (Senthilnath et al., 2012; Marchant et al., 2003; Omkar et al., 2010). This is also used to solve the prediction based problem. MLP-NN is an adaptive non-linear system that formulates a function for output from the observed values of input parameters. MLP-NN uses the back-propagation algorithm. The number of input neurons represents the number of input parameters or independent variables (in this chapter it is bandwidth, average end-to-end delay and average jitter) and the output neurons represent the response (in this chapter its throughput). Using MLP-NN technique, the authors predicted the values of throughput considering bandwidth, average end-to-end delay and average jitter as input parameters.

From the literature (Senthilnath et al., 2014; Omkar et al., 2015), we have understood that the MLP-NN technique converge to only local optima. Hence, in this chapterto the considered prediction based problem the authors have applied GEP technique, which converges to global optima.

MAIN FOCUS OF THE CHAPTER

In this chapter, the authors have proposed an efficient QoS of traffic prediction mechanism for the WiMAX network using GEP technique. Here, the throughput analysis of the WiMAX network is done with respect to real time services such as CBR based traffic and non-real-time services such as file transfer application. Further, this study also focuses on the QoS of traffic prediction of the network. To perform this study, the researchers have generated two datasets using QUALNET® 7.1 network simulator for CBR based traffic and file transfer applications.

The considered QoS parameters are bandwidth, average end-to-end delay and average jitter as input parameters and throughput as the output parameter. The GEP techniques have been applied to analyze and predict the QoS of traffic in both CBR based traffic and file transfer applications. From the literature (Senthilnath et al. 2014; Omkar et al., 2013; Kubusada et al., 2013; Lee et al., 2013), it is observed that GEP technique is more efficient in predicting the future values of QoS parameters when compared with other nature inspired techniques by generating mathematical expression. The GEP technique is applied to the CBR based traffic and file transfer datasets obtained from the network simulator to formulate the mathematical expressions for throughput in terms of bandwidth, average end-to-end delay and average jitter. The performance evaluation of the obtained results from the CBR based traffic and file transfer applications are compared with the MLP-NN technique.

Further, this study also focuses on sensitivity analysis. The sensitivity analysis is carried out with GEP technique for checking whether the throughput is sensitive to considered input parameters in both CBR based traffic and file transfer applications. To the best of our knowledge, the GEP technique has not been previously used to solve the QoS of traffic prediction mechanism in WiMAX networks. This study was identified as being importance to researchers and network engineers in providing them the necessary background for their works. The principal advantages of this chapter are: efficient utilization of networks, proper monitoring of network, efficiently routing the packets in the network and providing the good QoS to a large number of users.

SOLUTIONS AND RECOMMENDATIONS

In this chapter, the authors are focusing on analyzing the throughput performance of the WiMAX network, by considering bandwidth, average end-to-end delay and average jitter as input parameters. Using these, the QoS of traffic of the given network is predicted. To solve these issues, the Gene Expression Programming (GEP) technique is used. The GEP technique is applied on CBR based traffic and file transfer applications. The results obtained from GEP are compared with the MLP-NN technique. Further, the sensitivity analysis for the both CBR based traffic and file transfer applications are carried out.

Dataset Preparation Using Network Simulator

The datasets are generated using QUALNET® 7.1 network simulator for WiMAX network by considering two applications namely CBR based traffic and file transfer. These datasets are segregated into 69 training samples and 71 testing samples. These samples contain one output parameter: throughput and a set of three input parameters: bandwidth, average end-to-end delay and average jitter. The training samples are used in GEP technique to generate expression tree. The performance of the expression tree is analyzed by using the testing samples.

Gene Expression Programming for WiMAX Network

The GEP technique (Sangeetha et al., 2016) is applied on the datasets to obtain the mathematical expressions for throughput in terms of bandwidth, average end-to-end delay and average jitter. To employ the GEP technique, the fitness function is defined. The authors have considered the most preferred fitness function known as relative Mean Squared Error (rMSE) (Kubusada et al., 2013) for the function finding problem. The rMSE fitness function Ei of an individual program i is evaluated by the Equation 4.

$$E_i = \frac{1}{n} \sum_{j=1}^{n} \left(\frac{P_{(ij)} - T_j}{T_j} \right)^2 \qquad (4)$$

where P(ij) is the value predicted by the individual program i for fitness case j (out of n fitness cases) and Tj is the target value for fitness case j.

The considered rMSE fitness function gives more weight to higher errors as square term is used. This function helps to arrive at more accurate model which predicts throughput values much closer to target values. This function also helps to calculate error relative to the target values, hence when the target values are low even the low errors in prediction results in high rMSE value. Minimum the rMSE value; better is the expression tree obtained.

The other parameters such as mutation rate, transposition rate and recombination rate, number of generations, linking function, population size (i.e. number of chromosomes), number of genes and fitness function have to be fixed to carry out the symbolic regression using GEP technique. The researchers have empirically analyzed the values of these parameters after executing the GEP for different runs. Here, the authors have observed the most favorable values of genetic operators after several runs and this is as shown in Table 6, by considering least rMSE values for a given dataset.

If the number of genes is less, then the variation in the successive generation is less and so it takes more number of generations to arrive at the favorable result. If the number of genes is more, then the chances of variation over successive generation will be very high and hence the chances of getting unfavorable results are high. From the trial and error method and after several runs the authors conclude three genes per chromosome and two constants per gene as the favorable result. Hence, three Sub-expression trees (i.e. 3 genes) with six numerical constants in the Expression Tree (ET)of both CBR based traffic and file transfer applications are obtained.

CBR Based Traffic

In this case, a total of 100 data items, each of 512 bytes is transferred using CBR based traffic. The GEP technique is applied on training datasets of CBR based traffic. From Figure 4, it is observed that, for five different runs carried out, the best run is selected by comparing the mean and standard deviation values of rMSE in each run. The 3rd run resulted in minimum rMSE values compared to all other runs. Hence, the mean and standard deviation of rMSE values for the training dataset are 68.21 and 50.50 respectively and for the testing dataset the mean and standard deviation values are 71.12 and 48.66 respectively.

Table 6. Values of the GEP parameters

GEP Parameter	Value
Number of generations	2000
Population size	30
Mutation rate	0.044
Recombination rate	0.1
Transposition rate	0.1
Linking function	+
Number of genes	3
Fitness function	rMSE
Function set	+, -, *, /, sqrt, x2, x3, natural logarithm

Figure 4. Mean and standard deviation of rMSE values in CBR based traffic using the GEP technique for the training and testing dataset

Training Dataset   Testing Dataset

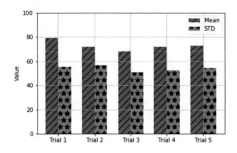 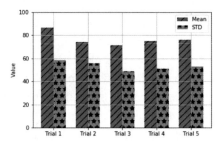

Sub-expression trees, mathematical expressions and numerical constant values obtained from 3[rd]run for throughput (T_{CBR}) evaluated using training dataset of CBR based traffic in terms of bandwidth (b), average end-to-end delay (d) and average jitter (j). The Sub-expression trees are shown in Figure 5. The mathematical expressions are shown in Equations 5, 6, 7 and 8.

The authors have considered 30 chromosomes and 3 genes per chromosome. Hence, totally 90 genes are generated randomly. The 90 genes get evolved (undergo mutation, recombination and transposition) over the assumed 2000 generations. The best 3 genes are selected based on the model and target values matching with the least rMSE value and are shown below in the Equations:

$$T_{CBR1} = \left(G_1C_1\right) + \left(\left(G_1C_0 \times G_1C_1\right)^2 + \left(\frac{d - G_1C_1}{d}\right)\right) \tag{5}$$

Figure 5. Sub-expression trees for the CBR based traffic

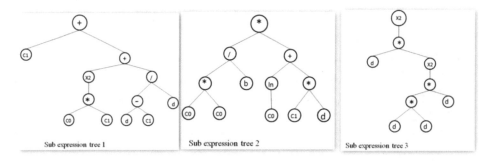

50

$$T_{CBR2} = \left(\frac{\left(G_2 C_0\right)^2}{b}\right) \times \left(\left(\ln\left(G_2 C_0\right)\right) + \left(G_2 C_1 \times d\right)\right) \tag{6}$$

$$T_{CBR3} = \left(\left(d \times \left(d^2 \times d\right)^2\right)^2\right) \tag{7}$$

where b is bandwidth and d is average end-to-end delay are the input parameters, the numerical constant values such as $G_1 C_0$, $G_1 C_1$, $G_2 C_0$, $G_2 C_1$, $G_3 C_0$, $G_3 C_1$ are given in Table 7.

The 'addition' as the linking function is used in GEP; the expression tree obtained is as shown in Figure 6. The mathematical expression for throughput of the given network for CBR based traffic is given below:

$$T_{CBR} = T_{CBR1} + T_{CBR2} + T_{CBR3} \tag{8}$$

From Figure 7, it is shown, the variation of model throughput values (obtained using GEP technique) and target throughput values (obtained from QUALNET 7.1 network simulator) in the CBR based traffic. It is observable that model and target values match very closely. During approximation, the GEP technique generates mathematical expression by mapping input parameter with the respective output parameter using training dataset. The mathematical expression (i.e. Equation 8) is validated with the testing dataset. Similarly, from the Figure 8 we observe that model values match with target values with better approximation for testing dataset.

Table 7. Values of constants used in expression for throughput in CBR based traffic

Constant	Value	Explanation of the constant
$G_1 C_0$	7.223358	1st constant of Gene 1
$G_1 C_1$	9.026275	2nd constant of Gene 1
$G_2 C_0$	7.223358	1st constant of Gene 2
$G_2 C_1$	6.719025	2nd constant of Gene 2
$G_3 C_0$	0.125396	1st constant of Gene 3
$G_3 C_1$	7.150665	2nd constant of Gene 3

Figure 6. Expression tree for the CBR based traffic

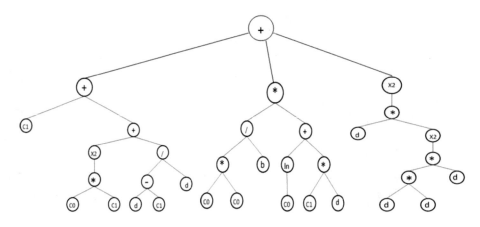

Figure 7. Network throughput for training samples in CBR based traffic

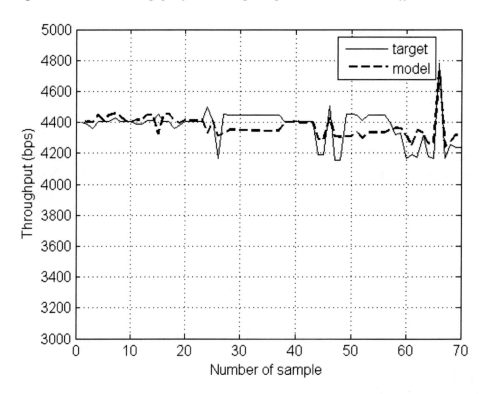

Figure 8. Network throughput for testing samples in CBR based traffic

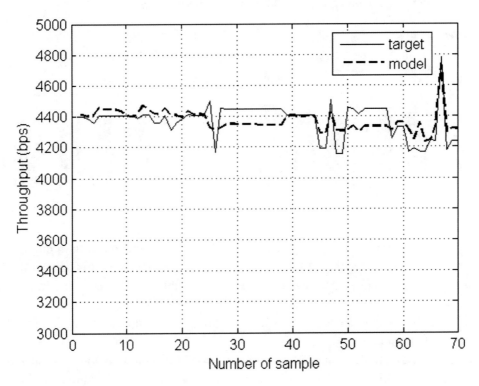

Comparison Between GEP and ANN
Techniques for CBR Based Traffic

The authors have compared the proposed GEP technique with Multi-Layer Perceptron Neural Network (MLP-NN) (Omkar et al., 2010; Senthilnath et al., 2012). Under CBR based traffic using the GEP technique, for the training dataset, the mean and standard deviation values are 68.21 and 50.50 respectively and for the testing dataset the mean and standard deviation values are 71.12 and 48.66 respectively. Using the MLP-NN technique, the values for mean and standard deviation for the training and testing dataset is computed and given in Figure 9.

From Figure 9, it is observed that, for five different runs carried out, the best run is selected by comparing the mean and standard deviation values of rMSE in each run. The 3[rd]run resulted in minimum rMSE values compared to all other runs. Hence, for the training dataset the mean and standard deviation values are 58.42 and 68.36 respectively and for the testing dataset the mean and standard deviation values are 66.92 and 67.22respectively.

Figure 9. Mean and Standard deviation of rMSE values in CBR based traffic using the MLP-NN technique for the training and testing dataset

Training Dataset

Testing Dataset

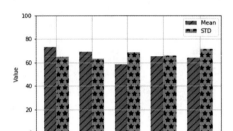
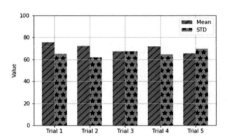

The throughput values obtained using MLP-NN are compared with throughput values obtained using the GEP technique. From the comparison, it is noticed that using the GEP technique we can generate a model which has better approximation with target values of throughput. Table 8 shows the mean and standard deviation of error between model and target values of throughput obtained through GEP and MLP-NN techniques.

From Table 8, the values of mean for MLP-NN technique is lower compared to values for GEP technique but MLP-NN has larger standard deviation values in comparison with the GEP technique. This suggests that MLP-NN is not appropriate to provide consistent model values for the throughput when compared to the GEP for the CBR based traffic. From the obtained result, it is noticed that the MLP-NN technique converge to only local optima. Hence, for the considered problem the authors conclude that the GEP has better performance than the MLP-NN.

File Transfer Application

Similar to the CBR based traffic, a total of 100 data items, each of 512 bytes is transferred. Apply the GEP technique for the training datasets of file transfer

Table 8. Comparison between GEP and MLP-NN techniques for CBR based traffic

Technique	Training		Testing	
	Mean	Standard Deviation	Mean	Standard Deviation
GEP	68.21	50.50	71.12	48.66
MLP-NN	58.42	68.36	66.92	67.22

application. From Figure 10, it is noticeable that for five different runs carried out, the best run is selected by comparing the mean and standard deviation values of rMSE in each run. The 1st run resulted in minimum error values compared to all other runs. Hence, the mean and standard deviation of rMSE values for the training dataset are 2.1393e003 and 2.1690e003 respectively and for the testing dataset the mean and standard deviation values are 1.9023e003 and 2.0748e003 respectively.

The Sub-expression trees obtained from 1st run for throughput (T_{FT}) evaluated using training dataset of file transfer applications in terms of bandwidth (b), average end-to-end delay (d) and average jitter (j). The Sub-expression trees are shown in Figure 11.

Figure 10. Mean and Standard deviation of rMSE values in file transfer application using the GEP technique for the training and testing dataset

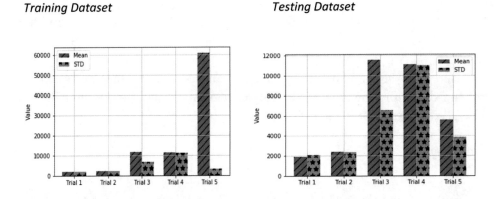

Figure 11. Sub-expression trees for the file transfer application

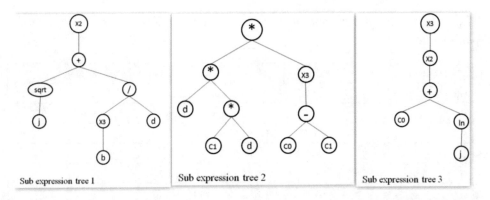

Similar to the CBR based traffic, the authors have selected the best 3 genes (i.e. mathematical expressions) are shown in the below Equations 9, 10, 11 and 12.

$$T_{FT1} = \left(\sqrt{j} + \left(\frac{b^3}{d} \right) \right)^2 \qquad (9)$$

$$T_{FT2} = \left(d^2 \times G_2C_1 \times \left(G_2C_0 - G_2C_1 \right)^3 \right) \qquad (10)$$

$$T_{FT3} = \left(\left(G_3C_0 + \ln(j) \right)^2 \right)^3 \qquad (11)$$

where b (i.e. bandwidth), d (i.e. average end-to-end delay) and j (i.e. average jitter) are the input parameters, the numerical constant values such as G_1C_0, G_1C_1, G_2C_0, G_2C_1, G_3C_0, G_3C_1 are given in Table 9.

Here also the 'addition' as the linking function is used; the expression tree obtained is as shown in Figure 12. The mathematical expression for throughput of the given network for file transfer application is:

$$T_{FT} = T_{FT1} + T_{FT2} + T_{FT3} \qquad (12)$$

In the file transfer application, from the Figure 13 the model and target values match with better approximation. The GEP technique generates mathematical

Table 9. Values of constants used in expression for throughput in file transfer application

Constant	Value	Explanation of the Constant
G_1C_0	-6.524719	1st constant of Gene 1
G_1C_1	3.18808	2nd constant of Gene 1
G_2C_0	2.508759	1st constant of Gene 2
G_2C_1	-6.651825	2nd constant of Gene 2
G_3C_0	-4.350281	1st constant of Gene 3
G_3C_1	-7.314789	2nd constant of Gene 3

Figure 12. Expression tree for the file transfer application

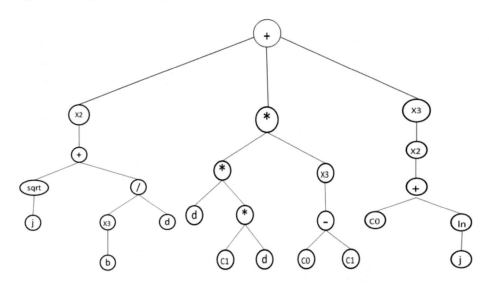

expression (i.e. Equation 12) by mapping input parameter with the respective output parameter using the training dataset. This expression is validated with the testing dataset. Similarly, for the testing dataset from Figure 14, it is observed that the model and target values almost match.

Comparison Between GEP and ANN Techniques for File Transfer Application

The authors have similarly compared the GEP technique with MLP-NN for the file transfer application. Under file transfer application using the GEP technique, for the training dataset the mean and standard deviation values are 2.1393e003 and 2.1690e003 respectively and for the testing dataset the mean and standard deviation values are 1.9023e003 and 2.0748e003 respectively. The values of mean and standard deviation for this training and testing dataset using the MLP-NN techniques is computed and shown in Figure 15. From Figure 15, we find that the 4[th]run resulted in least rMSE values. Hence, for the training dataset the mean and standard deviation values using the MLP-NN technique are 2.7355e004 and 1.5944e004 respectively and for the testing dataset the mean and standard deviation values are 2.9672e004 and 1.6232e004 respectively.

From the comparison, the authors have found that the GEP technique generates model which has better approximation with target values of throughput. From Table 10, it is noticed that the values of mean and standard deviation for error obtained

Figure 13. Network throughput for training samples in file transfer application

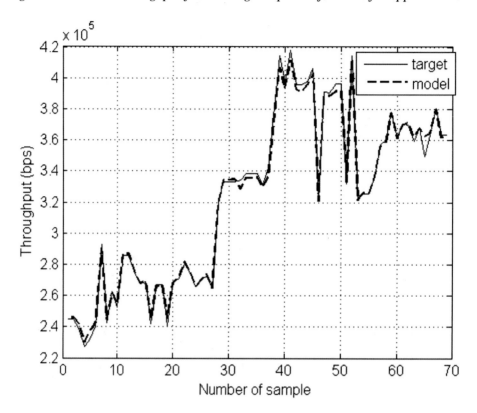

through GEP technique is lower than the values obtained through MLP-NN. From the obtained result, here also it is observed that the MLP-NN technique converge to only local optima. Hence, here also the authors conclude that the GEP perform better than the MLP-NN technique.

Sensitivity Analysis

In the previous cases, the researchers tried to obtain the mathematical expression by mapping input parameters (i.e. bandwidth, average end-to-end delay and average jitter) with output parameter (i.e. throughput) for CBR based traffic and file transfer applications. From the Equations 5, 6, 7 and 8, it is observed that the mathematical expressions are independent of average jitter (i.e. the throughput in the CBR based traffic is least sensitive to average jitter compared to the other parameters).

Hence, the sensitivity analysis is carried out with GEP technique by training the samples considering bandwidth and average end-to-end delay (i.e. ignoring average jitter) as input parameters with their output parameter to obtain the expression trees.

Figure 14. Network throughput for testing samples in file transfer application

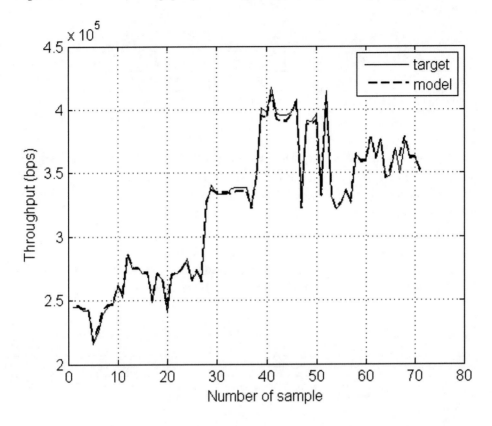

Figure 15. Mean and Standard deviation of rMSE values in file transfer application using the MLP-NN technique for the training and testing dataset

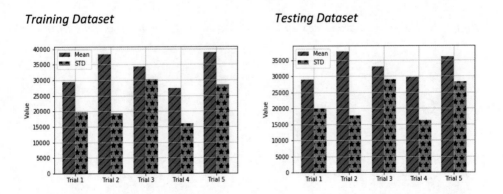

Table 10. Comparison between GEP and MLP-NN techniques for file transfer application

Technique	Training		Testing	
	Mean	Standard Deviation	Mean	Standard Deviation
GEP	2.1393×10^3	2.1690×10^3	1.9023×10^3	2.0748×10^3
MLP-NN	2.7355×10^4	1.5944×10^4	2.9672×10^4	1.6232×10^4

The authors conducted this experiment for several runs and the best run is selected and this is compared to the CBR based traffic with all input parameters. From Table 11, it is observed that CBR based traffic with two input parameters (i.e. bandwidth and average end-to-end delay) has lower rMSE values.

The Sub-expression trees are as shown in Figure 16 and the mathematical expressions are shown in Equations 13, 14, 15 and 16.

Similar to other applications (i.e. CBR based traffic and file transfer), here also the authors have selected the best 3 genes which are shown below:

Table 11. Mean and Standard deviation of rMSE values in CBR based traffic

Case	Training		Testing	
	Mean	Standard Deviation	Mean	Standard Deviation
CBR application with all input parameters	68.21	50.50	71.12	48.66
CBR application with two input parameters (i.e. bandwidth and average end-to-end delay)	66.30	49.44	69.36	48.82

Figure 16. Sub-Expression trees for the CBR based traffic with two input parameters

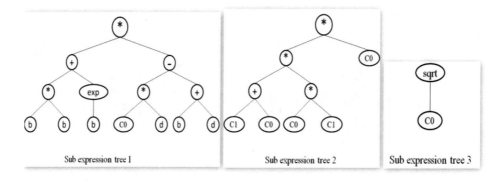

$$T_{CBR\_SA1} = \left(b^2 + e^b\right) \times \left(\left(G_1 C_0 \times d\right) - \left(b + d\right)\right) \tag{13}$$

$$T_{CBR\_SA2} = \left(\left(\left(G_2 C_1 + G_2 C_0\right) \times \left(G_2 C_0 \times G_2 C_1\right)\right) \times G_2 C_0\right) \tag{14}$$

$$T_{CBR\_SA3} = \sqrt{G_3 C_0} \tag{15}$$

where b (bandwidth) and d (average end-to-end delay) are the input parameters, the numerical constant values such as $G_1 C_0$, $G_1 C_1$, $G_2 C_0$, $G_2 C_1$, $G_3 C_0$, $G_3 C_1$ are given and explained in Table 12.

Here also the linking function (i.e. addition) is used in GEP. The obtained expression tree is as shown in Figure 17. The mathematical expression for throughput is:

$$T_{CBR\_SA} = T_{CBR\_SA1} + T_{CBR\_SA2} + T_{CBR\_SA3} \tag{16}$$

Here also from the Figure 18, it can be concluded that model and target values match with better approximation. Using the training dataset, here also the mathematical expression (i.e. Equation 16) is generated and is validated with the testing dataset. For the testing dataset also it is found that the model values match with the target with better approximation and this is shown in Figure 19.

From the sensitivity analysis, the authors conclude that in the CBR based traffic, after ignoring the average jitter parameter from both training and testing dataset, the value of rMSE decreased and the throughput values obtained from the mathematical expression matched better with target values. Hence, throughput is least sensitive to

Table 12. Values of constants used in expression for throughput in CBR based traffic

Constant	Value	Explanation of the Constant
$G_1 C_0$	5.814789	1st constant of Gene 1
$G_1 C_1$	-0.279754	2nd constant of Gene 1
$G_2 C_0$	-8.953431	1st constant of Gene 2
$G_2 C_1$	-4.159057	2nd constant of Gene 2
$G_3 C_0$	5.814789	1st constant of Gene 3
$G_3 C_1$	-0.279754	2nd constant of Gene 3

Figure 17. Expression tree for the CBR based traffic with two input parameters

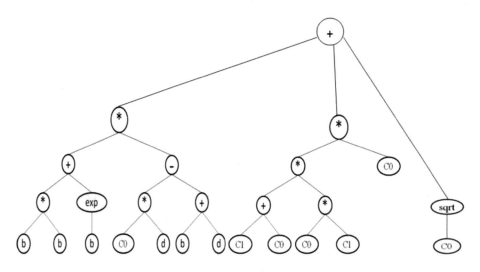

Figure 18. Network throughput for training samples in CBR based traffic with two input parameters

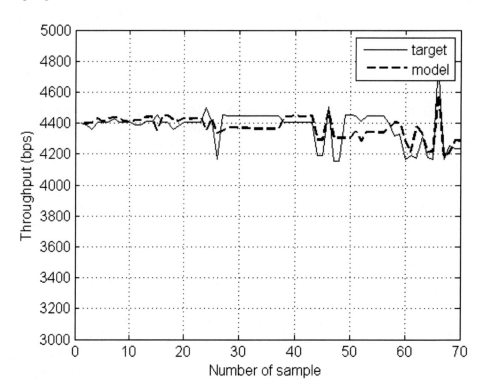

Figure 19. Network throughput for testing samples in CBR based traffic with two input parameters

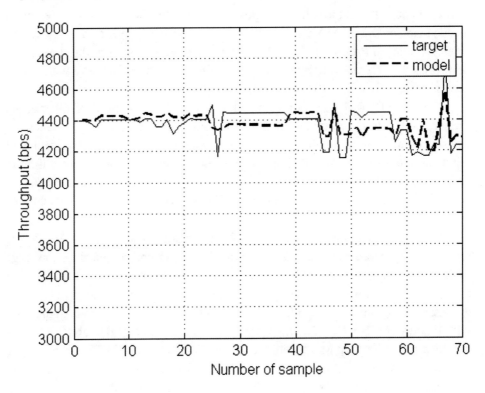

the average jitter parameter. Further, from the Equations 9, 10 and 11 it is observed, in the file transfer application the throughput is sensitive to all the input parameters (i.e. bandwidth, average end-to-end delay and average jitter).

FUTURE RESEARCH DIRECTIONS

This chapter mainly focuses on predicting QoS of traffic for the given WiMAX network. The mathematical equations obtained using GEP technique can also be used in decision making. The throughput values which can be predicted using the formulated mathematical equations can be used as reference while making the decisions in scenarios such as network management and QoS monitoring. This technique can be implemented in diverse field of networks such as MANETs, Cognitive networks and EPONs.

CONCLUSION

In this chapter, the authors have proposed an efficient QoS of traffic prediction mechanism for the WiMAX network using a nature inspired technique such as Gene Expression Programming (GEP). Here, the authors analyze the throughput performance of the network by predicting the QoS of traffic. The two datasets have been generated, one in CBR based traffic and the other in file transfer applications using QUALNET® 7.1 network simulator. The datasets consist of 69 training samples and 71 testing samples, totally 140 samples in each dataset. The generated datasets contain the throughput as the output parameter for the several values of input parameters such as bandwidth, average end-to-end delay and average jitter in both CBR based traffic and file transfer applications. This dataset is subjected to symbolic regression using GEP technique. The key point in using GEP technique is the future prediction that it offers.

The proposed technique is used to obtain the mathematical expressions for the QoS defining parameters such as bandwidth, average end-to-end delay, average jitter and throughput in both CBR based traffic and file transfer applications. The experimental results show that the model values (i.e. obtained from mathematical expressions) are almost matching with the target values (i.e. the generated data set) with the low rMSE value. The low rMSE values indicate that the model which is obtained from the proposed technique for throughput of both CBR based traffic and file transfer applications is efficient. The results from GEP technique are also compared with artificial neural network technique, namely multi-layer perceptron neural network for both CBR based traffic and file transfer applications and it is found that GEP technique provides model values which have better approximation with target values.

Further, this study also focuses on sensitivity analysis in both CBR based traffic and file transfer applications. The sensitivity analysis is carried out with the GEP technique. In CBR based traffic, throughput is least sensitive to the average jitter parameter and in file transfer application the throughput is sensitive to all the input parameters (i.e. bandwidth, average end-to-end delay and average jitter). From the obtained results, the authors conclude that the proposed technique is efficient and reliable, for analyzing the performance of the WiMAX networks by the QoS of traffic prediction mechanism.

ACKNOWLEDGMENT

The authors are profoundly grateful to Prof. V. Mani, Department of Aerospace Engineering, IISC, Bangalore for providing the honorable opportunity to work in their Evolutionary Computations Lab. The authors would like to thank PES University for providing the resource to complete this work. Author J. Sangeetha, would like to express her sincere gratitude to Dr. Shylaja. S. S, HOD, Department of Information Science & Engineering, PESIT, Bangalore for her extensive support in the completion of the proposed work. This research received no specific grant from any funding agency in the public, commercial, or not-for-profit sectors.

REFERENCES

Acharjya, D., & Anitha, A. (2017). A Comparative Study of Statistical and Rough Computing Models in Predictive Data Analysis. *International Journal of Ambient Computing and Intelligence*, 8(2), 32–51. doi:10.4018/IJACI.2017040103

Akashdeep, K., Kahlon, K. S., & Kumar, H. (2014). Survey of scheduling algorithms in IEEE 802.16 PMP networks. *Egyptian Informatics Journal*, 15(1), 25–36. doi:10.1016/j.eij.2013.12.001

Akyildiz, I. F., Wang, X., & Wang, W. (2005). Wireless mesh networks: A survey. *Computer Networks Journal (Elsevier)*, 47(4), 445–487. doi:10.1016/j.comnet.2004.12.001

Ali, N. A., Dhrona, P., & Hassanein, H. (2009). A performance study of uplink scheduling algorithms in point-to-multipoint WiMAX networks. *Computer Communications*, 32(3), 511–521. doi:10.1016/j.comcom.2008.09.015

Anderson, J. A. (1972). A simple neural network generating an interactive memory. *Mathematical Biosciences*, 14(3-4), 197–200. doi:10.1016/0025-5564(72)90075-2

Bag, V., & Kulkarni, U. V. (2017). Stock Price Trend Prediction and Recommendation using Cognitive Process. *International Journal of Rough Sets and Data Analysis*, 4(2), 36–48. doi:10.4018/IJRSDA.2017040103

Bakhshaii, A., & Stull, R. (2009). Deterministic ensemble forecasts using gene-expression programming. *Weather and Forecasting*, 24(5), 1431–1451. doi:10.1175/2009WAF2222192.1

Bashiri, M., & Geranmayeh, A. F. (2011). Tuning the parameters of an artificial neural network using central composite design and genetic algorithm. *Scientia Iranica*, 18(6), 1600–1608. doi:10.1016/j.scient.2011.08.031

Binh, H. T. T., Hanh, N. T., & Dey, N. (2016). Improved Cuckoo Search and Chaotic Flower Pollination optimization algorithm for maximizing area coverage in Wireless Sensor Networks. *Neural Computing & Applications*, 1–13.

Carvalho, T., Junior, J. J., Valente, W., Natalino, C., Francês, R., & Dias, K. L. (2013). *A Mobile WiMAX Mesh Network with Routing Techniques and Quality of Service Mechanisms. In Selected Topics in WiMAX* (pp. 61–84). InTech.

Chatterjee, S., Sarkar, S., Hore, S., Dey, N., Ashour, A. S., & Balas, V. E. (2016). Particle swarm optimization trained neural network for structural failure prediction of multistoried RC buildings. *Neural Computing & Applications*, 1–12.

Cicconetti, C., Lenzini, L., Mingozzi, E., & Eklund, C. (2006). Quality of Service Support in IEEE 802.16 Networks. *IEEE Network*, *20*(2), 50–55. doi:10.1109/MNET.2006.1607896

Deng, S., Yue, D., Fu, X., & Zhou, A. (2015). Security risk assessment of cyber physical power system based on rough set and gene expression programming. *IEEE/CAA Journal of Automatica Sinica, 2*(4), 431-439.

Dey, N., Ashour, A. S., Beagum, S., Pistola, D. S., Gospodinov, M., Gospodinova, E. P., & Tavares, J. M. R. (2015). Parameter optimization for local polynomial approximation based intersection confidence interval filter using genetic algorithm: An application for brain MRI image de-noising. *Journal of Imaging*, *1*(1), 60–84. doi:10.3390/jimaging1010060

Dey, N., Samanta, S., Chakraborty, S., Das, A., Chaudhuri, S. S., & Suri, J. S. (2014). Firefly algorithm for optimization of scaling factors during embedding of manifold medical information: An application in ophthalmology imaging. *Journal of Medical Imaging and Health Informatics*, *4*(3), 384–394. doi:10.1166/jmihi.2014.1265

El Hassani, H., Benkachcha, S., & Benhra, J. (2017). New genetic operator (jump crossover) for the traveling salesman problem. In Nature-Inspired Computing: Concepts, Methodologies, Tools, and Applications (pp. 1739-1752). IGI Global.

Ferreira, C. (2001). Gene Expression Programming: A New Adaptive Algorithm for Solving Problems. *Complex Systems*, *13*(2), 87–129.

Ferreira, C. (2002). Gene Expression Programming: Mathematical Modeling by an Artificial Intelligence. Angra do Heroismo.

Goldberg, D. E. (1989). *Genetic Algorithms in Search, Optimization and Machine Learning*. Addison-Wesley Publishing Company.

Grewal, V., & Sharma, A, K. (2010). On Performance Evaluation of Different QoS Mechanisms and AMC scheme for an IEEE 802.16 based WiMAX Network. *International Journal of Computer Applications*, *6*(7), 12 – 17.

Hamdan, M., & Abderrazzaq, M. H. (2016). Optimization of Small Wind Turbines using Genetic Algorithms. *International Journal of Applied Metaheuristic Computing*, *7*(4), 50–65. doi:10.4018/IJAMC.2016100104

Hore, S., Chatterjee, S., Santhi, V., Dey, N., Ashour, A. S., Balas, V. E., & Shi, F. (2017). Indian Sign Language Recognition Using Optimized Neural Networks. In *Information Technology and Intelligent Transportation Systems* (pp. 553–563). Springer International Publishing. doi:10.1007/978-3-319-38771-0_54

Hu, J. J., Tang, C. J., Duan, L., Zuo, J., Peng, J., & Yuan, C. A. (2007). The strategy for diversifying initial population of gene expression programming. *Chinese Journal of Computers-Chinese Edition*, *30*(2), 305.

Jeffrey, G. A., Ghosh, A., & Muhamed, R. (2007). *Fundamentals of WiMAX: Understanding Broadband Wireless Networking*. Prentice-Hall.

Kas, M., Yargicoglu, B., Korpeoglu, I., & Karasan, E. (2010). A survey on scheduling in IEEE 802.16 mesh mode. *IEEE Communications Surveys and Tutorials*, *12*(2), 205–221. doi:10.1109/SURV.2010.021110.00053

Koza, J. R. (1994In press). *Genetic programming II: automatic discovery of reusable programs*. Cambridge, MA: MIT Press.

Kubusada, Y., Mohan, G., Manjappa, K., & Reddy, G. R. M. (2013). *A Gene Expression Based Quality of Service Aware Routing Protocol for Mobile Ad Hoc Networks. In Computer Networks & Communications* (pp. 283–290). NetCom.

Kuran, M. S., & Tugcu, T. (2007). A survey on emerging broadband wireless access technologies. *Computer Networks*, *51*(11), 3013–3046. doi:10.1016/j.comnet.2006.12.009

Lee, J. Y., Hwang, I. S., Liem, A. T., Lai, K. R., & Nikoukar, A. (2013). Genetic expression programming: A new approach for QoS traffic prediction in EPONs. *Photonic Network Communications*, *25*(3), 156–165. doi:10.1007/s11107-013-0399-x

Li, B., Qin, Y., Low, C. P., & Gwee, C. L. (2007). Wireless Broadband Access: A survey on Mobile WiMAX. *IEEE Communications Magazine*, 70–75. doi:10.1109/MCOM.2007.4395368

Liu, Q., Wang, X., & Giannakis, G. B. (2006). A Cross-Layer Scheduling Algorithm with QoS Support in Wireless Networks. *IEEE Transactions on Vehicular Technology*, *55*(3), 839–846. doi:10.1109/TVT.2006.873832

Manogaran, G., & Lopez, D. (2017). Disease Surveillance System for Big Climate Data Processing and Dengue Transmission. *International Journal of Ambient Computing and Intelligence*, *8*(2), 88–105. doi:10.4018/IJACI.2017040106

Marchant, J. A., & Onyango, C. M. (2003). Comparison of a Bayesian classifier with a multilayer feed-forward neural network using the example of plant/weed/soil discrimination. *Computers and Electronics in Agriculture*, *39*(1), 3–22. doi:10.1016/S0168-1699(02)00223-5

Nayak, S. C., Misra, B. B., & Behera, H. S. (2016). An Adaptive Second Order Neural Network with Genetic-Algorithm-based Training (ASONN-GA) to Forecast the Closing Prices of the Stock Market. *International Journal of Applied Metaheuristic Computing*, *7*(2), 39–57. doi:10.4018/IJAMC.2016040103

Ni, Q., Vinel, A., Xiao, Y., Turlikov, A., & Jiang, T. (2007). Wireless Broadband Access: WiMax and Beyond - Investigation of bandwidth request mechanisms under point-to-multipoint mode of WiMax networks. *IEEE Communications Magazine*, *45*(5), 132–138. doi:10.1109/MCOM.2007.358860

Omkar, S. N., John, R. L., Choudhry, N., Kubusada, Y & Bhageshpur, G. (2013). *Crop Classification using Gene Expression Programming Technique*. Springer-Verlag Berlin Heidelberg.

Omkar, S. N., Mudigere, D., Senthilnath, J., & Kumar, M. V. (2015). Identification of Helicopter Dynamics based on Flight Data using Nature Inspired Techniques. *International Journal of Applied Metaheuristic Computing*, *6*(3), 15. doi:10.4018/ijamc.2015070102

Omkar, S. N., Ramaswamy, N., Senthilnath, J., Bharath, S., & Anuradha, N. S. (2012). Gene expression programming-fuzzy logic method for crop type classification. In *Genetic and Evolutionary Computing (ICGEC), 2012 Sixth International Conference on* (pp. 136-139). IEEE. doi:10.1109/ICGEC.2012.97

Omkar, S. N., Sivaranjani, V., Senthilnath, J., & Mukherjee, S. (2010). Dimensionality Reduction and Classification of Hyperspectral Data. *International Journal of Aerospace Innovations Multi-Science*, *2*(3), 157–163.

Sabar, N. R., Ayob, M., Kendall, G., & Qu, R. (2015). Automatic design of a hyper-heuristic framework with gene expression programming for combinatorial optimization problems. *IEEE Transactions on Evolutionary Computation*, *19*(3), 309–325. doi:10.1109/TEVC.2014.2319051

Sangeetha, J., Nagaraj, K., Murthy, K. B., & Rustagi, R. P. (2016). A New Approach for Analyzing the Performance of the WiMAX Networks based on QoS Traffic Prediction Routing Protocol using Gene Expression Programming. *International Journal of Applied Metaheuristic Computing*, 7(2), 16–38. doi:10.4018/IJAMC.2016040102

Sekercioglu, Y. A., Ivanovich, M., & Yegin, A. (2009). A survey of MAC based QoS implementations for WiMAX networks. *Computer Networks*, 53(14), 2517–2536. doi:10.1016/j.comnet.2009.05.001

Senthilnath, J., Bajpai, S., Omkar, S. N., Diwakar, P. G., & Mani, V. (2012). An approach to multi-temporal MODIS image analysis using image classification and segmentation. *Advances in Space Research, Elsevier*, 50(9), 1274–1287. doi:10.1016/j.asr.2012.07.003

Senthilnath, J., Omkar, S. N., Mani, V., Vanjare, A., & Diwakar, P. G. (2014). Multi-Temporal Satellite Image Analysis Using Gene Expression Programming. *Proceedings of Second International Conference on Soft Computing for Problem Solving*, 236, 1039 – 1045. doi:10.1007/978-81-322-1602-5_109

Sharma, S., Kumar, S., & Singh, B. (2014). AntMeshNet: An ant colony optimization based routing approach to wireless mesh networks. *International Journal of Applied Metaheuristic Computing*, 5(1), 20–45. doi:10.4018/ijamc.2014010102

Sharma, S., & Malik, A. (2017). Routing in Wireless Mesh Networks based on Termites Intelligence. *International Journal of Applied Metaheuristic Computing*, 8(2), 1–21. doi:10.4018/IJAMC.2017040101

Song, D., Ru-Chuan, W., Xiong, F., & Le-Chan, Y. (2010). Gene expression programming for attribution reduction in rough set. *International Journal of Computers and Applications*, 32(2), 226–231. doi:10.2316/Journal.202.2010.2.202-2842

Xu, L., Huang, Y., Shen, X., & Liu, Y. (2017). Parallelizing Gene Expression Programming Algorithm in Enabling Large-Scale Classification. *Scientific Programming, 2017*.

Zadshakoyan, M., & Pourmostaghimi, V. (2015). Cutting tool crater wear measurement in turning using chip geometry and genetic programming. *International Journal of Applied Metaheuristic Computing*, 6(1), 47–60. doi:10.4018/ijamc.2015010104

Zuo, J., Tang, C., Li, C., Yuan, C., & Chen, A. (2002). Time series prediction based on gene expression programming. *International Conference on Advances in WebAge Information & Management*, 3129(1), 55–56.

KEY TERMS AND DEFINITIONS

Constant Bit Rate Based Traffic: A real time multimedia application in which the bit rate must be maintained same throughout the entire data transfer. It is useful for multimedia streaming.

Empirical Value: Values that are obtained by observation, experience, and experimentation rather than by scientific proof.

Expression Tree: Tree structures which contains the variables at the leaves, mathematical functions at other branches, and a linking function at the root and which can be converted into mathematical expressions.

File Transfer Application: A non-real-time multimedia application which supports the transfer of data without the need to maintain constant data rate and is used to transfer multimedia files between network nodes.

Linking Function: A mathematical function such as addition, subtraction or multiplication that is used to connect various sub-branches of an expression tree.

Mutation Rate: The rate at which random and drastic changes occur in chromosomes during the process of evolution.

Recombination Rate: The rate at which the parent genetic material re-arranges due to crossover between chromosomes that might result in traits for offspring completely different from parents.

Sensitivity Analysis: A study of understanding the dependence of mathematical model's output uncertainty on uncertainty of its input parameters.

Symbolic Regression: A type of regression analysis in which initially mathematical expressions are randomly generated and are improved successively in an iterative process to best fit a given dataset.

Transposition Rate: The rate at which a part of chromosome changes its position resulting in chromosomes of different genetic property.

WiMAX: WiMAX stands for Worldwide Interoperability for Microwave Access which is a point-to-multipoint broadband wireless technology concentrated mainly around IEEE 802.16e standard and aims at providing high speed data access over a wide area.

Chapter 3

Chaotic Differential–Evolution–Based Fuzzy Contrast Stretching Method

Krishna Gopal Dhal
Midnapore College (Autonomous), India

Sanjoy Das
University of Kalyani, India

ABSTRACT

This study concentrates to develop one novel parameterized Bi-Histogram Fuzzy Contrast Stretching (BHFCS) method for enhancing the contrast of the grey level as well as color images properly. The parameters of this method have been optimized by employing one modified Chaotic Differential Evolution (CDE) with the combined assistance of Fractal Dimension (FD) and Quality Index based on Local Variance (QILV) as objective function. Experimental results prove that the modified DE gives better result than particle swarm optimization (PSO), genetic algorithm (GA) and traditional DE in this enhancement domain and the used objective function is also very useful to preserve the image's original brightness which is the one of the main criterion of the consumer electronics field.

INTRODUCTION

In the realm of digital image processing all the indigenous algorithms must be cognizant of the two main aspects viz. contrast enhancement and brightness preservation of the images experimented. The endeavour of the enhancement algorithms is to achieve an optimal condition using an objective function where the image attains a state

DOI: 10.4018/978-1-5225-4151-6.ch003

of maximum clarity such that it can have a good visual analysis. Then only it can be differentiated from the original image having poor contrast and other technical anomalies.

The first ever approach is to achieve contrast enhancement was Histogram Equalization (HE) technique (Gonzalez, R.C., Woods, R.E. (2002)). HE based techniques have been used in medical image processing, satellite image processing etc. Basically HE procedure flattens the histogram of the original image. Theoretically the entire grey levels are distributed with uniform distribution. As a result of this it improves the contrast of the image, maximizes the image entropy. As the histogram of the output image is uniformly distributed the mean brightness is approximately changed to the middle of the grey level regardless of the mean of the input image (Chen, S. D., Ramli, A. R. (2004), Kim, Y.T. (1997)). To overcome the flattering effect of the histogram in HE method which sometimes results in giving washed-out images, unnatural enhancement and also some undesirable artefacts a new procedure was put forward by Kim (Kim, Y.T. (1997)) known as Brightness Preserving Bi-Histogram Equalization (BBHE). In BBHE, histogram of the image was separated around its mean and then the two divided parts were equalized separately (Chen, S. D., Ramli, A. R. (2004), Shanmugavadivu, P., Balasubramanian, K., Muruganandam, A. (2014)). In Dualistic Sub-Image Histogram Equalization (DSIHE) proposed by Wan (Chen, S. D., Ramli, A. R. (2004), Shanmugavadivu, P., Balasubramanian, K., Muruganandam, A. (2014)), the procedure was same as BBHE, but the histogram was separated by median instead of mean (Chen, S. D., Ramli, A. R. (2004), Shanmugavadivu, P., Balasubramanian, K., Muruganandam, A. (2014), Chen, S. D., Ramli, A. R. (2003), Chen, S. D., Ramli, A. R. (2003)). Chen and Ramli proposed Minimum Mean Brightness Error Bi-Histogram Equalization (MMBEBHE) method (Chen, S. D., Ramli, A. R. (2004), Chen, S. D., Ramli, A. R. (2003)), in which the histogram was separated using a specified threshold which preserved the minimum mean brightness error between input and output images and then the two parts were equalized independently. This technique was better than BBHE and DSIHE, but it still suffered from deficiency of contrast and brightness (Shanmugavadivu, P., Balasubramanian, K., Muruganandam, A. (2014)). In literature, parameterized contrast stretching function was also reported for image enhancement and produced better result than traditional HE (Gorai, A., Ghosh, A. (2009), Gorai, A., Ghosh, A. (2011), Barik, M., Sheta, A., Ayesh, A. (2007), Dhal, K.G, Quraishi, I. M., Das, S. (2015), Dhal, K., G., Das, S. (2015), Dhal, K.G, Quraishi, I. M., Das, S. (2015), Dhal, K.G, Quraishi, I. M., Das, S. (2015)) . The optimal values of these parameters had been found by employing different metaheuristic algorithms with the assistance of properly selected objective function (Gorai, A., Ghosh, A. (2009), Gorai, A., Ghosh, A. (2011), Barik, M., Sheta, A., Ayesh, A. (2007), Dhal, K.G,

Quraishi, I. M., Das, S. (2015), Dhal, K., G., Das, S. (2015), Dhal, K.G, Quraishi, I. M., Das, S. (2015), Dhal, K.G, Quraishi, I. M., Das, S. (2015)) . In this study, one novel parameterized fuzzy based bi-histogram contrast stretching function has been employed for enhancing the grey as well as color images and optimal parameters are computed by formulating the enhancement problem as optimization problem.

Recently nature inspired optimization algorithms are widely employed in different fields such as in finance (VijayalakshmiPai, G. A., Michel, T. (2017)), clustering (Benmounah, Z., Meshoul, S., Batouche, M. (2017), NizarBanu, P.K., Andrews, S. (2015), Hamou, R. M., Bouarara, H. A., Amine, A. (2015)), networking (Binh (2016)), medical field (Dey (2013), Dey (2014a), Dey (2014b), Dey (2015)), image processing (Pal, S.,K., Bhandari, D., Kundu, M., K. (1994), Hashemi, S. (2010), Coelho, L. D. S., Sauer, J.G., Rudek, M. (2009), Samantaa et. al. (2013), Dhal, K.G, Quraishi, I. M., Das, S. (2015), Gorai, A., Ghosh, A.(2009), Ashour (2015)), Neural network field (Hore (2017)) etc. In image enhancement field, optimal parameters of different parameterized transformation functions are optimized by minimizing or maximizing the proper objective functions. Evolutionary algorithms such as Genetic Algorithm (GA) (Pal, S.,K., Bhandari, D., Kundu, M., K. (1994), Hashemi, S., et. al. (2010)) and Differential Evolution (DE) (Coelho, L. D. S., Sauer, J.G., Rudek, M. (2009), Dhal, K.G, Quraishi, I. M., Das, S. (2015)) had been applied successfully in this domain. Pal et al. developed one GA based image enhancement procedure by considering entropy, compactness, index area coverage and their combinations as objective functions (Pal, S.,K., Bhandari, D., Kundu, M., K. (1994)). Hashemi et. al. also proposed one GA based method but the objective function was developed based on edge information (Hashemi, S. (2010)). Coelho et. al. proposed one variant of DE algorithm by modifying the crossover rate (CR) and mutation factor (MF) with the help of chaotic sequence which outperformed the traditional DE (Coelho, L. D. S., Sauer, J.G., Rudek, M. (2009)). Dhal et. al. proposed two variants of DE algorithms by incorporating Lévy flight, chaotic sequence and population diversity information and the modified DEs outperform the traditional one (Dhal, K.G, Quraishi, I. M., Das, S. (2015)). Both authors considered the combination of entropy and edge information as objective function. Swarm optimization algorithms like PSO have also been widely applied in image enhancement field (Gorai, A., Ghosh, A.(2009), Gorai, A., Ghosh, A. (2011), Barik, M., Sheta, A., Ayesh, A.(2007), Quraishi, I. M. (2014), Quraishi, I. M. (2013), Dhal, K, G.(2015), Eutamene, A. (2017)). PSO based brightness preserving enhancement model with entropy as an objective function had been proposed by Shanmugavadivu et. al. (Shanmugavadivu, P. (2014)). Chaotic sequence, Lévy flight and population making mechanism had been incorporated in Firefly Algorithm (FA) to increase its efficiency in image enhancement field (Dhal, K.G, Quraishi, I. M., Das, S. (2015)). The modified

FA outperformed the FA via Lévy flight algorithm, PSO and GA by maximizing the combination of entropy, energy and contrast as objective function. Artificial Bee Colony (ABC) algorithm based edge image enhancement model had been proposed by Benala et. al. and ABC outperformed GA in this field (Benala, T., R. et. al. (2009)). Chaotic sequence based ABC algorithm had also been applied for brightness preserving image enhancement domain (Dhal, K., G., Das, S. (2015)). The proposed ABC outperformed the traditional ABC and PSO by considering the efficiency of the used objective function. CS algorithms with Lévy flight and chaotic sequence had been employed in image enhancement field (Dhal, K.G, Quraishi, I. M., Das, S. (2017), Dhal, K. G., Sen, M., Das, S. (2017), Dhal, K. G., Das, S. (2017), Bhandaria, A. K. (2014)). A chaotic version of Bat algorithm was presented by the authors (Dhal, K.G, Quraishi, I. M., Das, S. (2015), Dhal, K.G, Quraishi, I. M., Das, S. (2015)) which outperformed the chaotic CS algorithm and chaotic version of FA in image enhancement field. The next section describes the proposed image enhancement method.

PROPOSED BI-HISTOGRAM FUZZY CONTRAST STRETCHING (BHFCS) METHOD

This paper demonstrates a new parameterized Bi-Histogram Fuzzy Contrast Stretching model (BHFCS) for image enhancement which is discussed below:

1. Find the histogram of the corresponding image.
2. Divide the histogram based on threshold X_T which yields minimum brightness error between input and output images (Chen, S. D., Ramli, A. R. (2004), Chen, S. D., Ramli, A. R. (2003)). It is proved that this threshold helps to preserve the original brightness of the image (Dhal, K. G., Sen, S., Sarkar, K., Das, S. (2016), Dhal, K. G., Das, S.(2017a)).
3. If any pixel i.e. $X_i \leq X_T$ then $X_i \in C_1$ and if $X_i \geq X_T$ then $X_i \in C_2$ where C_1, C_2 are classes corresponding to background and foreground respectively. Therefore, the fuzzy membership for the pixels corresponding to the classes C_1 and C_2 have been computed as follows

$$\mu_{c1}\left(X_i\right) = 1 - \frac{X_T - X_i}{X_T}, \ \mu_{c2}\left(X_i\right) = 1 - \frac{E - X_i}{E - X_T} \tag{1}$$

Where, $E \leq 255$ and it is set by optimization. μ_{c1} and μ_{c2} are fuzzy memberships for classes C_1 and C_2 respectively and membership values lie between

$$0 \leq \begin{Bmatrix} \mu_{c1}\left(X_i\right) \\ \mu_{c2}\left(X_i\right) \end{Bmatrix} \leq 1$$

4.   The enhanced pixel values for classes C_1 i.e. X_{ie}^{c1} and C_2 i.e. X_{ie}^{c2} have been computed as follows

$$X_{ie}^{c1} = X + \mu_{c1}\left(X_i\right).K_1,$$

$$X_{ie}^{c2} = X_i.\mu_{c2}\left(X_i\right) + \left(E - \mu_{c2}\left(X_i\right)\right). K_2 \tag{2}$$

if $\left(X_{ie}^{c1} \text{ or } X_{ie}^{c2} > 255\right)$ then normalization has been performed.

Here X_{ie}^{c1} and X_{ie}^{c2} are the enhanced pixel values which are crucially depended on the parameters K_1 and K_2 which are belongs to [0, 255] and optimized by modified DE algorithm.

5.   Combine both X_{ie}^{c1} and X_{ie}^{c2} component and get the enhanced image.

Therefore, the proposed enhancement method clearly reveals that the proper enhancement significantly depends on the associated three parameters which are E, K_1 and K_2 with diverse ranges. The optimal values of these parameters are computed by employing one modified DE algorithm with the help of the combination of FD and QILV as objective function which is discussed in the next section.

OBJECTIVE FUNCTION

This paper also concentrates on finding one proper objective function to preserve the original brightness of the image. In this study one novel objective function has been proposed to accomplish that necessity. The proposed objective function is the combination of Fractal Dimension (FD) (Al-Kadi, O., S., Watson, D. (2008)) and Quality Index based Local Variance (QILV) (Aja-Fern´andez, S. (2006)).

Fractal Dimension (FD)

The fractal is based on the self-similarity and the fractal dimension is the quantitative expression of the inherent dimension of the images (Al-Kadi, O., S., Watson, D. (2008)). The basic method of deriving fractal dimension is box-counting method. Box counting is making the whole dimension by Figure uring out the points within determined box or grid. Mathematically, FD is computed using the following formula:

$$D = \frac{\log N_r}{\log\left(\dfrac{1}{r}\right)} \tag{3}$$

Where, D is the fractal dimension. Maximum and minimum intensity for each box (2×2) are obtained to sum their difference, which gives the N and r as follows:

$$r = \frac{s}{M} \text{Where, } M = min\ (R,\ C) \tag{4}$$

where s denotes scale factor, R and C denote the number of rows and number of columns respectively when the grid size gets doubled, R and C reduces to half of its original value and above procedure is repeated iteratively until $max(R,C)$ is greater than 2. Linear regression model uses to fit the line from plot $log\ (N)$ *vs. log (1/r)* and the slope gives the FD as:

$$logN_r = D\log\left(\frac{1}{r}\right) \tag{5}$$

Quality Index Based on Local Variance (QILV)

QILV is used to measure the structural information of the image (Aja-Fern´andez, S. (2006)). A great amount of the structural information of an image is coded in its local variance distribution. Local variances features of an image can help to compare two images properly. The local variance of an image I is defined as $Var\left(I_{i,j}\right) = E\left(\left(I_{i,j} - \overline{I_{i,j}}\right)^2\right)$, being $\overline{I_{i,j}} = E\left(I_{i,j}\right)$ the local mean of the image. It may be estimated using a weighted neighbourhood $\eta_{i,j}$ pixel under analysis with respective weights ω_p as:

$$Var\left(I_{i,j}\right) = \frac{\sum_{p\in\eta i,j}\omega_p\left(I_{i,j}-\overline{I_{i,j}}\right)^2}{\sum_{p\in\eta i,j}\omega_p} ; \overline{I_{i,j}} = \frac{\sum_{p\in\eta i,j}\omega_p I_p}{\sum_{p\in\eta i,j}\omega_p} \tag{6}$$

The estimated local-variance of the image will be used as a quality measure of the structural similarity between two images. The mean of the local variance μ_{V_I} is estimated as:

$$\mu_{V_I} = \frac{1}{MN}\sum_{i=1}^{M}\sum_{j=1}^{N} Var\left(I_{i,j}\right) \tag{7}$$

The (global) standard deviation of the local variance is defined as:

$$\sigma_{V_I} = \left(\frac{1}{MN-1}\sum_{i=1}^{M}\sum_{j=1}^{N}\left(Var\left(I_{i,j}\right)-\mu_{V_I}\right)^2\right)^{\frac{1}{2}} \tag{8}$$

Finally, the covariance between the variances of two images I and J is defined as:

$$\sigma_{V_I V_J} = \frac{1}{MN-1}\sum_{i=1}^{M}\sum_{j=1}^{N}\left(\text{Var}\left(I_{i,j}\right)-\mu_{V_I}\right)\left(\text{Var}\left(J_{i,j}\right)-\mu_{V_J}\right) \tag{9}$$

Quality Index based on Local Variance (QILV) between two images I and J as follows:

$$\text{QILV}\left(I, J\right) = \frac{2\mu_{V_I}\mu_{V_J}}{\mu_{V_I}^2+\mu_{V_J}^2} \cdot \frac{2\sigma_{V_I}\sigma_{V_J}}{\sigma_{V_I}^2+\sigma_{V_J}^2} \cdot \frac{\sigma_{V_I V_J}}{\sigma_{V_I}\sigma_{V_J}} \tag{10}$$

Where, $0 < QILV \leq 1$

The first term of QILV equation carries out a comparison betweenthe mean of the local variance distributions of both images. The second one compares the standard deviation of then local variances. The third term is the one to introducespatial coherence. To avoid some computational problemswith small values, some constants may be added to every term in equation.

Fractal Dimension (FD) measures the roughness of the image. It was reported that local variance distribution gives the information about the structure of the image (Dhal, K. G., Sen, M., Das, S. (2017)). If QILV increases then the structural information of the enhanced image is preserved. Therefore, In order to perform the proper enhancement, the combination of FD and QILV is taken as objective function. The Objective Function is defined as:

$$Fit\left(E, K_1, \ K_2\right) = \left\{\exp\left(FD\right) + \exp\left(QILV\right)\right\} \tag{11}$$

Where, $Fit\left(.\right)$ is the objective function. FD and QILV represent the fractal dimension and quality index based on local variance of the corresponding image respectively. exp is the exponential operator. Therefore, from the definition of the objective function it can be easily verified that if the proposed objective function is maximized then the FD and QILV of the corresponding image are maximized i.e. the structural information and original brightness of the images are preserved. So, the optimization problem has been defined as:

$$\left\{E_0, K_{10}, K_{20}\right\} = \arg[\max_{E, K_1, \ K_2} \left\{Fit\left(E, K_1, \ K_2\right)\right\} \tag{12}$$

This maximization problem has been solved by employing the modified Chaotic DE which is discussed in the next section.

CHAOTIC DIFFERENTIAL EVOLUTION (CDE)

In this study one new step size has been employed to control the mutation factor of the Differential Evolution. The methodology behind this step size has been discussed below

$$Step \ Size \ (SS_i^t) \ = \left| \frac{Fit\left(X_{gbest}\right) - Fit^t\left(X_i\right)}{\max\left(Fit\left(X_{gbest}\right), \ Fit^t\left(X_i\right)\right)} \right| \tag{13}$$

Where, $Fit\left(X_{gbest}\right)$ is the fitness value of global best solution up to generation number t. $Fit^t\left(X_i\right)$ is the fitness value of ith individual at generation number t. It is easily understood that $\left(0 \leq SS \leq 1\right)$. It is also clear that *SS* performs the main criteria of any metaheuristic algorithm that the step size be decreased or increased depending upon whether the solution is good or bad very well. Hence *SS* may be called as *Fitness-based Step-size.*

Chaotic Sequence

Recently, chaotic sequence has been incorporated with nature inspired algorithms to enhance their capability (Dhal, K.G, Quraishi, I. M., Das, S. (2017), Dhal, K.G, Quraishi, I. M., Das, S. (2015), Dhal, K., G., Das, S. (2015), Leandro, C., S., d., Viviana, C., M. (2009), Sheikholeslami, R., Kaveh, A. (2013), Coelho, L. d. S., Mariani, V. C. (2008), Caponetto, R. (2003)). Chaotic sequences are used in metaheuristic algorithms for three purposes 1. To generate random numbers 2.To generate inertia weight 3. To perform the local search. In this study the chaotic sequence has been successfully applied to update the mutation factor and crossover rate of the DE algorithm which are responsible for controlling the trade-off between exploration and exploitation. There are several chaotic generators like logistic map, tent map, gauss map, sinusoidal iterator, lozi map, chua's oscillator etc (Dhal, K.G, Quraishi, I. M., Das, S. (2017), Sheikholeslami, R., Kaveh, A. (2013)). Among those logistic equation is used in this paper as it carries greater variance and outperforms others (Dhal, K.G, Quraishi, I. M., Das, S. (2017), Dhal, K. G., Das, S. (2017), Dhal, K., G., Das, S. (2015)). The equation of logistic map is given below:

$$L_{m+1} = aL_m \left(1 - L_m\right)$$

(14)

a is a control parameter and $0 < a \leq 4$, L_m is the chaotic value at m^{th} iteration. The behaviour of the system mostly depends on the variation of a. Value of *a* is set to 4 and L_0 does not belong to $\{0, 0.25, 0.5, 0.75, 1\}$ otherwise the logistic equation does not show chaotic behaviour (Coelho, L. D. S., Sauer, J.G., Rudek, M. (2009)).

Initial Population Generation

The initial population is usually created randomly. The equation of standard method is given below:

$$x_i = low + \left(up - low\right) \times \partial$$

(15)

x_i is the ith individual. up $\& low$ are the upper and lower bound of the search space of objective function. ∂ is the random variable that belongs to [0,1].

If the initial population carries a great variance then it helps to restrict the premature convergence of the algorithm. Average population diversity is good when ∂ is generated using logistic equation (Dhal, K.G, Quraishi, I. M., Das, S. (2017), Dhal, K., G., Das, S. (2015)). In this study, logistic equation based initial population has been used.

The algorithm of the Chaotic Differential Evolution is as follows

Step 1: Initialize the population by using the logistic equation.

Step 2: Take the Objective function Fit as per Equation 11

Step 3: initialize the mutation factor F and Crossover rate CR by the logistic equation based chaotic sequence.

Step 4: Mutation step: For every enhanced image, take any three randomly chosen images i.e. $X_{r1}^{(t)}$, $X_{r2}^{(t)}$ and $X_{r3}^{(t)}$.

Now, for every parameter, get a new parameter by

$$V_i^{(t+1)} = X_{r3}^{(t)} + F \times SS_i^t \cdot \left(X_{r1}^{(t)} - X_{r2}^{(t)} \right) \tag{16}$$

Where $r1 \neq r2 \neq r3$, SS_i^t is the step size at t^{th} iteration.

F = mutation factor which controls the amplification of the difference between two individuals so as to avoid search stagnation.

Step 5 Crossover: Crossover increases the diversity of the population.

$$H_i^{(t+1)} = V_i^{(t+1)} \text{ if } \text{rand}[0,1] \leq CR \text{ ,}$$

$$= X_i^{(t)} \qquad \text{if } \text{rand}[0,1] > CR \text{ .} \tag{17}$$

Step 6: Selection: Using parameter Hi create new enhanced image

$$X_i^{(t+1)} = H_i^{(t+1)} \qquad \text{if } H_i^{(t+1)} > Fit\left(X_i^{(t)} \right),$$

$$= X_i^{(t)} \qquad \text{if } H_i^{(t+1)} \leq Fit\left(X_i^{(t)} \right). \tag{18}$$

It means if modified parameters create an enhanced image which fitness value is greater than previous one replace it otherwise not.

Step 7: Update CR and F using logistic equation based chaotic sequence and find the global best solution.

Step 8: Repeat steps 4 to 7 until stopping criterion.

Stopping Conditions

Find the optimal stopping condition is a challenging matter. It has been chosen experimentally. It stopping conditions are:

1.   When the fitness value of the global best solution does not change for continuous 10 iterations for a specific image.
2.   But the maximum limit of iterations number is 150 to find the optimal parameters.

EXPERIMENTAL RESULTS

The experiment has been performed over 100 grey level images and 50 color images and the computed experimental results have been given below:

Quality Assessment Parameters

Quantitative performance measurements are significant to compare between different image enhancements techniques and employed models. The well-known original brightness preserving quality measurement metrics for grey level as well as for color images have been discussed below.

Absolute Mean-Brightness Error (AMBE)

AMBE is basically used to measure the degree of the brightness preservation (Dhal, K.G, Quraishi, I. M., Das, S. (2017), Dhal, K., G., Das, S. (2015). Let input image is f and output image is G then the AMBE is calculated as:

$$AMBE = \left| Mean_f - Mean_G \right| \tag{19}$$

Where, $Mean_f$ and $Mean_G$ are the mean of the input and output image respectively. If the value of AMBE is low then the brightness preservation is better.

Peak-Signal to Noise Ratio (PSNR)

This statistical metric is also used to measure the performance of the image enhancement methods. PSNR is the ratio between the maximum possible power of the signal and the power of the noise (Dhal, K.G, Quraishi, I. M., Das, S. (2017), Dhal, K., G., Das, S. (2015). It is actually distortion metric which is crucially depends on Mean-Squared Error (MSE). MSE defined as:

$$\mathrm{MSE}\left(f,G\right) = \frac{\sum_{i=0}^{N-1}\sum_{j=0}^{M-1}\left[f\left(i,j\right) - G\left(i,j\right)\right]^2}{M \times N} \tag{20}$$

Where, f and G are the input and output image respectively. M and N are the number of rows and columns of the image.

The PSNR is calculated as follows:

$$\mathrm{PSNR}\left(f,G\right) = 10 \log_{10}\left(\frac{\left(L-1\right)^2}{\mathrm{MSE}\left(f,G\right)}\right) \tag{21}$$

L is the number discrete grey level. For 8 bit image it is 256.

If the value of PSNR is increased then contrast of the image is also enhanced and Absolute Mean Brightness Error (AMBE) is also reduced to some extent.

Simple popular metrics for gray level image enhancement such as Absolute Mean Brightness Error (AMBE) cannot be used in color image domain as each color model has their own representation for the brightness component (Kong, N. S. P., Ibrahim, H. (2008)). Therefore, apart from the visual results one popular referenced image quality assessment metric, PSNR-HVS-M (Ponomarenko N. (2007)) and one well-known non-referenced quality assessment metric, Cube Root Mean Enhancement (CRME) (Gao, C., Panetta, K., Agaian, S. (2013), Panetta, K, Gao, C.,Agaian, S. (2013)) have been taken into consideration which are explained as follows:

Cube Root Mean Enhancement (CRME)

CRME is a contrast measurement technique for color image which measures the contrast not only within each color plane but also across the color planes (Gao, C., Panetta, K., Agaian, S. (2013), Panetta, K, Gao, C.,Agaian, S. (2013)). CRME computes the contrast by measuring the relative difference of color cube center and all the neighbours in that cube. It is also correlated with HVS property. So, greater value of CRME represents greater contrast with natural enhancement (Gao, C., Panetta, K., Agaian, S. (2013), Panetta, K, Gao, C., Agaian, S. (2013)).

PSNR-HVS-M

This metric is developed by considering the DCT basis function (Ponomarenko N. (2007)). PSNR-HVS-M has been used to evaluate the quality as it represents two significant features of HVS. First, it reveals the fact that sensitivity to distortions in low spatial frequencies is larger than to distortions in high spatial frequencies. Second, masking effect (worse ability of human vision to notice distortions in heterogeneous and textural image areas) has been taken into consideration.

Result Section for Grey Level Images

The Chaotic DE algorithm with BHFCS has been applied over 100 grey level images and enhanced image are given as Figure 1. The average values of the quality parameters over 100 images are presented in Table 1.

The experiment has been done using MATLAB R2012b with x64-based PC using 100 images. The average execution times of different methods and Friedman rankings (Derrac, J. (2011)) are given in Table 2.

Figure 1. Aircraft Image (a) original (b) Result of CDE (c) Result of DE (d) Result of PSO (e) Result of GA (f) Result of BBHE (g) Result of DSIHE (h) Result of MMBEBHE (i) Result of HE

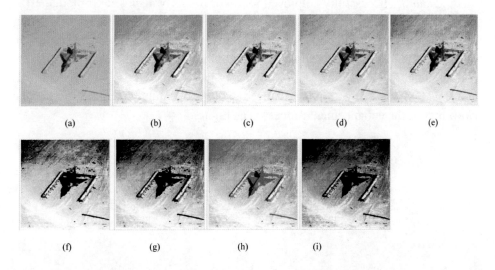

(a)   (b)   (c)   (d)   (e)

(f)   (g)   (h)   (i)

Table 1. Values of the quality parameters for grey level image enhancement

Variants	Average Fitness	Average AMBE	Average PSNR	Average QILV
Chaotic DE	**8.6799**	**2.030**	**26.2767**	**0.9523**
DE	8.6510	2.8706	25.9078	0.9501
PSO	8.6432	2.9892	25.7787	0.9411
GA	8.4770	4.001	25.715	0.9403

Table 2. Friedman ranking and average execution time

Variants	Average Fitness Over 100 images	Friedman ranking based on Average Fitness	Average Execution time (in sec.)	Friedman ranking based on Execution time
Chaotic DE	**8.6799**	**1**	**30.21**	**1**
DE	8.6510	2	35.56	2
PSO	8.6432	3	36.01	3
GA	8.4770	4	61.17	4

Result Section for Color Images

In this study, proposed grey level image enhancement methodology is also applied in color image enhancement domain. Chien et.al. proposed exact Hue-Saturation-Intensity (eHSI) model to enhance the color images (Chien, C. L., Tseng, D. C. (2011), Chien, C. L., Tsai, W. H. (2014)). Any gray level contrast enhancement method can be successfully employed for color image by using eHSI model. eHSI model is a hue preserving model which has the capability to resolve the out-of-gamut problem i.e. the pixel values of output RGB image always lie within their respective intervals. Traditional HE was applied by the author for enhancement purpose (Chien, C. L., Tseng, D. C. (2011)). But in this paper proposed BHFCS with Chaotic DE and stated objective function is employed to obtain a natural enhanced image. The flowchart of the enhancement process is as Figure 2.

Figure 2. Block Diagram of the color image enhancement scheme

$$\begin{bmatrix} r \\ g \\ b \end{bmatrix} \xrightarrow{RGB\ to\ eHSI} \begin{bmatrix} eH \\ S \\ I \end{bmatrix} \xrightarrow{I\ part} I \xrightarrow{grey\ level\ enhancement\ method} I' \rightarrow \begin{bmatrix} eH \\ S \\ I' \end{bmatrix} \xrightarrow{Inverse} \begin{bmatrix} r' \\ g' \\ b' \end{bmatrix}$$

The enhanced color images are given as Figure 3 and the average values of the quality parameters over 50 color images are given as Table 3.

Consistency Analysis of the Employed Metaheuristic Algorithms

Consistency of the CDE has been measured by maximizing the proposed objective function iteratively. Each variant has been executed 10 times for each image and

Figure 3. Woman Image (a) original (b) Result of CDE (c) Result of DE (d) Result of PSO (e) Result of GA (f) Result of eHSI with HE (g) Result of Naik's model (Naik, S. K., Murthy, C. A. (2003)) (h) Result of Automatic Color Equalization (ACE) method (Gatta, C., Rizzi, A., Marini, D. (2002)).

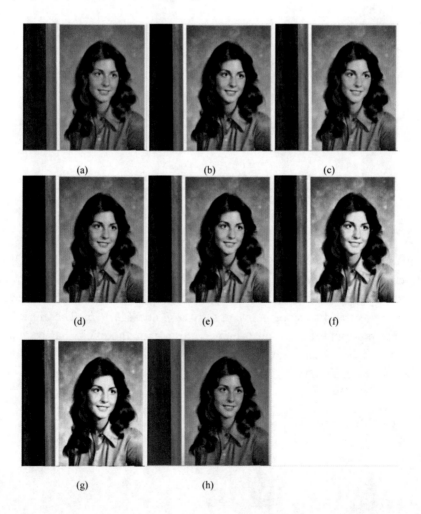

Table 3. Average values of the quality parameters over 50 color images

Parameters	Chaotic DE	DE	PSO	GA	eHSI with HE	Naik's model With HE	Automatic Color Equalization (ACE)
Average CRME	**0.8553**	0.8401	0.8387	0.8187	0.4007	0.4012	0.6270
Average PSNR-HVS-M	**26.82**	26.75	26.71	24.10	21.97	22.01	23.71

Figure 4. Changes of AMBE and PSNR with respect to objective function

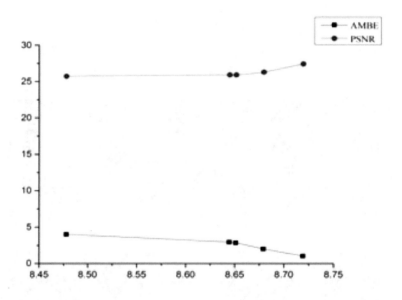

the maximum fitness value (*Max Obj.*), Minimum fitness value (*Min Obj.*) and difference between *Max Obj.* and *Min Obj.* i.e. *Diff* for those 10 runs are measured. Consistency represents the stability or the robustness of the algorithm. Here, it has been taken as the difference between *Max Obj.* and *Min Obj..*Therefore, the less difference represents better consistency. The same methodology has been used for 100 images. Then the average difference (*AD*) over 100 images has been computed by the following equation:

$$\text{Average Difference}(\text{AD}) = \frac{1}{p} \sum_{i=1}^{p} \text{Diff}(X_i),$$

$$\text{Diff}\left(X_i\right) = \left[\text{MaxObj}\left(X_i\right) - \text{MinObj}\left(X_i\right)\right]; \quad p = 100. \tag{22}$$

where, $MaxObj\left(X_i\right)$ and $MinObj\left(X_i\right)$ are the maximum and minimum objective function values over 10 iterations for i^{th} image respectively and $Diff\left(X_i\right)$ is the difference between these two. The values AD for each algorithm have been given in table 4 and their ranking is also done based on AD. Chaotic DE gets the best rank according to AD and therefore, it can be said that the chaotic DE is also very consistent metaheuristic algorithm.

Analysis of the Results

Visual analysis of the Figure 1 reveals that proper brightness preserved enhancement of grey level images occurs when proposed BHFCS is applied with metaheuristic algorithms and stated objective function. That's why Figures 1(b)-(e) are far better than other enhanced results using existing methods such as BBHE, DSIHE, MMBEBHE and HE. But the chaotic DE produces the best enhanced image visually and quantitatively as per Table 1 which also states that chaotic DE has the finest efficiency of fitness function maximization. Besides that the enhanced images with chaotic DE also carry lowest AMBE value and highest PSNR value. Table 2 represents the Friedman ranking depending upon the efficiency of fitness function maximization ability and execution time. Here the chaotic DE also gets the best rank.

The proposed grey level image enhancement model is employed for enhancing the color images through eHSI model which produces hue preserving and gamut problem free enhanced images. Figure 3 represents the enhanced color images using different methods such as well-known Naik's model (Naik, S. K., Murthy, C. A. (2003)) and Automatic Color Equalization (ACE) method (Gatta, C., Rizzi, A., Marini, D. (2002)). Visual analysis and quality parameters of Table 3 demonstrate that the proposed enhancement model also very fruitful for producing the natural enhanced color images. Average CRME and PSNR-HVS-M for chaotic DE based model is superior to other metaheuristic based models. According to Tables 2 and 4, Chaotic DE is very consistent algorithm within less computation time.

Table 4. Ranking based on AD values

Variants	Chaotic DE	DE	PSO	GA
Rank	1	3	2	4
AD	0.1787	0.2063	0.1971	0.2998

The brightness preservation ability of the employed objective function is also measured and represented as Figure 4 which states that the AMBE always reduces and PSNR increases when value of objective function increases. Therefore, the usage of developed objective function is fruitful in brightness preservation image enhancement domain which is the main criterion in consumer electronics field.

CONCLUSION

In this paper, one parameterized Bi-Histogram Fuzzy Contrast Stretching (BHFCS) method has been proposed where the proper enhancement of the image crucially depends on associated three parameters with diverse ranges. Therefore, the enhancement model has been formulated as maximization problem and one modified Chaotic DE with one novel objective function has been employed for optimizing the three parameters within reasonable time. The main aim of this study is to enhance the images by preserving its original brightness. Visual analysis and values of the quality parameters prove that the proposed enhancement model significantly performed very well. In addition to that the proposed grey level image enhancement model is also applied for color images through eHSI color model. Here, it also produces natural enhanced color images and outperforms some other well-known color image enhancement method such as Automatic Color Equalization (ACE) method. It is also proved in this study that the employed chaotic DE is very consistent and takes less time than the traditional DE algorithm. The chaotic sequence based mutation factor and crossover rate with the proposed step size assist the traditional DE to increase its efficiency. In the case of metaheuristic algorithm based image enhancement model, the proper enhancement also significantly depends on used objective function. Here, the brightness preservation ability of the employed objective also measured quantitatively in this study which proves that the objective function is very productive in the above said field. In future, this enhancement model can be applied in other kinds of image enhancement domain and the Chaotic DE can be compared with other existing metaheuristic algorithm in different optimization domain.

REFERENCES

Aja-Fern'andez, S., Jos'eEst'epar, R. S., Alberola-L'opez, C., & Westin, C. F. (2006). Image Quality Assessment based on Local Variance. *28th IEEE EMBS Annual International Conference*, 4815-4818.

Al-Kadi, O. S., & Watson, D. (2008). Texture analysis of Aggressive and non-aggressive lung tumor CE CT images. *IEEE Transaction on Biomedical Engineering, 55*, 1822-1830.

Ashour, A. S., Samanta, S., Dey, N., Kausar, N., Abdessalemkaraa, W. B., & Hassanien, A. E. (2015). Computed tomography image enhancement using cuckoo search: A log transform based approach. *Journal of Signal and Information Processing, 6*(03), 244–257. doi:10.4236/jsip.2015.63023

Barik, M., Sheta, A., & Ayesh, A. (2007). Image Enhancement Using Particle Swarm Optimization. *Proceedings of the World Congress on Engineering.*

Benala, T. R., Jampala, S. D., Villa, S. H., & Konathala, B. (2009). A novel Approach to Image Edge Enhancement Using Artificial Bee Colony Optimization Algorithm for Hybridized Smoothening Filters. *World Congress on Nature & Biologically Inspired Computing (NaBIC),* 1071-1076. doi:10.1109/NABIC.2009.5393866

Benmounah, Z., Meshoul, S., & Batouche, M. (2017). *Scalable Differential Evolutionary Clustering Algorithm for Big Data Using Map-Reduce Paradigm. Int. Jr. Applied Metaheuristic Computing,* 8(1).

Bhandaria, A. K., Sonia, V. A., Kumar, A., & Singh, G. K. (2014). Cuckoo search algorithm based satellite image contrast and brightness enhancement using DWT–SVD. *ISA Transactions, 53*, 1286–1296.

Binh, H. T. T., Hanh, N. T., & Dey, N. (2016). Improved Cuckoo Search and Chaotic Flower Pollination optimization algorithm for maximizing area coverage in Wireless Sensor Networks. *Neural Computing & Applications,* 1–13.

Caponetto, R., Fortuna, L., Fazzino, S., & Xibilia, M. G. (2003). Chaotic Sequences to Improve the Performance of Evolutionary Algorithms. *IEEE Transactions on Evolutionary Computation, 7*(3), 289–304. doi:10.1109/TEVC.2003.810069

Chen, S. D., & Ramli, A. R. (2003). Minimum Mean Brightness Error Bi-Histogram Equalization in Contrast Enhancement. *IEEE Transactions on Consumer Electronics, 49*(4), 1310–1319. doi:10.1109/TCE.2003.1261234

Chen, S. D., & Ramli, A. R. (2003). *Contrast Enhancement using Recursive Mean Separated Histogram Equalization for Scalable Brightness Preservation.* Academic Press.

Chen, S. D., & Ramli, A. R. (2004). Preserving Brightness in histogram equalization based contrast enhancement techniques. *Digital Signal Processing, 14*(5), 413–428. doi:10.1016/j.dsp.2004.04.001

Chien, C. L., & Tsai, W. H. (2014). Image Fusion with no Gamut Problem by Improved Nonlinear HIS Transforms for Remote Sensing. *IEEE Trans. on Geoscience and Remote Sensing, 52*, 651-663.

Chien, C. L., & Tseng, D. C. (2011). Color image enhancement with exact HIS color model. *Int. J. of Innovative Computing, Information and Control, 7*, 6691-6710.

Coelho, L. D. S., Sauer, J. G., & Rudek, M. (2009). Differential evolution optimization combined with chaotic sequences for image contrast enhancement. *Chaos, Solitons, and Fractals, 42*(1), 522–529. doi:10.1016/j.chaos.2009.01.012

Coelho, L. S., & Mariani, V. C. (2008). Use of chaotic sequences in a biologically inspired algorithm for engineering design optimization. *Expert Systems with Applications, 34*(3), 1905–1913. doi:10.1016/j.eswa.2007.02.002

Derrac, J., Garcia, S., Molina, D., & Herrera, F. (2011). A practical tutorial on the use of nonparametric statistical tests as a methodology for comparing evolutionary and swarm intelligence algorithms. *Swarm and Evolutionary Computation, 1*, 3-18.

Dey, N., Ashour, A. S., Beagum, S., Pistola, D. S., Gospodinov, M., Gospodinova, E. P., & Tavares, J. M. R. (2015). Parameter optimization for local polynomial approximation based intersection confidence interval filter using genetic algorithm: An application for brain MRI image de-noising. *Journal of Imaging, 1*(1), 60–84. doi:10.3390/jimaging1010060

Dey, N., Chakraborty, S., & Samanta, S. (2014b). Optimization of watermarking in biomedical signal. *Lambert Publication. Heinrich-Böcking-Straße, 6*, 66121.

Dey, N., Samanta, S., Chakraborty, S., Das, A., Chaudhuri, S. S., & Suri, J. S. (2014a). Firefly algorithm for optimization of scaling factors during embedding of manifold medical information: An application in ophthalmology imaging. *Journal of Medical Imaging and Health Informatics, 4*(3), 384–394. doi:10.1166/jmihi.2014.1265

Dey, N., Samanta, S., Yang, X. S., Das, A., & Chaudhuri, S. S. (2013). Optimisation of scaling factors in electrocardiogram signal watermarking using cuckoo search. *International Journal of Bio-inspired Computation, 5*(5), 315–326. doi:10.1504/IJBIC.2013.057193

Dhal, K. G., Namtirtha, A., Quraishi, I. M., & Das, S. (n.d.). Gray level image enhancement using Particle Swarm Optimization with Lévy Flight: An Eagle Strategy Approach. *International Journal of Innovative Research in Science, Engineering and Technology, 5*, 79-86.

Dhal, K. G., & Das, S. (2015). Diversity Conserved Chaotic Artificial Bee Colony Algorithm based Brightness Preserved Histogram Equalization and Contrast Stretching Method. *International Journal of Natural Computing Research, 5*, 45-73.

Dhal, K. G., & Das, S. (2017). Cuckoo search with search strategies. *Pattern Recognition and Image Analysis.* (accepted)

Dhal, K. G., & Das, S. (2017a). Combination of Histogram Segmentation and Modification to Preserve the Original Brightness of the Images. *Pattern Recognition and Image Analysis, 27*(2), 200–212. doi:10.1134/S1054661817020031

Dhal, K.G, Quraishi, I. M., Das, S.(2015). Performance Enhancement of Differential Evolution by Incorporating Lévy Flight and Chaotic Sequence for the Cases of Satellite Images. *Int. J. of Applied Metaheuristic Computing, 6*, 69-81.

Dhal, K. G., Quraishi, I. M., & Das, S. (2015). *Development of firefly algorithm via chaotic sequence and population diversity to enhance the image contrast. Natural Computing* , 14, 1–12.

Dhal, K. G., Quraishi, I. M., & Das, S. (2015). Performance Analysis of Chaotic Lévy Bat Algorithm and Chaotic Cuckoo Search Algorithm for Gray Level Image Enhancement. *Information Systems Design and Intelligent Applications*, 233-244.

Dhal, K. G., Quraishi, I. M., & Das, S. (2015). *A Chaotic Lévy flight Approach in Bat and Firefly Algorithm for Gray level image Enhancement. I.J. Image, Graphics and Signal Processing*, 7, 69–76.

Dhal, K. G., Quraishi, I. M., & Das, S. (2017). An improved cuckoo search based optimal ranged brightness preserved histogram equalization and contrast stretching method. *Int. Jr. of Swarm intelligence Research, 8*, 1-29.

Dhal, K. G., Sen, M., & Das, S. (2017). Cuckoo search based modified Bi-Histogram Equalizationmethod to enhance the cancerous tissues in Mammography images. *Int. Journal of Medical Engineering and Informatics.* (accepted)

Dhal, K. G., Sen, S., Sarkar, K., Das, S. (2016). Entropy based Range Optimized Brightness Preserved Histogram-Equalization for Image Contrast Enhancement. *Int. Jr. of Computer Vision and Image Processing, 6*(1), 59-72.

Eutamene, A., Kholladi, M. K., Gaceb, D., & Belhadef, H. (2017). *A Dual PSO-Adaptive Mean Shift for Preprocessing Optimization on Degraded Document Images. Int. Jr. Applied Metaheuristic Computing*, 8(1).

Gao, C., Panetta, K., & Agaian, S. (2013). No reference color image quality measures. *2013 Int. Conf. on Cybernetics*, 243-248.

Gatta, C., Rizzi, A., & Marini, D. (2002). ACE: An automatic color equalization algorithm. *Proceedings of the First European Conference on Color in Graphics Image and Vision (CGIV02).*

Gonzalez, R. C., & Woods, R. E. (2002). *Digital Image Processing* (2nd ed.). New York: Prentice Hall.

Gorai, A., & Ghosh, A. (2009). Gray-level Image Enhancement By Particle Swarm Optimization. *Proceedings of World Congress on Nature & Biologically Inspired Computing.* doi:10.1109/NABIC.2009.5393603

Gorai, A., & Ghosh, A. (2011). *Hue preserving color Image Enhancement by Particle Swarm Optimization.* IEEE. doi:10.1109/RAICS.2011.6069375

Hamou, R. M., Bouarara, H. A., & Amine, A. (2015). *Bio-Inspired Techniques in the Clustering of Texts: Synthesis and Comparative Study. Int. Jr. Applied Metaheuristic Computing,* 6(4).

Hashemi, S., Kiani, S., Noroozi, N., & Moghaddam, M. E. (2010). An image contrast enhancement method based on genetic algorithm. *Pattern Recognition Letters,* 31(13), 1816–1824. doi:10.1016/j.patrec.2009.12.006

Hore, S., Chatterjee, S., Santhi, V., Dey, N., Ashour, A. S., Balas, V. E., & Shi, F. (2017). Indian Sign Language Recognition Using Optimized Neural Networks. In *Information Technology and Intelligent Transportation Systems* (pp. 553–563). Springer International Publishing. doi:10.1007/978-3-319-38771-0_54

Kim, Y.T. (1997). Contrast enhancement using brightness preserving bi-histogram equalization. *IEEE Trans. Consum. Electron.,* 43(1), 1–8.

Kong, N. S. P., & Ibrahim, H. (2008). Color image enhancement using brightness preserving dynamic histogram equalization. *IEEE Trans. on Consumer Electronics,* 54, 1962-1968.

Leandro, C. (2009). A novel particle swarm optimization approach using Henon map and implicit filtering local search for economic load dispatch. *Chaos, Solitons, and Fractals,* 39(2), 510–518. doi:10.1016/j.chaos.2007.01.093

Naik, S. K., & Murthy, C. A. (2003). Hue Preserving Color Image Enhancement without Gamut Problem. *IEEE Trans. on Image Processing, 12,* 1591-1598.

NizarBanu. (2015). Gene Clustering Using Metaheuristic Optimization Algorithms. *Int. Jr. Applied MetaheuristicComputing,* 6(4).

Pal, S. K., Bhandari, D., & Kundu, M. K. (1994). Genetic algorithms for optimal image enhancement. *Pattern Recognition Letters*, *15*(3), 261–271. doi:10.1016/0167-8655(94)90058-2

Panetta, K., Gao, C., & Agaian, S. (2013). No reference color image contrast and quality measures. *IEEE Transactions on Consumer Electronics, 59*, 643-651.

Ponomarenko, N., Silvestri, F., Egiazarian, K., Carli, M., Astola, J., & Lukin, V. (2007). On between-coefficient contrast masking of DCT basis functions. *Proc. of the Third Int. Workshop on Video Proc. and Quality Metrics*.

Quraishi, I. M., De, M., Dhal, K.G, Mondal, S., & Das, G. (2013). *Novel hybrid approach to restore historical degraded documents*. IEEE. DOI: 10.1109/ISSP.2013.6526899

Quraishi, I. M., Dhal, K. G., Paul Chowdhury, J., Pattanayak, K., & De, M. (2012). *A novel hybrid approach to enhance low resolution images using particle swarm optimization*. IEEE. DOI: 10.1109/PDGC.2012.6449941

Samantaa, S., Dey, N., Das, P., Acharjee, S., & Chaudhuri, S. S. (2013). *Multilevel threshold based gray scale image segmentation using cuckoo search*. arXiv preprint arXiv:1307.0277

Shanmugavadivu, P., Balasubramanian, K., & Muruganandam, A. (2014). Particle swarm optimized bi-histogram equalization for contrast enhancement and brightness preservation of images. *The Visual Computer*, *30*(4), 387–399. doi:10.1007/s00371-013-0863-8

Sheikholeslami, R., & Kaveh, A. (2013). A Survey of Chaos Embedded Meta-Heuristic Algorithms. *Int. J. Optim. Civil. Eng.*, *3*(4), 617–633.

VijayalakshmiPai, G. A., & Michel, T. (2017). Metaheuristic Optimization of Constrained Large Portfolios using Hybrid Particle Swarm Optimization. *Int. Jr. Applied Metaheuristic Computing, 8*(1).

KEY TERMS AND DEFINITIONS

Chaotic Sequence: Chaos defines the complex behavior of non-linear deterministic system which has ergodicity property.

Fractal Dimension: Fractal dimension is the quantitative expression of the inherent dimension of the images.

Gamut Problem: The pixels values of the channels of the color space do not lie within their respective intervals.

Hue: Hue represents the kind of color i.e. the dominant wavelength that exists in mixture of colors.

Image Enhancement: Image enhancement is the technique of transforming one image into a better quality image according to the requirements.

Chapter 4

Protein Motif Comparator Using Bio-Inspired Two-Way K-Means

R. Gowri
Periyar University, India

R. Rathipriya
Periyar University, India

ABSTRACT

In this scientific world, the evolution of the disease is predominantly higher than the medicines. The diagnosis and prognosis of such diseases will differ from patient to patient. In this scenario, the protein motifs are very useful for understanding the functionality and lethality of the disease. Most of the existing techniques are supervised approaches which require prior knowledge of the data. As the protein sequences are unsupervised data, the unsupervised data mining techniques like Clustering and 2-way Clustering are chosen to mine the homologous protein motifs. The quality of the results is refined further using the bio-inspired computing models like Particle Swarm Optimization, Genetic Algorithm and Venus Flytrap Optimization in this research work. The existing approaches can mine homologous patterns with structure similarity of 75 percent which is increased in this proposed approach. The results from these three different approaches show that the bio-inspired based 2-way Clustering approaches can mine more homologous motifs than the clustering approaches.

DOI: 10.4018/978-1-5225-4151-6.ch004

INTRODUCTION

Proteins (Y.Vincent, Bernard, & SinanKockara) (Structures of life, 2007) are present in every cell of the organisms. They are involved virtually almost in all cellular activities. They are responsible for the various metabolic activities, nutrition transportation, regulations and etc. They exist as single chain molecule, as a three-dimensional structures or even in the bundle or complex forms. The protein plays a vital role in cellular processes. The protein consists of twenty amino acids. They possess different characteristics such as hydrophobic, hydrophilic, polar, non-polar, etc. It is the great challenge to the bioinformatics researchers that to find which combination of proteins are responsible for what kind of activities. The structure and function discovery of proteins in living organisms is vital role in understanding the background of various cellular processes. It is helpful in treating various diseases and in detecting the drugs to peculiar diseases.

The purpose of this motif comparator is to detect the motif information (Zhaoa-Xing-Ming, 2005) (Kunik.V, Solan.Z, Edelman.S, Ruppin.E, & Horn.D, 2005) from the protein sequences by clustering and 2-way clustering them. K-means is the benchmark clustering technique, used to group similar kind of data elements (Bapuji Rao, 2017). It is used to discover similar patterns from vast amount of data, a toy example is shown in the figure 1. It is widely used in many research areas like bioinformatics, pattern recognition, statistics, image analysis and machine learning. As all these areas are dealing with the unclassified data, the clustering is well suited to these kinds of research areas. The clusters can be found based on various similarities among the data such as intra distance and inter distance of the clusters (R.Gowri & R.Rathipriya, 2016-c) (Duggirala Raja Kishor, 2016). The quality of clusters will be evaluated based on our objective.

Figure 1. Clustering Approach: A toy example

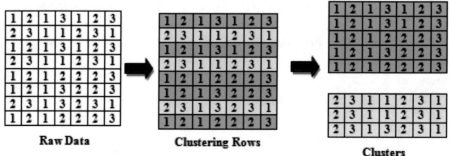

2-way clustering (Madeira.S.C & OliveiraA.L., 2004) is one of the data mining techniques. It is also named as co-clustering (R.Gowri & R.Rathipriya, 2017), biclustering. Biclustering and 2-way clustering are used synonymously in this chapter. This approach generates biclusters of different sizes and characteristics as shown in the figure 2. The process of grouping data based on both the samples and attributes. K-means is used for 2-way clustering in the proposed approach. K-means is applied to both rows and columns simultaneously and local patterns (Biclusters) are extracted by combining these row and column clusters.

The major difference (Madeira.S.C & OliveiraA.L., 2004) (Berkhin, 2002) between the clustering and 2-way clustering are as follows.

- Clustering applied to either rows or columns of the dataset, but biclustering is applied to both rows and columns.
- The size of any one of the dimensions of all the clusters will be same, but biclusters are of different size.
- 2-way clustering groups more similar element than the clustering process.
- 2-way clustering can predict both global and local models but clustering approach predicts global models only.

Normally, the results of the k-means approach are dependent on the initial seeds chosen. Thus the result will vary for different runs. So in this proposed approach, the bio-inspired optimization models (NizarBanu & Andrews, 2015) are used to refine the results based on the intra cluster distance. The Particle Swarm

Figure 2. 2-way Clustering: A toy example

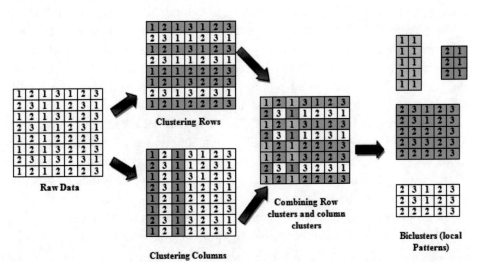

Optimization (PSO) (R.Gowri & R.Rathipriya, 2016-b), Genetic Algorithm (GA) (R.Gowri & R.Rathipriya, 2016-d) and Venus Flytrap Optimization (VFO) (R.Gowri & R.Rathipriya, 2015-a) (R.Gowri & R.Rathipriya, 2015-b) are attempted in this work. The PSO is one of the de-facto optimization techniques but stuck with local optimum. The Genetic Algorithm also has local optimum problem but they search optimal solution in a randomized scenario. So the local optimal problem is minimal than the PSO. Further, VFO algorithm is a recently upcoming optimization technique which is free from the local optimal problem is also chosen to refine the results. In this current work, the motifs are extracted from the clusters and biclusters that are detected using the proposed PSO k-means (R.Gowri & R.Rathipriya, 2016-b), GA k-means (R.Gowri & R.Rathipriya, 2016-d) and VFO k-means (R.Gowri & R.Rathipriya, 2015-a) approaches. The secondary structure similarity is used to measure the biological quality of the results. The quality of motifs extracted from clusters and biclusters are compared. There are various database are available for the protein sequence and motifs such as BLOCKS (S.Pietrokovski, JG.Henikoff, & S.Henikoff, 1996), PROSITE (Bairoch.A, 8ucher.P, & Hofmann.K, 1996), PISCES (Wang.G & Dunbrack.R, 2003)and so on. The protein sequence is preprocessed for both clustering and 2-way clustering processes. The clusters and biclusters are compared based on their secondary structural similarity.

BACKGROUND

In this work (Zhaoa-Xing-Ming, 2005), they have proposed an novel approach for extracting features from motif content and protein composition. They have used Support Vector Machine (SVM) along with the combination of Genetic Algorithm (GA) and Principal Component Analysis (PCA) for extracting the protein motif.

In this work (Y.Fujiwara & A.Konagaya, 2008), they have proposed a methodology for protein extraction in their work, they have used the Hidden Markov Model (HMM) to detect the protein motifs from the proteins with motifs unidentified. They train the HMM with test samples of protein motifs of various categories to detect the protein motifs as similar to the trained dataset.

In this work (B.Chen, S.Pellicer, P.C.Tai, R.Harrison, & Y.Pan, 2009), the authors have proposed a novel efficient granular computing models for protein sequence motif and structure information discovery. The protein sequence motifs are extracted using the granular computing with the Fuzzy improved K-Means model and Fuzzy greedy K-Means model.

In this work (B.Cheng, C.Hudson, M.Kim, A.Crawford, J.Wright, & D.Che, 2011), they have defined another method for protein sequence motif extraction using

Decision Forest. They have used the decision forest combined with fuzzy logic and granular computing to get more efficient results than their previous work.

In this work (Y.Vincent, Bernard, & SinanKockara)The authors have proposed a biclustering algorithm for extracting the protein motifs. They obtained the clusters using Fuzzy Greedy K-Means (FGK) model along with the Granular Computing. They used Cheng and Church methodology to shrink the clusters in order to get high quality biclusters.

In this work (Elayaraja, Thangavel, Ramya, & Chitralegha, 2011), the authors have devised a method for motif extraction process using the rough K-Means. They have used Rough K-Means to yield the better results than simple K-Means in their work, "Extraction of Motif Information from Protein Sequences using Rough K-Means" in 2011

In this work (Elayaraja E, 2012), they have further suggested another method for motif extraction process using the SVD in addition to the rough K-Means in order to attain better results. Their work is "Extraction of Motif Patterns from Protein Sequences Using SVD with Rough K-Means Algorithm" in 2011

In this work (Bill.C.H.Chang, 2012), they have suggested a method for Protein Motif Extraction Using Neuro-Fuzzy optimization in 2002, they attempted to improve the speed and flexibility of protein motif identification. They proposed an algorithm to extract both rigid and flexible protein motifs and to detect consensus pattern, or motif, from a group of related protein sequences.

In this work (Chen Yi-Cheng, 2011), they have suggested a method for the discovery of Protein Phosphorylation Motifs through Exploratory Data Analysis, they proposed an F-Motif algorithm for motif extraction using clustering methods in 2011.

In this work (R.Gowri & R.Rathipriya, 2015) they have suggested that the PSO algorithm can improvise the results further than the existing approaches. The biclustering approach can mine more local patterns than the clustering approach in 2015.

The various works in the literature show that the different hybrid methods were used for extracting the Motif Information. Those methods are any combination of Support Vector Machine (SVM), hidden Markov Model (HMM), Neural Networks, Fuzzy system, Rough set, Clustering technique and so on. Some authors were used optimization technique to improve the extraction process. From the literature, it shows the combination of optimization technique can improve the results but sometimes they stuck with local optimum. The clustering technique is better suits for unidentified data. The biclustering further improves results than the clustering process, the combination of bio-inspired models with clustering and 2-way clustering on protein sequences is proposed and yield better results. This proposed work is further discussed in the following sections.

PROTEIN MOTIF COMPARATOR

Objective of Motif Comparator

The objective of the Protein Motif Comparator is to detect Motifs either from the clusters are biclusters. The clusters (L. Youcheng, et al., 2012) (AshaGowdaKaregowda & SeemaKumari, 2013) and biclusters (Rathipriya, Thangavel, & J.Bagyamani, 2011) (Cui Xiaohui, 2005) (Das Shyama, 2010) are obtained by applying Bio-Inspired based approaches like Particle Swarm Optimization (PSO) k-means, Genetic Algorithm (GA) k-means and Venus Flytrap Optimization (VFO) k-means to the preprocessed Protein Sequences.

The main objective of these Bio-Inspired K-Means is to reduce the intra-distance and to increase the inter-distance of the clusters/biclusters. The structure similarity of the sequences is used to find the highly homologous sequences.

The significant amino acids (Chen Yi-Cheng, 2011) that play vital role in any cluster and bicluster can be visualized using sequence logo representation. The number of cluster/bicluster that present with selected similarity percentage can be detected. The work flow of the motif comparator is shown in the figure 3.

Figure 3. Overview of the Motif Comparator

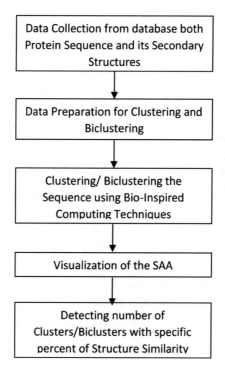

Bio-Inspired Computing Techniques

Genetic Algorithm

The Genetic algorithm (GA) (Holland) (Forrest, 1993) (DE, 1989)is one of the benchmark Meta-heuristic optimization technique almost suits for various types of problems in many domains. Genetic algorithm is devised by John Holland. The pseudo code of genetic algorithm is depicted in figure 4. It is one of the evolutionary algorithms, mimics the natural selection process. The individuals (chromosomes) of GA are represented as the string of bits generally but other kinds of representation are also possible. It is an iterative process starts with initial random population and terminates until the maximum generation. The fitness of the individuals is evaluated which is based on the objective function of optimization problem being discussed. It has various genetic evolution processes like Inheritance, mutation, selection and crossover.

Selection Operator is a process of selecting a proportion of individuals to breed the new generation in each successive generation (Holland) (Forrest, 1993) (DE, 1989). It is carried out based on the fitness of the solutions. The fitness function is problem dependent. The rate of fitness value is studied and the fitter individuals are likely to be selected. There are different selection operators are available.

The crossover and mutation operations are used for generating new generation (Holland) (Forrest, 1993) (DE, 1989). A pair of parent individuals is selected to generate new child individuals. Similarly, a pool of child individuals is generated. The characteristics of both parents are shared by the child individual. There are different types of crossover operators like single point crossover, multi-point crossover are available. The mutation operator is used to mutate the population for generating new traits. These processes ultimately result in the next generation population of chromosomes that is different from the initial generation. Although crossover and mutation are known as the main genetic operators, it is possible to use other operators such as regrouping, colonization-extinction, or migration in genetic algorithms.

This generational process is repeated until a termination condition has been reached. Common terminating conditions (Holland) (Forrest, 1993) (DE, 1989) are: a solution is found that satisfies minimum criteria, fixed number of generations reached, allocated budget (computation time/money) reached, the highest ranking solution's fitness is reaching or has reached a plateau such that successive iterations no longer produce better results, manual inspection or combinations of these conditions.

It is a most powerful unbiased optimization technique for sampling a large solution space. It is adaptive to any kind of environment with minimal changes. Typical optimization techniques require more space and time to mine all feasible solutions.

Figure 4. Pseudo code for Genetic Algorithm

Genetic algorithm
choose initial population
evaluate each individual's fitness
determine population's average fitness
repeat
select best-ranking individuals to reproduce
mate pairs at random
apply crossover operator
apply mutation operator
evaluate each individual's fitness
determine population's average fitness
until terminating condition

Particle Swarm Optimization

The particle swarm optimization (AshaGowdaKaregowda & SeemaKumari, 2013)is one of the swarm intelligence techniques. It is a stochastic optimization technique. It is a population based method that is designed based on the birds flocking behavior. Selecting the initial population is decided based on the problem criteria. The steps involved in PSO algorithm are given in the figure 5. The number of individuals in the population is decided based on the objective of the problem. The particle at each time interval updates its position and velocity based on its own best position achieved so far and the global best position achieved by any one of the particles in its swarm. The random terms are used to weigh the acceleration of the particle. The best position is evaluated based on the objective function of the problem. The basic particle swarm optimization algorithm (PriteshVora, 2013) (P.Riccardo, K.James, & B.Tim, 2007) is in 0.

The velocity of the particle is updated based on equation 1, here the first term is based on the velocity of the previous iteration t, second term is cognition part, based on the local best position of the particle and the third term is social part, based on the global best position of the particle. The w represents the inertia weight of the previous velocity of the particle; it is calculated using the equation 2. The c1 and c2 are constant values chosen randomly, the R1 and R2 are random numbers where R1, R2 [0, 1].

$$vel_{ij}\left(t+1\right) = wv_{ij}\left(t\right) + c_1 R_1 \left(pbest_{ij} - x_{ij}\left(t\right)\right) + c_2 R_2 \left(gbest_{ij} - x_{ij}\left(t\right)\right) \tag{1}$$

Figure 5. Pseudocode of Particle Swarm Optimization

Particle Swarm optimization
Create a swarm with P particles
Initialize the position and velocity of each particle randomly
Calculate fitness value of each position
Calculate pbest and gbest for each particle
Repeat
Update velocity and position of each particle
Evaluate the fitness of each particle
Update pbest and gbest for each particle
Until Stopping criteria is true;

Where,

$$w = W_{max} - \frac{W_{max} - W_{min}}{iter\left(max\right)} - iter\left(x\right) \tag{2}$$

The w_{max} is the initial weight of the particle and w_{min} is the final weight of the particle. The position of the particle at each iteration is updated using the equation 3 based on the updated velocity of the particle.

$$x_{ij}\left(t+1\right) = x_{ij}\left(t\right) + v_{ij}\left(t+1\right) \tag{3}$$

Venus Flytrap Optimization

The Venus Flytrap Optimization (R.Gowri & R.Rathipriya, 2015-b) is also a meta-heuristic algorithm that can be applied to any kind of optimization problems. The rapid closure behavior of the Venus Flytrap leaves (trap) to capture the prey is mimicked in this algorithm. The closure action is triggered through the stimulations of trigger hairs on the surface of the lobes, carried out by the prey (objects). The pseudo code of the VFO is discussed as in the figure. This algorithm has Initial phase, trapping phase and sealing phase. The pseudocode of the VFO algorithm is discussed in the figure 6.

Figure 6. Pseudo Code for VFO

Venus Flytrap Algorithm

                                                    //Initial phase

Objective function f(x), $x = (x_1, ..., x_d)^S$
Initialize a population of flytraps x_i (i = 1, 2, ..., n)
While iter < = S
  For i=1 : n all n flytraps   *//trapping phase*
    At t=0,   *//first stimulation*
    Evaluate Action Potential u_t of flytrap i
    Charge Accumulation C of flytrap i is determined by $f(x_i)$
    At t=rand()   *//second stimulation*
    if t<=T then
        update u_t, C of flytrap i
        evaluate the Object Status
      end if
  end for
Rank the flytraps and find the current best   *//sealing phase*
seal the best flytrap until another best flytrap arrives
end while
Post process results and visualization

The stimulation of trigger hairs generates the action potential required for the closure of the leaf. The potential generated is dissipated at a particular rate and reaches to zero. It is calculated using the equation (4).

$$u_t = \begin{cases} 0.15e^{-2000\,t}, \ t \geq 0 \\ \qquad 0, \ t < 0 \end{cases} \tag{4}$$

Where, t is the trigger time at which the trigger hairs are stimulated, t<0 before the first stimulation, t=0 for the first stimulation, t>0 for the second stimulation. The time between the two successive stimulations will be less than 30 seconds in order to initiate the flytrap closure. So the time before first stimulation is taken as less than zero, the time at the first stimulation is taken as zero and the time at which the trigger is stimulated for the second time is taken as greater than zero. Thus there is no action potential for the flytrap before the first stimulation. This is shown in the equation (4).

The charge accumulation may relate to the stepwise accumulation of a bioactive substance, resulting in ion channel activation by the action potential. It is evaluated using the equation (5).

$$C = -k_c C + k_a u_t \tag{5}$$

Where, C is the charge accumulated by the lobes for trap shutter. The k_a is the rate of accumulation of the charge, i.e., the rate at which the charge is builds up based on the action potential attained in the stimulation. For the first stimulation the dissipation part will be zero because the initial charge of the flytrap before first stimulation is zero, it will work for the second stimulation to sum up the previously gained charge with it. This is how the charge is calculated in the real flytraps. In these computational flytraps, the charge is calculated based on the objective function f(x).

The next parameter is the flytrap status (δ), used to know the current status of the flytraps. The status of the flytrap will be either 0 or 1 or 2(open or close or seal).

$$\delta\left(\text{ft}\right) = \begin{cases} 2, & S\left(C\right) = 1, \delta\left(\text{ft}\right) = 1 \\ 1, & 0 \leq t \leq T \\ 0, & otherwise \end{cases} \tag{6}$$

The flytrap will be initially in the opened the (0) state. If the trap closure is triggered by the prey (object) then the trap will be in closed (1) state. The time point of the first stimulation is taken as zero, here the t represents the second stimulation time. The T is the time threshold between two stimulations.

Hybrid Bio-Inspired K-Means

The hybrid bio-inspired k-means represents the k-means algorithm is optimized by adapting the bio-inspired optimization techniques (R.Gowri & R.Rathipriya, 2016-b) like PSO, GA and VFO as discussed in the previous sections. This combination of bio-inspired models as PSO k-means (R.Gowri & R.Rathipriya, 2016-a), GA k-means and VFO k-means improves the performance of k-means algorithm. These stochastic algorithms are used in order to search the optimal Motifs in a randomized solution space.

In the PSO k-means (R.Gowri & R.Rathipriya, 2015) algorithm the set of centroids are mapped as the position of the particle, the fitness of the particle is the intra cluster distance. The velocity of the particle is randomly initialized. The number of particles n_p is chosen as 50, these particles is iterated at the maximum of 1000 iterations (maxiter). In the PSO algorithm the particles are influenced by the global best and particle best positions so the particles has more possibility to stuck at local optimum values.

Figure 7. Workflow of Hybrid bio-Inspired K-Means

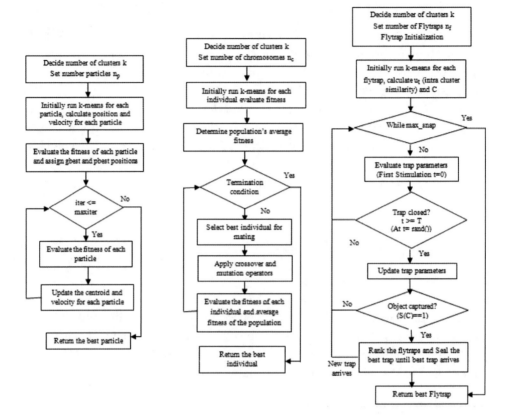

In the GA based k-means the chromosomes are represented as binary strings. The membership values of the set clusters are the individuals. The length of string is same as the number of residue fragments generated. The intra cluster distance is the fitness of the individuals. The crossover probability chosen is 0.7. The genetic algorithm has more random search nature compared to PSO. Even though it searches solution randomly, sometimes individuals may stuck with local optimum.

To avoid this local optimum problem the VFO is chosen to this approach. In the VFO algorithm the best solution is retained until the new best solution is obtained. Thus the local optimum problem is avoided in this optimization technique. The intra cluster distance is chosen as fitness measure. The charge accumulated (C) maps the intra cluster distance. The maximum fitness value is chosen as the charge threshold.

The distance (Elayaraja, K.Thangavel, M.Chitralega, & T.Chandrasekhar, 2012) (Y.Vincent, Bernard, & SinanKockara)between the different protein sequences is evaluated using the city block distance using equation (1). V_k is k^{th} sequence and V_c is the centroid sequence.

$$\text{city block distance} = \sum_{i=1}^{R}\sum_{j=1}^{A} V_k\left(i,j\right) - V_c\left(i,j\right) \tag{7}$$

The intra distance of the cluster is chosen as the fitness of all the three bio-inspired k-means approaches proposed for Motif Comparator. The distance is calculated using the equation (7). The mean of the distances between each sequence in the cluster and its centroid is taken as the fitness of the cluster. The fitness (Ahmadyfard.A & Modares.H, 2008) is calculated using the equation (8). Here V_k is the sequence in cluster k and cent is the centroid of the cluster.

$$\text{fitness} = 1 / n\left(\sum_{i=1}^{n}\text{distance}(V_k\left(i\right), \text{cent})\right) \tag{8}$$

The structure similarity (Y.Vincent, Bernard, & SinanKockara) of each cluster and bicluster is calculated using the equation (9). Here ws is the window size and $P_{i,H}$ shows the frequency of occurrence of helix among the segments for the cluster in position i. $P_{i,E}$ and $P_{i,C}$ are defined in a similar way. The motifs are

$$\text{similarity} = \frac{\sum_{i=1}^{ws}\max\left(P_{i,H}, P_{i,E}, P_{i,C}\right)}{ws} \tag{9}$$

Dataset Description

The protein sequences and their secondary structures are collected from different databases. Normally, the Secondary structures are taken from DSSP. Yeast Proteins and its structure are taken. The proteins and their secondary structures are stored in separate files, in the same order. The file is stored as FASTA format in a text file. Those files are loaded into this tool. The comparator is used to simulate the results of the first approach PSO k-means. The remaining two approaches are implemented similarly using MATLAB without GUI.

Data Preparation

The protein sequences are of different length and it is collection of Amino acids. In order to equalize the sequence length and to convert it to the numerical data the sequence is arranged into 9 or 10 residues (columns). The frequency profiles of these amino acid residues are taken to implement the proposed approach. The columns and rows represent Amino acids and residues. Now each sequence (Elayaraja, K.Thangavel, M.Chitralega, & T.Chandrasekhar, 2012) (Y.Vincent, Bernard, & SinanKockara) is now converted into 9 by 20 matrixes. These are used for clustering purpose it is shown in the figure 8.

For 2-way clustering the sequence these matrixes are further normalized into a single row as in the figure 9 using average normalization.

There are eight classes in secondary structure which is mapped to three classes by using the following conversion model: assigning H, G, and I to H (Helices), assigning B and E to E (Sheets), and assigning all others to C (Coils).

Clustering the Sequential Data

The protein sequences are clustered in order to group the highly homologous sequences together and detect the significant amino acids in it. These significant amino acids are used for the further research in finding the functionality of the proteins.

Figure 8. Motif Comparator preprocessing protein sequence for clustering

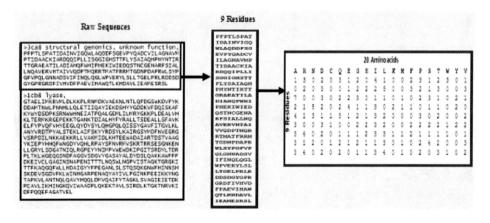

Figure 9. Motif Comparator preprocessing protein sequence for 2-way clustering

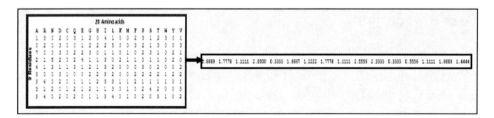

The PSO k-means is performed as follows: The number of clusters to be detected and number of particles to be handled are given as input for the clustering besides the sequence data in the interface as in figure 10(a). The result button is clicked to cluster the sequences given and visualizing panel will be displayed as in the figure 10(b). The remaining two approaches are implemented and the comparative results are visualized in the figure 10.

Figure 10. Motif Comparator (PSO k-means): (a) Cluster Specification (b)Results Obtained

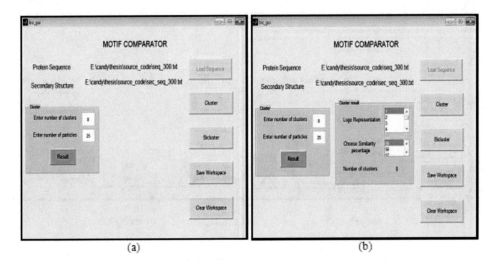

(a)   (b)

Figure 11. Motif Comparator(PSO k-means) – (a) Entering bicluster specification (b) and Bicluster results

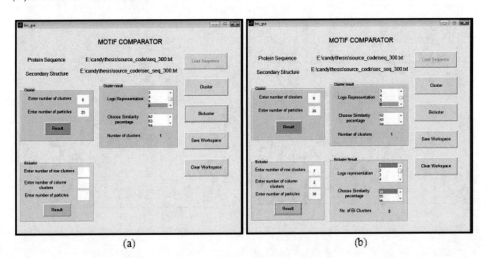

(a)   (b)

Bi-Clustering the Sequential Data

The protein sequences are biclustered (Madeira.S.C & OliveiraA.L., 2004) in order to group the highly homologous sequences together and detect the significant amino acids in it better than the clustering process. These significant amino acids are used for the further research in finding the functionality of the proteins. The number of row clusters and column clusters to be detected and number of particles to be handled are given as input for the 2-way clustering process besides the sequence data as in the figure 11 (a). The result button is clicked to bicluster the given sequences and visualizing panel will be displayed as in the figure 11 (b). The remaining two approaches are implemented and the comparative results are visualized in the figure 11.

Figure 12. Logo representation of some common motifs found by all the proposed approaches

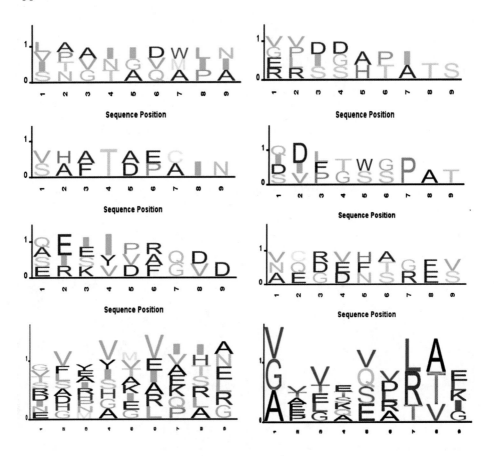

Visualizing Motifs and Comparative Analysis

The obtained clusters are visualized using the logo representation. The significant amino acids that are present in each cluster will be displayed in logo window by selecting the cluster id given in the list on the cluster result panel. The sample logo representations of some common motifs extracted are shown in the figure 12.

The obtained biclusters are visualized using the logo representation. The significant amino acids that are present in each cluster will be displayed in logo

Figure 13. Logo representation of some common motifs found by all the proposed approaches

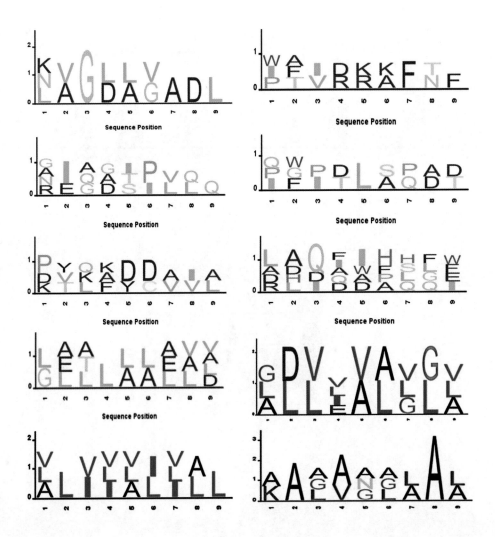

Figure 14. Comparison of number of cluster and biclusters extracted using the proposed Bio-Inspired k-means approaches based on structure similarity

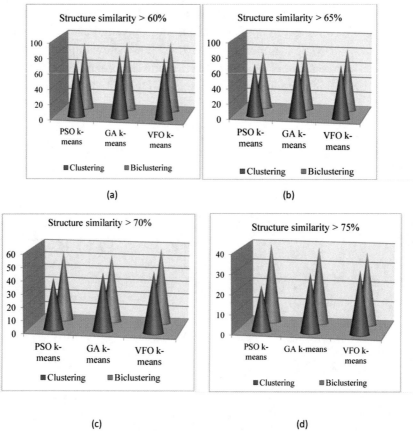

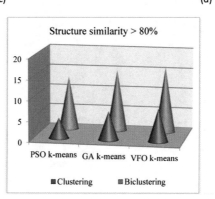

window by selecting the bicluster id given in the list on the bicluster result panel. The sample logo representations of some common bicluster extracted by all the proposed approaches are shown in the figure 13. The number of biclusters with required similarity percentage can be detected by selecting the similarity value displayed in the list as in the figure 11.

The comparative analysis is carried out by comparing the number of clusters and biclusters predicted by all the proposed approaches at specified structure similarity percent value. The results show that the GA and VFO based k-means approach can predict more patterns with more structure similarity than the PSO k-means. The 2-way clustering outperforms the clustering approach in all the three proposed approaches. The results are shown in the figure 14.

CONCLUSION

The protein motifs plays important role in studying the characteristics of the biological system. The existing approaches require prior knowledge to predict the protein motifs. They can mine motifs with structure similarity up to 75 percent. As the protein sequences are unsupervised data, the clustering and 2-way clustering approaches were proposed for protein motif prediction in this research work. The bio-inspired computing models like PSO, GA and VFO based k-means has been proposed for further refinement of the results. The experimental results evident that the 2-way clustering model can predict more homologous protein motifs than the clustering models. The GA k-means and VFO-k-means approaches perform well than the PSO k-means approach. The secondary structure similarity measure is used to extract the biologically significant patterns from the clusters and biclusters obtained. In future, this measure can be further incorporated in these approaches as fitness measure for more refined results.

REFERENCES

Ahmadyfard, A., & Modares, H. (2008). Combining PSO and K-Means to enhance data clustering. *International Symposium on Telecommunication*, 688 - 691. doi:10.1109/ISTEL.2008.4651388

Bairoch, A., Bucher, P., & Hofmann, K. (1996). PROSITE: New developments. *Nucleic Acids Research*, 189-196.

Bapuji Rao, B. K. (2017). An Approach to Clustering of Text Documents Using Graph Mining Techniques. *International Journal of Rough Sets and Data Analysis*, 4(1).

Berkhin, P. (2002). *Survey of Clustering Data Mining Techniques*. Accrue Software.

Bill, C. H., & Chang, S. (2012). Protein Motif Extraction Using Neuro-Fuzzy optimization. *Bioinformatics (Oxford, England)*, *18*(8), 1084–1090. PMID:12176831

Chen, Pellicer, Tai, Harrison, & Pan. (2009). Novel efficient granular computing models for protein sequence motifs and structure information discovery. *International Journal of Computational Biology and Drug Design*.

Chen Yi-Cheng, K. Y.-W.-T.-F. (2011). Discovery of Protein Phosphorylation Motifs through Exploratory Data Analysis. *Discovery of Protein Phosphorylation Motifs (PLoS ONE)*, 6.

Cheng, B., Hudson, C., Kim, M., Crawford, A., Wright, J., & Che, D. (2011). Protein Sequence Motif Extraction using Decision Forest. *World Congress in Computer Science, Computer Engineering*.

Cui Xiaohui, P. T. (2005). Document Clustering Analysis Based on Hybrid PSO K-means Algorithm. *Journal of Computer Sciences*, 27-33.

Das Shyama, I. S. (2010). Greedy Search-Binary PSO Hybrid for Biclustering Gene Expression Data. *International Journal of Computers and Applications*, *2*(3), 1–5. doi:10.5120/651-908

De, G. (1989). Genetic Algorithms in Search, Optimization, and Machine Learning. Reading, MA: Addison-Wesley.

Duggirala Raja Kishor, N. V. (2016). A Novel Hybridization of Expectation-Maximization and K-Means Algorithms for Better Clustering Performance. *International Journal of Ambient Computing and Intelligence*, *7*(2).

Elayaraja, E., Thangavel, K., Chitralega, M., & Chandrasekhar, T. (2012). Extraction of Motif Patterns from Protein Sequences Using SVD with Rough K-Means Algorithm. *IJCSI International Journal of Computer Science Issues*, *9*(6), 350–356.

Elayaraja, E., Thangavel, K., Ramya, B., & Chitralegha, M. (2011). Extraction of Motif Patterns from Protein Sequence using Rough K-Means Algorithm. *Procedia Engineering*, *30*, 814–820. doi:10.1016/j.proeng.2012.01.932

Forrest, S. (1993). Genetic algorithms: Principles of natural selection applied to Computation. *Science*, 872–878.

Fujiwara & Konagaya. (2008). Protein Motif Extraction using Hidden Markov Model. *Genome Informatics*, 57-64.

Gowri & Rathipriya. (2015). Extraction of Protein Sequence Motif Information using PSO K-Means. *Journal of Network and Information Security.*

Gowri & Rathipriya. (2015a). Biclustering using Venus Flytrap Optimization Algorithm. Computational Intelligence in Data Mining—Volume 1. *Advances in Intelligent Systems and Computing Series, 410.*

Gowri, R., & Rathipriya, R. (2016d). MR-GABiT: MapReduce based Genetic Algorithm for Biclustering Time Series Data. *International Conference on Advances in Computer Applications.* IEEE.

Gowri, R., & Rathipriya, R. (2017). Cohesive Sub-Network Mining in Protein Interaction Networks using Score Based Co-Clustering with MapReduce Model (MR-CoC). *International Conference on Big Data Analytics and Cloud Computing.* Springer.

Gowri, R., & Rathipriya, R. (2016b). Extraction of Protein Sequence Motif Information using Bio-Inspired Computing. In *Handbook of Research on Computational Intelligence Applications in Bioinformatics* (pp. 240–262). IGI Global.

Gowri, R., & Rathipriya, R. (2016c). Quality based Clustering using MapReduce Framework. *International conference on Green Engineering and Technologies.* IEEE.

Gowri, R., & Rathipriya, R. (2015b). Venus Flytrap Optimization Algorithm. International Conference on Computational Intelligence, Cyber Security and Computational Models. *Advances in Intelligent Systems and Computing Series, 412.*

Gowri & Rathipriya. (2016a). Protein Motif Comparator using PSO K-Means. *International Journal of Applied Metaheuristic Computing, 7*(3), 56–68.

Holland, J. H. (n.d.). Genetic Algorithms and Adaptation. *Adaptive Control of Ill-Defined Systems, NATO Conference Series,* 16, 317-333.

Karegowda & Kumari. (2013). Particle Swarm Optimization Algorithm Based K-Means and Fuzzy c-means clustering. *International Journal of Advanced Research in Computer Science and Software Engineering, 3*(7).

Kunik, V., Solan, Z., Edelman, S., Ruppin, E., & Horn, D. (2005). Motif Extraction and Protein Classification: Computational Systems. *Proceedings of IEEE Computational Systems Bioinformatics / Life Sciences Society.*

Madeira, S. C., & Oliveira, A. L. (2004). Biclustering Algorithms for Biological Data Analysis. *Survey (London, England),* 1–31. PMID:17048406

NizarBanu, P. K., & Andrews, S. (2015). Gene Clustering Using Metaheuristic Optimization Algorithms. *International Journal of Applied Metaheuristic Computing*, *6*(4).

Pietrokovski, S., Henikoff, J. G., & Henikoff, S. (1996). The BLOCKS database - a system for protein classification. *Nucleic Acids Research*, *24*(1), 197–200. doi:10.1093/nar/24.1.197 PMID:8594578

PriteshVora. (2013). A Survey on K-mean Clustering and Particle Swarm Optimization. *International Journal of Science and Modern Engineering*, *1*(3), 24–26.

Rathipriya, R., Thangavel, K., & Bagyamani, J. (2011). Binary Particle Swarm Optimization based Biclustering of Web usage Data. *International Journal of Computers and Applications*, *25*(2), 43–49. doi:10.5120/3001-4036

Riccardo, P., James, K., & Tim, B. (2007). Particle swarm optimization An Overview. *Swarm Intelligence*, 33–57.

Structures of life. (2007). US Department of Health and Human Services.

Vincent, , & Bernard, , & Kockara. (n.d.). *Extraction of Protein Sequence Motifs Information by Bi-Clustering Algorithm. Academic Press.*

Wang.G, & Dunbrack.R. (2003). PISCES: A protein sequence culling server. *Bioinformatics*, 1589-1591.

Youcheng, Nan, Majie, Kedi, Yuan, & Qu. (2012). K-means optimization clustering algorithm based on Particle swarm optimization and multiclass merging. *Advances in CSIE, 1*, 569-578.

Zhaoa-Xing-Ming. (2005). A novel approach to extracting features from motif content and protein composition for protein sequence classification. *Neural Networks*, 1019–1028. PMID:16153801

KEY TERMS AND DEFINITIONS

Amino Acid: Amino acids are the organic compounds that are fundamental elements of protein sequence or peptides. The protein consists of twenty amino acids. They possess different characteristics such as hydrophobic, hydrophilic, polar, non-polar and etc.

Homologous Proteins: The Homologous proteins are set of proteins having similar characteristic either structurally or functionally.

Logo Representation: It is one of the graphical representations of amino acids, nucleic acids used for protein sequence alignment processing. The weights of amino acids in a particular position are represented by the height of the amino acids.

Meta-Heuristic Model: A meta-heuristic model is a high-level problem-independent algorithmic framework that provides a set of guidelines or strategies to develop heuristic optimization algorithms.

Protein Motif: A consecutive sequence of amino acids present in a protein sequence, which possesses some specific characteristic.

Protein Sequence: Protein sequences are the fundamental determinants of biological structure and function. It is a sequence of Amino Acids.

Significant Amino Acid (SAA): SAA are present protein motifs, possess specific characteristics in homologous protein motifs. The SAA are highlighted using the Logo representation.

Chapter 5

Metaheuristics in Manufacturing:
Predictive Modeling of Tool Wear in Machining Using Genetic Programming

Mohammad Zadshakoyan
University of Tabriz, Iran

Vahid Pourmostaghimi
University of Tabriz, Iran

ABSTRACT

The state of a cutting tool is an important factor in any metal cutting process as additional costs in terms of scrapped components, machine tool breakage and unscheduled downtime result from worn tool usage. Therefore, tool wear prediction plays an important role in industry automation for higher productivity and acceptable product quality. Therefore, in order to increase the productivity of turning process, various researches have been made recently for tool wear estimation and classification in turning process. Chip form is one of the most important factors commonly considered in evaluating the performance of machining process. On account of the effect of the progressive tool wear on the shape and geometrical features of produced chip, it is possible to predict some measurable machining outputs such as crater wear. According to experimentally performed researches, cutting speed and cutting time are two extremely effective parameters which contribute to the development of the crater wear on the tool rake face. As a result, these parameters will change the chip radius and geometry. This chapter presents the development

DOI: 10.4018/978-1-5225-4151-6.ch005

of the genetic equation for the tool wear using occurred changes in chip radius in turning process. The development of the equation combines different methods and technologies like evolutionary methods, manufacturing technology, measuring and control technology with the adequate hardware and software support. The results obtained from genetic equation and experiments showed that obtained genetic equations are correlated well with the experimental data. Furthermore, it can be used for tool wear estimation during cutting process and because of its parametric form, genetic equation enables us to analyze the effect of input parameters on the crater wear parameters.

INTRODUCTION

Manufacturing processes like drilling, milling, or turning can be optimized significantly using reliable and flexible tool monitoring systems. The most important tasks in this context are (Golz, Schillo, Wolf, & Kaufeld, 1995):

- The fast detection of collisions, i.e. unintended contacts between the tool or the tool-holder and the work piece or components of the machine tool,
- The identification of tool fracture (breakage), e.g. outbreaks at cutting edges,
- The estimation or classification of tool wear caused by abrasion or other influences.

While collision and tool fracture are sudden and mostly unexpected events which require reactions in real-time, the development of wear is more or less slowly proceeding. This chapter focuses on the determination of wear, the most difficult of the three tasks. The importance of tool wear monitoring is implied by the possible economic advantages. By exchanging worn tools in time (considering the current machining process such as rough or finish turning, for instance), it is possible to avoid the production of waste. Furthermore, tools costs can be reduced noticeably with a precise exploitation of a tool's life time. With an accurate estimation of tool wear, it is even possible to adjust the tool position in order to meet geometric specifications and to control the tool wear rate in order to guarantee a certain surface quality of the work piece or roughness.

Chip form and tool wear are two of the major machining performance measures that have been the subject of extensive studies over several decades. It must be said that having the true conception of chip formation and chip movement is an essential task in the prediction of chip breakability. Furthermore, geometrical features of produced chip give us valuable information about tribological phenomena in cutting zone such as tool wear, cutting zone temperature, etc.

On the other hand, tool wear and economical estimations related to tool life are among essential issues associated with machining optimization, because in automated manufacturing operations, tool must be removed from the cutting process well before it fails, otherwise the parts produced become out of the allowable tolerance (Devillez, Lesko, & Mozer, 2004). Therefore, tool wear is of great significance in manufacturing since it affects the quality of the components, tool life and machine costs.

Mechanisms responsible for tool failure are abrasive, adhesive and diffusion wear (Devillez et al., 2004). Considering that the chip radius has a direct relation with the form of crater wear and this type of wear is formed due to adhesive and diffusion factors, so it can be resulted that these factors affect chip geometry impressively.

By considering the basic nature of the various wear mechanisms that are generally observed in machining operations, it has been showed that during the progressive tool wear, some major wear parameters contribute to the variation in chip flow, chip curl and chip breakability in metal machining, typically in a turning operations. Figure 1 shows various wear features studied in mentioned research.

To predict the tool crater wear in this work, two independent data sets are obtained on the basis of measurements: training data set and testing data set. Chip radius is used as independent input variable, while crater wear is the dependent output variable. An equation for the tool crater wear is developed on the basis of training data set and the accuracy of obtained model is proved on the testing data set by using fitness functions.

So in this chapter, on the basis of results obtained from practical experiments, the interrelationship between the chip radius and tool crater wear using their geometrical

Figure 1. Major tool wear parameters affecting chip geometry in a turning operation, VB: major flank wear; KT: crater wear depth; KB: crater wear length; KS: wear retract of the cutting edge; KK: crater wear width; N: tool nose wear (Devillez et al., 2004).

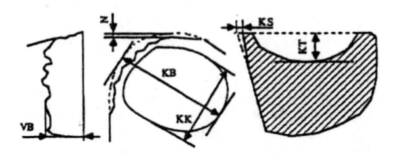

Figure 2. A schematic overview of the methodology used in present study

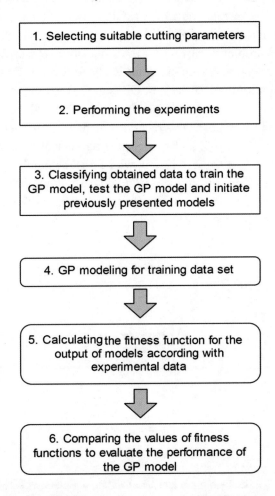

features has been studied and then using GP, a model has been presented to estimate the values of crater wear depth, *KT*, and crater wear length, *KB*.

Genetic Programming (GP)

Genetic algorithms (GA) are generally used as an optimization technique to search the global optimum of a function. However, this is not the only possible use for GA. Other fields of applications where robustness and global optimization are needed could also benefit greatly from GA. The two most important alternative domains applying GA are genetic based machine learning (GBML) and genetic programming (Settea & Boullartb, 2001). GP is basically a GA which is applied to a population of members or computer programs, while a GA usually operates on (coded) strings of numbers a GP has to operate on members. GP allows, in comparison with GA, the optimization of much more complicated structures and can therefore be applied to a greater diversity of problems (Koza, 1992). A schematic overview of GP model which shows its different stages is given in Figure 3. The following steps are performed in each stage of programming. The aim of GP is to find out the member or offspring that best solves the problem. Possible solutions in GP are all the possible computer programs that can be composed in a recursive manner from a set of function genes which is as $F = \{f_1, f_2, \ldots, f_m\}$, where m is the number of function genes, and the set of terminal genes $T = \{a_1, a_2, \ldots, a_n\}$, where n is the number of terminal genes. Each individual function fi from the set F has a certain number of arguments $z(f_i)$. The appropriate number of arguments for function genes from the set F is thus determined with the list $\{z(f_1), z(f_2), \ldots, z(f_m)\}$.

Figure 3. Schematic overview of GP model application (Zadshakoyan & Pourmostaghimi, 2013)

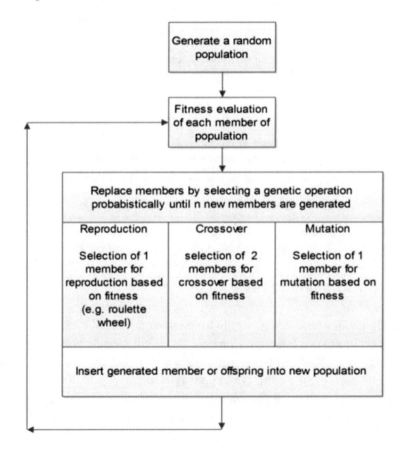

The set of function genes *F* can include basic mathematical functions, Boolean functions, relation functions, program flow control functions, functions for recursion, and functions defined with respect to the problem area studied. The set of terminal genes *T* can include numerical constants, logical constants, variables, etc. Terminal genes are, in fact, function genes without arguments. An example of such a tree using the *F* and *T* is given in Figure 4.

The initial population is obtained with the randomly creation of members by the use of available function genes from the set *F* and the available terminal genes from the set *T*. Each member of generation represents a random point in the searching space.

The creation of the initial population is a blind random search for solutions in the huge space of possible solutions. The next step is the calculation of adaptation of individuals to the environment (i.e., calculation of fitness for each member of generation). Fitness is a guideline for modifying the structures undergoing adaptation. In GP, the computer programs change, in particular, with two genetic operations: reproduction and crossover. The reproduction operation gives a higher probability of selection to more successful organisms.

In each generation the best chromosome is copied unchanged into the next generation. The crossover operation ensures the exchange of genetic material between the offsprings. Figure 5 shows the crossover operation of two parents' chromosomes consisting of several function and terminal genes and mutation operation.

Each cycle includes: (I) creation of initial population, (II) calculation of fitness for each individual of the population, and (III) genetic modification of contents of

Figure 4. An example tree representation of a member corresponding with the equation (2-x)*(y+5)

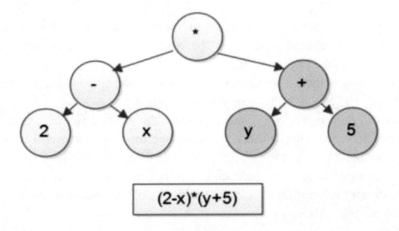

Figure 5. GP method mathematical operations (Zadshakoyan & Pourmostaghimi, 2013)

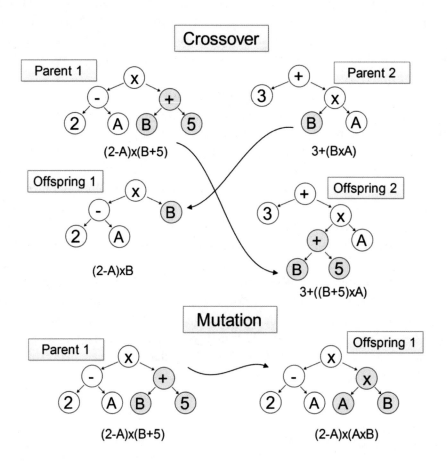

the computer programs, an iterative repetition of second and third stages follows. After a certain number of generations, the newly born offsprings are usually much better adapted to the environment.

The meaning of the environment depends on the problem dealt with. The evolution is terminated when a termination criterion is fulfilled.

This can be a prescribed number of generations or sufficient quality of the solution. Since evolution is a non-deterministic process, it does not end with a successful solution in each run. In order to obtain a successful solution, the problem must be processed in several independent runs. The number of runs required for the satisfactory solution depends on the difficulty of the problem (Zadshakoyan & Pourmostaghimi, 2013).

In this chapter, for determination of the relationship between crater wear parameters and chip radius a genetic equation with genetic programming has been developed. The genetic equations for the wear characteristics were developed as follows:

$$KT = F_1(R) \tag{1}$$

$$KB = F_2(R) \tag{2}$$

In which *KT* is crater wear depth, *KB* is crater wear length and F1 and F2 are functions which relates chip radius, *R*, to *KT* and *KB* respectively. The evolutionary parameters for the determination of the genetic equation are population size (number of chromosomes) Ms=40 and number of generations G=3000. The number of chromosomes is selected 30, that is, a very small population, as it produces very good results for virtually all problems, even for such high dimensional problems as DNA microarrays with more than 25000 variables. The genetic operations, crossover and mutation are used. The mutation rate is P_m=0.044 and crossover rate was P_c=0.1. Moreover, arithmetic operations, according to the nature of wear mechanism and wear rate, set as follows:

$$F = \{+, -, \times, Ln, exp\} \tag{3}$$

BACKGROUND

Today's scientific approaches in the area of tool wear monitoring usually measure several process parameters which are indirectly correlated with tool wear (such as force or vibration signals). These signals are measured on-line, i.e. during a cutting process. The process itself is influenced by many cutting conditions such as tool geometry or work material. A detailed description of metal-cutting manufacturing processes can be found in(Milton & Shaw, 1984), for instance. Very often, artificial neural networks (ANN), fuzzy systems, or combinations of both are used to model the non-linear dependencies between features extracted from the measured signals and cutting conditions on the one hand and tool wear or tool fracture on the other hand. A lot of promising research has been performed within the last years. However, particularly due to insufficient generalization capabilities (e.g. the use is restricted to a specific machine tool, only a small range of cutting conditions is allowed, or time-consuming 'teach-in' cycles are needed) or simply a lack of precision even promising methods are not marketable up to now. These shortages purse researchers to examine other modeling and analytical methods.

Tool wear estimation can be discussed in two categories:

1. On-line or sensor-based monitoring system which is aimed to measure the wear during the machining process.
2. Off-line or sensorless monitoring process which presents a predictive modeling of tool wear (Sick, 2002).

First category which consists of on-line tool wear monitoring methods can be classified into two categories: direct and indirect methods. Direct methods are based upon direct measurements of the tool wear using optical (Jianfeng, Yongqing, Fangrong, Zhiren, & Yao), radioactive, electrical resistance methods or vision systems (Sortino, 2003) (Lanzetta, 2001), etc. These methods present the advantage of high accuracy but they have not yet proven to be very attractive either economically or technically. Indirect methods are based on the relationship between tool conditions and measurable signals from the cutting process. Different measurable signals have been used, including force (Ghosh et al., 2007), vibration (Abu-Mahfouz, 2003), acoustic emission (Lu & Kannatey-Asibu, 2004), cutting temperature (D'Errico, 1998), etc. for detecting tool wear. However, very few reliable indirect methods have been established for industrial applications. This is mainly because the monitoring signals can be considered stochastic and non-stationary in nature rather than deterministic, and because of the non-linear relationship between the measured features and tool wear.

A number of approaches have been evolved for efficient TCM, some of which are being employed successfully in the industry. The sensor-based systems have been found to be more advantageous and are preferred for collecting information about the condition of the tool during machining. The information or signals from the sensors are processed by different methods and significant parameters are identified to determine the state of tool wear. Based on these parameters, efficient decision-making strategies are designed. A number of policies and methods of TCM are in practice, but most of those methods are capable of detecting tool wear and failure related to certain specific types of faults only. A universal approach to differentiate amongst the variety of failure modes is yet to be developed (Dan & Mathew, 1990). Direct methods can be described as follows:

1. Use of sensors to collect information about the state of tool wear: Either single or multiple sensors are used to sense signals related to the tool wear states during machining. Multiple sensors seem to be more advantageous as a part of subsequent sensor fusion strategy. Sensor fusion is the process of combining

sensory data obtained from several sources into a single element of information or knowledge (Tanner & Loh, 1992).

2. Extraction of significant features from the sensory information: Sometimes it is essential to analyze the information collected through the sensors and extract some relevant features significantly related to the states of tool wear. This information is either a direct indication of the state of failure or they are further processed as a part of subsequent decision-making strategy.

3. Development of a decision-making strategy for controlling the machining process and to indicate the requirement of a tool change state: Neural networks enjoy a very popular status as a part of decision-making strategy, on account of their efficient classification and optimization capabilities. Developments in computer technology have made faster computation possible and economically viable for common users. Moreover, the inherent nature of fault tolerance, noise suppression and the limitations of other methods have made neural networks a very popular choice in TCM (Dutta, Paul, & Chattopadhyay, 2000).

Second category which is sensorless and is based on predictive models can be divided in two classes: Empirical modeling and intelligent modeling. Taylor's tool-life equation, for example, belongs to the first class(see, e.g. (Ghani, Rizal, Nuawi, Ghazali, & Haron, 2011)). Other mathematical models such as regression can be grouped in this class. Other class uses intelligent modeling techniques such as genetic programming, artificial neural networks, and other modeling methods. Examples for sensorless monitoring techniques are lifetime prediction by means of multilayer perceptrons (Chao & Hwang, 1997), prediction of flank wear width and crater wear depth with multilayer perceptrons (Prasad & Ramamoorthy, 2001), and lifetime prediction by means of multilayer perceptrons and optimization of cutting conditions (Li & Nee, 1996), tool wear modeling in drilling by genetic programming (Zakeri & Pourmostaghimi, 2017), and other intelligent methods. However the majority of these methods are designed to evaluate the flank wear, VB, and progress in modeling the crater wear has slightly been done (Sick, 2002).

There has been some research on tool wear estimation over the past several years, and some analytical (Dawson & Kurfess, 2005) and empirical models were proposed for the evaluation of crater depth and length, however most of them lack practical applications.

Several direct and indirect measurement techniques have been proposed for evaluating crater wear in carbide inserts. Direct methods are based upon direct measurements of the worn area of the tool using optical (Dawson & Kurfess, 2005) and vision systems (Jurkovic, Korosec, & Kopac, 2005). These methods have advantage of high-measuring accuracy, but cannot be easily adopted for online applications, mainly because of interruption of coolant and chips (Lister & Barrow, 1986). For this reasons, several authors have proposed indirect techniques for wear monitoring.

In spite of the fact that numerous researches have been done in the field of chip radius and tool wear, there is a few works which has considered the effect of tool wear on the produced chip radius. Fang and Jawahir (Fang & Jawahir, 1993) investigated the effects of progressive tool wear on chip breakability and chip form in turning operations. The experimental results from this research showed that developing crater wear on the tool rake face acts as a chip breaking groove and so by passing time and expanding crater, chip radius will reduce.

K.C.Ea et al. investigated tool wear mechanisms and their effects on chip curl/ chip form in machining with grooved tools using equivalent tool face (ET) model. In mentioned work, a new methodology is extended to correlate chip curling when machining with progressive tool wear mechanism in grooved tools (Ee, Balaji, & Jawahir, 2003).

For the present time, due to the shortage of studies in this field and being difficult to establish an ideal analytical model, using intelligent or metaheuristic methods such as genetic programming is inevitable.

In computer science and mathematical optimization, a metaheuristic is a higher-level procedure or heuristic designed to find, generate, or select a heuristic (partial search algorithm) that may provide a sufficiently good solution to an optimization problem, especially with incomplete or imperfect information or limited computation capacity. Metaheuristics sample a set of solutions which is too large to be completely sampled. Metaheuristics may make few assumptions about the optimization problem being solved, and so they may be usable for a variety of problems (Osman & Kelly, 1996).

Metaheuristics have been used in wide area of research such as supervised machine learning (Abinash & Santanu Kumar, 2017), Forecasting Exchange Rates (Ahmed, Mahmoud, Mohammed, & Aboul Ella, 2015), Architecture (Alexiei, Daniel, & Ruben, 2012), genetic engineering (Banu & Andrews, 2015), elderly people care (Claas, Daniel, Michael, & Gerrit, 2011), medical purposes (Ashour et al., 2015), health science (Nilanjan Dey, Samanta, Yang, Das, & Chaudhuri, 2013), optimization algorithms (Gerald, 2016), recognizing human behavior (Hans & Stephen, 2016), Wi-Fi systems (Heba & Moustafa, 2014), manufacturing (Z. Mohammad & Vahid, 2015), energy and wind turbines (H. Mohammad & Mohammad Hassan, 2016), image processing (Samantaa, Dey, Das, Acharjee, & Chaudhuri, 2013), intelligent language recognition (Hore et al., 2017),complex mathematical problems (Hicham El, Said, & Jamal, 2015), learning techniques (Jennifer, Tom, & Paul Mc, 2011), data clustering (Kanungo, Janmenjoy, Bighnaraj, & Behera, 2016), wireless sensor networks (Binh, Hanh, & Dey), bio engineering technologies for example electrocardiography (Nilanjan Dey et al., 2013), retinal imaging (Nilanjan Dey et al., 2014), medical signals processing (N Dey, Chakraborty, & Samanta, 2014), MRI de-noising (Nilanjan Dey et al., 2015), brain disease detection (Ashour et al., 2015), civil engineering (Rahul, Senthilnath, Omkar, & Narendra, 2016), tracking systems (Sean & Kevin, 2014), prediction of stock price (Vipul & Kulkarni, 2017), educational methods (Vladimír, Petr, Peter, Karel, & Petr, 2016), and big data analytics (Zakaria, Souham, & Mohamed, 2017).

Belonging to the family of evolutionary computation and metaheuristic methods, GP imitates biological evolution of living organisms in nature. This relatively new automatic programming technique was first described by Koza in his methods which combined efficiently the concepts of evolutionary computation and automatic programming (Koza, 1992). In engineering, especially manufacturing engineering, GP is frequently applied to model various processes and conditions. Some applications of GP have been reported in prediction of surface roughness (Brezocnik, Kovacic, & Ficko, 2004), nonlinear system modeling (Metenidis, Witczak, & Korbicz, 2004), investigation of the cutting force (Milfelner, Kopac, Cus, & Zuperl, 2005), tool-chip contact length modeling (Zadshakoyan & Pourmostaghimi, 2013), and machine scheduling problems (Dimopoulos & Zalzala, 2001).

MAIN FOCUS OF THE CHAPTER

The manufacturing community is always striving to reduce operating costs while trying to improve product quality and meeting or exceeding customer satisfaction. These goals are behind the drive towards automation and the use of high production unmanned equipment. The metal cutting process is highly nonlinear involving such phenomena as plastic deformation, fracture, impact, continuous and intermittent multi contact points, friction, and wear. Direct visual inspection of the cutting edge during machining is not feasible because the work piece and chips obstruct the view. To overcome this difficulty indirect methods are required. On the other hand, using sensory systems is expensive and has some limitations. Therefore, finding a reliable model which can predict the wear and determine the relation between cutting parameters and tool wear is extremely needed.

In this chapter, a precise and quicker method for the estimation of tool life is proposed, which requires less consumption of work piece material and tools. In this method the tool life is estimated by using genetic programming and finding the time till tool failure by extrapolation. Genetic programming is used to predict tool crater wear. Tool wear estimation involves a number of tests to be carried out at various cutting conditions till the failure of the cutting tool. The wear after each cutting pass is noted and the time for a limiting crater wear is estimated by extrapolating the wear-time curve.

Experimental Work

All the experimental tests were performed on a CNC lathe machine and under dry conditions. To decrease the variation of cutting speed across the cutting edge, a large diameter work piece were used. In order to establish the genetic equation, different values of cutting speed, V, and cutting time, t, were selected while feed rate and depth of cut were selected constant values of 0.07 mm/rev and 1.5 mm respectively. The values of cutting speed selected were 65 (m/min), 75 (m/min) and 85 (m/min) and cutting times were 1 (min), 3 (min), 5 (min) and 7 (min). In addition to 12 mentioned experiments which were performed to train the genetic equation, 5 extra experiments were done to test the equation quantitatively which are according to conditions shown in Table 1.

Commercially available uncoated cemented carbide insert (Tizit, TNMA 220408, grade P20) were used in these tests. AISI 4104 with hardness about 187 BHN were selected as a work piece material because of its widespread application and acceptable machinability. For the measurement of the wear parameters, cutting inserts were examined carefully using an optical microscope equipped with image processing software.

The radii of obtained chips were measured by vernier caliper, however, profile projector were used to measure accurately chips with bigger radius.

The accuracy of developed equations was analyzed in terms of two statistical measures. These measures are the root mean square error, *RMSE*, and absolute friction of variance, R^2, which are defined as below:

$$RMSE = \sqrt{\sum_{m=1}^{n} \frac{\left(Y_{predicted,m} - Y_{experimental.m}\right)^2}{n}} \tag{4}$$

$$R^2 = 1 - \frac{\sum_{m=1}^{n}\left(Y_{predicted,m} - Y_{experimental.m}\right)^2}{\sum_{m=1}^{n}\left(Y_{experimental.m}\right)^2} \tag{5}$$

Table 1. Cutting parameters for testing step of GP

	Test 1	Test 2	Test 3	Test 4	Test 5
V(m/min)	80	60	50	60	70
t (min)	3	2	4	4	3

Where *n* is the number of data points, *Ypredicted,m* and *Yexperimental,m* respectively indicate the predicted value and the target value from experimental data of one data point m. *RMSE* indicates the deviation between the experimental and predicted values. A very good fit yields R^2 value of 1, where as a poor fit results in a value near zero.

RESULTS AND DISCUSSION

In this chapter to modeling the condition of crater wear in turning by using chip radius, the evolutionary algorithm of GP has been used. 12 practical experiments have been performed to train and modeling of the equation and 5 other experiments to qualify established model. The experimental results corresponding with cutting conditions have been shown in Figure 6.

Figure 7 illustrates produced chips in the cutting speed of 75 (m/min) in various times. In Figures 8 and 9 tool wear measurement results for cutting conditions have been presented. As it can be seen, by passing time and increasing cutting speed, crater depth *KT* and crater length *KB* will increase. The value of crater depth *KT* increases more rapidly than the other. This rapid increase will lead to an increase in the chip

Figure 6. Chip radii obtained from experiments
t=1(min) t=3(min) t=5(min) t=7(min)

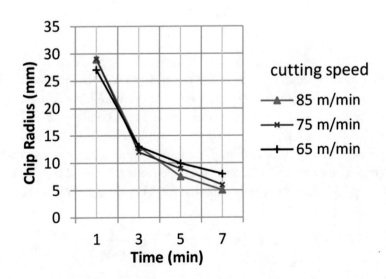

Figure 7. Produced chips in cutting speed of 75 (m/min)

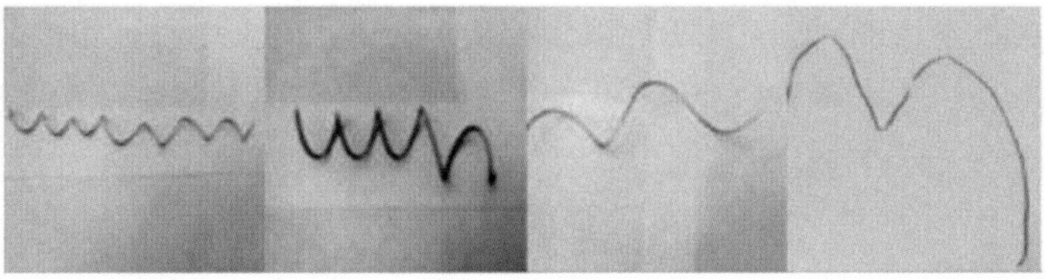

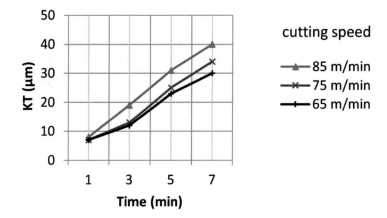

t=1(min)   t=3(min)   t=5(min)   t=7(min)

Figure 8. Experimental data For KT (training data set)

curvature. In other hand, the deeper the crater depth *KT*, the smaller the chip curl radius. Generally, the crater length *KB* and crater width *KK* are formed quickly on the tool rake face within the first few minutes and then continue to develop slowly. The results for performed tests have been shown in table 2.

To perform genetic programming, various arithmetic operations can be used. In this chapter, arithmetic-functional set is as equation 3. Based on values obtained for *RMSE* and R^2, the best genetic equation for *KT* and *KB* are obtained as follows:

$$KT = 77.77 - 3.17R - 28Ln(R) + \exp(0.06R) + \frac{816}{\exp(R)} - \frac{20952}{\exp(2R)} \qquad (6)$$

Figure 9. Experimental data For KB (training data set)

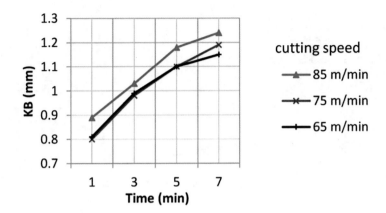

Table 2. Experimental data and conditions for testing data set

	Test 1	Test 2	Test 3	Test 4	Test 5
V (m/min)	80	60	50	60	70
t (min)	3	2	4	4	3
R (mm)	12.96	17.27	12.33	11.76	12.64
KT (μm)	15	10	15	18	17
KB (mm)	1	0.89	0.99	1.03	0.98

$$KB = 1.008 - 0.009R + \frac{1.63}{R + 0.75} + \frac{\exp(R)}{\exp(32)} + 2\exp(R) \tag{7}$$

In which *R* is chip radius, *KT* is crater wear depth and *KB* is crater wear length. In Figures 10 and 11 the plot corresponding with obtained genetic equations is represented. As shown, any decrease in chip radius corresponds with increase in both *KT* and *KB* values. Therefore, it can be concluded that the developed genetic equations indicate wear manner during turning process of AISI 4140 accurately.

Table 3 shows the values of *RMSE* and R^2 for selected genetic equations. According to this table, it can be concluded that the genetic equation presented for *KT* and *KB* corresponds well with experimental data in given range of cutting parameters, so it has unique ability in prediction of the chip radius with progressive tool crater wear.

Figure 10. Variation of KT versus chip radius, R, according to Equation 6

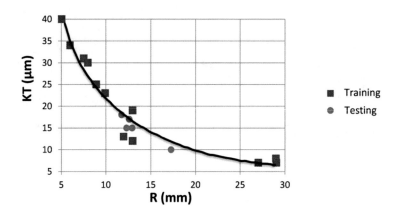

Figure 11. Variation of KB versus chip radius, R, according to Equation 7

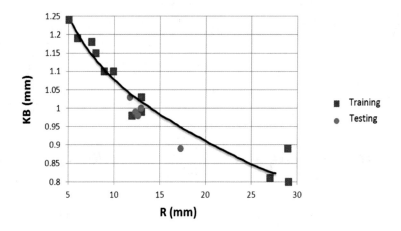

Table 3. RMSE and R^2 for selected genetic models

KT(μm)				KB(mm)			
train		test		train		test	
R^2	RMSE	R^2	RMSE	R^2	RMSE	R^2	RMSE
0.95	2.56	0.98	2.11	0.96	0.029	0.95	0.036

FUTURE RESEARCH DIRECTIONS

Although a lot of work has been done in this field, there is still a great demand in presenting reliably applicable models in machining industry which could predict the effect of various parameters on tool wear. As an outline of future work these guidelines can be noted:

- Comparing the accuracy and reliability of various intelligent and metaheuristic methods.
- Extending the models with more materials and tools.
- Modeling of tool wear in other machining practices such as milling and drilling.
- Finding a relationship between various types of wear in machining processes.
- Finding optimized cutting parameters by using various metaheuristic methods.
- Integration of the proposed approach with an intelligent manufacturing system

CONCLUSION

In this chapter, the interaction between the two major machining performance measures, chip form and tool wear, have been studied. The work investigates the variation of chip radius at different stages of progressive tool wear giving experimental evidence for the inter-relationships of these two major machining performance factors. The reduction of chip radius with tool wear progression shows a consistent pattern for the flat faced tool under all cutting conditions used in this experiment.

This chapter also presents the development of the genetic equation in machining process. The results obtained from the proposed genetic programming approach prove its effectiveness. The implication of the encouraging results obtained from the present approach is that such approach can be integrated on-line, with an intelligent manufacturing system for automated process planning. Since the genetic programming based approach can obtain near optimal solution, it can be used for machining parameter selection of complex machined parts that require many machining constraints. Integration of the proposed approach with an intelligent manufacturing system will lead to reduction in production cost and production time and improvement of product quality.

REFERENCES

Abinash, T., & Santanu Kumar, R. (2017). Classification of Sentiment of Reviews using Supervised Machine Learning Techniques. *International Journal of Rough Sets and Data Analysis*, *4*(1), 56–74. doi:10.4018/IJRSDA.2017010104

Abu-Mahfouz, I. (2003). Drilling wear detection and classification using vibration signals and artificial neural network. *International Journal of Machine Tools & Manufacture*, *43*(7), 707–720. doi:10.1016/S0890-6955(03)00023-3

Ahmed, R., Mahmoud, K., Mohammed, Y. D., & Aboul Ella, H. (2015). Forecasting Exchange Rates: A Chaos-Based Regression Approach. *International Journal of Rough Sets and Data Analysis*, *2*(1), 38–57. doi:10.4018/ijrsda.2015010103

Alexiei, D., Daniel, A., & Ruben, M. (2012). Turning Homes into Low-Cost Ambient Assisted Living Environments. *International Journal of Ambient Computing and Intelligence*, *4*(2), 1–23. doi:10.4018/jaci.2012040101

Ashour, A. S., Samanta, S., Dey, N., Kausar, N., Abdessalemkaraa, W. B., & Hassanien, A. E. (2015). Computed tomography image enhancement using cuckoo search: A log transform based approach. *Journal of Signal and Information Processing*, *6*(03), 244–257. doi:10.4236/jsip.2015.63023

Banu, P. K. N., & Andrews, S. (2015). Gene Clustering Using Metaheuristic Optimization Algorithms. *International Journal of Applied Metaheuristic Computing*, *6*(4), 14–38. doi:10.4018/IJAMC.2015100102

Binh, H. T. T., Hanh, N. T., & Dey, N. (n.d.). Improved Cuckoo Search and Chaotic Flower Pollination optimization algorithm for maximizing area coverage in Wireless Sensor Networks. *Neural Computing and Applications*, 1-13.

Brezocnik, M., Kovacic, M., & Ficko, M. (2004). Prediction of surface roughness with genetic programming. *Journal of Materials Processing Technology*, *157*, 28–36. doi:10.1016/j.jmatprotec.2004.09.004

Chao, P. Y., & Hwang, Y. D. (1997). An improved neural network model for the prediction of cutting tool life. *Journal of Intelligent Manufacturing*, *8*(2), 107–115. doi:10.1023/A:1018552620196

Claas, A., Daniel, K., Michael, L., & Gerrit, K. (2011). IT-ASSIST: Towards Usable Applications for Elderly People. *International Journal of Ambient Computing and Intelligence*, *3*(1), 33–41. doi:10.4018/jaci.2011010104

Dan, L., & Mathew, J. (1990). Tool wear and failure monitoring techniques for turning—a review. *International Journal of Machine Tools & Manufacture*, *30*(4), 579–598. doi:10.1016/0890-6955(90)90009-8

Dawson, T. G., & Kurfess, T. R. (2005). Quantification of tool wear using white light interferometry and three-dimensional computational metrology. *International Journal of Machine Tools & Manufacture*, *45*(4), 591–596. doi:10.1016/j.ijmachtools.2004.08.022

Derrico, G. (1998). An adaptive system for turning process control based on tool temperature feedback. *Journal of Materials Processing Technology*, *78*(1), 43–47. doi:10.1016/S0924-0136(97)00461-5

Devillez, A., Lesko, S., & Mozer, W. (2004). Cutting tool crater wear measurement with white light interferometry. *Wear*, *256*(1), 56–65. doi:10.1016/S0043-1648(03)00384-3

Dey, N., Ashour, A. S., Beagum, S., Pistola, D. S., Gospodinov, M., Gospodinova, E. P., & Tavares, J. M. R. (2015). Parameter optimization for local polynomial approximation based intersection confidence interval filter using genetic algorithm: An application for brain MRI image de-noising. *Journal of Imaging*, *1*(1), 60–84. doi:10.3390/jimaging1010060

Dey, N., Chakraborty, S., & Samanta, S. (2014). Optimization of watermarking in biomedical signal. *Heinrich-Böcking-Straße*, *6*, 66121.

Dey, N., Samanta, S., Chakraborty, S., Das, A., Chaudhuri, S. S., & Suri, J. S. (2014). Firefly algorithm for optimization of scaling factors during embedding of manifold medical information: An application in ophthalmology imaging. *Journal of Medical Imaging and Health Informatics*, *4*(3), 384–394. doi:10.1166/jmihi.2014.1265

Dey, N., Samanta, S., Yang, X.-S., Das, A., & Chaudhuri, S. S. (2013). Optimisation of scaling factors in electrocardiogram signal watermarking using cuckoo search. *International Journal of Bio-inspired Computation*, *5*(5), 315–326. doi:10.1504/IJBIC.2013.057193

Dimopoulos, C., & Zalzala, A. M. (2001). Investigating the use of genetic programming for a classic one-machine scheduling problem. *Advances in Engineering Software*, *32*(6), 489–498. doi:10.1016/S0965-9978(00)00109-5

Dutta, R., Paul, S., & Chattopadhyay, A. (2000). Applicability of the modified back-propagation algorithm in tool condition monitoring for faster convergence. *Journal of Materials Processing Technology*, *98*(3), 299–309. doi:10.1016/S0924-0136(99)00295-2

Ee, K., Balaji, A., & Jawahir, I. (2003). Progressive tool-wear mechanisms and their effects on chip-curl/chip-form in machining with grooved tools: An extended application of the equivalent toolface (ET) model. *Wear*, *255*(7), 1404–1413. doi:10.1016/S0043-1648(03)00112-1

Fang, X., & Jawahir, I. (1993). The effects of progressive tool wear and tool restricted contact on chip breakability in machining. *Wear*, *160*(2), 243–252. doi:10.1016/0043-1648(93)90427-N

Gerald, S. (2016). Gene Expression Analysis based on Ant Colony Optimisation Classification. *International Journal of Rough Sets and Data Analysis*, *3*(3), 51–59. doi:10.4018/IJRSDA.2016070104

Ghani, J. A., Rizal, M., Nuawi, M. Z., Ghazali, M. J., & Haron, C. H. C. (2011). Monitoring online cutting tool wear using low-cost technique and user-friendly GUI. *Wear*, *271*(9), 2619–2624. doi:10.1016/j.wear.2011.01.038

Ghosh, N., Ravi, Y., Patra, A., Mukhopadhyay, S., Paul, S., Mohanty, A., & Chattopadhyay, A. (2007). Estimation of tool wear during CNC milling using neural network-based sensor fusion. *Mechanical Systems and Signal Processing*, *21*(1), 466–479. doi:10.1016/j.ymssp.2005.10.010

Golz, H., Schillo, E., Wolf, A., & Kaufeld, M. (1995). Bewertung von Werkzeugüberwachungssystemen aus Sicht der Anwender. *VDI-Berichte*, *1179*, 309–309.

Hans, W. G., & Stephen, M. (2016). Using Contextual Information for Recognising Human Behaviour. *International Journal of Ambient Computing and Intelligence*, *7*(1), 27–44. doi:10.4018/IJACI.2016010102

Heba, A., & Moustafa, Y. (2014). An Analysis of Device-Free and Device-Based WiFi-Localization Systems. *International Journal of Ambient Computing and Intelligence*, *6*(1), 1–19. doi:10.4018/ijaci.2014010101

Hicham El, H., Said, B., & Jamal, B. (2015). New Genetic Operator (Jump Crossover) for the Traveling Salesman Problem. *International Journal of Applied Metaheuristic Computing*, *6*(2), 33–44. doi:10.4018/IJAMC.2015040103

Hore, S., Chatterjee, S., Santhi, V., Dey, N., Ashour, A. S., Balas, V. E., & Shi, F. (2017). *Indian Sign Language Recognition Using Optimized Neural Networks. In Information Technology and Intelligent Transportation Systems* (pp. 553–563). Springer. doi:10.1007/978-3-319-38771-0_54

Jennifer, H., Tom, L., & Paul Mc, K. (2011). AmbiLearn: Multimodal Assisted Learning. *International Journal of Ambient Computing and Intelligence*, *3*(1), 53–59. doi:10.4018/jaci.2011010106

Jianfeng, L., Yongqing, Z., Fangrong, C., Zhiren, T., & Yao, W. (n.d.). *Wear and Breakage Monitoring of Cutting Tools By Optic Method (1st Part: Theory).* Academic Press.

Jurkovic, J., Korosec, M., & Kopac, J. (2005). New approach in tool wear measuring technique using CCD vision system. *International Journal of Machine Tools & Manufacture*, *45*(9), 1023–1030. doi:10.1016/j.ijmachtools.2004.11.030

Kanungo, D. P., Janmenjoy, N., Bighnaraj, N., & Behera, H. S. (2016). Hybrid Clustering using Elitist Teaching Learning-Based Optimization: An Improved Hybrid Approach of TLBO. *International Journal of Rough Sets and Data Analysis*, *3*(1), 1–19. doi:10.4018/IJRSDA.2016010101

Koza, J. R. (1992). *Genetic programming: on the programming of computers by means of natural selection* (Vol. 1). MIT Press.

Lanzetta, M. (2001). A new flexible high-resolution vision sensor for tool condition monitoring. *Journal of Materials Processing Technology*, *119*(1), 73–82. doi:10.1016/S0924-0136(01)00878-0

Li, X., & Nee, A. (1996). Monitoring cutting conditions for tool scheduling in CNC machining. *Manuf Syst*, *25*(4), 377–383.

Lister, P., & Barrow, G. (1986). *Tool condition monitoring systems.* Paper presented at the Proceedings of the Twenty-sixth International Machine Tool Design and Research Conference. doi:10.1007/978-1-349-08114-1_36

Lu, M.-C., & Kannatey-Asibu, E. (2004). Flank wear and process characteristic effect on system dynamics in turning. *Transactions-American Society of Mechanical Engineers Journal of Manufacturing Science and Engineering*, *126*(1), 131–140. doi:10.1115/1.1643082

Metenidis, M. F., Witczak, M., & Korbicz, J. (2004). A novel genetic programming approach to nonlinear system modelling: Application to the DAMADICS benchmark problem. *Engineering Applications of Artificial Intelligence*, *17*(4), 363–370. doi:10.1016/j.engappai.2004.04.009

Milfelner, M., Kopac, J., Cus, F., & Zuperl, U. (2005). Genetic equation for the cutting force in ball-end milling. *Journal of Materials Processing Technology*, *164*, 1554–1560. doi:10.1016/j.jmatprotec.2005.02.147

Milton, C., & Shaw, M. (1984). *Metal cutting principles.* Oxford Science Publication.

Mohammad, H., & Mohammad Hassan, A. (2016). Optimization of Small Wind Turbines using Genetic Algorithms. *International Journal of Applied Metaheuristic Computing, 7*(4), 50–65. doi:10.4018/IJAMC.2016100104

Mohammad, Z., & Vahid, P. (2015). Cutting Tool Crater Wear Measurement in Turning Using Chip Geometry and Genetic Programming. *International Journal of Applied Metaheuristic Computing, 6*(1), 47–60. doi:10.4018/ijamc.2015010104

Osman, I. H., & Kelly, J. P. (1996). *Meta-heuristics: an overview. In Meta-heuristics* (pp. 1–21). Springer. doi:10.1007/978-1-4613-1361-8

Prasad, K. N., & Ramamoorthy, B. (2001). Tool wear evaluation by stereo vision and prediction by artificial neural network. *Journal of Materials Processing Technology, 112*(1), 43–52. doi:10.1016/S0924-0136(00)00896-7

Rahul, K., Senthilnath, J., Omkar, S. N., & Narendra, S. (2016). A Novel Multiobjective Optimization for Cement Stabilized Soft Soil based on Artificial Bee Colony. *International Journal of Applied Metaheuristic Computing, 7*(4), 1–17. doi:10.4018/IJAMC.2016100101

Samantaa, S., Dey, N., Das, P., Acharjee, S., & Chaudhuri, S. S. (2013). *Multilevel threshold based gray scale image segmentation using cuckoo search.* arXiv preprint arXiv:1307.0277

Sean, C., & Kevin, C. (2014). An Active Low Cost Mesh Networking Indoor Tracking System. *International Journal of Ambient Computing and Intelligence, 6*(1), 45–79. doi:10.4018/ijaci.2014010104

Sick, B. (2002). On-line and indirect tool wear monitoring in turning with artificial neural networks: A review of more than a decade of research. *Mechanical Systems and Signal Processing, 16*(4), 487–546. doi:10.1006/mssp.2001.1460

Sortino, M. (2003). Application of statistical filtering for optical detection of tool wear. *International Journal of Machine Tools & Manufacture, 43*(5), 493–497. doi:10.1016/S0890-6955(02)00266-3

Tanner, R., & Loh, N. K. (1992). A toxonomy of multi-sensor fusion. *Journal of Manufacturing Systems, 11*(5), 314–325. doi:10.1016/0278-6125(92)90060-S

Vipul, B., & Kulkarni, U. V. (2017). Stock Price Trend Prediction and Recommendation using Cognitive Process. *International Journal of Rough Sets and Data Analysis, 4*(2), 36–48. doi:10.4018/IJRSDA.2017040103

Vladimír, B., Petr, T., Peter, M., Karel, M., & Petr, B. (2016). Application of Ambient Intelligence in Educational Institutions: Visions and Architectures. *International Journal of Ambient Computing and Intelligence*, 7(1), 94–120. doi:10.4018/IJACI.2016010105

Zadshakoyan, M., & Pourmostaghimi, V. (2013). Genetic equation for the prediction of tool–chip contact length in orthogonal cutting. *Engineering Applications of Artificial Intelligence*, 26(7), 1725–1730. doi:10.1016/j.engappai.2012.10.016

Zakaria, B., Souham, M., & Mohamed, B. (2017). Scalable Differential Evolutionary Clustering Algorithm for Big Data Using Map-Reduce Paradigm. *International Journal of Applied Metaheuristic Computing*, 8(1), 45–60. doi:10.4018/IJAMC.2017010103

KEY TERMS AND DEFINITIONS

Crater Wear: Crater wear in which contact with chips erodes the rake face. This is somewhat normal for tool wear, and does not seriously degrade the use of a tool until it becomes serious enough to cause a cutting-edge failure.

Genetic Programming: In artificial intelligence, genetic programming (GP) is a technique whereby computer programs are encoded as a set of genes that are then modified (evolved) using an evolutionary algorithm (often a genetic algorithm, "GA") – it is an application of (for example) genetic algorithms where the space of solutions consists of computer programs.

Machining: Machining is the broad term used to describe removal of material from a work piece, it covers several processes, which we usually divide into the following categories: Cutting, generally involving single-point or multipoint cutting tools, each with a clearly defined geometry.

Metaheuristics: Metaheuristics is a higher-level procedure or heuristic designed to find, generate, or select a heuristic (partial search algorithm) that may provide a sufficiently good solution to an optimization problem, especially with incomplete or imperfect information or limited computation capacity.

Predictive Modeling: Is a process that uses data mining and probability to forecast outcomes. Each model is made up of a number of predictors, which are variables that are likely to influence future results. Once data has been collected for relevant predictors, a statistical model is formulated.

Tool Wear: Tool wear describes the gradual failure of cutting tools due to regular operation. It is a term often associated with tipped tools, tool bits, or drill bits that are used with machine tools.

Turning: Turning is a machining process in which a cutting tool, typically a non-rotary tool bit, describes a helix tool-path by moving more or less linearly while the work piece rotates.

Chapter 6
Intelligent Computing in Medical Imaging:
A Study

Shouvik Chakraborty
University of Kalyani, India

Sankhadeep Chatterjee
University of Calcutta, India

Amira S. Ashour
Tanta University, Egypt

Kalyani Mali
University of Kalyani, India

Nilanjan Dey
Techno India College of Technology, India

ABSTRACT

Biomedical imaging is considered main procedure to acquire valuable physical information about the human body and some other biological species. It produces specialized images of different parts of the biological species for clinical analysis. It assimilates various specialized domains including nuclear medicine, radiological imaging, Positron emission tomography (PET), and microscopy. From the early discovery of X-rays, progress in biomedical imaging continued resulting in highly sophisticated medical imaging modalities, such as magnetic resonance imaging (MRI), ultrasound, Computed Tomography (CT), and lungs monitoring. These biomedical imaging techniques assist physicians for faster and accurate analysis and treatment. The present chapter discussed the impact of intelligent computing methods for biomedical image analysis and healthcare. Different Artificial Intelligence (AI)

DOI: 10.4018/978-1-5225-4151-6.ch006

based automated biomedical image analysis are considered. Different approaches are discussed including the AI ability to resolve various medical imaging problems. It also introduced the popular AI procedures that employed to solve some special problems in medicine. Artificial Neural Network (ANN) and support vector machine (SVM) are active to classify different types of images from various imaging modalities. Different diagnostic analysis, such as mammogram analysis, MRI brain image analysis, CT images, PET images, and bone/retinal analysis using ANN, feed-forward back propagation ANN, probabilistic ANN, and extreme learning machine continuously. Various optimization techniques of ant colony optimization (ACO), genetic algorithm (GA), particle swarm optimization (PSO) and other bio-inspired procedures are also frequently conducted for feature extraction/selection and classification. The advantages and disadvantages of some AI approaches are discussed in the present chapter along with some suggested future research perspectives.

INTRODUCTION

Medical image analysis has a major role in detecting and diagnosis of different diseases. Recently, researchers are interested with biomedical image analysis (Doi, 2007). Mainly, techniques based on machine learning including artificial neural networks (ANNs), and bio-inspired algorithms have drawn the attention of several researchers. Computer aided diagnosis (CAD) is considered a promptly developing active areas with the help of modern computer based methods, and new medical imaging modalities. Decision-support tools and intelligent analysis frameworks are significant in biomedical imaging for CAD, detection and evaluation where accuracy is one of the major issues. CAD helps physicians by the results obtained from a computerized system for detecting and diagnosing different diseases, such as lesions, and tumors as well as measuring the extent and effect of specific disease. One of the foremost goals of these artificial systems is to improve the consistency and accuracy of diagnosis in such a way that the rate of false negative will be reduced. Generally, CAD systems involve initial selection of samples for training, image pre-processing for enhancement, selection of region of interests (ROI), features extraction, feature selection, classification and segmentation. The CAD system generally tries to localize and to identify the disease for diagnosis. CAD systems consist of two most important processes, namely image segmentation and image classification. During the image segmentation, pixels are grouped into some domains based on some feature of the image producing a set of distinct regions or objects that can be studied and quantified separately, representing specific ROC (Receiver Operating

Characteristics) of the actual image. In the classification stage, features are extracted and depending on those features classification of objects are performed, i.e. normal or abnormal, malignant or benign.

The prime goal of computational intelligence is to understand and to learn the principles and logics that can help a machine or artificial systems to behave intelligently. General approaches and methods applied in medical image analysis at various stages are shown in Figure 1.

For applying the preceding medical image analysis/processing stages, the ANN is considered one of the popular, effective nonlinear information processing systems that designed from interconnected basic processing modules, namely neurons. Some of the basic advantages of the ANN include fault tolerance, adaptive learning, parallelism, and self-adjustment. ANN has several applications in knowledge extraction and classification, pattern recognition, forecasting of some results depending on some current results, clinical diagnosis and analysis. In this chapter, a study is conducted on the uses of NN and other AI systems to diagnostic science.

Ideally, the main objective the biomedical imaging system is to upgrade the efficiency in monitoring the conditions of humans and other biological species efficiently for possible illness and/or diseases detection and treatment. Techniques based on AI are widely used for biomedical imaging improvement. In order to perform biomedical image analysis for useful information retrieving with a certain amount of uncertainty related to it. It is generally performed using artificial computational intelligence methods, such as fuzzy logic (FL), GA, bio-inspired algorithms, SVM, ANN and deep neural networks. Recent research deals with different tools and methods based on AI, which are effective and known for very high classification accuracy. Some related tasks, such as biological features identification and segmentation are performed more precisely by applying the AI based methods. Consequently, these techniques are precious in biomedical image analysis for accurate analysis (Rastgarpour, & Shanbehzadeh, 2013). Thus, advanced procedures and systems for automated biomedical image analysis are very helpful in increasing the consistency and precise interpretation of the biomedical images. AI approaches integrated with fuzzy logic, machine learning, and deep learning are so precious in interpretation, analysis and mining some useful information from biomedical image data. AI has been tested to obtain promising results in digital imaging. Moreover, the structural information nature for biomedical images may efficiently be approached by using tools and techniques of AI. In biomedical imaging domain; conflicting, ambiguous, uncertain, imprecise, and complementary are very common and data fusion techniques can efficiently cope up with these issues.

The following sections illustrate in detail how the ANN is employed for image classification and analysis. Typically, the ANN has a important role in the medical image analysis domain (Miller *et al.*, 1992). Thus, the major focus of the current

Figure 1. Different stages of biomedical image analysis

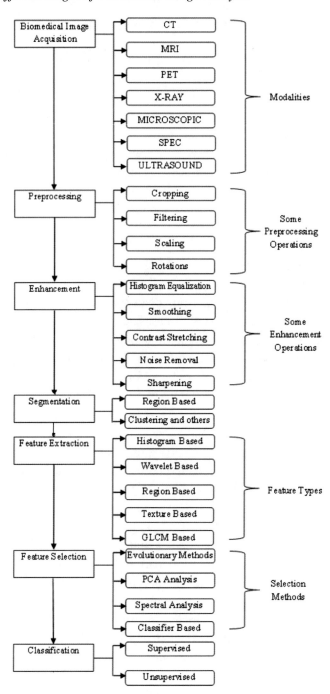

chapter is on preprocessing of the biomedical images, segmentation, and object recognition from biomedical images instead of attempting to cover the research aspects of artificial computing in biomedical image analysis.

NEURAL NETWORKS IN BIOMEDICAL IMAGING

ANNs are very popular and massively used for their high performance and accuracy in classification and approximation of functions. ANNs have been employed with success in various applications of biomedical image analysis, more specifically in the preprocessing, segmentation, recognition and classification. An overview of some types of the ANN used in this domain is reported in Table 1.

Artificial Neural Network Assisted Biomedical Image Pre-Processing

ANN assisted biomedical image pre-processing for image restoration including noise removal/quality enhancement and reconstruction. Hopfield neural network is considered as an efficient neural work for the reconstruction stage of biomedical images (Warsito, & Fan, 2001). The reconstruction process can be considered as an optimization problem using NN by allowing it to converge to a stable state through

Table 1. Some types of NN used in biomedical image processing

	Image Pre-processing	Image Segmentation	Classification/ Recognition
Feed Forward Neural Network	Yes	Yes	Yes
Fuzzy Neural Network	Yes	Yes	Yes
Probabilistic Neural Network	X	Yes	Yes
Convolution Neural Network	X	X	Yes
Radial basis function based Neural Network	X	X	Yes
Hopfield Neural Network	Yes	Yes	Yes
Self-organizing feature based Neural Network	Yes	Yes	Yes
Adaptive resonance theory based Neural Network	X	X	Yes
Artificial Neural ensemble	X	Yes	Yes
Massive training Neural Network	Yes	X	Yes
Cellular Neural Network	Yes	X	X

optimizing the energy function. Wang *et al.* (2003) conducted a comparative study of reconstructed shapes with the output generated from conventional convolution techniques and algebraic reconstruction methods. This study established the Hopfield neural networks efficiency in biomedical image reconstruction.

Acquired images reconstruction from electrical impedance tomography necessitates the removal of the nonlinear inverse on the data corrupted with noise. This requires some assumptions or generalization depending on some previous knowledge. The feed-forward ANN and the self-organizing ANN can be more advantageous for the reconstruction of such medical images compared to some other methods (Adler, & Guardo, 1994). Generally, noise is one of the major issues in biomedical images and in restoration stage, noise removal is performed. Suzuki *et al.* (2003) suggested a filter based on NN to solve this issue. An ANN has been employed in the proposed filter with multiple layers. This filter can obtain the function of different linear and nonlinear filters by proper training.

Edge detection is very popular and has popular effective solutions. For example the Laplace, Prewitt, Sobel and some other advanced operators. Suzuki *et al.* (2003) developed a neural edge enhancement approach based on an adapted NN with multiple layers. It can enhance desired edges prominently from noisy images. This method is verified to be robust and less sensitive to noise and superior compared to other conventional methods. It has the capability to enhance continuous edges from noisy images.

Neural Network Based Biomedical Image Segmentation

Feed-forward ANN based segmentation are powerful and less noisy than the conventional segmentation methods similar to the methods based on Maximum Likelihood Classifier (MLC). Feed-forward ANN is insensitive to the training set selection compared to the MLC classifier. An overview of the ANNs used in biomedical image segmentation is given in table 2.

From the preceding literature review, it can be concluded that the NN is effective for biomedical image segmentation. However, it undergoes slow convergence rate and its learning parameters should be defined in advance. These disadvantages restrict the use of feed- forward ANN in biomedical image segmentation. However, recent studies have revealed that the ANNs performance can be improved by using metaheuristics. Training ANNs essentially means to find the optimal set of weight vector for the network for which some error function is minimized. Thus, the training can be framed as an optimization problem. Traditional backpropagation based learning algorithms may lead to a set of weight vectors for the ANN, which are not optimal. This happens due to the convergence to local optima while finding the optimal weight vectors. The problem has been addressed in several literatures

Table 2. Overview of the artificial neural networks applied for biomedical image segmentation

Algorithm	Description
Du–Yih *et al.* (1994)	Applied on CT images of liver structure. A three layer BP artificial neural network has been used for segmentation.
Hasegawa *et al.* (1998)	Employed on the radiographic images of the chest. A shift invariant ANN has been used.
Ozkan *et al.* (1993)	Tested on the Magnetic Resonance Images acquired from brain tissues. A BP NN based method has been employed for characterization.
Li *et al.* (1999)	A method based on LSB ANN has been illustrated.
Middleton, & Damper (2004)	Applied on Magnetic Resonance Images. Here, Multilayer Perceptron has been combined with Active Contour model.
Koss *et al.* (1999)	Employed on CT images acquired from abdominal region. Images of liver have been taken for consideration. Hopfield NN has been used for segmentation.
Chang, & Ching (2002)	A fuzzy Hopfield NN based segmentation technique has been described.
Cheng *et al.* (1996)	A competitive Hopfield neural network has been discussed for biomedical image segmentation
Sun, & Wang (2005)	Applied on MRI, where Fuzzy Gaussian basis NN has been used for segmentation.
Lee, & Chung (2002)	A contextual NN based segmentation method has been described.
Wang *et al.* (1998)	A probabilistic NN based segmentation method has been described.
Pitiot *et al.* (2002)	Applied on MRI/CT images, where Hybrid NN has been presented.

(Chatterjee *et al.*, 2016a; 2016b; 2017; Hore *et al.*, 2015a; 2016a; 2017). It can be solved by solving the optimization problem regarding the training phase of ANN using metaheuristics (Hore *et al.*, 2016b; Chatterjee *et al.*, 2017a). Several metaheuristics have been proposed to train ANNs leading to hybrid ANN models that are extremely effective in image processing applications. Typically, the Hopfield ANN has been proposed as a tool for computing efficient output to difficult optimization problems. This sorts it an attractive option to conventional optimization procedures for the reconstruction process of the biomedical image reconstruction. Some other ANNs, such as fuzzy Gaussian basis ANN, contextual ANN, hybrid ANN based method is also employed for medical image segmentation.

Neural Network Based Object Detection

In biomedical imaging, detection and recognition of different shapes and object, such as tumors is considered significant and prerequisite in various applications. It is also important in disease detection and useful in interpretation and retrieval of information from the biomedical images. Sometimes it is also the final stage in the biomedical image analysis. It is potentially the brightest area for the application of ANN because it is possible to combine several preceding phases (e.g. preprocessing, and feature extraction) by applying a NN. The main advantage is its capability to train the whole as a single system. A summary of the ANN that has been employed in object detection and recognition are reported in Table 3.

Feed-forward NN based techniques have proved their efficiency and preferred over conventional image detection and recognition methods due to their accuracy in terms of recognition. ANN ensembles are engaged for detecting cancer using two-level constructions, which are applied to find whether a cell is normal containing high confidence. Each network can produce two outputs related to normal cell or abnormal cell. In addition, the second-level is employed to handle the cancer cells as computed by the first level. The judgment of those separate networks is combined

Table 3. Summary of the AA applied for biomedical image detection

Algorithm	Description
Maclin, & Dempsey (1992)	A feed-forward neural network based technique has been applied on liver images obtained from ultrasonography and has been used for liver images classification.
Wu *et al.* (1993)	A feed-forward NN based technique has been proposed for the interpretation and recognition of mammograms.
Tourassi, & Floyd (1993)	A feed-forward NN based technique has been developed for localization of cold lesion and the images are of SPECT modality.
Ercal *et al.* (1994)	This method has been based on BP NN with skin dataset for Melanoma detection.
Wolberg *et al.* (1995)	A feed-forward NN based technique has been carried out for breast cancer diagnosis.
Kadah *et al.* (1996)	A neural network based on radial basis function has been developed for diagnosis of liver related diseases obtained from ultrasonic modality.
Zhu, & Yan (1997)	This approach has been based on Hopfield NN to detect boundaries of brain tumor.
Innocent *et al.* (1997)	An ART NN based method has been proposed for radiographic image classification.
Chan *et al.* (1997)	A convolution NN has been applied for the detection of clustered micro calcifications.
Chen *et al.* (1998)	A probabilistic NN based model has been developed for the recognition of liver tumors.
Ashizawa *et al.* (1999)	A BP NN method has been tested on lung diseases classification.
Pavlopoulos *et al.* (2000)	A fuzzy NN based model has been employed on the ultrasound image of the liver.
Verma, & Zakos (2001)	A fuzzy NN based model has been used to detect micro calcifications in mammogram images.
Suzuki *et al.* (2005)	A modified BP NN based approach has been discussed to reduce the false positives. This method has been illustrated in computerized detection of lung nodules.

by a plurality voting method. Experimental results proved that the ANN ensemble can achieve a good rate of classification and recognition as well as can minimize the false negatives.

ADVANTAGES OF ARTIFICIAL NEURAL NETWORKS IN BIOMEDICAL IMAGE ANALYSIS

From the preceding literatures, it can be concluded that the Hopfield ANN and the feed-forward ANN are the two mostly adapted models that can be used efficiently in biomedical image analysis. The main advantage of Hopfield ANN model in the domain of biomedical image analysis is that the problem in this domain can be considered as an optimization problem. The major advantages of this type of NN based techniques are their efficient capability to handle the tradeoff between the noise sensitivity and image reconstruction resolution. Furthermore, the self-organization feature map (SOM) is one of the attractive alternatives to supervised methods. It has the ability to learn and to classify biomedical image information.

Disadvantages of Artificial Neural Networks in Biomedical Image Analysis

Beside the success history, ANN based methods have several disadvantages compared to some other methods. The first problem that can be mentioned is the choice of the best ANN model and its related architecture. There are no appropriate data that can select the ANN type to be used for a certain application and no proper guidelines found that assures the best trade-off between the variance and bias for a specific volume of the training samples. These networks have to be developed by empirical trial and error method and it is hard to surmount. Moreover, there is chance of over fitting an ANN. Sometimes optimizing the objective measure does not lead to obtain a generalized ANN. The second issue is that the internal implementation is hidden such as the black-box. For a certain input, a corresponding output is generated without explanation of the taken decision. The third problem related with biomedical image analysis is the large volume of input data. If a neural network is trained with a few number of test instances, then the generalization power will be degraded and may not be useful for test cases. In order to ensure high reliability sufficient training samples is essential. In biomedical image analysis, the accuracy is imperative for computer aided diagnostic systems.

Finally, training with large number of data may consume huge amount of time, while time is very important in diagnostic profession and timely accurate results. Moreover, there is a prominent necessity for a detailed validation of the proposed algorithms. In addition, in case of Hopfield ANN for biomedical image analysis, the actual problem is the requirement to its modification before being placed for a solution to the Hopfield network organization.

IMPACT OF THE BIO-INSPIRED AND EVOLUTIONARY ALGORITHMS IN BIOMEDICAL IMAGING

Evolutionary algorithms are inspired by living organisms. One of the effective optimization techniques based on the evolution theory is the Genetic Algorithm (GA). Learning technique of GA uses computational models of natural adaptation to increase their efficiency by mimicking the population genetics. The GA is known as a population-based method because it does to consider only a single potential solution. It has several applications in biomedical imaging, which are proved to be efficient and effective. In mammogram image classification, physicians are interested about three types of classes i.e. normal, benign and malignant. A hybrid method has been developed by Vasantha *et al.* (2010) for feature selection and reduction. This method can reduce up to 75% of the features. A hybrid method of Greedy stepwise technique and GA has been developed to choose the optimal features for further classification.

Cartesian genetic programming (CGP) is an efficient method where more than one networks is employed to classify the mammograms (Nandi *et al.*, 2006), genetic programming has been adapted for implicit feature selection. Now to select the features from the available pool, feature selection approach with three statistical parameters, namely Kolmogorov–Smirnov test, Student's t-test, and Kullback–Leibler divergence has been employed. The proposed method achieved system accuracy of 98%. Hernández-Cisneros, & Terashima-Marín (2006) developed a classification method for micro calcification clusters in using consecutive difference of Gaussian filters (DoG). Three evolutionary ANNs has been compared against a back-propagation feed forward ANN. The GA has been employed to find the optimal weights for ANN.

Das, & Bhattacharya (2008) developed a computer guided treatment development system using Neuro-fuzzy method based on GA. The tumor features have been extracted based on the boundary using Fourier descriptors to represent the features. The proposed approach achieved 87% classification accuracy. Kharrat *et al.* (2010) proposed a hybrid method for brain tissues classification obtained from MRI images. This approach was based on GA and SVM classifier using texture features that based on wavelet. Spatial gray level dependence method is used to extract the features from both normal and tumor segments. These acquired features have been supplied to SVM. The RBF Kernel has been employed with accuracy range 96.38% to 98.78%. Hong, & Cho (2006) developed an advanced technique to select features using GA. Yeh, & Fu (2008) developed an optimization method based on hierarchical GA associated with a fuzzy learning-vector quantization network to perform segmentation of multi-spectral human-brain images of MRI modality. The HGALVQ method has been compare to some other well-known methods, namely fuzzy c-means, k-means, FALVQ, and LVQ. The HGALVQ provided an exact number of clusters. Moreover, it outperformed some other techniques in terms of specificity. Saha & Bandyopadhyay (2007) proposed an automatic segmentation method based on genetic clustering. This clustering method has been based on fuzzy point symmetry and has been applied on the multispectral MRI of the brain. The proposed fuzzy-VGAPS method can automatically iterate and can evolve total number of clusters within the data set. This method used elitist GA with fixed number of generations.

Kishore *et al.* (2000) studied the efficiency of the GA for various multiclass problems using association rules. This method has been compared with the maximum likelihood classifier. A classification function has been evolved through the training samples, where those samples that belong to same class are assigned with association strengths in terms of association degrees. A distinct expression-tree has been evolved through every class. It checked whether unknown test samples belong to the class under test. Parthiban, & Subramanian, (2008) proposed an automated analysis system based on coactive neuro-fuzzy inference system (CANFIS) to predict the heart disease using the ANN adaptive nature. Fuzzy logic qualitative approach has been used along with GA to detect the disease. GA has been used to improve the learning capability of CANFIS. It is used to optimize the number of membership function for separate inputs and other control parameters including the rate of learning, and momentum coefficient. A power spectral based hybrid GA has been proposed by Khazaee & Ebrahimzadeh (2010), where the SVM classifier has been employed to classify five different types of electrocardiogram (ECG) signals. These five classes are normal and four manifestations of heart arrhythmia. In case of SVM, the free parameters have great impact on the accuracy of the classification. This method could achieve up to 96.0% accuracy.

Apart from GA, other bio-inspired method, such as PSO, ABC, and cuckoo search have great impact in the biomedical image analysis. PSO has been inspired by social behavior of bird flocking, where the possible solutions are termed as particles. This technique is easy to implement and computationally cheap. Its system requirements (i.e. mainly CPU and memory) are low. A new method has been developed by Dheeba,& T. Selvi (2010) to detect micro calcification from mammograms. This method has been based on PSO and clustering. Fuzzy c-means clustering method has been used with the PSO to find the center of the clusters automatically. This approach avoids the minimum local value. Geetah *et al.* (2010) developed a model to enhance the mammogram images. A median filter has been used for enhancement and normalization. In this study, the GA has been used to enhance the border; in addition, the PSO has been applied to find the nipple position in the mammogram. The algorithm effectiveness has been measured by true and false positive, where the Corel image database has been used to compute the efficiency of the classification. Ibrahim *et al.* (2010) applied the PSO algorithm to detect abnormalities in brain tissue. This technique is based on four main stages, namely an initially generated population particle, and then the computed fitness using the fitness function, afterward the position and velocity has been updated and finally the stopping criterion has been applied. Typically, PSO based methods worked efficiently on the light abnormalities but gives poor output in dark abnormalities segmentation.

Maitra, & Chatterjee (2008) developed a new multilevel thresholding procedure for MRI brain images segmentation based on bacterial forging algorithm, where thresholding based on image histogram has been used. Jude *et al.* (2010) offered a modified counter propagation NN for brain MRI classification. In order to increase the efficiency, the PSO has been used with addition to the CPN. Alba *et al.* (2007) empirically evaluated a modified PSO namely Geometric PSO. This method has been evaluated by employing a binary representation in Hamming space. This approach has been tested on high dimensional microarray data. A comparative study has been given to compare PSO and GA. Both of them are associated with SVM with 10- fold cross-validation for the classification purpose. Generally, several researchers have been interested to apply several image processing techniques in various applications that can be applied in the medical domain (Setiawan, 2014; Kumar *et al.*, 2014; Hore *et al.*, 2016; Sambyal, & Abrol, 2016; Ang *et al.*, 2016; Naik *et al.*, 2016, Mohanpurkar, & Joshi, 2016; Wang *et al.*, 2016; Dey *et al.* 2016; Manogaran, & Lopez, 2017; Li *et al.*, 2017; Khachane, 2017; Tian *et al.*, 2017; Boulmaiz *et al.*, 2017; Satapathy *et al.*, 2017; Juneja *et al.*, 2017; Sharma, & Virmani, 2017).

CONCLUSION

In this chapter, a study has been conducted on the impact and different application area of intelligent computing methods for biomedical image analysis. Different methods along with their basic features, limitations and advantages have been addressed. These methods can be used as the platform for future development and the problems associated with the discussed method can be eliminated. More efficient systems will ensure better and faster performance of the health care industry.

Moreover, some modifications in ANN for biomedical and other image analysis applications have also been noticed in recent past years. Several advanced techniques, such as SVM are used to get more efficient results. ANN is not always considered as the only solution to the classification or regression related applications. There are some modified versions of the NN that seems to be promising. The use of some emergent ANN techniques in biomedical image processing, e.g. ANN ensembles, the hybrid ANN combined with some intelligent agents, the combination of bio-inspired methods with fuzzy fitness and ANN represent a promising choice to enhance efficiency and accuracy in biomedical image analysis.

REFERENCES

Adler, A., & Guardo, R. (1994). A neural network image reconstruction technique for electrical impedance tomography. *IEEE Transactions on Medical Imaging, 13*(4), 594–600. doi:10.1109/42.363109 PMID:18218537

Alba, E., Garcia-Nieto, J., Jourdan, L., & Talbi, E. G. (2007, September). Gene selection in cancer classification using PSO/SVM and GA/SVM hybrid algorithms. In *Evolutionary Computation, 2007. CEC 2007. IEEE Congress on* (pp. 284-290). IEEE.

Ang, L. M., Seng, K. P., & Heng, T. Z. (2016). Information Communication Assistive Technologies for Visually Impaired People. *International Journal of Ambient Computing and Intelligence, 7*(1), 45–68. doi:10.4018/IJACI.2016010103

Ashizawa, K., Ishida, T., MacMahon, H., Vyborny, C. J., Katsuragawa, S., & Doi, K. (1999). Artificial neural networks in chest radiography: Application to the differential diagnosis of interstitial lung disease. *Academic Radiology, 6*(1), 2–9. doi:10.1016/S1076-6332(99)80055-5 PMID:9891146

Boulmaiz, A., Messadeg, D., Doghmane, N., & Taleb-Ahmed, A. (2017). Design and Implementation of a Robust Acoustic Recognition System for Waterbird Species using TMS320C6713 DSK. *International Journal of Ambient Computing and Intelligence, 8*(1), 98–118. doi:10.4018/IJACI.2017010105

Chan, H. P., Sahiner, B., Petrick, N., Helvie, M. A., Lam, K. L., Adler, D. D., & Goodsitt, M. M. (1997). Computerized classification of malignant and benign microcalcifications on mammograms: Texture analysis using an artificial neural network. *Physics in Medicine and Biology, 42*(3), 549–567. doi:10.1088/0031-9155/42/3/008 PMID:9080535

Chang, C. L., & Ching, Y. T. (2002). Fuzzy Hopfield neural network with fixed weight for medical image segmentation. *Optical Engineering (Redondo Beach, Calif.), 41*(2), 351–358. doi:10.1117/1.1428298

Chatterjee, S., Ghosh, S., Dawn, S., Hore, S., & Dey, N. (2016b). Forest Type Classification: A hybrid NN-GA model based approach. In Information Systems Design and Intelligent Applications (pp. 227-236). Springer India. doi:10.1007/978-81-322-2757-1_23

Chatterjee, S., Hore, S., Dey, N., Chakraborty, S., & Ashour, A. S. (2017). Dengue Fever Classification Using Gene Expression Data: A PSO Based Artificial Neural Network Approach. In *Proceedings of the 5th International Conference on Frontiers in Intelligent Computing: Theory and Applications* (pp. 331-341). Springer. doi:10.1007/978-981-10-3156-4_34

Chatterjee, S., Nag, R., Sen, S., & Sarkar, A. (2017a, June). Towards Golden Rule of Capital Accumulation: A Genetic Algorithm Approach. In *IFIP International Conference on Computer Information Systems and Industrial Management* (pp. 481-491). Springer. doi:10.1007/978-3-319-59105-6_41

Chatterjee, S., Sarkar, S., Hore, S., Dey, N., Ashour, A. S., & Balas, V. E. (2016a). Particle swarm optimization trained neural network for structural failure prediction of multistoried RC buildings. *Neural Computing & Applications*, 1–12.

Chen, E. L., Chung, P. C., Chen, C. L., Tsai, H. M., & Chang, C. I. (1998). An automatic diagnostic system for CT liver image classification. *IEEE Transactions on Bio-Medical Engineering*, *45*(6), 783–794. doi:10.1109/10.678613 PMID:9609943

Cheng, K. S., Lin, J. S., & Mao, C. W. (1996). The application of competitive Hopfield neural network to medical image segmentation. *IEEE Transactions on Medical Imaging*, *15*(4), 560–567. doi:10.1109/42.511759 PMID:18215937

Das, A., & Bhattacharya, M. (2008, September). GA based neuro fuzzy techniques for breast cancer identification. In *Machine Vision and Image Processing Conference, 2008. IMVIP'08. International* (pp. 136-141). IEEE. doi:10.1109/IMVIP.2008.19

Dey, N., Ashour, A. S., Chakraborty, S., Samanta, S., Sifaki-Pistolla, D., Ashour, A. S., & Nguyen, G. N. et al. (2016). Healthy and unhealthy rat hippocampus cells classification: A neural based automated system for Alzheimer disease classification. *Journal of Advanced Microscopy Research*, *11*(1), 1–10. doi:10.1166/jamr.2016.1282

Dheeba, J., & Selvi, T. (2010, December). Bio inspired swarm algorithm for tumor detection in digital mammogram. In *International Conference on Swarm, Evolutionary, and Memetic Computing* (pp. 404-415). Springer Berlin Heidelberg. doi:10.1007/978-3-642-17563-3_49

Doi, K. (2007). Computer-aided diagnosis in medical imaging: Historical review, current status and future potential. *Computerized Medical Imaging and Graphics*, *31*(4), 198–211. doi:10.1016/j.compmedimag.2007.02.002 PMID:17349778

Du–Yih, T. S. A. I. (1994). Automatic segmentation of liver structure in CT images using a neural network. *IEICE Transactions on Fundamentals of Electronics, Communications and Computer Science*, *77*(11), 1892–1895.

Ercal, F., Chawla, A., Stoecker, W. V., Lee, H. C., & Moss, R. H. (1994). Neural network diagnosis of malignant melanoma from color images. *IEEE Transactions on Bio-Medical Engineering*, *41*(9), 837–845. doi:10.1109/10.312091 PMID:7959811

Hasegawa, A., Lo, S. C. B., Lin, J. S., Freedman, M. T., & Mun, S. K. (1998). A shift-invariant neural network for the lung field segmentation in chest radiography. *The Journal of VLSI Signal Processing*, *18*(3), 241–250. doi:10.1023/A:1007937214367

Hemanth, D. J., Vijila, C. K. S., & Anitha, J. (2010). Performance improved PSO based modified counter propagation neural network for abnormal MR brain image classification. *Int. J. Advance. Soft Comput. Appl*, *2*(1), 65–84.

Hernández-Cisneros, R., & Terashima-Marín, H. (2006). Classification of individual and clustered microcalcifications in digital mammograms using evolutionary neural networks. *MICAI 2006. Advances in Artificial Intelligence*, 1200–1210.

Hong, J. H., & Cho, S. B. (2006). Efficient huge-scale feature selection with speciated genetic algorithm. *Pattern Recognition Letters*, *27*(2), 143–150. doi:10.1016/j.patrec.2005.07.009

Hore, S., Chakraborty, S., Chatterjee, S., Dey, N., Ashour, A. S., Van Chung, L., & Le, D. N. (2016a). An Integrated Interactive Technique for Image Segmentation using Stack based Seeded Region Growing and Thresholding. *Iranian Journal of Electrical and Computer Engineering*, *6*(6), 2773–2780.

Hore, S., Chatterjee, S., Chakraborty, S., & Shaw, R. K. (2016b). Analysis of Different Feature Description Algorithm in object Recognition. *Feature Detectors and Motion Detection in Video Processing*, 66.

Hore, S., Chatterjee, S., Santhi, V., Dey, N., Ashour, A. S., Balas, V. E., & Shi, F. (2017). Indian Sign Language Recognition Using Optimized Neural Networks. In *Information Technology and Intelligent Transportation Systems* (pp. 553–563). Springer International Publishing. doi:10.1007/978-3-319-38771-0_54

Hore, S., Chatterjee, S., Sarkar, S., Dey, N., Ashour, A. S., Balas-Timar, D., & Balas, V. E. (2016). Neural-based prediction of structural failure of multistoried RC buildings. *Structural Engineering & Mechanics*, *58*(3), 459–473. doi:10.12989/sem.2016.58.3.459

Hore, S., Chatterjee, S., Shaw, R., Dey, N., & Virmani, J. (2015a, November). Detection of chronic kidney disease: A NN-GA based approach. In *CSI—2015; 50th Golden Jubilee Annual Convention*.

Ibrahim, S., Khalid, N. E. A., & Manaf, M. (2010, March). Empirical study of brain segmentation using particle swarm optimization. In *Information Retrieval & Knowledge Management,(CAMP), 2010 International Conference on* (pp. 235-239). IEEE. doi:10.1109/INFRKM.2010.5466910

Innocent, P. R., Barnes, M., & John, R. (1997). Application of the fuzzy ART/MAP and MinMax/MAP neural network models to radiographic image classification. *Artificial Intelligence in Medicine*, *11*(3), 241–263. doi:10.1016/S0933-3657(97)00032-8 PMID:9413608

Juneja, D., Singh, A., Singh, R., & Mukherjee, S. (2017). A thorough insight into theoretical and practical developments in multiagent systems. *International Journal of Ambient Computing and Intelligence*, *8*(1), 23–49. doi:10.4018/IJACI.2017010102

Kadah, Y. M., Farag, A. A., Zurada, J. M., Badawi, A. M., & Youssef, A. B. (1996). Classification algorithms for quantitative tissue characterization of diffuse liver disease from ultrasound images. *IEEE Transactions on Medical Imaging*, *15*(4), 466–478. doi:10.1109/42.511750 PMID:18215928

Khachane, M. Y. (2017). Organ-Based Medical Image Classification Using Support Vector Machine. *International Journal of Synthetic Emotions*, *8*(1), 18–30. doi:10.4018/IJSE.2017010102

Kharrat, A., Gasmi, K., Messaoud, M. B., Benamrane, N., & Abid, M. (2010). A hybrid approach for automatic classification of brain MRI using genetic algorithm and support vector machine. *Leonardo Journal of Sciences*, *17*(1), 71–82.

Khazaee, A., & Ebrahimzadeh, A. (2010). Classification of electrocardiogram signals with support vector machines and genetic algorithms using power spectral features. *Biomedical Signal Processing and Control*, *5*(4), 252–263. doi:10.1016/j.bspc.2010.07.006

Kishore, J. K., Patnaik, L. M., Mani, V., & Agrawal, V. K. (2000). Application of genetic programming for multicategory pattern classification. *IEEE Transactions on Evolutionary Computation*, *4*(3), 242–258. doi:10.1109/4235.873235

Koss, J. E., Newman, F. D., Johnson, T. K., & Kirch, D. L. (1999). Abdominal organ segmentation using texture transforms and a hopfield neural network. *IEEE Transactions on Medical Imaging*, *18*(7), 640–648. doi:10.1109/42.790463 PMID:10504097

Kumar, S. U., Inbarani, H. H., Azar, A. T., & Hassanien, A. E. (2014). Identification of heart valve disease using bijective soft sets theory. [IJRSDA]. *International Journal of Rough Sets and Data Analysis*, *1*(2), 1–14. doi:10.4018/ijrsda.2014070101

Lee, C. C., & Chung, P. C. (2000). Recognizing abdominal organs in CT images using contextual neural network and fuzzy rules. In *Engineering in Medicine and Biology Society, 2000. Proceedings of the 22nd Annual International Conference of the IEEE* (Vol. 3, pp. 1745-1748). IEEE.

Li, Y., Wen, P., Powers, D., & Clark, C. R. (1999). LSB neural network based segmentation of MR brain images. In *Systems, Man, and Cybernetics, 1999. IEEE SMC'99 Conference Proceedings. 1999 IEEE International Conference on* (Vol. 6, pp. 822-825). IEEE.

Li, Z., Shi, K., Dey, N., Ashour, A. S., Wang, D., Balas, V. E., & Shi, F. et al. (2017). Rule-based back propagation neural networks for various precision rough set presented KANSEI knowledge prediction: A case study on shoe product form features extraction. *Neural Computing & Applications*, 1–18.

Maclin, P. S., & Dempsey, J. (1992). Using an artificial neural network to diagnose hepatic masses. *Journal of Medical Systems*, *16*(5), 215–225. doi:10.1007/BF01000274 PMID:1289469

Maitra, M., & Chatterjee, A. (2008). A novel technique for multilevel optimal magnetic resonance brain image thresholding using bacterial foraging. *Measurement*, *41*(10), 1124–1134. doi:10.1016/j.measurement.2008.03.002

Manogaran, G., & Lopez, D. (2017). Disease surveillance system for big climate data processing and dengue transmission. *International Journal of Ambient Computing and Intelligence*, *8*(2), 88–105. doi:10.4018/IJACI.2017040106

Middleton, I., & Damper, R. I. (2004). Segmentation of magnetic resonance images using a combination of neural networks and active contour models. *Medical Engineering & Physics*, *26*(1), 71–86. doi:10.1016/S1350-4533(03)00137-1 PMID:14644600

Miller, A. S., Blott, B. H., & Hames, T. K. (1992). Review of neural network applications in medical imaging and signal processing. *Medical & Biological Engineering & Computing*, *30*(5), 449–464. doi:10.1007/BF02457822 PMID:1293435

Mohanpurkar, A. A., & Joshi, M. S. (2016). A Traitor Identification Technique for Numeric Relational Databases with Distortion Minimization and Collusion Avoidance. *International Journal of Ambient Computing and Intelligence*, 7(2), 114–137. doi:10.4018/IJACI.2016070106

Naik, A., Satapathy, S. C., Ashour, A. S., & Dey, N. (2016). Social group optimization for global optimization of multimodal functions and data clustering problems. *Neural Computing & Applications*, 1–17.

Nandi, R. J., Nandi, A. K., Rangayyan, R. M., & Scutt, D. (2006). Classification of breast masses in mammograms using genetic programming and feature selection. *Medical & Biological Engineering & Computing*, 44(8), 683–694. doi:10.1007/s11517-006-0077-6 PMID:16937210

Ozkan, M., Dawant, B. M., & Maciunas, R. J. (1993). Neural-network-based segmentation of multi-modal medical images: A comparative and prospective study. *IEEE Transactions on Medical Imaging*, 12(3), 534–544. doi:10.1109/42.241881 PMID:18218446

Parthiban, L., & Subramanian, R. (2008). Intelligent heart disease prediction system using CANFIS and genetic algorithm. *International Journal of Biological, Biomedical and Medical Sciences, 3*(3).

Pavlopoulos, S., Kyriacou, E., Koutsouris, D., Blekas, K., Stafylopatis, A., & Zoumpoulis, P. (2000). Fuzzy neural network-based texture analysis of ultrasonic images. *IEEE Engineering in Medicine and Biology Magazine*, 19(1), 39–47. doi:10.1109/51.816243 PMID:10659429

Pitiot, A., Toga, A. W., Ayache, N., & Thompson, P. (2002). Texture based MRI segmentation with a two-stage hybrid neural classifier. In *Neural Networks, 2002. IJCNN'02. Proceedings of the 2002 International Joint Conference on* (Vol. 3, pp. 2053-2058). IEEE. doi:10.1109/IJCNN.2002.1007457

Rastgarpour, M., & Shanbehzadeh, J. (2013). The status quo of artificial intelligence methods in automatic medical image segmentation. *International Journal of Computer Theory and Engineering*, 5(1), 5–8. doi:10.7763/IJCTE.2013.V5.636

Saha, S., & Bandyopadhyay, S. (2007, September). MRI brain image segmentation by fuzzy symmetry based genetic clustering technique. In *Evolutionary Computation, 2007. CEC 2007. IEEE Congress on* (pp. 4417-4424). IEEE. doi:10.1109/CEC.2007.4425049

Sambyal, N., & Abrol, P. (2016). Feature based Text Extraction System using Connected Component Method. *International Journal of Synthetic Emotions*, 7(1), 41–57. doi:10.4018/IJSE.2016010104

Satapathy, S. C., Raja, N. S. M., Rajinikanth, V., Ashour, A. S., & Dey, N. (2017). Multi-level image thresholding using Otsu and chaotic bat algorithm. *Neural Computing & Applications*, 1–23.

Setiawan, N. A. (2014). Fuzzy decision support system for coronary artery disease diagnosis based on Rough set theory. *International Journal of Rough Sets and Data Analysis*, 1(1), 65–80. doi:10.4018/ijrsda.2014010105

Sharma, K., & Virmani, J. (2017). A Decision Support System for Classification of Normal and Medical Renal Disease Using Ultrasound Images: A Decision Support System for Medical Renal Diseases. *International Journal of Ambient Computing and Intelligence*, 8(2), 52–69. doi:10.4018/IJACI.2017040104

Sun, W., & Wang, Y. (2005). Segmentation method of MRI using fuzzy Gaussian basis neural network. *Neural Information Processing-Letters and Reviews*, 8(2), 19–24.

Suzuki, K., Horiba, I., & Sugie, N. (2003). Neural edge enhancer for supervised edge enhancement from noisy images. *IEEE Transactions on Pattern Analysis and Machine Intelligence*, 25(12), 1582–1596. doi:10.1109/TPAMI.2003.1251151

Suzuki, K., Shiraishi, J., Abe, H., MacMahon, H., & Doi, K. (2005). False-positive reduction in computer-aided diagnostic scheme for detecting nodules in chest radiographs by means of massive training artificial neural network 1. *Academic Radiology*, 12(2), 191–201. doi:10.1016/j.acra.2004.11.017 PMID:15721596

Tian, Z., Dey, N., Ashour, A. S., McCauley, P., & Shi, F. (2017). Morphological segmenting and neighborhood pixel-based locality preserving projection on brain fMRI dataset for semantic feature extraction: An affective computing study. *Neural Computing & Applications*, 1–16.

Tourassi, G. D., & Floyd, C. Jr. (1993). Artificial Neural Networks for Single Photon Emission Computed Tomography: A Study of Cold Lesion Detection and Localization. *Investigative Radiology*, 28(8), 671–677. doi:10.1097/00004424-199308000-00002 PMID:8375998

Vasantha, M., Bharathi, D. V. S., & Dhamodharan, R. (2010). Medical image feature, extraction, selection and classification. *International Journal of Engineering Science and Technology*, 1(2), 2071–2076.

Verma, B., & Zakos, J. (2001). A computer-aided diagnosis system for digital mammograms based on fuzzy-neural and feature extraction techniques. *IEEE Transactions on Information Technology in Biomedicine*, *5*(1), 46–54. doi:10.1109/4233.908389 PMID:11300216

Wang, D., He, T., Li, Z., Cao, L., Dey, N., Ashour, A. S., & Shi, F. et al. (2016). Image feature-based affective retrieval employing improved parameter and structure identification of adaptive neuro-fuzzy inference system. *Neural Computing & Applications*, 1–16.

Wang, Y., Adali, T., Kung, S. Y., & Szabo, Z. (1998). Quantification and segmentation of brain tissues from MR images: A probabilistic neural network approach. *IEEE Transactions on Image Processing*, *7*(8), 1165–1181. doi:10.1109/83.704309 PMID:18172510

Wang, Y., Heng, P. A., & Wahl, F. M. (2003). Image reconstructions from two orthogonal projections. *International Journal of Imaging Systems and Technology*, *13*(2), 141–145. doi:10.1002/ima.10036

Warsito, W., & Fan, L. S. (2001). Neural network based multi-criterion optimization image reconstruction technique for imaging two-and three-phase flow systems using electrical capacitance tomography. *Measurement Science & Technology*, *12*(12), 2198–2210. doi:10.1088/0957-0233/12/12/323

Wolberg, W. H., Street, W. N., & Mangasarian, O. L. (1995). Image analysis and machine learning applied to breast cancer diagnosis and prognosis. *Analytical and Quantitative Cytology and Histology*, *17*(2), 77–87. PMID:7612134

Wu, Y., Giger, M. L., Doi, K., Vyborny, C. J., Schmidt, R. A., & Metz, C. E. (1993). Artificial neural networks in mammography: Application to decision making in the diagnosis of breast cancer. *Radiology*, *187*(1), 81–87. doi:10.1148/radiology.187.1.8451441 PMID:8451441

Yeh, J. Y., & Fu, J. C. (2008). A hierarchical genetic algorithm for segmentation of multi-spectral human-brain MRI. *Expert Systems with Applications*, *34*(2), 1285–1295. doi:10.1016/j.eswa.2006.12.012

Zhou, Jiang, Yang, & Chen. (2002). Lung Cancer Cell Identification Based on Artificial Neural Network Ensembles. *Artificial Intelligence in Medicine, 24*, 25-36.

Zhu, Y., & Yan, Z. (1997). Computerized tumor boundary detection using a Hopfield neural network. *IEEE Transactions on Medical Imaging*, *16*(1), 55–67. doi:10.1109/42.552055 PMID:9050408

KEY TERMS AND DEFINITIONS

Classification: Defined as assigning a physical object or incident into a set of known groups. It is considered a numerical properties analysis of the image features for classification.

Feature Extraction: The attributes transformation into a lower dimensional space.

Feature Selection: The selection of the most significant attributes that provide important information about the object under concern.

Image Analysis: The extraction of expressive information from images using digital image processing procedures.

Image Processing: The manipulation and analysis of a digitized image for quality improvement.

Image Segmentation: The image partitioning process into several segments.

Magnetic Resonance Imaging: A medical device that employed nuclear magnetic resonance of protons to yield images.

Medical Imaging: The method that produces/captures medical images.

Medical Modalities: The medical instruments for capturing medical images of the internal organ of the body to support diagnosis.

Chapter 7
Effect of SMES Unit in AGC of an Interconnected Multi–Area Thermal Power System With ACO–Tuned PID Controller

K. Jagatheesan
Paavai Engineering College, India

B. Anand
Hindusthan College of Engineering and Technology, India

Nilanjan Dey
Techno India College of Technology, India

Amira S. Ashour
Tanta University, Egypt

ABSTRACT

Load changes in any one of interconnected power system that influence the system response from their nominal values. The Proportional–Integral- Derivative (PID) controller is employed to mitigate this issue as a secondary controller in addition to the Superconducting Magnetic Energy Storage (SMES) unit. In Automatic Generation Control (AGC), the current work proposed an Ant Colony Optimization (ACO) technique to tune PID controller gain values of multi-area interconnected thermal power system. The gain value of PID controller is tuned by using the ACO techniques. The system response is compared with and without considering SMES unit in the system. The comparative results clearly established that the system response with SMES unit improve the performance of system during sudden load disturbance.

DOI: 10.4018/978-1-5225-4151-6.ch007

INTRODUCTION

Nowadays, the electrical energy demand increases rapidly all over the world due to the enormous development in technology. Large scale power systems are created to achieve energy demand balance. The large scale power systems are incorporated with a number of control areas that are interconnected through the tie lines. In any one of power system, the increased load demand will lead to share the power between the connected areas to maintain the system in stable condition. The size and complexity are increased with large control areas' interconnections. The system complexity can be reduced with the help of recently developed modern control theory.

Many researchers reported the AGC of interconnected power systems performance that were related to AGC or LFC of two and three equal or unequal areas of thermal-thermal, and thermal-hydro systems. Several studies have been including various optimization techniques (Samanta *et al.*, 2013a; 2013b; Jagatheesan, & Anand, 2014), while others have been directed with controller types with different optimization techniques that have been used in the LFC, such as classical, optimal, fuzzy logic (Ali, & Abd-Elazim, (2011), neural network (Anand, & Jeyakumar, 2009), Variable Structure Control (VSC) (Das *et al.*, 1991), Optimal Control (Moon *et al.*, 2000), and Decentralized Controller (Jagatheesan *et al.*, 2014). In LFC or AGC the optimal PID controller gain values are optimized by using recently developed evolutionary computation techniques, such as ACO (Hsiao *et al.*, 2004), Bacteria Foraging Optimization (BFO) (Ali, & Abd-Elazim, (2011), and Particle Swarm Optimization (PSO) (Ebrahim *et al.*, 2009), Artificial Bee Colony (ABC) (Debbarma *et al.*, 2013), Cuckoo Search (CS) (Dash *et al.*, 2014), and Teaching Learning Based Optimization (TLBO) (Chidambaram, & Paramasivam, 2012).

The AGC in 3-area equal Thermal–Thermal–Hydro system has been investigated with different classical controllers and the performance has been compared with fuzzy Integral double derivative (IDD) controller (Taher *et al.*, 2014). The optimal controllers' gain values are optimized using BFO associated to conventional PID controller. Imperialist Competitive Algorithm (ICA) is implemented with LFC of 3-area power system with Fractional Order PID (FOPID) controller (Debbarma *et al.*, 2013). The simulation result demonstrated the superiority of system performance with ICA based controller compared to the existing controller. The FOPID controller has been implemented under released environment using BF technique for optimization (Roy *et al.*, 2010). From the above discussion, it is very clear that the modern evolutionary computation techniques have been developed and implemented the three areas system in the load frequency control successfully. An energy storage device with the ability to decrease the system frequency oscillations andthe tie-line power flow within a quick period of time has been presented in (Tam, & Kumar,

1990). Many energy storage units, namely the capacitive energy storage (CES), battery energy storage, SMES and flywheels, have been modeled.

In the current chapter, super conducting magnetic energy storage unit is implemented, which stores the energy in the magnetic field model (Tam, & Kumar, 1990). The stored energy is suddenly released through power conversion system with the rise in load demand. Due to this demand, the turbine and other LFC arrangements are adjusted for the power balance and a new equilibrium. SMES coil absorbs the energy through the system steady state situation. The absorbed energy is released during sudden load changes. The control of SMES unit is based on changing the converter firing angle. Since the operative way of using SMES unit is based on the control strategy method, an efficient soft computing ACO technique is used for tuning the PID controller gain values in AGC of three areas interconnected reheat thermal power systems. The chief aims of the presented work are as follows:

1.   Design a 3-area interconnected reheat thermal power system without and with the consideration of SMES unit in association with PID controller as a secondary controller.
2.   Design a PID controller for AGC of 3 equal areas reheat thermal power system and to optimize the gain values of controller by ACO technique.
3.   Compute the Kp, Ki and Kd gain values of PID controller without and with the consideration of SMES unit.
4.   Investigate the performances of the AGC reheat thermal system with the SMES energy storage unit.
5.   Compare the AGC reheat thermal system performance without and with including the Superconducting Magnetic Energy Storage unit effect.

SYSTEM UNDER STUDY

The model of transfer function of uncontrolled 3-area interconnected reheat thermal power system is illustrated in Figure 1 (Anand, & Jeyakumar, 2009; Jagatheesan, & Anand, 2012). In this power system, each power plant is incorporated with speed regulator, a governor, turbine with reheater and generator. In addition, each plant has an equal rating of 2000MW.

All the power plants are interconnected with the help of tie-lines for interchanging the power among the plants during abnormal condition to keep the system stability. Increasing load demand in either plant of the system; affects the reactive/real system power. Changes in real power mainly affect (tie-line power flow and system frequency) stability of total interconnected power system compared to reactive power changes. The proper control signal that generated to enhance the system stability

Figure 1. Model of open loop 3-area transfer function with SMES

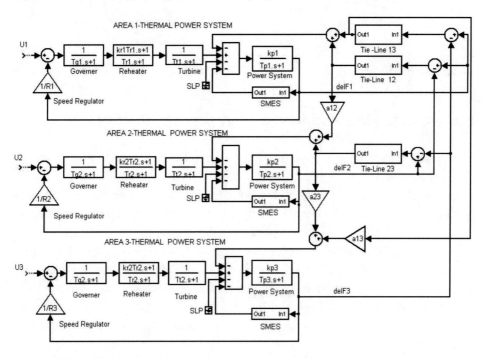

is very important that is fed to the connected plants. The generated control signal from PID controller is given by:

$$u_1(t) = - K_{p1} ACE_1 - K_{i1} \int ACE_1 dt - T_d K_{d1} \frac{d}{dt} ACE_1 \qquad (1)$$

$$u_2(t) = - K_{p2} ACE_2 - K_{i2} \int ACE_2 dt - T_d K_{d2} \frac{d}{dt} ACE_2 \qquad (2)$$

$$u_3(t) = - K_{p3} ACE_3 - K_{i3} \int ACE_3 dt - T_d K_{d3} \frac{d}{dt} ACE_3 \qquad (3)$$

The area control error (ACE) that generated in area 1, area 2 and area 3 is given by:

$$ACE_1 = \Delta F_1 . B_1 + \Delta P_{tie12} \qquad (4)$$

$$ACE_2 = \Delta F_2 . B_2 + \Delta P_{tie\,23} \qquad (5)$$

$$ACE_3 = \Delta F_3 . B_3 + \Delta P_{tie\,31} \qquad (6)$$

Superconducting Magnetic Energy Storage (SMES) Unit

SMES is a DC current device that uses the magnetic field as a form to store the energy (Tam, & Kumar, 1990). Figure 2 illustrates the basic component of this unit is shown. It contains the cryogenic system, superconducting coil, transformer, Power Conversion System (PCS) with proper control. From these components, superconducting coil is the heart of SMES unit. It incorporates with vacuum vessels and liquid vessels for the cooling arrangement of coil. A cryogenic system is employed for keeping the temperature of coil within the permissible limits. The power conversion system is used for two purposes, namely the conversion of electrical energy from DC to AC and the charging/discharging of the oil. The power system is connected to the PCS with the help of transformer to reduce the operating voltage into acceptable level for the PCS.

The energy is stored in the super conducting coil (E) in the SMES unit, and the rated power (P) is given by (Tam, & Kumar, 1990):

$$E = \frac{1}{2} L I^2 \qquad (7)$$

Figure 2. Components of SMES unit

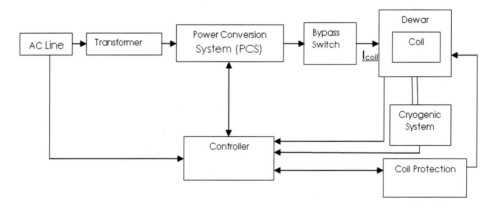

$$P = \frac{dE}{dt} = LI\frac{dI}{dt} = VI \tag{8}$$

where, L is the coil (H) inductance, V is voltage across coil and I is DC current flowing over a coil (A). As the superconducting coil reaches the rated current, the SMES unit is equipped for AGC/LFC control. ACE is sensed. It is conducted for the voltage control of SMES unit by changing the duty cycle of the chopper. Table 1 reports the few noteworthy applications of SMES in LFC/AGC issue of multi-area interconnected power systems.

The preceding studies involved applications of SMES units in interconnected power system, it is clearly shows that sudden power surplus in power system is overcome by deriving power from large inductor coil. It improved the inclusive dynamic system performance and stability.

Proportional-Integral-Derivative (PID) Controller

An industrial PID controller is used to solve the AGC problem. The ACO procedure is utilized to obtain the gain values of PID controller and discussed in section 4. PID controller structure is illustrated in Figure 3.

Table 1. Applications of SMES unit in LFC/AGC issue of multi-area interconnected power systems

Size of the Power System	Authors	Remarks
Two area	Pothiye *et al.* (2007)	AGC problem of 2-area reheat thermal power system has been discussed using fuzzy logic based PID controller with applying multiple Tabu Search algorithms.
Two area (multi-unit)	Bhatt *et al.*(2010)	Multi-area multiple unit hydrothermal power system operation has been improved by TCPS coordinated SMES units in all areas with integral controller.
Two area	Joseph *et al.* (2011)	Damping oscillations in tie-line power and frequency in two area thermal has been discussed with SMES and TCPS coordination.
Two area (multi-unit)	Roy *et al.*(2014)	Dynamic performance two area hydro power system with three multiple units in each area has been improved by introducing SMES units in both units.
Two area (multi-unit)	Padhan *et al.*(2014)	Multi-area multiple unit thermal power system has been deliberated in with fuzzy based PID controller. It improved system response with less settling time and overshoots.
Two area	Chine,& Tripathy (2015)	The real power surplus in two area power system compensated by deriving same amount of power from large indictor coil. By the use of SMES unit in interconnected two area power system.

Figure 3. PID controller

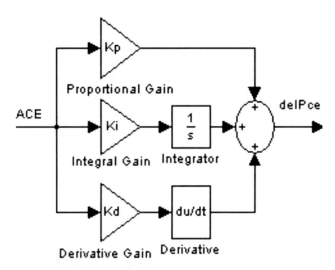

The PID controller structure entails 3-different control terms (Integral, Proportional and Derivative terms). In power system, all are connected together to solve AGC problematic. Here, Integral Time Absolute Error (ITAE) objective function is applied to obtain the optimal gain values of integral (K_i), Proportional (K_p), and Derivative (K_d) controller gain values. The ITAE expression is given as follows:

$$J = \int_{0}^{T} t \left| \left\{ \Delta f_i + \Delta P_{tie\ i-j} \right\} \right| dt \tag{9}$$

where, J represents performance index, t is simulation time period, Δf is frequency deviation, ΔP_{tie} is tie-line power deviation and $i,j = 1, 2, 3$.

Ant Colony Optimization Technique

Real ants' performance stimulated several researchers to solve many discrete optimization problems. When ants are searching their food, originally the ants are explored random manner around their nest. The explored ants are finding a food source as soon as possible. The quality/quantity of the food source is evaluated. It deposits some pheromone chemical trial on the ground. The indirect communication between the ants using chemical trials enables shortest path between food and their nest. These characteristics of real ants are used to find the solution for many optimization problems. Transition probability from town i and j for the kth ant is expressed by:

$$p_{ij}(t) = \frac{\tau_{ij}(t)^\alpha \left(\eta_{ij}\right)^\beta}{\sum\limits_{j \in nodes} \tau_{ij}(t)^\alpha \left(\eta_{ij}\right)^\beta} \qquad (10)$$

The pheromone value against heuristic η_{ij} information is:

$$\eta_{ij} = \frac{1}{d_{ij}} \qquad (11)$$

The global updating rule is applied based on the following expression:

$$\tau_{ij}(t+1) = (1-\rho)\tau_{ij}(t) + \sum\limits_{\substack{k \in colony\ that \\ used\ edge\ (i,j)}} \frac{Q}{L_k} \qquad (12)$$

here, P_{ij} is the probability between the town i and j, τ_{ij} is pheromone related to edge linking cities i and j, Q is constant, d_{ij} is distance between cities i and j, L_k is the tour length that performed by K^{th} ant, α, β are constants to determine the relative time between heuristic values and pheromone and ρ is the evaporation rate.

During the optimization of PID controller parameters using ACO algorithm consists of several steps. The first step is initialization simulation parameters, including the number of ants, pheromone and iteration. After running initialization simulation model, ants are start moving from source to node (nest to food source) on the ground by pasting pheromone chemicals. The chemicals concentrations are varied based on the food quantity and quality. During this tour shortest path having higher chemical concentration and longer path having lesser concentration, it evaporates after few iteration. The simulation is stops when it has maximum value of the iteration. The optimal control gain values and results comparisons are as follows.

SIMULATION RESULTS AND DISCUSSIONS

MATLAB 7.5(R2007b) is conducted to gain dynamic response of power system in all areas with and without considering SMES unit. The PID controller parameters are tuned by applying ACO technique, it is discussed in the section IV and gain values are illustrated in the Table 2.

In this section, the simulation performance comparison of AGC multi-area interconnected reheat thermal power system without and with considering SMES unit in all the areas is shown in Figures 4-12. In these figures, the response comparison dashed line illustrates the response system without considering SMES unit and solid line illustrates the system of response with considering SMES unit.

Table 2. Gain values of PID controller optimized using ACO

	PID Controller Gain Values								
	Ki			Kp			Kd		
	Ki$_1$	Ki$_2$	Ki$_3$	Kp1	Kp2	Kp3	Kd1	Kd2	Kd3
Without Considering SMES Unit	9.6	6.7	5.7	10	9.6	8	1.3	4.3	2.1
Considering SMES Unit	0.8	9.6	9.6	6.3	9.6	9.8	8.7	2.3	3.3

Figure 4. Change in frequency deviation comparisons in area 1 with and without considering SMES unit

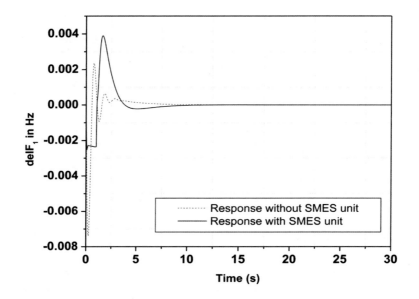

Figure 5. Change in frequency deviation comparisons in area 2 with and without considering SMES unit

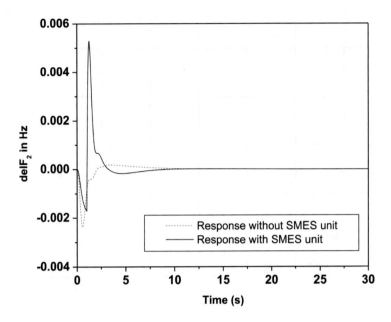

Figure 6 demonstrates the frequency deviation system assessments in three areas with ACO based PID controller with and without considering SMES unit in all areas. It is shows that system response including SMES unit response settled quickly without considering energy storage unit.

Figure 9 show the tie-line power flow response between connected power systems with and without considering SMES unit in all area for 1% SLP in area 1. It is effectively regulated with superior settling time and minimum damping oscillations in comparison with the system response without taking into account the SMES unit in all areas.

Figures 10-12 show the performance comparison of area control error with and without considering SMES unit in all the areas. It is clearly evident that the ACE is settled quickly compared to system response without considering SMES unit. Table 3 reported the performance analysis is made by time domain specifications and numerical values.

Simulation result comparisons in plot and time domain specification parameters comparison in the table of the interconnected power system establish that the SMES unit including system response settled faster with lesser damping oscillations compared to system response without considering SMES unit in all interconnected area.

Figure 6. Frequency deviation change comparison in area 3 with and without considering SMES unit

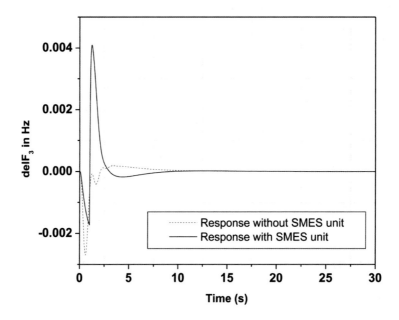

Figure 7. Tie-line power flow deviations in between area 1 & 2 with and without considering SMES unit

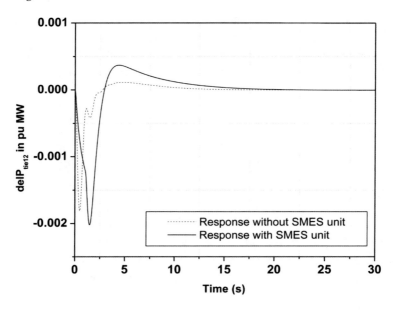

Figure 8. Tie-line power flow deviations in between area 1 & 3 with and without considering SMES unit

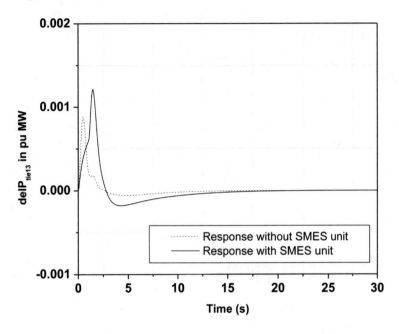

Figure 9. Tie-line power flow deviations in between area 2 & 3 with and without considering SMES unit

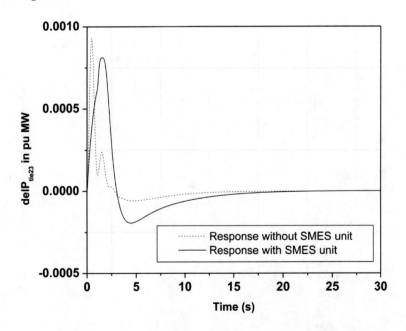

Figure 10. Area control error deviation in area 1 with and without considering SMES unit

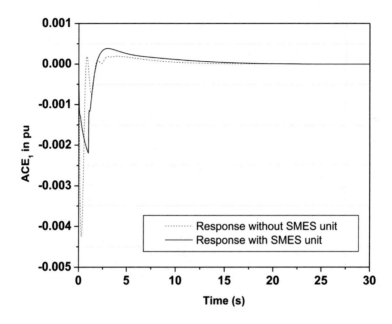

Figure 11. Area control error deviation in area 2 with and without considering SMES unit

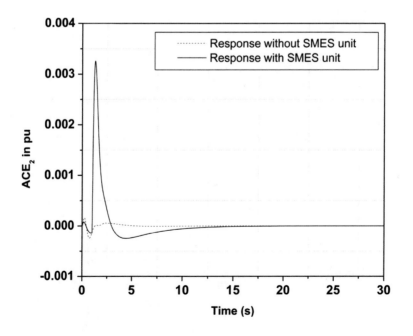

Figure 12. Area control error deviation in area 3 with and without considering SMES unit

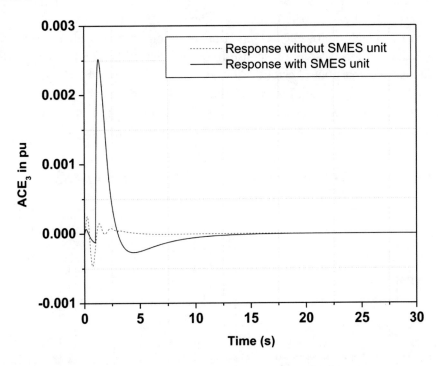

Table 3. Comparison of numerical values of settling time with and without considering SMES unit

Settling Time Comparison With and Without Considering SMES Unit			
Fig.No	Response	Without Considering SMES Unit	With Considering SMES Unit
4	delF1	10.1	10
5	delF2	19	16
6	delF3	16.5	10.1
7	delPtie12	21.5	20
8	delPtie13	19	18
9	delPtie23	18.5	17
10	ACE1	14.5	13.5
11	ACE2	13	12.5
12	ACE3	15.5	14.5

The settling time bar chart comparisons of system with and without considering SMES is shown in Figures 13-15. It is clearly evident that the SMES unit equipped system settled quick compare to system without SMES unit response.

The percentage improvement comparisons of system with and without considering SMES unit equipped system response frequency deviations, tie-line power flow deviations and area control error is shown in following Tables 4 through 6.

Tables 4 through 6 and Figures 16 through 18 clearly proved that SMES unit equipped system response enhanced in terms of minimum settling time in comparison with the system response without SMES unit during sudden load demand.

Figure 13. Bar chart comparisons of settling time in system frequency

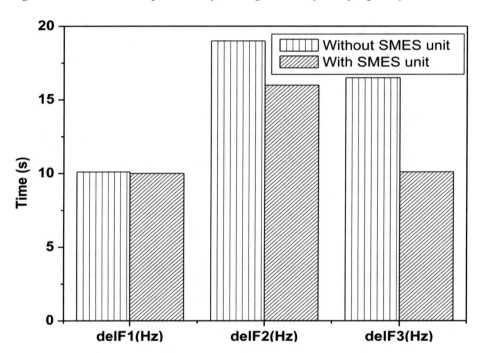

Table 4. Percentage of improvement of SMES unit over without SMES unit in settling time of delF

Response	% of Improvement Over Without SMES Unit
$delF_1$	0.99
$delF_2$	15.79
$delF_3$	38.79

Figure 14. Bar chart comparisons of settling time in tie-line power flow

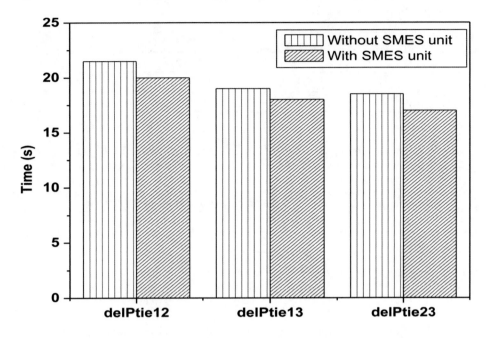

Figure 15. Bar chart comparisons of settling time in area control error

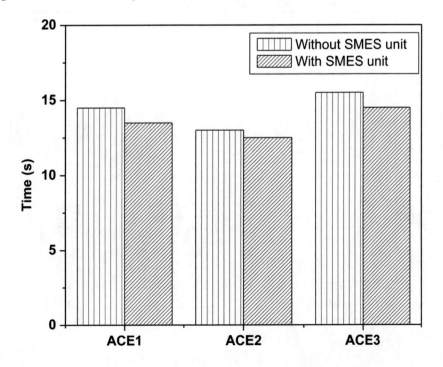

Table 5. Percentage of improvement of SMES unit over without SMES unit in settling time of delPtie

Response	% of Improvement Over Without SMES Unit
$delP_{12}$	6.98
$delP_{13}$	5.26
$delP_{23}$	8.11

Table 6. Percentage of improvement of SMES unit over without SMES unit in settling time of ACE

Response	% of Improvement Over Without SMES Unit
ACE_1	6.90
ACE_2	3.85
ACE_3	6.45

Figure 16. Bar chart comparisons of percentage of improvement in settling time of delF

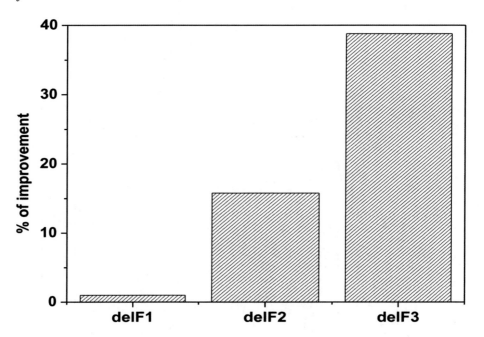

Figure 17. Bar chart comparisons of percentage of improvement in settling time of delPtie

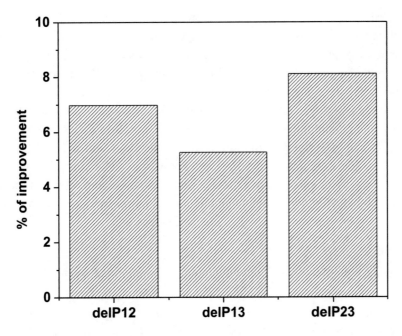

Figure 18. Bar chart comparisons of percentage of improvement in settling time of ACE

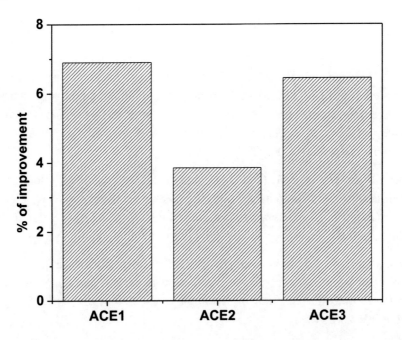

CONCLUSION

In the present work, AGC of three area interconnected reheat thermal power system is investigated with PID controller considered as secondary controller. The ACO is used for optimizing the gain values of PID controller using ITAE objective function. The optimization process is performed without and with SMES energy storage unit in all the three interconnected areas.

The system performance with SMES energy storage unit is associated with performance of system without the energy storage unit. Simulation results depicted that SMES unit effectively damping out the oscillations and reduced the system response settling time during sudden load disturbance. The numerical values and response comparisons are given in the table and plot. It is clearly proved that system response with SMES unit settled quick response in comparison with the system response without considering SMES unit in all areas.

REFERENCES

Ali, E. S., & Abd-Elazim, S. M. (2011). Bacteria foraging optimization algorithm based load frequency controller for interconnected power system. *International Journal of Electrical Power & Energy Systems*, *33*(3), 633–638. doi:10.1016/j. ijepes.2010.12.022

Anand, B., & Jeyakumar, A. E. (2009). Load frequency control with fuzzy logic controller considering non-linearities and boiler dynamics. *ICGST-ACSE Journal*, *8*(111), 15–20.

Bhatt, P., Ghoshal, S. P., & Roy, R. (2010). Load frequency stabilization by coordinated control of Thyristor Controlled Phase Shifters and superconducting magnetic energy storage for three types of interconnected two-area power systems. *International Journal of Electrical Power & Energy Systems*, *32*(10), 1111–1124. doi:10.1016/j.ijepes.2010.06.009

Chaine, S., & Tripathy, M. (2015). Design of an optimal SMES for automatic generation control of two-area thermal power system using cuckoo search algorithm. *Journal of Electrical Systems and Information Technology*, *2*(1), 1–13. doi:10.1016/j. jesit.2015.03.001

Chidambaram, I. A., & Paramasivam, B. (2012). Control performance standards based load-frequency controller considering redox flow batteries coordinate with interline power flow controller. *Journal of Power Sources*, *219*, 292–304. doi:10.1016/j. jpowsour.2012.06.048

Das, D., Kothari, M. L., Kothari, D. P., & Nanda, P. J. (1991, November). Variable structure control strategy to automatic generation control of interconnected reheat thermal system. *IEE Proceedings. Control Theory and Applications, 138*(6), 579–585. doi:10.1049/ip-d.1991.0080

Dash, P., Saikia, L. C., & Sinha, N. (2014). Comparison of performances of several Cuckoo search algorithm based 2DOF controllers in AGC of multi-area thermal system. *International Journal of Electrical Power & Energy Systems, 55*, 429–436. doi:10.1016/j.ijepes.2013.09.034

Debbarma, S., Saikia, L. C., & Sinha, N. (2013). AGC of a multi-area thermal system under deregulated environment using a non-integer controller. *Electric Power Systems Research, 95*, 175–183. doi:10.1016/j.epsr.2012.09.008

Ebrahim, M. A., Mostafa, H. E., Gawish, S. A., & Bendary, F. M. (2009, November). Design of decentralized load frequency based-PID controller using stochastic particle swarm optimization technique. In *Electric Power and Energy Conversion Systems, 2009. EPECS'09. International Conference on* (pp. 1-6). IEEE.

Hsiao, Y. T., Chuang, C. L., & Chien, C. C. (2004, September). Ant colony optimization for designing of PID controllers. In *Computer Aided Control Systems Design, 2004 IEEE International Symposium on* (pp. 321-326). IEEE.

Jagatheesan, K., & Anand, B. (2012, December). Dynamic performance of multi-area hydro thermal power systems with integral controller considering various performance indices methods. In *Emerging Trends in Science, Engineering and Technology (INCOSET), 2012 International Conference on* (pp. 474-484). IEEE. doi:10.1109/INCOSET.2012.6513952

Jagatheesan, K., & Anand, B. (2014). Automatic generation control of three area hydro-thermal power systems considering electric and mechanical governor with conventional controller and ant colony optimization technique. *Advances in Natural and Applied Sciences, 8*(20), 25–34.

Jagatheesan, K., Anand, B., & Ebrahim, M. A. (2014). Stochastic particle swarm optimization for tuning of PID controller in load frequency control of single area reheat thermal power system. *International Journal of Electrical and Power Engineering, 8*(2), 33–40.

Joseph, R., Abraham, A., Das, D., & Patra, A. (2011). Damping oscillations in tie power and area frequencies in a thermal power system with SMES-TCPS combinations. *Journal of Electrical System, 1*(1), 71–80.

Moon, Y. H., Ryu, H. S., Kim, B., & Song, K. B. (2000). Optimal tracking approach to load frequency control in power systems. In *Power Engineering Society Winter Meeting, 2000. IEEE* (Vol. 2, pp. 1371-1376). IEEE.

Padhan, S., Sahu, R. K., & Panda, S. (2014). Automatic generation control with thyristor controlled series compensator including superconducting magnetic energy storage units. *Ain Shams Engineering Journal*, *5*(3), 759–774. doi:10.1016/j.asej.2014.03.011

Pothiya, S., Ngamroo, I., & Kongprawechnon, W. (2007, December). Design of optimal fuzzy logic-based PID controller using Multiple Tabu Search algorithm for AGC including SMES units. In *Power Engineering Conference, 2007. IPEC 2007. International* (pp. 838-843). IEEE.

Roy, A., Dutta, S., & Roy, P. K. (2014, January). Automatic generation control by SMES-SMES controllers of two-area hydro-hydro system. In *Non Conventional Energy (ICONCE), 2014 1st International Conference on* (pp. 302-307). IEEE. doi:10.1109/ICONCE.2014.6808731

Roy, R., Bhatt, P., & Ghoshal, S. P. (2010). Evolutionary computation based three-area automatic generation control. *Expert Systems with Applications*, *37*(8), 5913–5924. doi:10.1016/j.eswa.2010.02.014

Samanta, S., Acharjee, S., Mukherjee, A., Das, D., & Dey, N. (2013a, December). Ant weight lifting algorithm for image segmentation. In *Computational Intelligence and Computing Research (ICCIC), 2013 IEEE International Conference on* (pp. 1-5). doi:10.1109/ICCIC.2013.6724160

Samanta, S., Chakraborty, S., Acharjee, S., Mukherjee, A., & Dey, N. (2013b, December). Solving 0/1 knapsack problem using ant weight lifting algorithm. In *Computational Intelligence and Computing Research (ICCIC), 2013 IEEE International Conference on* (pp. 1-5). IEEE.

Taher, S. A., Fini, M. H., & Aliabadi, S. F. (2014). Fractional order PID controller design for LFC in electric power systems using imperialist competitive algorithm. *Ain Shams Engineering Journal*, *5*(1), 121–135. doi:10.1016/j.asej.2013.07.006

Tam, K. S., & Kumar, P. (1990). Application of superconductive magnetic energy storage in an asynchronous link between power systems. *IEEE Transactions on Energy Conversion*, *5*(3), 436–444. doi:10.1109/60.105266

Chapter 8

Meta–Heuristic Algorithms in Medical Image Segmentation:
A Review

Nilanjan Dey
Techno India College of Technology, India

Amira S. Ashour
Tanta University, Egypt

ABSTRACT

Artificial intelligence is the outlet of computer science apprehensive with creating computers that perform as humans. It compromises expert systems, playing games, natural language, and robotics. However, soft computing (SC) varies from the hard (conventional) computing in its tolerant of partial truth, uncertainty, imprecision, and approximation, thus, it models the human mind. The most common SC techniques include neural networks, fuzzy systems, machine learning, and the meta-heuristic stochastic algorithms (e.g., Cellular automata, ant colony optimization, Memetic algorithms, particle swarms, Tabu search, evolutionary computation and simulated annealing. Due to the required accurate diseases analysis, magnetic resonance imaging, computed tomography images and images of other modalities segmentation remains a challenging problem. Over the past years, soft computing approaches attract attention of several researchers for problems solving in medical data applications. Image segmentation is the process that partitioned an image into some groups based on similarity measures. This process is employed for abnormalities volumetric analysis in medical images to identify the disease nature. Recently, meta-heuristic algorithms are conducted to support the segmentation techniques. In the current chapter, different segmentation procedures are addressed. Several meta-heuristic approaches are reported with highlights on their procedures. Finally, several medical applications using meta-heuristic based-approaches for segmentation are discussed.

DOI: 10.4018/978-1-5225-4151-6.ch008

INTRODUCTION

Image analysis, pattern recognition, image disciplines are the foremost domains of computer engineering and computer science in several domains, such as medical, military, astronomy and real-world applications. In the medical applications, image-guided therapy is one of the vital methods for accurate diagnosis. Medical image computing has a rising prominence for medical diagnosis. Image analysis systems incorporating with innovative image computing procedures carried out to extract quantifiable parameters from the medical image in order to support the diagnosis and treatment. In order to achieve accurate clinical routine, automated and robust medical image computing techniques become an active research area. Model-based image analysis as well as image-based modelling methods becomes significant tools for accurate assessable analysis of the objects in the medical image. These methods require earlier information about the medical images' structures, including bones, tumours, tissue, vessels and organs. Afterward, the image-based modelling approaches applied to extract the significant features automatically. For complex visualization and quantitative measures, processing of digital indicative imaging data carried out to support disease progression monitoring, diagnosis and pre-operative planning. Nevertheless, successful image analysis requires optimized and complex processing systems, which is a challenging aspect. Currently, research in medical image analysis pursued by an ongoing stream of successful new clinical applications to achieve robust solutions based on computing techniques (Dey,& Ashour, 2016; Kotyk *et al.*, 2016; Saba *et al.* (2016); Ahmed *et al.*, 2017; Ashour *et al.*, 2016; Dey *et al.*, 2017).

Medical image segmentation and classification are considered the main image processing approaches. High soft tissue contrast of magnetic resonance (MR) images segmentation has a significant role for evaluating the brain tumors' therapy. Manual segmentation by physicians still the segmentation gold standard of atypical brain images, however, it is disposed to human bias/error as well as its tedious process. An endeavor for reliable computerization of medical image segmentation is consequently extremely desired. This leads to the necessity to used clustering algorithms to label the pixels of the medical image into a prearranged number of clusters, where the number of clusters is known a priori in most of the anatomic structures. Furthermore, medical image classification is extensively used to discriminate the abnormal and normal images. Automated classification process is highly desired to support the physicians in the analysis monotonous task.

Artificial intelligence and soft computing play a significant role in several applications (Mhetre *et al.*, 2016; Bureš *et al.*, 2016; Boulmaiz *et al.*, 2017; Acharjya, & Anitha, 2017; Sharma, & Virmani, 2017; Manogaran, & Lopez, 2017). Computing algorithms have an imperative role in medical image analysis and processing to solve the inherent uncertainties in the captured medical image data. Recently, researchers developed fuzzy methods for image segmentation, fuzzy clustering approaches, and fuzzy methods for object delineation and recognition (Pham *et al.*, 2000). Generally, computing methods comprise support vector machines, neural networks, fuzzy logic, probabilistic methods, chaos theory and evolutional computation. Medical image computing improves mathematical and computational approaches to solve related problems to medical images (Chan, T. F., & Shen, 2005). Clinically, the chief objective of the medical image computing is the extraction of relevant information from medical images. Medical image computing focuses on the images computational analysis. Generally, medical image computing methods can categorize into image segmentation-, image classification-, and image registration-based computational techniques. Typically, medical image computing works on sampled data with consistent spatial space. The data under concern is based on the used modality, namely, Computed Radiography (CT), magnetic resonance imaging (MRI), functional MRI (fMRI), X-ray, optical coherence tomography (OCT), positron emission tomography (PET), Single photon emisson computed tomography (SPECT), SPECT-CT, PET-MRI, and PET-CT. These imaging modalities capture images of the different human organs (Ahmad *et al.*, 2014). Recently, numerous meta-heuristic optimization algorithms have been developed and involved is several medical and real applications, namely cuckoo search (CS), Particle swarm optimization (PSO), genetic algorithms (GA), and Firefly algorithm (FA) (Samanta *et al.*, 2016; Satapathy *et al.*, 2016; Dey *et al.*, 2016b; Chakraborty *et al.*, 2017).

MEDICAL IMAGE SEGMENTATION TECHNIQUES

Automation of image processing and analysis techniques is compulsory to to assist physicians in treatment planning and clinical diagnosis. Consistent algorithms are mandatory for the delineation of regions of interest (ROI) and the anatomical structures. Subsequently, computer-aided diagnosis (CAD) developed to acquire accurate medical images analysis process, to achieve fast results using high-speed computers and to support information technology for faster communication with patients at remote areas. Medical images segmentation techniques are specific to the used imaging modality, the application under concern, and type of the considered body part. However, there is no universal segmentation algorithm that used efficiently with all medical image types, where each imaging modality has its own definite limits.

Segmentation defined as the process of allotting an image into several regions having similar properties, including color, gray level, contrast brightness, and texture. Its basic role in the medical domain is to identify the ROI, such as lesion, tumor, and any abnormalities, to study the anatomical structures, to measure the tissue volume and to assist treatment planning. Automated medical images segmentation is complex; in addition, the inhomogeneous intensity, low contrast, partial volume effect, artifacts and the close gray level values of the different soft tissues affect the segmented images. Consequently, several segmentation techniques have been employed in the medical applications, which can be categorized into i) Shape-based segmentation, ii) interactive segmentation, iii) atlas-based segmentation and iv) shape-based segmentation. Another classification of the segmentation techniques is as follows, i) histogram based segmentation, region based segmentation and edge based segmentation, which based on the gray level features, and ii) texture features based segmentation (Heimann *et al.*, 2009).

Histogram Based Segmentation

Histogram based segmentation depends mainly on a thresholding value of the histogram. This technique used with uniform brightness regions within the image under consideration, where the threshold is employed to segment the ROI and background. The threshold can have single value or multiple values based on the number of ROI within the image (Tobias, & Seara, 2002). Several computing algorithms are used to perform thresholding segmentation effectively. Commonly, the whole image is scanned pixel by pixel to label the pixels into object or the background based on the gray level value compared to the thresholding function (T). The main steps of the global thresholding are as follows (Algorithm 1).

Algorithm 1. Global thresholding algorithm

Start
Chose an initial threshold value T
Apply T to segment the image leading to two groups of pixels
  R_1 are pixels with gray level $>T$
  R_2 are pixels with gray level $<=T$
Measure the average gray level values $mean_1$ and $mean_2$ for the pixels in R_1 and R_2.
Calculate the new threshold value $T_{new} = (mean_1 + mean_2)/2$
Repeat the previous steps till the difference in T is smaller than a pre-defined threshold T_0 in the successive iterations
  End

Region-Based Segmentation

In region-based segmentation, the main goal is to partition the image into dissimilar regions to determine the images' disjoint regions directly. Region split and merge segmentation as well as region growing segmentation are the major region-based segmentation techniques (Salembier, & Marqués, 1999). The main steps of the region-based segmentation are as follows (Algorithm 2).

Split and Merge Segmentation

Split and merge based segmentation depends on the quad quadrant tree data depiction, where the image segment is divided into four quadrants providing the non-uniform original segment. Afterward, the 4 neighboring squares are fused based on the segments uniformity (Freixenet *et al.*, 2002). This split/merge process is iterative and repeated until all possible split/merge occur using the following steps (Algorithm 3).

Edge-Based Segmentation

Edge-based segmentation is considered one of the vital segmentation methods, where edges embrace much information about the image. Edges represent the boundaries between any two dissimilar regions that provide information about the objects location, their size/shape, and their texture (Tsai *et al.*, 2003). Thus, the gradient can be calculated to determine the pixel values differences between the regions

Algorithm 2. Region-based segmentation algorithm (region growing)

```
Start
Merge iteratively an initial small area set based on similarity
Select an arbitrary pixel
Compare the arbitrary pixel with the neighboring pixel
  Add similar neighboring pixels that increase the region size
from the seed pixel
If one region growth stops
  Select another seed pixel that does not belong to any region
  Repeat
Endif
Repeat the whole process until all pixels fit some region
End
```

Algorithm 3. Split and merge segmentation algorithm

```
Start
Delineate homogeneity criterion.
Divide the image into 4 square quadrants
If inhomogeneous square result
    Split it further into 4 quadrants
Endif
Merge the two or more neighbouring regions that satisfy the
homogeneity condition at each level
Continue the split/merge until no further split/merge of region
is possible
End
```

at which the image intensity changes from high value to low value or vice versa. Hough transform based, border detection, edge relaxation are different methods of edge-based segmentation (Algorithm 4).

META-HEURISTIC

Global optimization (GO) algorithm is applied to find the global optimum of a fitness function in the search space. It has applications in several domains, including healthcare, economics, and engineering. The GO algorithms have two sets, namely evolutionary and deterministic. The deterministic approaches locate the local minimums of the fitness function, while the evolutionary procedures activate over the candidate solutions population, thus, can localize the global optimum faster than the deterministic ones. Recently, meta-heuristic (MHs) algorithms are applied for

Algorithm 4. Edge-based segmentation algorithm

```
Start
Use the derivative of the image for detecting the edges
Measure the gradient amplitude to calculate the edges strength
Preserve all edge with greater magnitude than a threshold T
Determine the crack edges
Repeat the previous two steps with different threshold values
to realize the closed boundaries
End
```

optimization, however, such approaches still deliberated as an open research problem due to several complexities, including the overcoming of the local optimum and the premature convergence (Voß *et al.,* 2012).

Metaheuristics are defined as a stochastic optimization procedure that use brute-force or random search to find the optimal solutions of the problems under consideration. The algorithmic MHs family includes simulated annealing, genetic algorithms, ant colony optimization, hill-climbing, and particle swarm optimization. The foremost aim of the MHs' learning/optimization algorithms is to realize a trade-off between diversification and intensification, where the exploration (diversification) denotes creating different solutions in order to discover the search space on a global scale, whereas, the exploitation (intensification) entails directing the search onto a local region at which good solutions have been established. These optimization algorithms have common characteristics, such as i) reliable and robust, ii) implied parallelism, iii) easy implementation, iv) approximate and non-deterministic, v) explore efficiently search spaces, and vi) global search ability. MHs techniques can categorize into, Memetic algorithms, Population-based methods, and Trajectory methods (Onwubolu, & Babu, 2013).

Memetic algorithms are hybrid local/global search approaches, where a local enhancement procedure is integrated into a population-based procedure (Moscato, & Cotta, 2003). The basic concept is to emulate the social interaction/learning effect of the individuals by a local enhancement procedures smeared to the established solutions by the global search operators. Thus, memetic algorithms contain a virtual several potential hybridizations of prevailing approaches. Population-based approaches handle a solutions' population in every iteration of the procedure. The search procedure can be considered as the progress in discrete time of a points' set of in the solution space. Such algorithms include genetic algorithms, evolutionary programming, evolution algorithms, and swarm intelligence techniques (e.g. particle swarm optimization). Generally, swarm intelligence approaches imitate the collective activities of dispersed, self-organized artificial systems at which global search is an evolving actions of the agents' population. Furthermore, the evolutionary algorithms depend on a computational model that imitates appliances inspired by the biological evolution, namely reproduction, mutation, recombination, and selection, in order to solve the optimization problems.

The most recent and popular procedure for continuous optimization is the differential evolution that inherits its characteristics from both the swarm intelligence algorithms and the evolutionary algorithms (Qin *et al.*, 2009). Moreover, the trajectory procedures can be considered as the evolution algorithms in the discrete time of a distinct dynamical system. In such algorithms, the search process designates a trajectory in the search space. Tabu search, iterated local search, variable neighborhood search and the simulated annealing are several types of the trajectory procedures

(Osman, & Christofides, 1994). Generally, each MHs category include a huge number of methods. Generally, the most prevalent swarm inspired algorithms are Bee colony optimization, ant colony optimization, particle swarm optimization, bacteria optimization algorithm, firefly algorithm, and cuckoo search algorithms.

Genetic Algorithm

The GA is a search procedure for optimizing common combinational problems. It is one of the most prevalent evolutionary algorithms that inspired by the evolution Darwins theory (i.e. survival of the fitness) to solve difficult optimization problems. A solution in the GA is called individual, while the term populations are used to refer to set of individuals (Leung, & Wang, 2001). The GA operators are the selection, cross over and mutation, where the selection associates to the fitness survival, the cross over signifies the mating between individuals, and the mutation presents random modifications. The genetic algorithm steps are as follows (Algorithm 5).

Algorithm 5. Genetic Algorithm

```
    Start
    Produce random population of n suitable solutions
(chromosomes)
        Assess the fitness f(x) of each solution in the population
            Generate a new population by reciting following
phases until completing the new population
            Choose from the population, two parent chromosomes
based on their fitness (Selection)
            Cross over the parents with a crossover probability
to form a new offspring (Crossover)
            Mutate new offspring with a mutation probability at
each position in the chromosome (Mutation)
            Place in a new population, new offspring
    Use new produced population
    Test if the end condition is satisfied
    stop, and return the best solution
    Repeat the previous steps
End
```

Particle Swarm Optimization

The PSO is one of the contemporary meta-heuristic population-based stochastic optimization that carried out to non- continuous and non-linear optimization problems. It delivers an evolutionary based search to discover the near optimal/ optimal solutions. The PSO behavior is envisioned from the searching strategy for optimal food sources by the bird swarms. The bird movement direction is influenced by its present movement to find the best food source. Typically, the birds are motivated by their personal knowledge, inertia, and the swarm knowledge. Thus, in the PSO algorithm, the particle movement is affected by its personal-/ global- best position, and its inertia (Eberhart, & Kennedy, 1995). The PSO algorithm consists of multiple particles, where each has its position, velocity and current objective value. It preserves the global best value, which is related to the best objective value, and the global best position at which the global best value achieved. The PSO algorithm consists of the following repeated steps until the pre-determined stopping condition is achieved (Algorithm 6).

Ant Colony Optimization

The ACO meta-heuristic algorithm is a modern population-based approach enthused by the real ants colony collective foraging behavior. The real ants capability to find the shortest path from a food source toward their nest is the main inspiration of the ACO. In ACO, a pheromone trail is known as the ants' movement in a straight line that joins the food source to their nests to obtain optimum value from a population. Problem solutions are constructed in a stochastic iterative process, where each individual ant creates a part of the solution using a pheromone (Dorigo *et al.*, 2006).

Algorithm 6. Particle Swarm Optimization

```
Start
Initialize the position and velocity of the particles
Determine stopping criteria
Assess the fitness of each particle using the objective
function
Update the individual/global best positions and finesses
Update position and velocity of each particle
Stop
```

Bat Optimization Algorithm

The BAT algorithm is based on the echolocation bats' behavior. The ability of microbats echolocation is attractive, where the bats can discover their prey and distinguish different insects' types even in complete darkness. This bats' behavior inspired the BAT algorithm based on the echolocation microbats' characteristics. Some realization rules are used in the BAT algorithm, namely i) all to sense distance, background barriers, and dissimilarity between prey/food, bats use echolocation, ii) bats fly randomly with certain velocity at specific position with a fixed frequency but varying wavelength to search for prey, and iii) the loudness changes from a large to a minimum constant value (Yang, 2010). The inclusive pseudocode of the BAT algorithm is as follows (Algorithm 7).

SEGMENTATION ALGORITHMS FOR MEDICAL IMAGES

Segmentation is an essential technique in medical image processing to extract suspicious regions from a medical image. Recently, several researches are interested in different organs segmentation in medical images (Pham *et al.*, 2000). Prevalent procedures using supervised algorithms include active appearance models (AAM), supervised support vector machine (SVMs), and artificial neural network (ANNs) are considered for medical image processing, which require training set. The ANNs and SVMs are non-linear statistical data exhibiting methods for modelling complex

Algorithm 7. Particle Swarm Optimization

```
Start
Delineate the initial population and velocities vector
Chose a pulse frequency, rates and loudness
Do until get to number of iterations
     Compute new solutions via frequency
     Update velocity and location for each particle (bat)
     Produce a random value and compare to
     If a solution is the best solutions, a new local solution
is produced
     Use a random bat's fly to generate a new solution
     Re-evaluate all particles to determine the current new
best
End
```

associations between inputs and outputs. The classifiers' weights are chosen using optimizing the energy function distinct by the features of organs, structures, cells, etc. These weights reorganized through handling each sample in the training set. Thus, meta-heuristic can be involved for optimal weights selection. From the training set, the extracted information offers essential cues of the structures, including shape, position and intensity that can be valued corresponding information for the test images segmentation. However, the AAM are statistical models of the structures' shape, where the training samples are employed to extract the shape parameters' ranges, mean appearance and mean shape. In order to ensure the similarity between the segmentation result and the training samples, restrictions on shape parameters is required, where the segmentation technique is to find the superior locations of the shape points based on the appearance information. Consequently, in medical images, the algorithms established on classifiers can be widely applied to segment organs, such as the brain and cardiac images.

Meta-Heuristic Based Segmentation of Magnetic Resonance Images

Brain tumor occurs when infrequent cells shape appear inside the cerebrum, which has two main types, namely benign tumors and harmful tumors. Malignant tumors can be categorized into basic tumors, and secondary tumors that spread elsewhere. Currently, the MRI is one of the unsurpassed technologies for brain tumor diagnosis. In addition, segmentation has a significant role to extract suspicious areas from complex brain medical images. Automated brain tumor detection through MRI can offer valued outlook and earlier accurate detection of the brain tumor. Gopal, N. N., & Karnan (2010) designed an intelligent system for brain tumor diagnosis through MRI exhausting image processing clustering procedures, namely Fuzzy-C Means along with optimization intelligent algorithms, including Particle Swarm Optimization (PSO), and Genetic Algorithm (GA). The tumor detection has been performed in several stages, namely enhancement, segmentation and classification.

Karnan, & Logheshwari (2010) employed a recent population-based approach, namely the Ant Colony Optimization (ACO) meta-heuristic, which is stimulated real ants colony and their collective foraging performance. The authors proposed hybrid technique of the ACO with Fuzzy segmentation. Initially, the MRI brain image has been segmented using the proposed approach to extract the suspicious region. Afterward, the pixel similarity and tumor position of the proposed segmented process and the radiologist report compared. Hamdaoui *et al.* (2014) compared the performance of two meta-heuristic swarm intelligence methods, namely the PSO and Shuffled Frog Leaping Algorithm (SFLA) for MR brain medical images segmentation. The performance of the Modified PSO (MPSO) and Modified SFLA

(MSFLA) techniques has been investigated through the segmentation process that consists of dividing an image into two regions.

Ladgham *et al.*, (2015) proposed a new meta-heuristic algorithm, called the modified Shuffled Frog Leaping algorithm (MSFLA) for fast MR brain image segmentation. The MSFLA allow the segmentation process without using de-noising filter. A new fitness function has been used to quickly evaluate the particle frogs to arrange them in descendent order. The results included a comparative study with other meta-heuristic for segmentation, namely Genetic Algorithm (GA), and 3D-Otsu thresholding with SFLA. It has been established that the proposed MSFLA is capable to realize superior segmentation quality with less execution time compared to the use of GA or the SFLA.

Si *et al.* (2015) proposed a novel segmentation method of MRI brain tumor images. Entropy maximization using Grammatical Swarm (GS) algorithm has been applied to attain a threshold values set. A threshold value is then selected with the expert knowledge to isolate the lesion part from the non-diseased cells in the image. A discrete wavelet transform (DWT)-based soft-thresholding procedure has been carried out to remove the noise form the MRI images. Afterward, intensity inhomogeneity (IIH) noise independent has been removed, followed by DWT to sharpen the IIH corrected and de-noised images. The wavelet decomposition has been used to decompose the image into first level and approximate values. The detailed image has been added with the pre-processed image to yield sharpened image.

Quantitative assessment of MRI lesion load of patients with multiple sclerosis is vital for a better understanding of the pathology history as well as for natural/ modified therapies. Numerous methods have been conducted for the MS lesions segmentation in MR images. Zangeneh, & Yazdi (2016) employed a constrained Gaussian Mixture Model (GMM) and GA to define the optimal highly non-linear model's parameters for the segmentation process. A pre-processing step has been executed for artifacts suppression and unwanted skull portions removal from the brain MRI. The proposed technique has been evaluated on real MR images proving the efficiency of the proposed method for segmenting the MS lesions in the MR images.

Meta-Heuristic Based Segmentation of Computed Tomography Images

For CT medical image segmentation, Bruyninckx et al. (2010) proposed an algorithm for segmenting the liver portal veins from an arterial stage. Using minimal mechanical energy, the physiological model stated that the vasculature pattern is arranged such that the entire organ is perfused. In the image, the proposed method has been locally detecting the possible candidate vessel segments. The segments subset that produces the most plausible vessel tree based on the physiological model and the image is subsequently sought by a global optimization technique. From CT images, the proposed technique has been applied for segmenting the lung vessel trees. In addition, a SVM has been used to cope with the low contrast to locally detect vessels. This proposed model can be applied to the liver, lungs, and kidney.

Bong *et al.* (2012) proposed a multi-objective clustering ensemble technique, called adaptive multi-objective archive-based hybrid scatter search (AMAHSS) to segment lung CT images for candidate nodule detection. Fuzzy clustering has been used with optimization of three objective functions, namely symmetry distance-based cluster validity index, global fuzzy clusters compactness, and fuzzy separation. The proposed AMAHSS empowers the search scheme to explore the search space to find the optimal solutions. The optimal solution is determined using the meta-clustering procedure. The results established that the proposed algorithm achieved positive predictive rate of 90%.

Active Contour Models (ACMs) has superior performance compared to the traditional low-level method to segment ill-defined medical images. However, it is sensitive to the contour initial position and the setup in the local minima. Sahoo, & Chandra (2013) considered the ACM based segmentation as an optimization problem find a minimal energy contour. A nature-inspired meta-heuristic procedure, namely the L'evy flight firefly algorithm (LFA) has been employed effectively to solve the global optimization problems. Thus, a hybrid technique based on integrating the ACM with LFA has been designed to improve its segmentation capability of real abdomen CT images.

Ramakrishnan, & Sankaragomathi (2017) proposed a technique for classifying CT images into tumor and the non-tumor images followed by the tumor region segmentation in CT images has been performed. The classification process has been carried out using SVM with different kernel functions and optimization procedures. The Sequential Minimal Optimization (SMO) based SVM classifier has a significant role. Modified Region Growing (MRG) based on threshold optimization has been applied for the segmentation process after the classification. Grey Wolf Optimization (GWO), Evolutionary Programming (EP) and Harmony Search (HS) have been used for threshold optimization. The experimental results reported 99.05% accuracy of the segmentation process using the GWO algorithm. It has been established that the proposed MRG-GWO achieved high accuracy with superior tumor detection compared to the HS and EP.

Liver segmentation is a challenging initial stage of liver diagnosis due to its likeness with other structures in terms of the intensity values. For liver image segmentation of the abdomen CT images, Mostafa et al. (2017) proposed a grey wolf optimization based approach. This approach carried out the grey wolf optimization, simple region growing, statistical image of liver, and Mean shift clustering method. Grey Wolf (GW) optimization algorithm has been applied on the pre-processed image to calculate the centroids of a pre-defined number of clusters. In the image, according to the intensity value of each pixel, the number of the nearest cluster has labeled the pixel. In order to extract the probable area of the liver, a binary liver statistical image has been used. Lastly, the mean shift clustering procedure has been applied to extract the ROI in the segmented liver.

CONCLUSION

In the medical domain, MRI, CT and other modalities are conducted to distinguish pathological tissues from normal ones, and to acquire images of the different body parts for further analysis and processing. Image segmentation is the most significant pre-processing task for several computer aided medical imaging applications. From MRI data, Tumor segmentation is considered an imperative process, while it is time consuming if accomplished manually. Thus, automated image analysis becomes essential to facilitate image-based diagnosis. In computer-aided systems, the analysed computer-based are used to support the radiologists and physicians in diagnosis in a faster mode. The current chapter reported different meta-heuristic approaches and their uses in the MRI and CT images segmentation, including Genetic Algorithm, Particle Swarm Optimization, Ant Colony Optimization, and Artificial Bee Colony Optimization (ABCO). These optimization algorithms are carried out to obtain the optimal parameters required during the segmentation process, where different segmentation methodologies are explained.

REFERENCES

Acharjya, D., & Anitha, A. (2017). A Comparative Study of Statistical and Rough Computing Models in Predictive Data Analysis. *International Journal of Ambient Computing and Intelligence*, 8(2), 32–51. doi:10.4018/IJACI.2017040103

Ahmad, H. A., Yu, H. J., & Miller, C. G. (2014). Medical imaging modalities. In *Medical Imaging in Clinical Trials* (pp. 3–26). Springer London. doi:10.1007/978-1-84882-710-3_1

Ahmed, S. S., Dey, N., Ashour, A. S., Sifaki-Pistolla, D., Bǎlas-Timar, D., Balas, V. E., & Tavares, J. M. R. (2017). Effect of fuzzy partitioning in Crohns disease classification: A neuro-fuzzy-based approach. *Medical & Biological Engineering & Computing*, 55(1), 101–115. doi:10.1007/s11517-016-1508-7 PMID:27106754

Ashour, A. S., Beagum, S., Dey, N., Ashour, A. S., Pistolla, D. S., Nguyen, G. N., & Shi, F. et al. (2016). Light microscopy image de-noising using optimized LPA-ICI filter. *Neural Computing & Applications*, 1–17.

Bong, C. W., Lam, H. Y., Khader, A. T., & Kamarulzaman, H. (2012). Adaptive multi-objective archive-based hybrid scatter search for segmentation in lung computed tomography imaging. *Engineering Optimization*, *44*(3), 327–350. doi:10.1080/03 05215X.2011.639369

Boulmaiz, A., Messadeg, D., Doghmane, N., & Taleb-Ahmed, A. (2017). Design and Implementation of a Robust Acoustic Recognition System for Waterbird Species using TMS320C6713 DSK. *International Journal of Ambient Computing and Intelligence*, *8*(1), 98–118. doi:10.4018/IJACI.2017010105

Bruyninckx, P., Loeckx, D., Vandermeulen, D., & Suetens, P. (2010, March). Segmentation of liver portal veins by global optimization. In *SPIE Medical Imaging* (pp. 76241Z–76241Z). International Society for Optics and Photonics. doi:10.1117/12.843995

Bureš, V., Tučník, P., Mikulecký, P., Mls, K., & Blecha, P. (2016). Application of ambient intelligence in educational institutions: Visions and architectures. *International Journal of Ambient Computing and Intelligence*, *7*(1), 94–120. doi:10.4018/IJACI.2016010105

Chakraborty, S., Chatterjee, S., Dey, N., Ashour, A. S., Ashour, A. S., Shi, F., & Mali, K. (2017). Modified cuckoo search algorithm in microscopic image segmentation of hippocampus. *Microscopy Research and Technique*. doi:10.1002/jemt.22900 PMID:28557041

Chan, T. F., & Shen, J. (2005). *Image processing and analysis: variational, PDE, wavelet, and stochastic methods*. Society for Industrial and Applied Mathematics. doi:10.1137/1.9780898717877

Dey, N., & Ashour, A. S. (Eds.). (2016). *Classification and clustering in biomedical signal processing*. IGI Global. doi:10.4018/978-1-5225-0140-4

Dey, N., Ashour, A. S., & Althoupety, A. S. (2017a). Thermal Imaging in Medical Science. In *Recent Advances in Applied Thermal Imaging for Industrial Applications* (pp. 87–117). IGI Global. doi:10.4018/978-1-5225-2423-6.ch004

Dey, N., Ashour, A. S., Chakraborty, S., Samanta, S., Sifaki-Pistolla, D., Ashour, A. S., & Nguyen, G. N. et al. (2016b). Healthy and unhealthy rat hippocampus cells classification: A neural based automated system for Alzheimer disease classification. *Journal of Advanced Microscopy Research*, *11*(1), 1–10. doi:10.1166/jamr.2016.1282

Dorigo, M., Birattari, M., & Stutzle, T. (2006). Ant colony optimization. *IEEE Computational Intelligence Magazine, 1*(4), 28–39. doi:10.1109/MCI.2006.329691

Eberhart, R., & Kennedy, J. (1995, October). A new optimizer using particle swarm theory. In *Micro Machine and Human Science, 1995. MHS'95., Proceedings of the Sixth International Symposium on* (pp. 39-43). IEEE. doi:10.1109/MHS.1995.494215

Freixenet, J., Muñoz, X., Raba, D., Martí, J., & Cufí, X. (2002). Yet another survey on image segmentation: Region and boundary information integration. *Computer Vision—ECCV 2002*, 21-25.

Gopal, N. N., & Karnan, M. (2010, December). Diagnose brain tumor through MRI using image processing clustering algorithms such as Fuzzy C Means along with intelligent optimization techniques. In *Computational Intelligence and Computing Research (ICCIC), 2010 IEEE International Conference on* (pp. 1-4). IEEE. doi:10.1109/ICCIC.2010.5705890

Hamdaoui, F., Mtibaa, A., & Sakly, A. (2014, December). Comparison between MPSO and MSFLA metaheuristics for MR brain image segmentation. In *Sciences and Techniques of Automatic Control and Computer Engineering (STA), 2014 15th International Conference on* (pp. 164-168). IEEE. doi:10.1109/STA.2014.7086725

Heimann, T., Van Ginneken, B., Styner, M. A., Arzhaeva, Y., Aurich, V., Bauer, C., & Bello, F. et al. (2009). Comparison and evaluation of methods for liver segmentation from CT datasets. *IEEE Transactions on Medical Imaging, 28*(8), 1251–1265. doi:10.1109/TMI.2009.2013851 PMID:19211338

Karnan, M., & Logheshwari, T. (2010, December). Improved implementation of brain MRI image segmentation using ant colony system. In *Computational Intelligence and Computing Research (ICCIC), 2010 IEEE International Conference on* (pp. 1-4). IEEE. doi:10.1109/ICCIC.2010.5705897

Kotyk, T., Dey, N., Ashour, A. S., Balas-Timar, D., Chakraborty, S., Ashour, A. S., & Tavares, J. M. R. (2016). Measurement of glomerulus diameter and Bowmans space width of renal albino rats. *Computer Methods and Programs in Biomedicine, 126*, 143–153. doi:10.1016/j.cmpb.2015.10.023 PMID:26796351

Ladgham, A., Hamdaoui, F., Sakly, A., & Mtibaa, A. (2015). Fast MR brain image segmentation based on modified Shuffled Frog Leaping Algorithm. *Signal. Image and Video Processing, 9*(5), 1113–1120. doi:10.1007/s11760-013-0546-y

Leung, Y. W., & Wang, Y. (2001). An orthogonal genetic algorithm with quantization for global numerical optimization. *IEEE Transactions on Evolutionary Computation, 5*(1), 41–53. doi:10.1109/4235.910464

Manogaran, G., & Lopez, D. (2017). Disease surveillance system for big climate data processing and dengue transmission. *International Journal of Ambient Computing and Intelligence*, 8(2), 88–105. doi:10.4018/IJACI.2017040106

Mhetre, N. A., Deshpande, A. V., & Mahalle, P. N. (2016). Trust Management Model based on Fuzzy Approach for Ubiquitous Computing. *International Journal of Ambient Computing and Intelligence*, 7(2), 33–46. doi:10.4018/IJACI.2016070102

Moscato, P., & Cotta, C. (2003). A gentle introduction to memetic algorithms. In Handbook of metaheuristics (pp. 105-144). Springer US. doi:10.1007/0-306-48056-5_5

Mostafa, A., Hassanien, A. E., & Hefny, H. A. (2017). Grey Wolf Optimization-Based Segmentation Approach for Abdomen CT Liver Images. In *Handbook of Research on Machine Learning Innovations and Trends* (pp. 562–581). IGI Global. doi:10.4018/978-1-5225-2229-4.ch024

Onwubolu, G. C., & Babu, B. V. (2013). *New optimization techniques in engineering* (Vol. 141). Springer.

Osman, I. H., & Christofides, N. (1994). Capacitated clustering problems by hybrid simulated annealing and tabu search. *International Transactions in Operational Research*, 1(3), 317–336. doi:10.1016/0969-6016(94)90032-9

Pham, D. L., Xu, C., & Prince, J. L. (2000). Current methods in medical image segmentation 1. *Annual Review of Biomedical Engineering*, 2(1), 315–337. doi:10.1146/annurev.bioeng.2.1.315 PMID:11701515

Pham, D. L., Xu, C., & Prince, J. L. (2000). Current methods in medical image segmentation 1. *Annual Review of Biomedical Engineering*, 2(1), 315–337. doi:10.1146/annurev.bioeng.2.1.315 PMID:11701515

Qin, A. K., Huang, V. L., & Suganthan, P. N. (2009). Differential evolution algorithm with strategy adaptation for global numerical optimization. *IEEE Transactions on Evolutionary Computation*, 13(2), 398–417. doi:10.1109/TEVC.2008.927706

Ramakrishnan, T., & Sankaragomathi, B. (2017). A professional estimate on the computed tomography brain tumor images using SVM-SMO for classification and MRG-GWO for segmentation. *Pattern Recognition Letters*, 94, 163–171. doi:10.1016/j.patrec.2017.03.026

Saba, L., Dey, N., Ashour, A. S., Samanta, S., Nath, S. S., Chakraborty, S., & Suri, J. S. et al. (2016). Automated stratification of liver disease in ultrasound: An online accurate feature classification paradigm. *Computer Methods and Programs in Biomedicine, 130,* 118–134. doi:10.1016/j.cmpb.2016.03.016 PMID:27208527

Sahoo, A., & Chandra, S. (2013, August). L'evy-flight firefly algorithm based active contour model for medical image segmentation. In *Contemporary Computing (IC3), 2013 Sixth International Conference on* (pp. 159-162). IEEE. doi:10.1109/IC3.2013.6612181

Salembier, P., & Marqués, F. (1999). Region-based representations of image and video: Segmentation tools for multimedia services. *IEEE Transactions on Circuits and Systems for Video Technology, 9*(8), 1147–1169. doi:10.1109/76.809153

Samanta, S., Choudhury, A., Dey, N., Ashour, A. S., & Balas, V. E. (2016). *Quantum inspired evolutionary algorithm for scaling factors optimization during manifold medical information embedding. InQuantum Inspired Computational intelligence: Research and Applications.* Elsevier.

Satapathy, S. C., Raja, N. S. M., Rajinikanth, V., Ashour, A. S., & Dey, N. (2016). Multi-level image thresholding using Otsu and chaotic bat algorithm. *Neural Computing & Applications,* 1–23.

Sharma, K., & Virmani, J. (2017). A Decision Support System for Classification of Normal and Medical Renal Disease Using Ultrasound Images: A Decision Support System for Medical Renal Diseases. *International Journal of Ambient Computing and Intelligence, 8*(2), 52–69. doi:10.4018/IJACI.2017040104

Si, T., De, A., & Bhattacharjee, A. K. (2015). Brain MRI segmentation for tumor detection via entropy maximization using Grammatical Swarm. *International Journal of Wavelets, Multresolution, and Information Processing, 13*(05), 1550039. doi:10.1142/S0219691315500393

Tobias, O. J., & Seara, R. (2002). Image segmentation by histogram thresholding using fuzzy sets. *IEEE Transactions on Image Processing, 11*(12), 1457–1465. doi:10.1109/TIP.2002.806231 PMID:18249714

Tsai, A., Yezzi, A., Wells, W., Tempany, C., Tucker, D., Fan, A., & Willsky, A. et al. (2003). A shape-based approach to the segmentation of medical imagery using level sets. *IEEE Transactions on Medical Imaging, 22*(2), 137–154. doi:10.1109/TMI.2002.808355 PMID:12715991

Voß, S., Martello, S., Osman, I. H., & Roucairol, C. (Eds.). (2012). *Meta-heuristic: Advances and trends in local search paradigms for optimization.* Springer Science & Business Media.

Yang, X. S. (2010). A new metaheuristic bat-inspired algorithm. *Nature inspired cooperative strategies for optimization (NICSO 2010)*, 65-74.

Zangeneh, D., & Yazdi, M. (2016, May). Automatic segmentation of multiple sclerosis lesions in brain MRI using constrained GMM and genetic algorithm. In *Electrical Engineering (ICEE), 2016 24th Iranian Conference on* (pp. 832-837). IEEE. doi:10.1109/IranianCEE.2016.7585635

Section 2

Genetic Algorithm Applications

Chapter 9

Optimized Crossover JumpX in Genetic Algorithm for General Routing Problems:
A Crossover Survey and Enhancement

Hicham El Hassani
ENSEM Casablanca, Morocco

Said Benkachcha
ENSEM Casablanca, Morocco

Jamal Benhra
ENSEM Casablanca, Morocco

ABSTRACT

Inspired by nature, genetic algorithms (GA) are among the greatest meta-heuristics optimization methods that have proved their effectiveness to conventional NP-hard problems, especially the traveling salesman problem (TSP) which is one of the most studied Supply chain management problems. This paper proposes a new crossover operator called Jump Crossover (JMPX) for solving the travelling salesmen problem using a genetic algorithm (GA) for near-optimal solutions, to conclude on its efficiency compared to solutions quality given by other conventional operators to the same problem, namely, Partially matched crossover (PMX), Edge recombination Crossover (ERX) and r-opt heuristic with consideration of computational overload. We adopt the path representation technique for our chromosome which is the most direct representation and a low mutation rate to isolate the search space exploration ability of each crossover. The experimental results show that in most cases JMPX can remarkably improve the solution quality of the GA compared to the two existing classic crossover approaches and the r-opt heuristic.

DOI: 10.4018/978-1-5225-4151-6.ch009

INTRODUCTION

NP-hard problems generally require exponential time depending on the problem size to find exact optimal solutions. This is why many metaheuristics are used to obtain approximate solutions to problems of such difficulty.To legitimate using metaheuristics to solve an optimization problem, a complexity analysis of a problem can be driven to give an indication on the hardness of the problem. It is also important to know the size of input instances the algorithm is supposed to solve. Even if a problem is NP-hard, small instances or even large-size instances with a specific structure may be solved in optimality by exact approach. Moreover, the required search time to solve a given problem is an important issue in the selection of an optimization algorithm. It is unwise to use metaheuristics to solve problems where efficient exact algorithms are available. For instance, one should not use a metaheuristic to find a minimum spanning tree or a shortest path in a graph. Known polynomial-time exact algorithms exist for those problems.

There are several powerful optimization techniques that are inspired by nature. Evolutionary algorithms (EAs) have been developed based on the principles of natural genetics to perform research and optimization in complex spaces. The most important components of the Evolutionary algorithms family are: Genetic Algorithms, Genetic Programming and Evolutionary Strategies.

Various other bio-inspired research and optimization techniqueswhich was created, developed, hybridized, enhanced and used in numerous fields of optimization, such as Particle Swarm Optimization (PSO) in (Shweta & Kamal, 2014; Soleimani & Kannan, 2015; Wang, Ma, Xu, Liu, & Wang, 2015), Ant Colony Optimization (ACO) in (Ahmed Hamza, Ahmad Taher, & Aboul Ella, 2014), A.hamza developed a New Heuristic Function, Differential Evolution (DE) in (Zhu, Fang, Tang, Zhang, & Du, 2012), Artificial Bee Colony (ABC) in (Rahul, Senthilnath, Omkar, & Narendra, 2016), Cuckoo Search and Chaotic Flower Pollination optimization algorithm in(Binh, Hanh, Van Quan, & Dey, 2016),(Dey, Samanta, Yang, Das, & Chaudhuri, 2013), (Ashour et al., 2015), Firefly algorithmin (Dey, Samanta, et al., 2014),Neural Networks in (Hore et al., 2017), and Simulated Annealing in (Bouttier et al., 2017), are also classified among the metaheuristics techniques. In (Reza, 2016), a new Meta heuristic algorithm inspired of the biologic nephron performance for optimization of objective functions in Np-hard problems is introduced (NAO).In (Dey, Chakraborty, & Samanta, 2014) the author is using Particle Swarm Optimization and Genetic Algorithm based techniques and offers MATLAB result sets, tables, flow charts and illustrations to exemplify the complicated concepts discussed in the text.

Over the past years, hybridization of metaheuristics has become an important issue, to the point that all the different metaheuristics that we have cited, and other techniques, are now seen as starting points for the development of new optimization algorithms. In (A. Meryem & Salim, 2016), authors present a new approach based on the cooperation of many variants of metaheuristics in order to solve the large existing benchmark instances of the capacitated vehicle routing problem (CVRP). (Amal Mahmoud & Sawsan, 2015) propose a new variation of ABC that uses multi-parent crossover named multi parent crossover operator artificial bee colony (MPCO-ABC). In the proposed technique the crossover operator is used to generate three new parents based on memory.

Also, Harmony search algorithm (HSA) which is a recent evolutionary algorithm used to solve several optimization problems. The algorithm mimics the improvisation behavior of a group of musicians to find a good harmony. Several variations of HSA have been proposed to enhance its performance. In (Iyad Abu, Faisal, Eslam Al, Mohammed Azmi, & Basima Hani, 2013), a new variation of HSA that uses multi-parent crossover is proposed (HSA-MPC). In (B. Meryem & Abdelmadjid, 2016), the authors present a new Quantum Inspired Harmony Search algorithm with Variable Population Size QIHSVPS for a complex variant of vehicle routing problem (VRP), called HVRPMBTW (Vehicle Routing Problem with Heterogeneous fleet, Mixed Backhauls and Time Windows). In (B. Meryem & Abdelmadjid, 2015), the author deals with a variant of the famous NP-hard (Laporte, 1992)vehicle routing problem called the Vehicle Routing Problem with Simultaneous Pickup and Delivery VRPSPD.

Genetic algorithms are stochastic search methods which mimic the natural biological evolution. They are widely used in NP-hard problems optimization(Mohammad & Mohammad Hassan, 2016).

Genetic algorithms were developed by John Holland of the University of Michigan in the early 1970s(Holland, 1975) and since then, the GAs continue to prove theoretically and empirically their efficiency and robustness to provide good solutions in complexes areas (David Edward Goldberg, 1989).

GA operates on a population (group of individuals) of possible solutions applying the principle of survival of the fittest, to generate new and improved estimates. In every generation, a new set of approximate solutions is created by the process of selecting individuals according to their fitness (objective) and the use of genetic operators inspired by natural genetics. This approach guarantees the evolution towards better populations(Eiben, Hinterding, & Michalewicz, 1999).

In the following, a description of the main genetic operators is given, namely: selection, crossover, mutation, and replacement. The emphasis here is on presenting a functional description of the principles, rather than giving a complete overview of the concepts of these operators; however, the focusin this work is on crossovers operators.

The selection mechanism is one of the main components of research in evolutionary algorithms. The overall principle of parent selection is that their probability of being chosen grows with their fitness. Such selection pressure will lead the population towards better solutions. However, the worst individuals should not be rejected and they have a chance to be selected. This can lead to useful genetic material. After the selection process, the crossing operator is applied to each parent pair (P1, P2) with a probability Pc (predetermined) and generates the child pair (E1, E2). The mutation operators are unary operators that act on a single individual and whose main action is the modification of an individual genotype and thus allow a better exploration of the solutions space. Finally, the replacement phase concerns the selection of survivors from the parents generation to maintain the size of population.

Evolutionary algorithms have shown their efficiency in solving optimization problems, but given their stochastic nature, these algorithms alone may sometimes not retain the correct solutions encountered during their execution until the end of the algorithm. The notion of elitism which advocates that the best individuals of the actual population will be saved in the next generation is then necessary. In (Kanungo, Janmenjoy, Bighnaraj, & Behera, 2016), an effort has been made with a recently developed population based metaheuristic called Elitist based teaching learning based optimization (ETLBO) for data clustering. The ETLBO has been hybridized with K-means algorithm (ETLBO-K-means) to get the optimal cluster centers and effective fitness values.

The TSP is one of the most famous combinatorial optimization problems (NP-hard for large size), it was treated by a large number of metaheuristic and approximate methods (Yong, 2015) and particularly genetic algorithms (Abdoun & Abouchabaka, 2011; Bontoux, Artigues, & Feillet, 2010; Dwivedi, Chauhan, Saxena, & Agrawal, 2012; Yuan, Skinner, Huang, & Liu, 2013).

Researchers have proposed several versions of genetic operators for this kind of ordered problems such as order based crossover (OBX) and uniform order based crossover (UOBX) chapitre 1 pages 1–101)(L. D. Davis, 1991), partially mapped crossover (PMX) (David E. Goldberg & Lingle, 1985) and many others that we cite afterwards.

Here, we propose a new crossover called Jump crossover (JMPX) then we compare it with some pretty powerful and classic methods.

This paper is organized into 4 sections. The first deals with some basic concepts of genetic algorithms and a brief description of the benchmark operators and methods. In the second section, we describe the proposed crossover operator. The third section presents the results and discussions in comparison with the benchmark, while the fourth section discusses the conclusions reached.

GENETIC ALGORITHMS FOR THE TRAVELING SALESMAN PROBLEM

Traveling Salesman Problem

The TSP is a classic combinatorial optimization problem, simple in its formulation but very difficult to solve. This problem is known to be NP-hard, in other words it cannot be solved exactly in a polynomial time. Many exact and heuristic algorithms have been developed in the field of Operations Research (OR) to solve it. The problem is to find the shortest possible tour through a set of n vertices in such a way that each vertex is visited once and only once.

This problem can be divided into two categories depending on the form of the costs matrix: symmetric and asymmetric. If the equality $C(i, j) = C(j, i)$ is satisfied, the TSP is symmetric, otherwise it is called an asymmetric TSP, **i** and **j** being any vertices. In a symmetric tsp of **n** cities, there are **(n-1)!/2** possible solutions and their inverses cyclic permutations with the same total cost. The purpose is then to find a Hamiltonian cycle of minimum total cost (Cicirello & Smith, 2000).

Mathematic Formulation

The tsp is formulated as a cost matrix in **n** dimensions of d_{ij} values Figure 1, where the purpose is to obtain a permutation of these values, as the sum of costs d_{ij} is minimal, for all **i** and **j**, where **i** is a node and **j** his next in a sequence.

More formally, we have:

$$MINIMIZE \sum_{i=1}^{n} \sum_{j=1}^{n} d_{ij} x_{ij} \tag{1}$$

With:

$$\sum_{j=1}^{n} x_{ij} = 1, \forall i, \quad \sum_{i=1}^{n} x_{ij} = 1, \forall j, \quad x_{ij} \in \{0,1\}, \forall i, j \tag{2}$$

$$\sum_{i,j \in S}^{n} x_{ij} \langle |S|, \forall S \subset V, S \neq \varnothing \tag{3}$$

Figure 1. distance matrix of symmetric tsp of 8 cities

	1	2	3	4	5	6	7	8
1	0	12	3	23	1	5	32	56
2	12	0	9	18	3	41	45	5
3	3	9	0	89	56	21	12	49
4	23	18	89	0	87	46	75	17
5	1	3	56	87	0	55	22	86
6	5	41	21	46	55	0	21	76
7	32	45	12	75	22	21	0	11
8	56	5	49	17	86	76	11	0

X_{ij} is the decision matrix (connection).

S is a vertex Set from the global set V.

We consider $\mathbf{d_{ij}} = \mathbf{d_{ji}}$, $\mathbf{\forall i, j}$ to work on the symmetric TSP (**STSP**);

Genetic Algorithm

Representation Methods

In this section we present the method of data representation which is best adapted to the handled problem.In recent decades there have been three vector representations considered within the tsp (Michalewicz, 1996):the adjacency representation, the ordinal representation and path representation.

Path Representation is the most natural representation of a tour; this is the one we adopt in this article. A path simply lists visited nodes using labels representing the successor and predecessor of each city. So a tour like $[1 \rightarrow 2 \rightarrow 3 \rightarrow 4 \rightarrow 5 \rightarrow 6]$can be represented as shown in Figure 2.

Figure 2. path representation

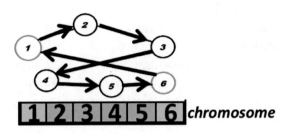

Crossover Operators

Several ways to do the crossing in tsp optimization context are described in the literature: Partially Mapped Crossover (**PMX**)(David Edward Goldberg, 1989), Order Crossover (**OX**) proposed by(L. Davis, 1985) which produces offspring that preserves the cities relative order of parents, Edge Crossover (**EX**) (L. D. Whitley, Starkweather, & Fuquay, 1989), Subtour Exchange Crossover (**SXX**) (Yamamura, Ono, & Kobayashi, 1992), Edge Exchange Crossover (**EXX**) (Murata & Itai, 2008), Edge Assembly Crossover (**EAX**) (J. Watson et al., 1998).

Various Others Crossover Operators and Their Variations

the Modified crossover(L. Davis, 1985),this crossover operator is an extension of the one-point crossover for permutation problems.The Order-based crossover (**OBX**) which focuses on the relative order of the cities on the parent chromosomes, used by G. Syswerda in (L. D. Davis, 1991);

Alternate Edges Crossover (**AEC**) is reported in (Grefenstette, Gopal, Rosmaita, & Van Gucht, 1985), the results with this operator have been uniformly discouraging. However, it was a good introduction to the other edge-preserving operators.(Deep & Mebrahtu, 2011) proposed three new additional variations of order crossover and their performance were far better than the existing variations. The variations are designed using cut point analysis on the standard ordered crossover operator.

Freisleben and Merz(Freisleben & Merz, 1996) and (Merz & Freisleben, 1997) suggested the distance-preserving crossover (DPX) for TSP.

- **More Specific Crossover for Ordered Problems**
  - **Position-Based Crossover Pperator (POS)** (Goel & Wadhwa, 2013)
  - **Voting Recombination Crossover Operator (VR)** (Muhlenbein, 1989)

- ○ **Alternating-Position Crossover Operator (AP)** (Larranaga, Kuijpers, Poza, & Murga, 1997)
  - ○ **Sequential Constructive Crossover Operator (SCX)** (Zakir, 2010)
- **Brief Description of Used Crossovers**
  - ○ **Partially Matched Crossover (PMX):** PMX is one of the most popular Crossovers for the tsp, (Kumar, Karambir, & Kumar, 2012)says it gives better results compared to other cross operators as Cyclic Crossover CX which has been proposed by (I.M.Oliver, D.J.Smith, &J.R.C.Holland, 1987) and the Order Crossover OX already introduced in the previous paragraph. PMX and many variants of it have proved their worth on the ordered problems such as TSP (Deep &Mebrahtu, 2012).

    In this method, two crossing points are randomly selected. Children completely inherit segments inside the cut points, while the borders of children are filled by a mapped matching with vertices in the two parents as shown in Figure 3. The complexity of this crossover is **O(n).**
  - ○ **Edge Recombination Crossover (ERX):** Since its introduction by (D. Whitley, Starkweather, &Shaner, 1990), this method is among the most used in the literature to solve various problems of planning and scheduling using GA. It tends to preserve inherited edges from parents. In this method, we select an initial city in one parent (it can be a random or guided choice by a defined criteria) and all occurrences of this city are eliminated from other cities neighborhoods. If this selected city still has neighbors (unvisited) then we choose the city with the least neighborhood (for exceptional cases random is carried out) and then redo the same process for the chosen city untill filling the current child Figure 4.

Figure 3. PMX

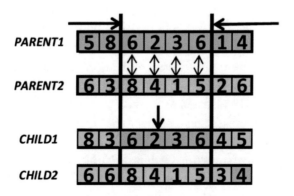

Figure 4. ERX

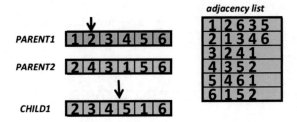

- ◦ **R-opt Heuristic:** First introduced by (Lin & Kernighan, 1973) is one of the most powerful heuristic algorithms for the TSP.It was proposed almost fifty years ago but even nowadays it is the state-of-the-art TSPlocal search(Johnson &McGeoch, 2002), (Rocki&Suda, 2012) and (Manthey&Veenstra, 2013).

  An R-opt operator consists of replacing r edges from a tour by r edges not in the tour if this decreases the length of the tour (Jog, Suh, & Gucht, 1989). For giving an example, a 2-opt strategy randomly selects two edges (1,2) and (3,4) from a tour and checks if $ED(1,2) + ED(3,4) > ED(1,4) + ED(2,3)$ (ED stands for Euclidiandistance).

  If this is the case, the new tour is obtained by removing the edges (1,2) and (3,4) and replacing them with the edges (1,4) and (3,2) as shown in Figure 5.

Genetic Algorithm Functioning

We use a simple but effective strategy, to get an elitist genetic algorithm using overlapped populations. This principle has been presented as a Steady State Genetic Algorithm(David Edward Goldberg, 1989)and (Vavak & Fogarty, 1996).

Figure 5. r-opt(2-opt)

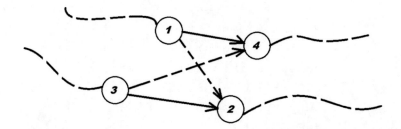

During GA Evolving from one generation to another, the population is preserved and new individuals are inserted only if they improve the average quality of the population and this is performed by replacing those less useful as described in the pseudocode in Figure 6.

ADOPTED APPROCH: JUMP CROSSOVER

A good crossover should mainly have two features: respect and edgetransmission (Surry & Radcliffe, 1996). Respect means that the common traits between both parents must be inherited and transmission implies that each inherited trait must belong to at least one of the two parents. (R. A. Watson & Pollack, 2000) states that effective Crossover must also introduce new characteristic into generated children.

In summary, it is necessary that our operator tends to inherit the traits of the parents and also to introduce new traits for children diversity.

Overview of the Jump Crossover

The Jump crossover operator is aimed at exchanging information between two parent chromosomes. The adjacency lists of the two parents are made then a starting item (city) and its link to a second item are chosen from one parent(it can be a random

Figure 6. Pseudo-code of a standard GA

```
BEGIN GA
gen=0 [ generation counter ]
Initialize population P(gen)
Evaluate population P(gen)
done:=false
WHILE not done DO
gen:=gen+1
Select P(gen) from P(gen -1)
Crossover P(gen)
Mutate P(gen)
Evaluate P(gen)
done:=Optimization criteria
END WHILE
Output of  best solutions
END GA.
```

or guided choice by a defined criteria), then the jump to the other parent is made taking the last selected entry (in the particular case where all its neighbors are already visited, we generate it randomly) then loop until filling the current Child. As described the jump crossover tend to keep the parents traits by its edge transmission procedure and apply as far as possible the two principles introduced above.

A probability is associated to the application of the crossover operator. If the operator is not applied to the selected parents, they are copied to the new population without any modification. In this way, good chromosomes can be preserved from one generation to the next.

Jump Crossover Processing

We have developed a process that builds new children inheriting as much information as possible from parents' structures as well as introducing new genes. The Figure 7 shows all steps of this operator:

RESULTS AND DISCUSSIONS COMPARED WITH THE BENCHMARK

The system was developed using the C + + language and tests were performed on a personal computer Core2 Duo with a speed of 4 GHz and 4GB RAM running on MS Windows 7.

The various operators of the genetic algorithm was written in C + + based on the Galib library (Wall, 1996). The initial population is generated randomly. The experiments were carried out **40** times for each instance. The quality of the solution is measured by the percentage of the error above the optimum solution value as reported in **TSPLIB**(Reinelt, 1991), as given by the formula:

$$Error \% = \frac{Solution - optimal\ solution}{Optimal\ Solution} * 100$$

The scale used for the fitness is linear (linear scaling); the selection method adopted in the simulations is the Roulette Wheel based on the fitness value. We apply different crossovers with a probability equal to 1, a relatively small mutation rate (probability equal to 0.3) to compare the ability of operators to diversify the offsprings, a moderate population size popsize = 60, a number of generations equal to 3000 iterations and a replacement rate of 0.5.

Table 1 includes all of the results for a set of 10 instances from the TSPLIB library.

Figure 7. JMP crossover

Initial state::	Step 1 :
Parents :	Choose a random item (city) from P1. Insert this element in the child

Initial state::

Parents :

parent1	1	2	3	4	5
Parent2	2	1	5	3	4

The adjacency lists of P1 and P2:

```
1    2 5      1  2 5
2    1 3      2  4 1
3    2 4      3  5 4
4    3 5      4  3 2
5    4 1      5  1 3
```

Step 1 :

Choose a random item (city) from P1.
Insert this element in the child

Child	2				

Step 2 :

Remove this item from adjacency lists then randomly select a 2nd one from its neighborhood:

```
1    2 5      1  2 5
2    1 3      2  4 1
3    2 4      3  5 4
4    3 5      4  3 2
5    4 1      5  1 3
```

We consider the element 1, we insert it then remove it from adjacency lists :

Child		2	1			

```
1    2 5      1  2 5
2    1 3      2  4 1
3    2 4      3  5 4
4    3 5      4  3 2
5    4 1      5  1 3
```

Step 3 :

We jump to the other parent taking the last selected entry (in the particular case where all its neighbors are already visited, we generate it randomly) :

```
1    2   5    1  2 5
2    1   3    2  4 1
3    2   4    3  5 4
4    3   5    4  3 2
5    4   1    5  1 3
```

Step 4 :

After selecting the element go to **Step 2**.
Then loop until filling the current Child.

To continue the Example, we take 5 which is not yet visited.

```
1    2   5    1  2 5
2    1   3    2  4 1
3    2   4    3  5 4
4    3   5    4  3 2
5    4   1    5  1 3
```

Child		2		1	5		

Then 4:

```
1    2   5    1  2 5
2    1   3    2  4 1
3    2   4    3  5 4
4    3   5    4  3 2
5    4   1    5  1 3
```

Child		2		1	5	4	

Then 3 :

```
1    2   5    1  2 5
2    1   3    2  4 1
3    2   4    3  5 4
4    3   5    4  3 2
5    4   1    5  1 3
```

Child		2		1	5	4	3

Table 1. Results summary

Instance	Optimal Solution	Cross	Best Solution	Worst Solution	Avg Solutions	Average Time(second)	Error (%)
a280	2579	PMX	7642,98	8514,24	8059,723	35,902225	196,35%
a280	2579	ERX	5760,51	6437,17	6144,11725	104,7723	123,36%
a280	2579	JMPX	7093,56	8357,93	7637,657	14,912925	175,05%
a280	2579	r-opt	10036,5	11073,1	10436,7975	14,144025	289,16%
berlin52	7542	PMX	7966,35	10460,4	8532,3585	3,16255	5,63%
berlin52	7542	ERX	7648,88	8823,12	8246,92675	10,0123	1,42%
berlin52	7542	JMPX	7913,37	8793,54	8257,745	2,895375	4,92%
berlin52	7542	r-opt	7854,82	9137,63	8391,71625	2,8926	4,15%
ch130	6110	PMX	9462,43	14098,9	10373,847	10,5164	54,87%
ch130	6110	ERX	7770,08	9342,48	8483,37325	31,5467	27,17%
ch130	6110	JMPX	7852,38	9763,67	8935,4725	6,79755	28,52%
ch130	6110	r-opt	11468	12995,7	12253,09	6,56115	87,69%
eil51	426	PMX	443,013	524,196	475,156175	3,13695	3,99%
eil51	426	ERX	442,092	483,868	458,106125	10,210875	3,78%
eil51	426	JMPX	435,612	495,813	461,0907	2,9425	2,26%
eil51	426	r-opt	450,453	488,379	469,802175	2,70975	5,74%
eil101	629	PMX	796,883	944,825	854,251125	7,43235	26,69%
eil101	629	ERX	717,073	820,35	765,862	23,818925	14,00%
eil101	629	JMPX	732,377	843,159	782,79155	5,179675	16,44%
eil101	629	r-opt	902,597	996,687	953,138225	5,13125	43,50%
d657	48912	PMX	289300	297417	293352,3333	178,0301667	491,47%
d657	48912	ERX	213492	232933	225224,4	473,099	336,48%
d657	48912	JMPX	339441	370123	354573,3333	40,85266667	593,98%
d657	48912	r-opt	358976	379768	370784,175	33,452125	633,92%
ch150	6528	PMX	11294,2	13230,6	12127,6175	15,4144	73,01%
ch150	6528	ERX	9061,53	10534,3	9835,223	46,2424	38,81%
ch150	6528	JMPX	9838,28	11443,2	10639,3445	7,926375	50,71%
ch150	6528	r-opt	13946,5	15593,5	14913,3175	7,482325	113,64%
bier127	118282	PMX	162001	186434	175763,325	10,373775	36,96%
bier127	118282	ERX	140174	163650	152040,25	30,659675	18,51%
bier127	118282	JMPX	143125	166566	157971,6	6,83695	21,00%
bier127	118282	r-opt	181965	210261	193874,525	6,3253	53,84%
eil76	538	PMX	620,46	870,146	673,722625	5,191925	15,33%
eil76	538	ERX	586,673	643,665	618,3357	16,9454	9,05%
eil76	538	JMPX	599,862	669,751	626,811175	4,141475	11,50%
eil76	538	r-opt	659,248	739,603	694,36385	4,69785	22,54%
pr76	108159	PMX	125910	170257	137975,175	5,0882	16,41%
pr76	108159	ERX	111779	132786	122628,9	15,9418	3,35%
pr76	108159	JMPX	113647	135422	124316,25	4,1669	5,07%
pr76	108159	r-opt	134193	157256	144516,525	4,04595	24,07%

We chose to take as a stop criterion for the genetic algorithm: the number of iteration to compare the trend and the evolution of the different results of studied crossovers. Figure 10 shows the evolution of the GA with JMPX during 3000 generations.

The results are illustrated globally in Figure 8 which shows clearly the contribution of our approach JMPX compared to PMX, ERX and r-opt heuristic.JMPX outperform PMX in all simulations in execution time and solutions accuracy.

Simulations on the ERX show an advantage for our approach in instances having moderate size and for ERX in instances having a significant size.

In most cases the JMPX consumes less execution time and have a better ratio reporting the solution quality and the time to reach it than required by ERX, PMX and r-opt heuristic (details Figure 9).

An execution of 100000 iterations clearly shows that the JMPX method compete well the benchmark at the beginning of the GA evolution and Ends up with override these methods as shown in Figure 11.

Based on the model structure, the basic logistic network design models can be summarized. In this classification approach Farahani(Farahani, Rezapour, Drezner, & Fallah, 2014) offers an overview of the classification of models and the techniques of resolutions.

In this scope we can introduce the use of GIS, financial information, demand, time, transport, networks, in strategic decisions as shown in Figure 12.

Figure 8. Quality percentage for each tested instance

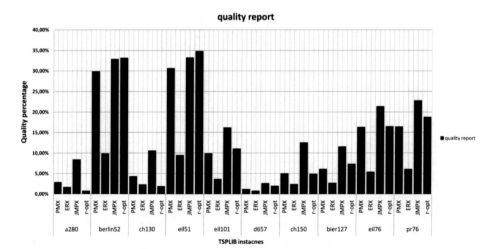

Figure 9. Simulations results on TSPLIB instances

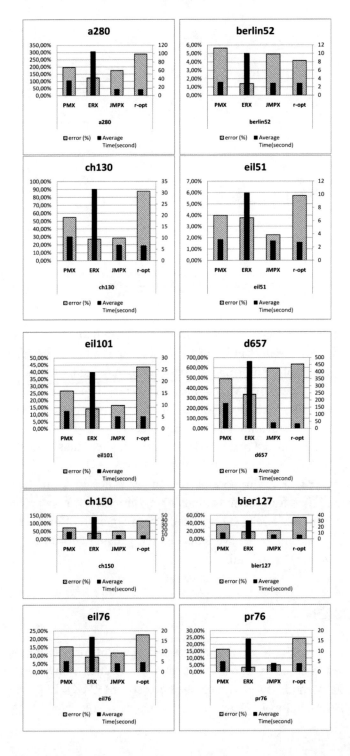

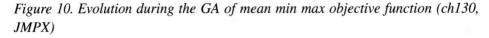

Figure 10. Evolution during the GA of mean min max objective function (ch130, JMPX)

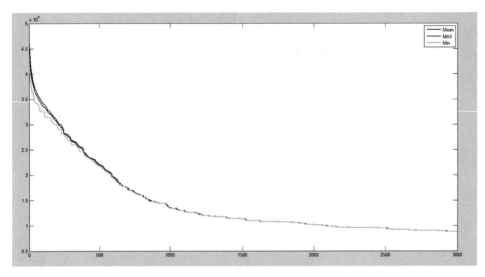

For the Moroccan context, Figure 13 shows a simulation of our algorithm, on a real instance with a real data set of the Moroccan road network. The concept of Volunteered Geographic Information has recently emerged with the new Web 2.0 technologies. The OpenStreetMap project is currently the most significant example of a VGI-based system (Girres & Touya, 2010). It aims to produce free geographic databases using the contributions of Internet users.

We cleaned the data and organized it for use, and then transformed it into a road graph in QGIS (Tsou & Smith, 2011).

We choose 128 of the important and largest cities in Morocco, in terms of population, and therefore the most demanding in terms of goods. Then we run a Dijkstra algorithm to find the shortest paths between each of the selected cities on the road graph, and then we have launched the genetic algorithm with that input data to optimize the overall path.

CONCLUSION

This paper presented a new genetic crossover operator for solving the TSP using GAs. The new method is tested and compared to other conventional crossover operators and methods: Partially matched crossover (PMX), Edge recombination Crossover (ERX) and r-opt Heuristic, To conclude on the overall performance of

Figure 11. Comparative convergence (eil76)

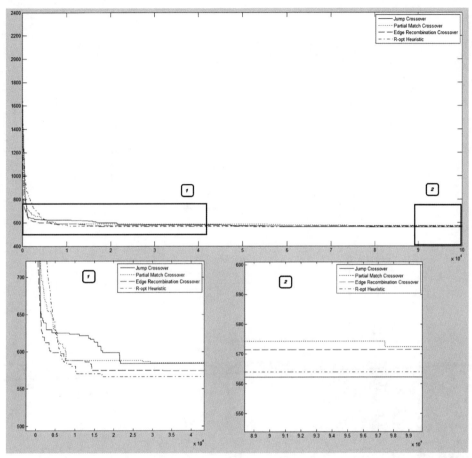

it, simulations study shows the remarkable performance of the proposed method of crossing (jump crossover).

Thus, we evaluate and compare the proposed JMPX with the three different methods for one TSP objective function namely, minimizing total travel distance. The benchmarking was performed using TSPLIB. The experimental results show that in most cases the JMPX operator enables the GA to produce high solution quality in less time than the existing crossover operators.

The crossover method proposed is simple to implement, it should help to solve other difficult problems quickly, reliably and accurately.

Our future work will focus on two main areas: Firstly, studying the contribution of classic mutation operators such as Inversion, Displacement, Insertion and Exchange

Figure 12. Multi-level approach to freight modeling (adaptedfrom Xu, Hancock, & Southworth, 2003)

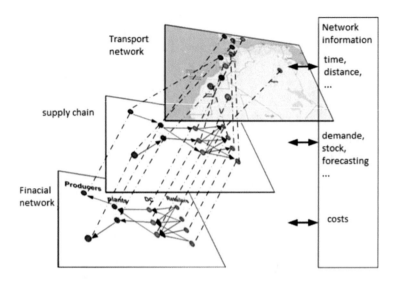

Figure 13. Simulation on 128 Moroccan cities

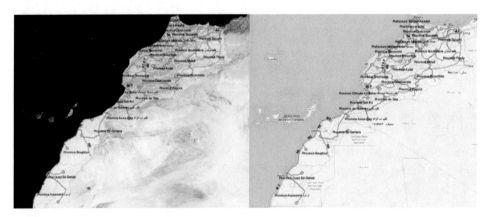

mutationused with the just studied crossovers and then, applying genetic algorithm to optimize design and management of a global supply chain. Secondly, since many practical problems can be modeled by the multi objective TSP (MTSP), we will use the JMPX operator into our existing GA for solving a large multi objective TSP problem in green supply chain management including minimizing green house gas into objective functions.

REFERENCES

Abdoun, O., & Abouchabaka, J. (2011). A Comparative Study of Adaptive Crossover Operators for Genetic Algorithms to Resolve the Traveling Salesman Problem. *International Journal of Computers and Applications, 31*(11), 49–57.

Ahmed Hamza, A., Ahmad Taher, A., & Aboul Ella, H. (2014). A New Heuristic Function of Ant Colony System for Retinal Vessel Segmentation. *International Journal of Rough Sets and Data Analysis, 1*(2), 15–30. doi:10.4018/ijrsda.2014070102

Amal Mahmoud, A., & Sawsan, A. (2015). Hybridizing Artificial Bee Colony Algorithm with Multi-Parent Crossover Operator. *International Journal of Applied Metaheuristic Computing, 6*(2), 18–32. doi:10.4018/IJAMC.2015040102

Ashour, A. S., Samanta, S., Dey, N., Kausar, N., Abdessalemkaraa, W. B., & Hassanien, A. E. (2015). Computed tomography image enhancement using cuckoo search: A log transform based approach. *Journal of Signal and Information Processing, 6*(03), 244–257. doi:10.4236/jsip.2015.63023

Binh, H. T. T., Hanh, N. T., Van Quan, L., & Dey, N. (2016). Improved Cuckoo Search and Chaotic Flower Pollination optimization algorithm for maximizing area coverage in Wireless Sensor Networks. *Neural Computing & Applications*, 1–13. doi:10.1007/s00521-016-2823-5

Bontoux, B., Artigues, C., & Feillet, D. (2010). A Memetic Algorithm with a large neighborhood crossover operator for the Generalized Traveling Salesman Problem. *Computers & Operations Research, 37*(11), 1844–1852. doi:10.1016/j.cor.2009.05.004

Bouttier, C., Babando, O., Gadat, S., Gerchinovitz, S., Laporte, S., & Nicol, F. (2017). Adaptive Simulated Annealing with Homogenization for Aircraft Trajectory Optimization. In K. Doerner, I. Ljubic, G. Pflug, & G. Tragler (Eds.), *Operations Research Proceedings 2015: Selected Papers of the International Conference of the German, Austrian and Swiss Operations Research Societies (GOR, ÖGOR, SVOR/ ASRO)* (pp. 569-574). Cham: Springer International Publishing. doi:10.1007/978-3-319-42902-1_77

Cicirello, V. A., & Smith, S. F. (2000). *Modeling GA Performance for Control Parameter Optimization.* Paper presented at the GECCO.

Davis, L. (1985). Applying Adaptive Algorithms to Epistatic Domains. San Francisco, CA: Academic Press.

Davis, L. D. (1991). *Handbook Of Genetic Algorithms.* Van Nostrand Reinhold.

Deep, K., & Mebrahtu, H. (2011). New Variations of Order Crossover for Travelling Salesman Problem. *International Journal of Combinatorial Optimization Problems and Informatics, 2*(1), 2–13.

Deep, K., & Mebrahtu, H. (2012). Variant of partially mapped crossover for the Travelling Salesman problems. *International Journal of Combinatorial Optimization Problems and Informatics, 3*(1), 47–69.

Dey, N., Chakraborty, S., & Samanta, S. (2014). *Optimization of Watermarking in Biomedical Signal*: Lambert Publication. *Heinrich-Böcking-Straße, 6*, 66121.

Dey, N., Samanta, S., Chakraborty, S., Das, A., Chaudhuri, S. S., & Suri, J. S. (2014). Firefly Algorithm for Optimization of Scaling Factors During Embedding of Manifold Medical Information: An Application in Ophthalmology Imaging. *Journal of Medical Imaging and Health Informatics, 4*(3), 384–394. doi:10.1166/jmihi.2014.1265

Dey, N., Samanta, S., Yang, X.-S., Das, A., & Chaudhuri, S. S. (2013). Optimisation of scaling factors in electrocardiogram signal watermarking using cuckoo search. *International Journal of Bio-inspired Computation, 5*(5), 315–326. doi:10.1504/IJBIC.2013.057193

Dwivedi, V., Chauhan, T., Saxena, S., & Agrawal, P. (2012). *Travelling Salesman Problem using Genetic Algorithm.* Paper presented at the National Conference on Development of Reliable Information Systems, Techniques and Related Issues.

Eiben, A. E., Hinterding, R., & Michalewicz, Z. (1999). Parameter control in evolutionary algorithms. *IEEE Transactions on Evolutionary Computation, 3*(2), 124–141. doi:10.1109/4235.771166

Farahani, R. Z., Rezapour, S., Drezner, T., & Fallah, S. (2014). Competitive supply chain network design: An overview of classifications, models, solution techniques and applications. *Omega, 45*, 92–118. doi:10.1016/j.omega.2013.08.006

Freisleben, B., & Merz, P. (1996). *New genetic local search operators for the traveling salesman problem. In Parallel Problem Solving from Nature—PPSN IV* (pp. 890–899). Springer. doi:10.1007/3-540-61723-X_1052

Girres, J.-F., & Touya, G. (2010). Quality Assessment of the French OpenStreetMap Dataset. *Transactions in GIS, 14*(4), 435–459. doi:10.1111/j.1467-9671.2010.01203.x

Goel, S., & Wadhwa, V. (2013). A comparative analysis of PMX, POS and OX crossover operators for solving. *International Journal of Latest Research in Science and Technology, 2*(2), 80–83.

Goldberg, D. E. (1989). Genetic Algorithms in Search, Optimization, and Machine Learning. Addison-Wesley Longman Publishing Co.

Goldberg, D. E., & Lingle, R. (1985). Alleles, loci, and the traveling salesman problem. *Proceedings of the First International Conference on Genetic Algorithms and Their Applications*, 154-159.

Grefenstette, J., Gopal, R., Rosmaita, B., & Van Gucht, D. (1985). Genetic algorithms for the traveling salesman problem. *Proceedings of the first International Conference on Genetic Algorithms and their Applications.*

Holland, J. H. (1975). *Adaption in Natural and Artificial Systems.* The University of Michigan Press.

Hore, S., Chatterjee, S., Santhi, V., Dey, N., Ashour, A. S., Balas, V. E., & Shi, F. (2017). Indian Sign Language Recognition Using Optimized Neural Networks. In V. E. Balas, L. C. Jain, & X. Zhao (Eds.), *Information Technology and Intelligent Transportation Systems: Vol. 2. Proceedings of the 2015 International Conference on Information Technology and Intelligent Transportation Systems ITITS 2015* (pp. 553-563). Cham: Springer International Publishing. doi:10.1007/978-3-319-38771-0_54

Iyad Abu, D., Faisal, A., Eslam Al, M., Mohammed Azmi, A.-B., & Basima Hani, F. H. (2013). Hybridizing Harmony Search Algorithm with Multi-Parent Crossover to Solve Real World Optimization Problems. *International Journal of Applied Metaheuristic Computing, 4*(3), 1–14. doi:10.4018/ijamc.2013070101

Jog, P., Suh, J. Y., & Gucht, D. v. (1989). The effects of population size, heuristic crossover and local improvement on a genetic algorithm for the traveling salesman problem. *Proceedings of the Third International Conference on Genetic Algorithms.*

Johnson, D. S., & McGeoch, L. A. (2002). *Experimental analysis of heuristics for the STSP. In The traveling salesman problem and its variations* (pp. 369–443). Springer.

Kanungo, D. P., Janmenjoy, N., Bighnaraj, N., & Behera, H. S. (2016). Hybrid Clustering using Elitist Teaching Learning-Based Optimization: An Improved Hybrid Approach of TLBO. *International Journal of Rough Sets and Data Analysis, 3*(1), 1–19. doi:10.4018/IJRSDA.2016010101

Kumar, N., Karambir, & Kumar, R. (2012). A Comparative Analysis of PMX, CX and OX Crossover operators for solving Travelling Salesman Problem. *International Journal of Latest Research in Science and Technology*, *1*(2), 98–101.

Laporte, G. (1992). The vehicle routing problem: An overview of exact and approximate algorithms. *European Journal of Operational Research*, *59*(3), 345–358. doi:10.1016/0377-2217(92)90192-C

Larranaga, P., Kuijpers, C. M. H., Poza, M., & Murga, R. H. (1997). Decomposing Bayesian Networks: Triangulation of the Moral Graph with Genetic Algorithms. *Statistics and Computing*, *7*(1), 19–34. doi:10.1023/A:1018553211613

Lin, S., & Kernighan, B. W. (1973). An effective heuristic algorithm for the traveling-salesman problem. *Operations Research*, *21*(2), 498–516. doi:10.1287/opre.21.2.498

Manthey, B., & Veenstra, R. (2013). *Smoothed analysis of the 2-Opt heuristic for the TSP: Polynomial bounds for Gaussian noise. In Algorithms and Computation* (pp. 579–589). Springer.

Meryem, A., & Salim, C. (2016). Cooperative Parallel Metaheuristics based Penguin Optimization Search for Solving the Vehicle Routing Problem. *International Journal of Applied Metaheuristic Computing*, *7*(1), 1–18. doi:10.4018/IJAMC.2016010101

Meryem, B., & Abdelmadjid, B. (2015). Resolution of a Vehicle Routing Problem with Simultaneous Pickup and Delivery: A Cooperative Approach. *International Journal of Applied Metaheuristic Computing*, *6*(3), 53–68. doi:10.4018/ijamc.2015070103

Meryem, B., & Abdelmadjid, B. (2016). Quantum Inspired Algorithm for a VRP with Heterogeneous Fleet Mixed Backhauls and Time Windows. *International Journal of Applied Metaheuristic Computing*, *7*(4), 18–38. doi:10.4018/IJAMC.2016100102

Merz, P., & Freisleben, B. (1997). *Genetic local search for the TSP: New results.* Paper presented at the Evolutionary Computation, 1997., IEEE International Conference on. doi:10.1109/ICEC.1997.592288

Michalewicz, Z. (1996). Genetic algorithms + data structures = evolution programs (3rd ed.). London: Springer-Verlag.

Mohammad, H., & Mohammad Hassan, A. (2016). Optimization of Small Wind Turbines using Genetic Algorithms. *International Journal of Applied Metaheuristic Computing*, *7*(4), 50–65. doi:10.4018/IJAMC.2016100104

Muhlenbein, H. (1989). *Parallel Genetic Algorithms, Population Genetics and Combinatorial Optimization.* Academic Press.

Murata, T., & Itai, R. (2008). Enhancing Solution Similarity in Multi-Objective Vehicle Routing Problems with Different Demand Periods. In T. Caric & H. Gold (Eds.), *Vehicle Routing Problem.* InTech. doi:10.5772/5619

Oliver, Smith, & Holland. (1987). *A Study of Permutation Crossover Operator on the TSP.* Academic Press.

Rahul, K., Senthilnath, J., Omkar, S. N., & Narendra, S. (2016). A Novel Multiobjective Optimization for Cement Stabilized Soft Soil based on Artificial Bee Colony. *International Journal of Applied Metaheuristic Computing, 7*(4), 1–17. doi:10.4018/IJAMC.2016100101

Reinelt, G. (1991). TSPLIB—A Traveling Salesman Problem Library. *ORSA Journal of Computing, 3*(4), 376–384. doi:10.1287/ijoc.3.4.376

Reza, B. (2016). Nephron Algorithm Optimization: Inspired of the Biologic Nephron Performance. *International Journal of Applied Metaheuristic Computing, 7*(1), 38–64. doi:10.4018/IJAMC.2016010103

Rocki, K., & Suda, R. (2012). *Accelerating 2-opt and 3-opt local search using GPU in the travelling salesman problem.* Paper presented at the High Performance Computing and Simulation (HPCS), 2012 International Conference on.

Shweta, T., & Kamal, K. B. (2014). A Particle Swarm Optimization Approach to Fuzzy Case-based Reasoning in the Framework of Collaborative Filtering. *International Journal of Rough Sets and Data Analysis, 1*(1), 48–64. doi:10.4018/ijrsda.2014010104

Soleimani, H., & Kannan, G. (2015). A hybrid particle swarm optimization and genetic algorithm for closed-loop supply chain network design in large-scale networks. *Applied Mathematical Modelling, 39*(14), 3990–4012. doi:10.1016/j.apm.2014.12.016

Surry, P. D., & Radcliffe, N. J. (1996). *Formal Algorithms + Formal Representations = Search Strategies.* Paper presented at the Parallel Problem Solving from Nature IV, London, UK.

Tsou, M.-H., & Smith, J. (2011). *Free and Open Source software for GIS education.* San Diego, CA: Academic Press.

Vavak, F., & Fogarty, T. C. T. C. (1996). *Comparison of Steady State and Generational Genetic Algorithms for Use in Nonstationary Environments.* Academic Press.

Wall, M. (1996). *GAlib: A C ++ Library of Genetic Algorithm Components.* Academic Press.

Wang, Y., Ma, X., Xu, M., Liu, Y., & Wang, Y. (2015). Two-echelon logistics distribution region partitioning problem based on a hybrid particle swarm optimization–genetic algorithm. *Expert Systems with Applications*, *42*(12), 5019–5031. doi:10.1016/j.eswa.2015.02.058

Watson, J., Ross, C., Eisele, V., Denton, J., Bins, J., Guerra, C., . . . Howe, A. (1998). *The Traveling Salesrep Problem, Edge Assembly Crossover, and 2-opt.* Academic Press.

Watson, R. A., & Pollack, J. B. (2000). Recombination without respect: Schema combination and disruption in genetic algorithm crossover. *Proceedings of the 2000 Genetic and Evolutionary Computation Conference.*

Whitley, D., Starkweather, T., & Shaner, D. (1990). *The Traveling Salesman and Sequence Scheduling: Quality Solutions Using Genetic Edge Recombination.* Academic Press.

Whitley, L. D., Starkweather, T., & Fuquay, D. A. (1989). *Scheduling problems and traveling salesmen: The genetic edge recombination operator.* Paper presented at the ICGA.

Xu, J., Hancock, K., & Southworth, F. (2003). Simulation of regional freight movement with trade and transportation multinetworks. *Transportation Research Record*, *1854*, 152–161. doi:10.3141/1854-17

Yamamura, M., Ono, I., & Kobayashi, S. (1992). Character-preserving genetic algorithms for traveling salesman problem. *Journal of Japanese Society for Artificial Intelligence*, *7*(6), 1049–1059.

Yong, W. (2015). An Approximate Algorithm for Triangle TSP with a Four-Vertex-Three-Line Inequality. *International Journal of Applied Metaheuristic Computing*, *6*(1), 35–46. doi:10.4018/ijamc.2015010103

Yuan, S., Skinner, B., Huang, S., & Liu, D. (2013). A new crossover approach for solving the multiple travelling salesmen problem using genetic algorithms. *European Journal of Operational Research*, 228(1), 72–82. doi:10.1016/j.ejor.2013.01.043

Zakir, H. A. (2010). Genetic algorithm for the traveling salesman problem using sequential constructive crossover operator. *International Journal of Biometrics & Bioinformatics*, 3(6), 96–105.

Zhu, W., Fang, J., Tang, Y., Zhang, W., & Du, W. (2012). Digital IIR Filters Design Using Differential Evolution Algorithm with a Controllable Probabilistic Population Size. *PLoS ONE*, 7(7), e40549–e40549. doi:10.1371/journal.pone.0040549 PMID:22808191

KEY TERMS AND DEFINITIONS

Combinatorial Optimization: In applied mathematics and theoretical computer science, combinatorial optimization is a topic that consists of finding an optimal object from a finite set of objects.

Meta-Heuristics: In computer science and mathematical optimization, a metaheuristic is a higher-level procedure or heuristic designed to find, generate, or select a heuristic (partial search algorithm) that may provide a sufficiently good solution to an optimization problem.

NP-Hardness: (Non-Deterministic Polynomial-Time Hard), In computational complexity theory, is the defining property of a class of problems that are, informally, "at least as hard as the hardest problems in NP".

Optimization: In mathematics, computer science and operations research, optimization is the selection of a best element (with regard to some criterion) from some set of available alternatives. In the simplest case, an optimization problem consists of maximizing or minimizing a real function by systematically choosing input values and computing the value of the function. More generally, optimization includes finding "best available" values of some objective function given a defined domain (or input), including a variety of different types of objective functions and different types of domains.

Routing Problem Optimization: Combinatorial optimization and integer programming problem which asks "What is the optimal set of routes for a fleet of agents to traverse in order to deliver to a given set of nodes?".

Supply Chain: A system of organizations, people, activities, information, and resources involved in moving a product or service from supplier to customer.

Volunteered Geographic Information (VGI): The harnessing of tools to create, assemble, and disseminate geographic data provided voluntarily by individuals (Goodchild, 2007).

ENDNOTE

[1]   VGI is a special case of the larger Web phenomenon known as user-generated content.

Chapter 10

On Developing and Performance Evaluation of Adaptive Second Order Neural Network With GA–Based Training (ASONN–GA) for Financial Time Series Prediction

Sarat Chandra Nayak
Kommuri Pratap Reddy Institute of Technology, India

Bijan Bihari Misra
Silicon Institute of Technology, India

Himansu Sekhar Behera
Veer Surendra Sai University of Technology, India

ABSTRACT

Financial time series forecasting has been regarded as a challenging issue because of successful prediction could yield significant profit, hence require an efficient prediction system. Conventional ANN based models are not competent systems. Higher order neural networks have several advantages over traditional neural networks such as stronger approximation, higher fault tolerance capacity and faster convergence. With the aim of achieving improved forecasting accuracy, this article develops and evaluates the performance of an adaptive single layer second order neural network with GA based training (ASONN-GA). The global search ability of

DOI: 10.4018/978-1-5225-4151-6.ch010

GA has been incorporated with the better generalization ability of a second order neural network and the model is found quite capable in handling the uncertainties and nonlinearities associated with the financial time series. The model takes minimal input data and considered the partially optimized weight set from previous training, hence a significant reduction in training time. The efficiency of the model has been evaluated by forecasting one-step-ahead closing prices and exchange rates of five real stock markets and it is revealed that the ASONN-GA model achieves better forecasting accuracy over other state of the art models.

1. INTRODUCTION

Stock market behaves very much like a random walk process and the stock market index prediction has been considered as an important and challenging task for the researchers. Due to the influence of uncertainties involved in the movement of the market, the stock market forecasting is regarded as a difficult task. Stock movement prediction is also difficult due to its nonlinearities, highly volatile in nature, discontinuities, movement of other stock markets, political influences and other many macro-economical factors and even individual psychology. Various economic factors such as oil prices, exchange rates, interest rates, stock price indices in other countries, domestic as well as global economic situations, etc. have been influencing the market behavior. As more and more money is being invested in the stock market by common investors, brokers and speculators, they get anxious about the future trend of the stock prices in the market. Hence, an effective and accurate forecasting model is necessary in order to predict the stock market behavior. If the direction of the market is successfully predicted, the investors may be better guided and also monetary rewards will be substantial. In recent years, many new methods for the modeling and forecasting the stock market have been developed including linear as well as nonlinear models.

Exchange rate prediction is relevant to all sorts of firms and interesting for international companies which want to decrease exchange exposure. The foreign exchange rates have an important role in the financial market as well as economy of a country. Its area of influence includes not only interest rate and inflation but also the economic stability of any country. While deciding the monetary policies of any country FOREX rates acts as a vital factor. Global economy also comes under the influence of FOREX rate. Various massive economic crises such as The Asian crisis of 1997-98, China's undervalued Yuan (1994-2004) and Japanese yen's gyrations from 2008 to mid-2013, portrays the influence of FOREX rate on global economy. Hence to maintain the national as well as international economic stability numerous research activities have been carried out in this area. Till now it is one of the most demanding fields of research due to the highly volatile nature of FOREX rate. The dependency of FOREX rates on various fundamental and technical factors such as, inflation, interest rate differentials, capital flows, technical support and resistance levels, and so on, is the root cause of its dynamic nature.

For many decades linear models have been the basis of traditional statistical forecasting models in financial engineering. The Box-Jenkins method using autoregressive moving average (ARMA) linear models have extensively been used in many areas of time series forecasting (Box & Jenkins, 1976). Several statistical techniques such as moving averages (MA), auto-regressive integrated moving average (ARIMA), auto-regressive heteroscedastic (ARCH), generalized ARCH (GARCH) have been used extensively for stock market prediction. They have been successfully applied to different engineering, economic and social applications. Nonlinear dynamics proposes that in financial time series, past prices help to determine future prices, but not in a straightforward way. The relationship between past prices and future prices is nonlinear, and this nonlinearity implies that past price change can have wide ranging effects on future prices. Due to the presence of noise and nonlinearity in the financial time series, such traditional methods have seldom proved to be effective. These models were lacking in capturing the nonlinearity of other types of time series, since they have developed to model certain types of problems. This paves the path toward adopting nonlinear models. The popular nonlinear models used for financial forecasting include artificial neural networks, support vector machine, Bayesian networks, fuzzy system models etc. Amongst these frequently adopted methods, artificial neural networks have drawn significant interests from several researchers in the stock market behavior forecasting.

Artificial neural network (ANN) is one of the important approaches in machine learning methods. ANNs are software constructs designed to mimic the way the human brain learns. The neural network can imitate the process of human's behavior and solve nonlinear problems, which have made it widely used in calculating and predicting complicated systems. The quality of non linearity mapped achieved in ANN is difficult with the conventional calculating approaches. It has the capability of dealing with complex problems of structural instability. They are analogous to nonparametric, nonlinear regression models. Their novelty lies in their ability to model nonlinear processes with few a priori assumptions about the nature of the generating process. Neural networks extensively used in medical applications such as image/signal processing (Miller,

1992), pattern and statistical classifiers (Maglaveras, 1998) and for modeling the dynamic nature of biological systems. ANNs are relatively recent method for business forecasting and has been successfully applied to wide range of forecasting problems such as exchange rate, credit scoring, business failure, bankruptcy, interest rate, stock return, stock market index, portfolio management and option & future prices. ANNs have been successfully applied in financial engineering and gained wide acceptance due to their better learning abilities and approximation capabilities. ANNs are considered to be an effective modeling procedure when the mapping from the input to the output contains both regularities and exceptions. This is particularly useful in financial engineering applications where much is assumed and little is known about the nature of the processes determining asset prices. The neural networks have the ability to discover nonlinear relationships in the input data set without a priori assumption of the knowledge of relation between the input and the output. ANNs are found to be good universal approximator which can approximate any continuous function to any desire accuracy. They are considered to be an effective modeling procedure when the mapping from the input to the output contains both regularities and exceptions which is the way the stock market behaves. It also allows the adaptive adjustment to the model and nonlinear description of the problems. These advantages of ANN attract researchers to develop ANN based forecasting models to the area of stock market prediction. These forecasting models incorporate prior knowledge in ANN to improve the prediction accuracy. Gradient based methods are one of the most widely used error minimization methods used to train back propagation networks. Back propagation algorithm is a classical domain dependent technique for supervised training. It works by measuring the output error, calculating the gradient of this error, and adjusting the ANN weights and biases in the descending gradient direction. Back propagation is the most commonly used and the simplest feed forward algorithm used for classification. Back propagation based ANNs are very popular methods to predict stock market with better calculation, spreading abilities and stronger nonlinear mapping ability. But the stock market is not only with nonlinearity but also chaos, and it is a dynamic system related to time. Therefore the network for predicting itself is a dynamic system. Back propagation neural networks, particularly the multilayer perceptron (MLP) has many shortcomings such as the slow learning rate, more computational overhead, larger memory size, easy to get into local minimum, bigger randomicity and so on. This affects the predicted results of the stock price. These shortcomings force researchers toward developing hybrid models by combining linear and nonlinear models. These hybrid models that have been developed by many researchers combining nonlinear models such as ANN and evolutionary soft computing techniques such as Particle Swarm Optimization (PSO), Genetic Algorithm (GA) and other nature and bio-inspired search techniques, have better accuracies. ANN and its hybridization with other soft computing techniques have been successfully applied to the potential corporate finance applications and found to be appropriate. Over the decades, a number of forecasting models based on soft computing techniques such as ANN (White, 1998; Chiang, 1996), fuzzy logic and its hybridization (Romahi & Shen, 2000; Abraham, 2002), GA based ANN (Nayak, 2012) have been applied to the stock index forecasting. Several nature-inspired population-based algorithms such as GA, PSO, differential evolution (DE), and evolutionary algorithm (EA) have shown their promising ability as learning algorithm utilized for forecasting purpose. A hybrid version of harmony search algorithm (HSA) with multi-parent crossover is proposed in (Doush, 2013) and applied to solve a set of real world numerical optimization problem. Their experimental results show superiority over other. A GA based hybrid RBF models have been proposed for classification (Dash, 2013) and an ANN-RBF hybrid model used for estimation (Nourani, 2013) and claimed to be superior over conventional models. A discrete artificial bee colony optimization has been used for financial classification problem and found to be performing better as compared to other nature inspired methods (Marinakis, 2011).There are several applications of nature-inspired optimization techniques found in literature such as Cuckoo Search (Binh et al., 2016; Dey et al., 2013; Samantaa et al., 2013; Ashour et al., 2015), Firefly Algorithm (Dey et al., 2014a; Dey et al., 2014b), GA and PSO (Hore et al., 2017; Dey et al., 2015).

Pai and Michel proposed a hybrid PSO strategy in which the global best particle position arrived at by the hybrid PSO acts as the initial point to the Sequential Quadratic Programming (SQP) algorithm (Pai& Michel, 2017)). The superiority of the hybrid model has been demonstrated on portfolio set selection of BSE200 index and Nikkei225 index. A highly scalable DE algorithm based on map-reduce programming model has been proposed by Benmounah et al. (2017). for clustering large sets of data with reduced time consumption. A comparative analysis between statistical, rough computing, and hybridized techniques based models in predictive data analysis has been proposed by Acharjya and Anitha (2017).The comparative analysis was carried out over financial bankruptcy data set and it was found that the hybridized computing techniques provides better accuracy as compared to rough and statistical based computing. A Novel Hybridization of Expectation-Maximization and K-Means Algorithms for Better Clustering Performance has been proposed by Raja Kishor and Venkateswarlu (2016). The method was taking less execution time by producing results with higher clustering fitness and lesser SSE than other algorithms. Prediction of stock price trend and recommendation using cognitive process has been proposed by Bag and Kulkarni (Bag, & Kulkarni, 2017). They used a Naïve bays classification algorithm to classify the news sentiments. A News Sentiment Index (NSI) was calculated and effect of the news on particular stock was calculated to predict the trend. The results were compared with traditional systems and showed significant improvement. Rough Set Theory was used to analyze the understanding of complex shopping behavior of retail consumers of India in grocery segment (Senthilnathan, 2016).

It has been found in most of the research work in financial forecasting area used ANN, particularly multilayer perceptron (MLP). Suffering from slow convergence, sticking to local minima are the two well known lacuna of a MLP. In order to overcome the local minima, more number of nodes added to the hidden layers. Multiple hidden layers and more number of neurons in each layer also add more computational complexity to the network. In the other hand, HONN are type of feed forward network which provide nonlinear decision boundaries, hence offering better classification capability as compared to linear neuron (Guler & Sahin, 1994). They are different from ordinary feed forward networks by the introduction of higher order terms into the network. HONN have fast learning properties, stronger approximation, greater storage capacity, higher fault tolerance capability and powerful mapping of single layer trainable weights (Wang, 2006). In most of neural network models, neural inputs are combined using summing operation, where in HONN, not only summing units, but also units that find the product of weighted inputs called as higher order terms. Due to single layer of trainable weights needed to achieve nonlinear separability, they are simple in architecture and require less number of weights to capture the associated nonlinearity (Shin & Ghosh, 1995; Park, 2000). As compared to networks utilizing summation units only, higher order terms in HONN can increase the information capacity of the network. This representational power of higher order terms can help solving complex nonlinear problems with small networks as well as maintaining fast convergence capabilities (Leerink, 1995). A novel application of Ridge polynomial network formed by adding different degrees of Pi–Sigma neural networks has been suggested by (Ghazali, 2006) for financial time series prediction. The model is able to find an appropriate input output mapping of various chaotic financial time series data with a good performance in learning speed and generalization capability.

In the expedition of enhancing the accuracy of the prediction evolutionary algorithms or optimization techniques such as GA, PSO, Ant Colony Optimization (ACO), and so on, were used along with ANNs. Sermpinis et al. (2013) investigated the performance of an adaptive radial basis neural network along with PSO in the field of FOREX rate forecasting (Chen & Zhang, 2013). The experimental result shows that the hybrid model performs better than other traditional models in terms of both statistical and trading efficiency. Another investigation lead by Chen and Zhang (2013) used GA based on Mendel's principle of evolution to predict the FOREX rate. The outcome shows that the Mendel's-GA model works as a valuable tool for FOREX rate prediction in case of high-frequency data. A back propagation neural network was employed by Chang et al. (2009) to predict the buy/sell points for a stock. The study applied a case based dynamic window for improved forecast accuracy. Some compressive reviews of data mining applications in stock market forecasting were found in articles (Atsalakis & Valavanis, 2009; Venugopal et al., 2010). It was observed that neural networks, neuro-fuzzy models and other soft computing techniques outperform conventional models in most of cases. The prediction of stock closing prices of NSE and SENSEX using hybrid ANN model of functional link fuzzy logic neural models was found in the article (Kumaran, & Kailas, 2012). Forecasting currency exchange rates using an adaptive ARMA model with differential evolution based training was proposed by Rout et al. (2014). A novel knowledge guided artificial neural network (KGANN) was proposed by Jena et al. (2015) for exchange rate prediction. The prediction results of their proposed models were compared with that of the individual FLANN and LMS based models and found better. Performance evaluation of ANN based model for exchange rate prediction was conducted by Svitlana Galeshchuk in 2016 (Galeshchuk, 2016). The author claims the superiority of a MLP based model for one-step-ahead prediction of daily, monthly, and quarterly collected samples. Some applications of higher order neural networks for financial forecasting are proposed by Nayak et al. (2016a, 2016b, 2016c, 2016d, 2015a, 2015b) and Sahu et al. (2016).

The motivation of this research work is to develop and apply some of the most promising new neural networks such as HONNs to stock market data with improved forecasting accuracies. In order to overcome the disadvantages of gradient descent based training algorithm, an evolutionary global search optimization technique such as GA has been chosen for optimizing the parameters of the HONN based model. The prediction of short term (one-day-ahead), closing prices of BSE, DJIA, FTSE and NASDAQ have been carried out for financial year 2012 data. Similarly the prediction of one-step-ahead exchange rates also carried out by employing the same model. The sliding window technique has been used to select the training pattern for the network instead of dividing the whole data set into training and test pattern. Instead of normalizing the whole data set before training, we normalize the current training data. Also, for each current training pattern, a previously optimized weight set has been utilized adaptively and hence there is a significant reduction in training time.

The rest of the paper is organized as follows. Section 2 describes the GA based evolutionary training. Section 3 describes the model architecture of the forecasting models. Section 4 presents the experimental results and discussion. Finally Section 5 gives the concluding remarks followed by a list of references.

2. GENETIC ALGORITHM

Genetic algorithm has been considered as a popular global search optimization works on a population of potential solutions in the form of chromosomes, attempting to locate the best solution through the process of artificial evolution. GA are based on biological evolutionary theory and used to solve optimization problems which work with encoding parameter instead of parameter itself. It consists of the following repeated artificial genetic operations: evaluation, selection, crossover, and mutation.

In general the genetic evolution process consist the following basic steps as described by Algorithm 1. A complete discussion about GA can be found in (Goldberg, 1989; Holland, 1975).

The basic GA has six fundamental issues such as *individual representation, creation of the initial population, selection, reproduction using genetic operators, evaluation, and termination criteria.* Each part is described in the following sub section as follows:

2.1 Individual Representation

The representation scheme of GA determines how the problem is structured and the genetic operators used. To describe each individual in the population of interest i.e. search space, they are represented in the form of chromosome, which is made up of a sequence of genes from a certain alphabet. An alphabet can be binary, integers, floating point or symbols.

2.2 Creation of Initial Population

The most common method to supply an initial population to GA is randomly generated population. Since there can be improvement in the existing solution iteratively, the first solution can be a potentially good solution followed by randomly generated solutions for rest of the population. However, initial population may be created in the infeasible region, or all chromosomes in population may be far to the optimal solution, or search of solution may get a local solution and this local solution cannot get rid of. Uniform population generation can be another possible method for creation of initial mating pools in the population. In this method, instead of randomly generated initial population, a uniform population that forces the initial population to be not far away from the solutions and distributes it in the feasible region uniformly can be used.

Algorithm 1. Basic steps of Genetic Algorithm

```
1. Initialization of the search node randomly.
2. Evaluation of fitness of individuals.
3. Application of selection operator.
4. Application of crossover operator.
5. Application of mutation operator.
6. Repetition of the above steps until convergence.
```

2.3 Selection

The selection of better fit individuals to produce more suitable offspring in the successive generations is called as the selection mechanism in GA. This can act as the most important feature of GA. Based upon the individual's fitness; a probabilistic selection can be performed with the hope of creating better individuals in the next generation. There are several selection schemes that can be adopted in GA, such as tournament selection, roulette wheel selection, rank selection, and elitism method. In case of roulette wheel selection, the probability Pi, for each individual can be defined by:

$$P[individualchoosen] = \frac{F_i}{\sum_{j=1}^{popsize} F_j} \tag{1}$$

where F_i is the fitness of individual *i*.

2.4 Genetic Operators

The basic search mechanism of GA can be achieved through two genetic operators such as crossover and mutation. These two operators used to create new individuals from the existing individuals of the population. The crossover operator takes two individuals, exchange their genetic characteristics and produce two new solutions. The mutation takes one individual, alters it and produces one new solution. The mechanism of crossover and mutation depends upon the individual representation. For two individuals X and Y (*m* dimension vector) with binary representation, the crossover and mutation operators can be defined as follows:

Simple crossover: it generates a random number r from a uniform distribution from 1 to m and creates two new individuals x' and y' as shown by Equation 2 and Equation 3.

$$x'_i = \begin{cases} x_i & if\ i < r \\ y_i & otherwise \end{cases} \tag{2}$$

$$y'_i = \begin{cases} y_i & if\ i < r \\ x_i & otherwise \end{cases} \tag{3}$$

Binary mutation: it flips each bit in every individual in the current population with probability p_m according to Equation 4.

$$x'_i = \begin{cases} 1 - x_i & if U(0,1) < p_m \\ x_i & otherwise \end{cases} \tag{4}$$

There are several crossover methods such as single point, 2-point, multi point, uniform, arithmetic, and matrix crossover. Similarly, there can be uniform, non uniform, multi non uniform, boundary mutation etc., based upon the type of chromosome representation used.

2.5 Evaluation and Termination

The evaluation function is independent of the GA and can be used in many forms. The evaluation mechanism is subject to the minimal requirement that the function can map the population into a partially ordered set. GAs will force much of the entire population to converge to a single solution.

As the GA moves from generation to generation, there is chance of producing better solutions. The GA stopped by meeting the stopping criteria, which can be the maximum number of generation or population convergence criteria.

3. MODEL ARCHITECTURE

3.1 Multilayer Perceptron

The architecture of the MLP based forecasting model developed is discussed by this subsection. MLP is the most popular and frequently used neural model used for financial forecasting purpose. The better approximation and generalization capability of MLP has been established by many research works. The MLP model developed in this research work has only one hidden layer. The first layer is the input layer and the number of neurons/nodes in this layer corresponds to a fixed number of past closing prices selected by a sliding window. The optimal number of input to the model is a matter of trail. The last layer is called as the output layer and the number of neurons in this layer corresponds to the number of response variables. In this work the number of output neuron is fixed to one since it is going to predict the next day's closing prices. The number of neurons in the hidden layer defines the amount of complexity the model is capable of fitting. Apart from this there is an extra node having a fixed value of one to the hidden and output layer. This is called as a bias node. Each node in one layer has connected to all nodes in the immediate next layer. Each node connection represents a weight factor. Each node in the higher layer receives a weighted sum of input and weight factors from the previous layer. Each node in the hidden and output layer passes the information through a nonlinear activation function. In this way the information passes through the network and an output signal is produced at the output neuron called as an estimated closing price. Now the actual/desired price is provided at the output neuron and an error signal is calculated by finding difference between the estimated and actual price. This error value act as a feedback to the network and the weight vector and biases are adjusted accordingly. The learning process is the process of finding optimal weight and bias values for the MLP model so that it will able to map the input value of the training data to the corresponding output value. Figure 1 shows the standard MLP model developed for this experimental work.

Where:

$X = [x_1, x_2, \cdots, x_n]$ represents the network input.

$W = [w_{01}, w_{02}, \cdots, w_{mn}]$ is the adjustable weight vector between input and hidden layer.

Figure 1. Architecture of MLP with one hidden layer

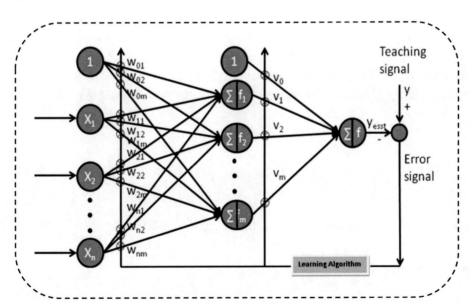

$V(n) = [v_0, v_1, \cdots, v_n]$ is the adjustable weight vector between hidden and output layer.

Σ is the weighted sum of input signals.

$F = (f_1, f_2, \cdots, f_n)$ is the transfer sigmoid activation: $S(x) = \dfrac{1}{1 + e^{-x}}$

y_{esst} is the estimated closing price by the model.

y is the actual/desired closing price

3.2. Second Order Neural Network: ASONN-GA

This subsection presents the architecture of the proposed ASONN-GA forecasting model and GA based adaptive training for ASONN-GA.

3.2.1 ASONN-GA Architecture

Figure 2 presents the standard ASONN-GA based forecasting model. The network has single layer architecture. The input signal contains the original closing prices as selected by the sliding window and product of these input signals resulting higher order terms of degree two. The neuron at the output layer receives the weighted sum of the input values along with a bias value of fixed weight one. This weighted sum is passed through a nonlinear activation which is a sigmoid function and produces an estimated closing price. The optimal weight vector and bias values are selected by GA and the GA based training is explained in the section *ASONN-GA Based Forecasting*.
   Where:

$X = [x_0, x_1, \cdots, x_m, x_0x_1, x_0x_2, \cdots x_0x_m, \cdots, x_{m-1}x_m]^T$ is the model input (including the input bias).

$y(n)$ is the estimated closing price by the forecasting model.

$d(n)$ is the desired closing price.

$w(n)$ is the adjustable weight vector.

Figure 2. Architecture of single layer ASONN-GA trained with genetic algorithm

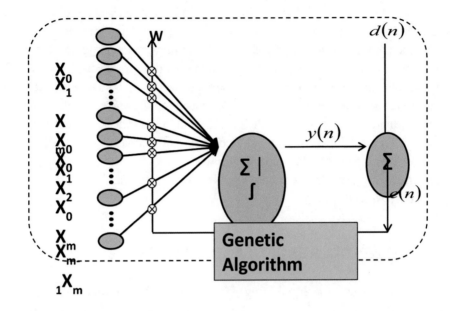

$e(n)$ is the error signal generated by the forecasting model

Σ is the weighted sum of input signals at the output neuron.

3.2.2 ASONN-GA Based Forecasting

This section explains about incorporation global search capability of GA to the above developed ASONN-GA based models. The basic of GA has been discussed in section 2.

In this research work, first we define a network structure with a fixed number of inputs, and a single output as shown in the Figure 1. The higher order signals terms are generated from the original input signals. Hence the input data contains the original signal and the second order terms generated from them. In order to keep the network architecture simple, the higher order terms are limited to second order only. Second we employed the GA in the learning phase of the network, as it is capable to search in a large search space. The hybridization of neural network and GA is able to select the optimal weight sets as well as the bias value for the forecasting model. The genetic algorithm performs search over the whole solution space, finds the optimal solution relatively easily, and it does not requires continuous differentiable objective functions. The problem of finding an optimal parameter set to train the model could be seen as a search problem into the space of all possible parameters. The fitness of the best and average individual in each generation increases towards a global optimum. It can be used as the tool for decision making in order to solve the complex nonlinear problems such as stock index prediction here. The chromosomes of GA represent the weight and bias values for a set of ASONN-GA models. Input data along with the chromosome values are fed to the set of ASONN-GA models. The fitness is obtained from the absolute difference between the target and the estimated output. The less the fitness value of an individual, GA considers it better fit. Figure 3 shows the general architecture of GA based adaptive ASONN-GA model developed for this experimental work.

The major steps of the GA based ASONN-GA models can be summarized and described by Algorithm 2.

4. EXPERIMENTAL RESULTS AND DISCUSSION

This section presents the forecasting results obtained by employing the above models. Different steps such as data collection, input design and normalization, and

Figure 3. Adaptive ASONN-GA forecasting model trained with Genetic Algorithm

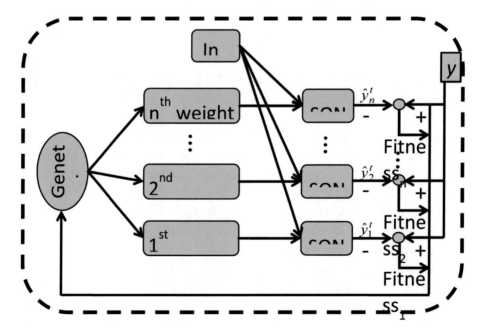

Algorithm 2. ASONN-GA Training

```
1. Random initialization of search spaces, i.e. populations.
   Initialize each search space, i.e. chromosome with values
   from the domain [0, 1].
2. Setting training data, i.e. choosing number of closing
   prices as input vector for the network.
3. Mapping of input patterns.
   Map input pattern from the lower dimension to higher
   dimension by incorporating second order terms.
4. While (termination criteria not met)
       For each chromosome in the search space
           Calculate the weighted sum and feed as an input to the
           node of output layer.
           Present the desired output, calculate the error signal
           and accumulate it.
           Fitness of the chromosome is equal to the accumulated
           error signal.
       End
       Apply crossover operator.
       Apply mutation operator.
       Select better fit solutions.
    End
5. Present the testing input vector, immediate to the training
   vectors.
   Calculated the weighted sum and calculate the error value.
6. Repeat the steps 2-5 for all training and testing patterns,
   calculate the mean absolute error signals.
```

experimental setup are discussed first followed by result analysis and discussion. Results obtained from closing prices forecasting and exchange rate forecasting are discussed separately.

4.1 Data Collection

The closing prices are collected from four fast growing stock markets such as BSE, DJIA, FTSE and NASDAQ for each transaction day of the stock exchange for the year 2016. The descriptive statistics for the closing prices are summarized in Table 1.

Table 1. Descriptive statistics of closing prices for different stocks

Stock Index	Descriptive Statistics						
	Minimum	Maximum	Mean	Standard deviation	Skewness	Kurtosis	Jarque-Bera test statistics
BSE	1.1024e+004	792.1800	4.6235e+003	2.6947e+003	0.1154	1.7908	236.0430(h=1)
DJIA	1.7138e+004	6.5471e+003	1.1400e+004	2.1801e+003	0.6644	3.0512	253.8134(h=1)
NASDAQ	4.5982e+003	1.1141e+003	2.3858e+003	709.7888	1.0392	4.0027	764.3663(h=1)
FTSE	6.8785e+003	3287	5.4165e+003	836.2381	-0.2837	2.1378	158.4568(h=1)

The positive skewness value of the closing price as observed from Table 1 implies that all the data sets except FTSE are spread out more toward right. The kurtosis analysis implies that stock price of DJIA, and NASDAQ are more outlier prone whereas all other financial time series are less outlier prone. Also, from the Jarque-Bera test statistics, it can be observed that all the stock price data sets are non-normal distributed.

For experimental purpose real data from five exchange rates have been collected from the website www.forecasts.org. (Financial Forecast Center, LLC., 2017). The data set consists of exchange rates of European Euro, British Pound, Indian Rupees, Japanese Yen, and Australian Dollar. The data show the average of daily figures on the 1st day of each month and collected for the period of 1999 to 2016. The number of data in each set is 214. The descriptive statistics of the exchange rate series are summarized in Table 2. It can be observed that except Yen to Dollar and Pound to Dollar dataset all other datasets show positive skewness value. This means, these

Table 2. Descriptive statistics from all financial time series

Dataset	Descriptive Statistics						
	Minimum	Maximum	Mean	Standard deviation	Skewness	Kurtosis	Jarque-Bera test statistics
US Dollar to Rupees	39.2680	68.2400	49.5192	7.5903	1.0952	2.9765	42.7875(h=1)
US Dollar to Euro	0.6345	1.1723	0.8430	0.1344	0.8812	2.8473	27.9051(h=1)
US Dollar to Yen	76.6430	133.6430	106.2796	14.0317	-0.5481	2.3795	14.1480(h=1)
US Dollar to Pound	0.9276	1.9920	1.3393	0.2888	0.6141	2.4885	15.7831(h=1)
US Dollar to Australian Dollar	0.4831	0.7886	0.6161	0.0619	-0.2110	2.6432	2.7234(h=0)

datasets are spread out more toward right and suggest investment opportunities. The kurtosis analysis implies that exchange rate of all datasets are less outlier prone than the normal distribution. Again from the Jarque-Bera test statistics, it can be observed that all the stock price datasets are non-normal distributed.

Each model is simulated for 10 times for each training set, in order to reduce the stochastic behavior of the model and the average error is considered for comparative analysis of results. Since each time the sliding window moves one step ahead, only one new closing price data has been included into the training set. So there may not be significant change in nonlinearity behavior of the training data set. For that reason, instead of considering another random weight set, we have used the previously optimized weight set for the successive training. In this way, after the first training set, the number of iteration has been fixed to a small value, hence significant reduction in training time. For comparison purpose the same set of training and testing data are fed to all the models. Also another statistical based model, i.e. Multi linear regression (MLR) has been considered for comparative study.

The experiment was carried out by a system with Intel ® core TM i3 CPU, 2.27 GHz and 2.42 GB memory. The programming language used MATLAB-2009 Version-7.8.0.347.

4.2 Input Design and Data Normalization

The sliding window method has been used to decide the input pattern for the model. An initial window with size 6 containing the present day closing prices and past 5 days closing price data is used. Subsequently the sliding window is shifted by one position in the financial time series to extract the next training pattern. The sliding window size is chosen 6 as it provides best prediction accuracy in the simulation experiment. Figure 4 shows an example of training and testing pattern is generated in this study. Table 1 presents the total number of closing prices and the number of windows generated by the sliding window for each financial time series.

Figure 4. Training window generation for short term prediction

						Target Data
	X_1	X_2	X_3	X_4	X_5	X_6
Training Data	X_2	X_3	X_4	X_5	X_6	X_7
	X_3	X_4	X_5	X_6	X_7	X_8
Test Data	X_4	X_5	X_6	X_7	X_8	X_9

The sigmoid normalization method has been used to normalize the original input signals as shown by Equation 5 (Nayak et al., 2012, 2014).

$$x_{norm} = \frac{1}{1 + e^{-\left(\frac{x_i - x_{min}}{x_{max} - x_{min}}\right)}} \tag{5}$$

Where x_{norm} is the normalized price, x_i is the current day closing price, x_{max} and x_{min} are the maximum and minimum price of the window respectively. The data within the current training set are normalized within [0, 1].

4.3 Experimental Setup

The normalized values are now considered as the input vector to the model. Let $X(n) = [x_1, x_2, \cdots, x_n]$ be the normalized closing prices. Let $W(n) = [w_1, w_2, \cdots, w_n]$ $W(n) = [w_{11}, w_{12}, w_{13} \cdots, w_{n1}, w_{n2}, w_{n3}]$ represent the elements of a weight vector associated with the input vector $X(n)$ at the summing unit neuron as shown in Figure 3. Each input pattern $X(n)$ is applied to the model sequentially and the desired closing prices value is supplied at the output neuron. Given the input, the model produces an output $y(n)$, which acts as an estimate to the desired value.

The error signal $e(n)$ is calculated as the difference between the desired response and the estimated output of the model. This is represented as in Equation 6.

$$e(n) = d(n) - y(n) \tag{6}$$

The error signal $e(n)$ and the input vectors are employed to the weight update algorithm to compute the optimal weight vector.

Figure 5 shows the individual representation in GA for both MLP and RNN as they have one hidden layer.

Figure 6 presents the individual representation for ASONN-GA.

Figure 5. Individual representation of MLP and RNN model

Weight Vector								Bias Values	
Input and Hidden Layer				Hidden and Output Layer				hidden	output
w_{11}	W_{12}	...	w_{mn}	V_1	V_1	...	V_n	$B_1 \, \text{----} \, B_n$	B_0

Figure 6. Individual representation of ASONN-GA model

Weight Vector								Bias Values	
Input and Hidden Layer				Hidden and Output Layer				hidden	output
W_{11}	W_{12}	...	W_{mn}	V_1	V_1	...	V_n	B_1 ... . B_n	B_0

To overcome the demerits of GD based back propagation, we employed the GA which is a popular global search optimization. We adopted the binary encoding for GA. Each weight and bias value constitute of 15 binary bits. For calculation of weighted sum at output neuron, the decimal equivalent of the binary chromosome is considered. A randomly initialized population with 50 genotypes is considered. GA was run for maximum 100 generations with the same population size. Parents are selected from the population by elitism method in which first 10% of the mating pools are selected from the best parents and the rest are selected by binary tournament selection method. A new offspring is generated from these parents using uniform crossover followed by mutation operator. In this experiment the crossover probability is taken as 0.5 and mutation probability is taken as 0.003. In this way the new population generated replaces the current population and the process continues until convergence occurs. The fitness of the best and average individuals in each generation increases towards a global optimum. The uniformity of the individuals increases gradually leading to convergence. Extensive experiments have been conducted and average results of 10 simulations have been collected. The same data sets are provided to each forecasting model and the computation time have been recorded. Table 2 summarizes the computation times for different models for different financial time series. It can be observed that the RNN model requires more computational time as compared to MLP due to more number of weight values. There is a substantial reduction in computational time in case of ASONN-GA as compared to MLP and RNN due to absence of hidden layer and simple architecture. The mean absolute errors (MAE) of 10 simulations from each model are considered for comparison and represented by Equation 7.

$$MAE = \frac{1}{10} \sum_{j=1}^{10} \left(\frac{1}{N} \sum_{i=1}^{N} \left| actual - estimated \right| \right) \tag{7}$$

$$MAE = \frac{1}{10} \sum_{j=1}^{10} \left(\frac{1}{N} \sum_{i=1}^{N} \left| actual\ closing\ prices - estimated\ closing\ prices \right| \right)$$

Further, to find out the exact benefit of using higher order neural network based forecasting model over other models for different stock indices, performance gain is evaluated as follows at Equation 8.

$$Performance\ Gain = \frac{(MAE\ of\ existing\ model - MAE\ of\ SONN\ model)}{MAE\ of\ existing\ model}$$

(8)

4.4 Results Analysis From Closing Price Data

This sub section presents and analyses the prediction accuracies obtained from all the three forecasting models for the prediction of one-step-ahead closing price. Separate experiments have been conducted for the aforementioned real stock market time series. Table 3 presents the prediction error signals.

Table 3. Prediction error generated by MLP, RNN, and ASONN-GA for all closing price series

		MLP	RNN	ASONN-GA
BSE	Minimum	0.000140	0.000100	0.000100
	Maximum	0.057200	0.060200	0.063700
	Average	**0.014433**	**0.013958**	**0.013100**
	Std.Deviation	0.011398	0.011247	0.011114
DJIA	Minimum	0.000000	0.000100	0.000000
	Maximum	0.030400	0.032000	0.031400
	Average	**0.008060**	**0.008632**	**0.008024**
	Std.Deviation	0.006975	0.006857	0.006928
NASDAQ	Minimum	0.000000	0.000000	0.000000
	Maximum	0.063400	0.057300	0.050300
	Average	**0.016045**	**0.012511**	**0.010741**
	Std.Deviation	0.013033	0.010415	0.008918
FTSE	Minimum	0.000000	0.000100	0.000000
	Maximum	0.073900	0.031100	0.032100
	Average	**0.014741**	**0.008106**	**0.007910**
	Std.Deviation	0.012637	0.006813	0.006802

From Table 3 it can be observed for BSE data set that the ASONN-GA model generates minimum average error, i.e. 0.013100 values as compared to MLP and RNN. RNN has an overall performance similar to that of MLP model. Comparing the performance of ASONN-GA to MLP and RNN, there is a gain in performance of 9.23515% and 6.147012% respectively.

For DJIA, MLP gives superior results as compared to RNN. However, the performance of ASONN-GA dominates that of MLP and RNN generating a minimal error of 0.008024. By adopting ASONN-GA, there is a % gain in performance of 0.445635% and 7.036159% as compared to MLP and RNN respectively.

The NASDAQ data set is provided to MLP, RNN and ASONN-GA model separately. Here also the ASONN-GA performs better than MLP and RNN. It can be observed that the ASONN-GA model generates lowest error value. It achieves significant better result over MLP and RNN. The % gain in error values are 33.05931% and 14.14995% when compared with MLP and RNN respectively.

The three forecasting models are employed to forecast the next day's closing prices of FTSE financial time series. Here the RNN and ASONN-GA model give quite superior results as compared to MLP. The ASONN-GA model achieves 46.3386% and 2.4176% gain in performance as compared to MLP and ASONN-GA respectively. From the results the superiority of the ASONN-GA forecasting model has been very clearly established.

From the above discussed empirical results, it can be clearly establish that the ASONN-GA model achieves better forecasting accuracies over other two conventional neural based models. To make it more clear the performance gain of ASONN-GA over MLP and RNN are calculated as in Equation 8. It can be observed that the ASONN-GA model gains a highest performance improvement over MLP for FTSE data, i.e. 46.3385% and lowest in case of DJIA, i.e. 0.445635%. The trend repeats for performance gain of ASONN-GA over RNN. There is a maximum performance gain over RNN in case of NASDAQ, i.e. 33.05931% and a minimum of 2.417577% in case of FTSE. On an average ASONN-GA achieves 22.26965% performance gain over MLP and 7.437674% over RNN while considering all the four data sets.

The actual v/s estimated prices by the proposed ASONN-GA model are plotted and presented by Figure 7 – 10 for BSE, DJIA, NASDAQ, and FTSE respectively. From these figures it can be observed that the proposed model is quite able to estimate future prices very closer to the actual values.

4.5 Results Analysis From Exchange Rate Data

This sub section presents and analyses the prediction accuracies obtained from all the three forecasting models for the prediction of one-step-ahead exchange rate price.

Figure 7. Actual vs. estimated closing prices by ASONN-GA from BSE stock data

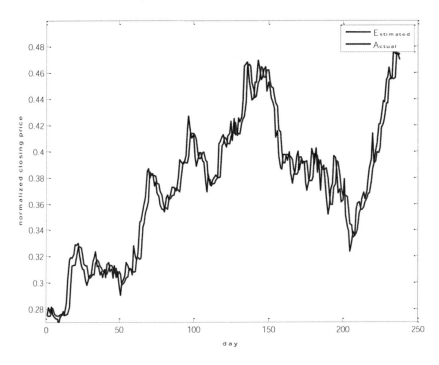

Figure 8. Actual vs. estimated closing prices by ASONN-GA from DJIA stock data

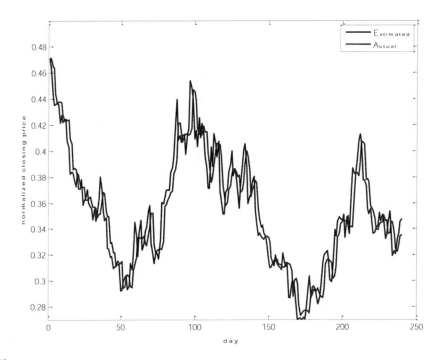

Figure 9. Actual vs. estimated closing prices by ASONN-GA from NASDAQ stock data

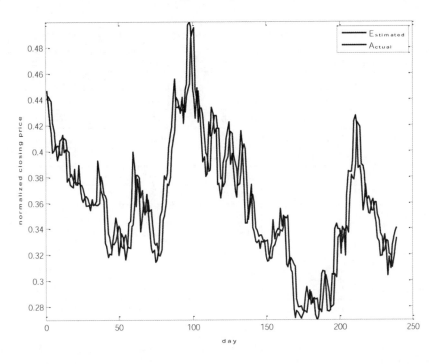

Figure 10. Actual vs. estimated closing prices by ASONN-GA from FTSE stock data

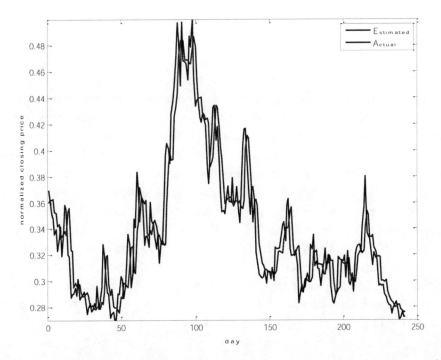

Table 4. Prediction error generated by MLP, RNN, and ASONN-GA for all exchange rate series

		MLP	**RNN**	**ASONN-GA**
US Dollar to Rupees	Minimum	0.001160	0.000102	8.2553e-005
	Maximum	0.054720	0.064202	0.049700
	Average	0.017033	0.014257	**0.007400**
	Std.Deviation	0.013318	0.012045	0.008000
US Dollar to Euro	Minimum	0.000030	0.000162	2.0725e-004
	Maximum	0.032300	0.032101	0.039700
	Average	**0.008351**	0.008601	0.011000
	Std.Deviation	0.006377	0.006127	0.008100
US Dollar to Yen	Minimum	0.000020	0.000001	4.4548e-005
	Maximum	0.061200	0.046303	0.050400
	Average	0.018142	0.013418	**0.011900**
	Std.Deviation	0.013130	0.010315	0.010100
US Dollar to Pound	Minimum	0.000000	0.000100	5.8760e-006
	Maximum	0.082900	0.053100	0.075800
	Average	0.034843	0.080106	**0.011100**
	Std.Deviation	0.015607	0.002813	0.011000
US Dollar to Australian Dollar	Minimum	0.014030	0.011001	1.1901e-006
	Maximum	0.000550	0.000010	0.076300
	Average	0.051930	0.046101	**0.010500**
	Std.Deviation	0.044245	0.070105	0.010300

Separate experiments have been conducted for the aforementioned real exchange rate time series from the stock market. Table 4 presents the prediction error signals.

From Table 4 it can be observed that, the ASONN-GA achieves lowest average error for all the exchange rate series except US Dollar to Euro data set, where the MLP generated the lowest. In case of US Dollar to Rupees data, ASONN-GA obtained 56.5549% and 48.0956% less error as compared to MLP and RNN respectively. In case of US Dollar to Yen data, the proposed model generated 34.4063% and 11.3131% less error as compared to MLP and RNN. For US Dollar to Pound series data the percentage of less error as compared to MLP and RNN are found to be 68.1428% and 86.1433% respectively. Similarly for US Dollar to Australian Dollar data the ASONN-GA model generated 79.7804% and 77.2239% less error over MLP and RNN forecasting model respectively. For more clarity on the performance of the proposed model, the actual v/s estimated prices are plotted and presented by the Figure 11 – 15.

Figure 11. Comparison of actual and predicted values for dollar to rupees exchange rates for 1 month ahead prediction

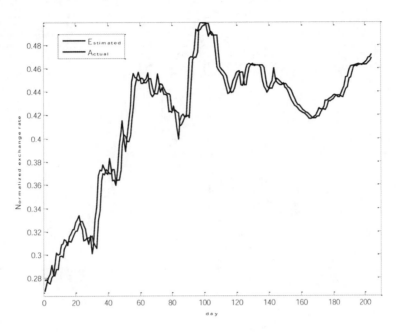

Figure 12. Comparison of actual and predicted values for dollar to euro exchange rates for 1 month ahead prediction

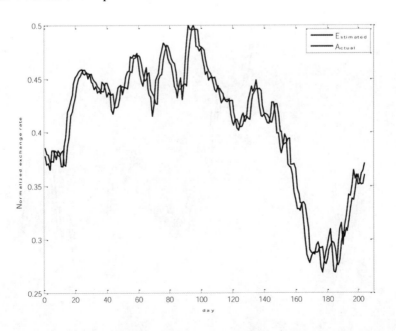

Figure 13. Comparison of actual and predicted values for dollar to pound exchange rates for 1 month ahead prediction

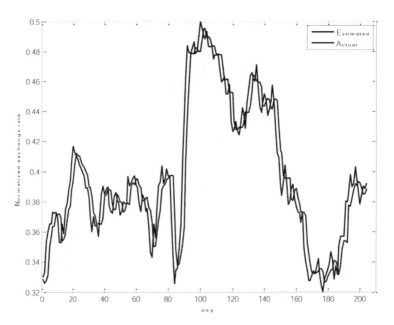

Figure 14. Comparison of actual and predicted values for dollar to yen exchange rates for 1 month ahead prediction

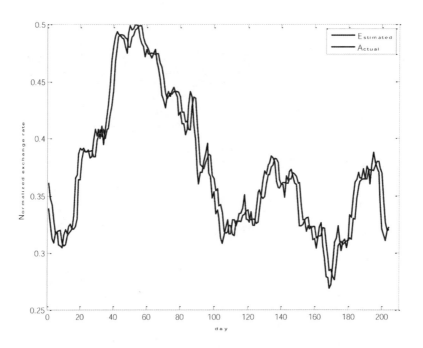

Figure 15. Comparison of actual and predicted values for dollar to Australian dollar exchange rates for 1 month ahead prediction

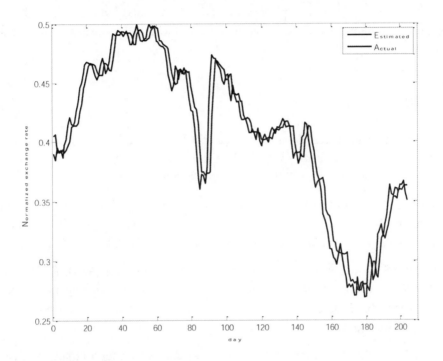

5. CONCLUSION

With the objective of achieving more forecasting accuracy, a second order neural network (ASONN-GA) based forecasting model trained with a global optimization technique has been proposed. The single layer architecture of the proposed model makes it simpler, requires less training time and provides white box visualization as compared to multilayer approach. The dimensions of input signals are limited to a degree of two in order to avoid the complexity and the model is quite capable to handle the high nonlinearity associated with the stock market data. For comparison purpose, two multilayer approach based networks such as a MLP and a RNN with one hidden layer have developed. The optimal parameters of the three models are fine tuned by genetic algorithm. The models are employed to forecast the next day's closing prices of four real stock market data and one-step-ahead exchange rates of five real stock markets. These models are trained adaptively and hence there is a reduction in training time. From extensive simulation results, it can be observed that the prediction capabilities of the three models are found to be satisfactory and acceptable. However, it can be established that the ASONN-GA model requires less training time and gives an overall better forecasting accuracies over other two models.

The future work may explore other HONN models, hybridizing with other evolutionary algorithms as well as application of the model toward other forecasting and data mining problems.

REFERENCES

Abraham, A., Nath, B., & Mahanti, P. K. (2002). Hybrid Intelligent Systems for Stock Market Analysis. *Proceedings of the International Conference on Computational Science*, 337-345. doi:10.1109/FUZZY.2000.838709

Acharjya, D., & Anitha, A. (2017). A Comparative Study of Statistical and Rough Computing Models in Predictive Data Analysis. *International Journal of Ambient Computing and Intelligence*, 8(2), 32–51. doi:10.4018/IJACI.2017040103

Ashour, A. S., Samanta, S., Dey, N., Kausar, N., Abdessalemkaraa, W. B., & Hassanien, A. E. (2015). Computed tomography image enhancement using cuckoo search: A log transform based approach. *Journal of Signal and Information Processing*, 6(03), 244–257. doi:10.4236/jsip.2015.63023

Atsalakis, G. S., & Valavanis, K. P. (2009). Surveying stock market forecasting techniques – part II: Soft computing methods. *Expert Systems with Applications*, 36(3), 5932–5941. doi:10.1016/j.eswa.2008.07.006

Bag, V., & Kulkarni, U. V. (2017). Stock Price Trend Prediction and Recommendation using Cognitive Process. *International Journal of Rough Sets and Data Analysis*, 4(2), 36–48. doi:10.4018/IJRSDA.2017040103

Benmounah, Z., Meshoul, S., & Batouche, M. (2017). Scalable Differential Evolutionary Clustering Algorithm for Big Data Using Map-Reduce Paradigm. *International Journal of Applied Metaheuristic Computing*, 8(1), 45–60. doi:10.4018/IJAMC.2017010103

Binh, H. T. T., Hanh, N. T., & Dey, N. (2016). Improved Cuckoo Search and Chaotic Flower Pollination optimization algorithm for maximizing area coverage in Wireless Sensor Networks. *Neural Computing & Applications*, 1–13.

Box, G. E. P., & Jenkins, G. M. (1976). *Time Series Analysis-Forecasting and Control*. San Francisco, CA: Holden-Day Inc.

Chang, P.-C., Liu, C.-H., Lin, J.-L., Fan, C.-Y., & Ng, C. S. P. (2009). A neural network with a case based dynamic window for stock trading prediction. *Expert Systems with Applications, 36*(3), 6889–6898. doi:10.1016/j.eswa.2008.08.077

Chen, Y., & Zhang, G. (2013). Exchange rates determination based on genetic algorithms using Mendels principles: Investigation and estimation under uncertainty. *Information Fusion, 14*(3), 327–333. doi:10.1016/j.inffus.2011.12.003

Chiang, W. C., Urban, T. L., & Baldridge, G. W. (1996). A Neural Network Approach to Mutual Fund Net Asset Value Forecasting. *Omega, 24*(2), 205–215. doi:10.1016/0305-0483(95)00059-3

Dash, Ch. S. K., Dash, A. P., Dehuri, S., & Cho, S. B. (2013). Feature Selection for Designing a Novel Differential Evolution Trained Radial Basis Function Network for Classification. *International Journal of Applied Metaheuristic Computing, 4*(1), 32–49. doi:10.4018/jamc.2013010103

Dey, N., Ashour, A. S., Beagum, S., Pistola, D. S., Gospodinov, M., Gospodinova, E. P., & Tavares, J. M. R. (2015). Parameter optimization for local polynomial approximation based intersection confidence interval filter using genetic algorithm: An application for brain MRI image de-noising. *Journal of Imaging, 1*(1), 60–84. doi:10.3390/jimaging1010060

Dey, N., Chakraborty, S., & Samanta, S. (2014b). Optimization of watermarking in biomedical signal.Lambert Publication. *Heinrich-Böcking-Straße, 6*, 66121.

Dey, N., Samanta, S., Chakraborty, S., Das, A., Chaudhuri, S. S., & Suri, J. S. (2014a). Firefly algorithm for optimization of scaling factors during embedding of manifold medical information: An application in ophthalmology imaging. *Journal of Medical Imaging and Health Informatics, 4*(3), 384–394. doi:10.1166/jmihi.2014.1265

Dey, N., Samanta, S., Yang, X. S., Das, A., & Chaudhuri, S. S. (2013). Optimisation of scaling factors in electrocardiogram signal watermarking using cuckoo search. *International Journal of Bio-inspired Computation, 5*(5), 315–326. doi:10.1504/IJBIC.2013.057193

Doush, I. A., Alkhateed, F., & Al Maghayreh, E. (2013). Hybridizing Harmony Search Algorithm with Multi-Parent Crossover to Solve Real World Optimization Problems. *International Journal of Applied Metaheuristic Computing, 4*(3), 1–14. doi:10.4018/ijamc.2013070101

Financial Forecast Center, LLC. (2017). *Why do the stock markets keep going up?*. Retrieved from www.forecasts.org

Galeshchuk, S. (2016). Neural networks performance in exchange rate prediction. *Neurocomputing*, *172*, 446–452. doi:10.1016/j.neucom.2015.03.100

Ghazali, R., Hussain, A., & El-Deredy, V. (2006). Application of ridge polynomial neural networks to financial time series prediction. *2006 International Joint Conference on Neural Networks*, 913–20. doi:10.1109/IJCNN.2006.246783

Goldberg, D. (1989). *Genetic Algorithms in Search, Optimization, and Machine Learning*. Addison Wesley.

Guler, M., & Sahin, E. (1994). A new higher-order binary-input neural unit: Learning and generalizing effectively via using minimal number of monomials. *Third Turkish Symposium on Artificial Intelligence and Neural Networks Proceedings*. Middle East Technical University.

Holland, J. (1975). *Adaptation in natural and artificial systems*. Ann Arbor, MI: The University of Michigan Press.

Hore, S., Chatterjee, S., Santhi, V., Dey, N., Ashour, A. S., Balas, V. E., & Shi, F. (2017). Indian Sign Language Recognition Using Optimized Neural Networks. In Information Technology and Intelligent Transportation Systems (pp. 553-563). Springer International Publishing. doi:10.1007/978-3-319-38771-0_54

Jena, P. R., Majhi, R., & Majhi, B. (2015). Development and performance evaluation of a novel knowledge guided artificial neural network (KGANN) model for exchange rate prediction. *Journal of King Saud University-Computer and Information Sciences*, *27*(4), 450–457. doi:10.1016/j.jksuci.2015.01.002

Kishor, D. R., & Venkateswarlu, N. B. (2016). A Novel Hybridization of Expectation-Maximization and K-Means Algorithms for Better Clustering Performance. *International Journal of Ambient Computing and Intelligence*, *7*(2), 47–74. doi:10.4018/IJACI.2016070103

Kumaran Kumar, J., Kailas, A., 2012. Prediction of future stock close price using proposed hybrid ANN model of functional link fuzzy logic neural model (FLFNM). *Int. J. Comput. Appl. Eng. Sci.*, *2*(1).

Leerink, L. R., Giles, C. L., Horne, B. G., & Jabri, M. A. (1995). Learning with product units. In G. Tesaro, D. Touretzky, & T. Leen (Eds.), Advances in Neural Information Processing Systems 7. Cambridge, MA: MIT Press.

Maglaveras, N., Stamkopoulas, T., Pappas, C., & Strintzis, M. (1998). An Adaptive back-propagation neural network for real time ischemia episodes detection Development and performance using the European ST-T databases. *IEEE Trans., Biomed Engng.*, 805-813.

Marinakis, Y., & Magdalene, N. (2011). Discrete Artificial Bee Colony Optimization Algorithm for Financial Classification Problems. *International Journal of Applied Metaheuristic Computing, 2*(1), 1–17. doi:10.4018/jamc.2011010101

Miller, A. S., Blott, B. H., & Hames, T. K. (1992). Review of neural network applications in medical imaging and signal processing. *Medical & Biological Engineering & Computing, 30*(5), 449–464. doi:10.1007/BF02457822 PMID:1293435

Nayak, S. C., Misra, B. B., & Behera, H. S. (2012). Stock Index Prediction With Neuro-Genetic Hybrid Techniques. *Intenational Journal of Computer Science and Informatics, IJCSI, 2*(3), 27–34.

Nayak, S. C., Misra, B. B., & Behera, H. S. (2012, October). Evaluation of normalization methods on neuro-genetic models for stock index forecasting. In *Information and Communication Technologies (WICT), 2012 World Congress on* (pp. 602-607). IEEE. doi:10.1109/WICT.2012.6409147

Nayak, S. C., Misra, B. B., & Behera, H. S. (2014). Impact of data normalization on stock index forecasting. *Int. J. Comp. Inf. Syst. Ind. Manag. Appl, 6*, 357–369.

Nayak, S. C., Misra, B. B., & Behera, H. S. (2015a). A Pi-Sigma Higher Order Neural Network for Stock Index Forecasting. In *Computational Intelligence in Data Mining-Volume 2* (pp. 311–319). Springer India. doi:10.1007/978-81-322-2208-8_29

Nayak, S. C., Misra, B. B., & Behera, H. S. (2015b). Comparison of Performance of Different Functions in Functional Link Artificial Neural Network: A Case Study on Stock Index Forecasting. In *Computational Intelligence in Data Mining-Volume 1* (pp. 479–487). Springer India. doi:10.1007/978-81-322-2205-7_45

Nayak, S. C., Misra, B. B., & Behera, H. S. (2016a). Adaptive Hybrid Higher Order Neural Networks for Prediction of Stock Market Behavior. In Applied Artificial Higher Order Neural Networks for Control and Recognition (pp. 174-191). IGI Global. doi:10.4018/978-1-5225-0063-6.ch007

Nayak, S. C., Misra, B. B., & Behera, H. S. (2016b). Improving Performance of Higher Order Neural Network using Artificial Chemical Reaction Optimization: A Case Study on Stock Market Forecasting. In *Applied Artificial Higher Order Neural Networks for Control and Recognition* (pp. 253–280). IGI Global. doi:10.4018/978-1-5225-0063-6.ch011

Nayak, S. C., Misra, B. B., & Behera, H. S. (2016c). An Adaptive Second Order Neural Network with Genetic-Algorithm-based Training (ASONN-GA) to Forecast the Closing Prices of the Stock Market. *International Journal of Applied Metaheuristic Computing*, 7(2), 39–57. doi:10.4018/IJAMC.2016040103

Nayak, S. C., Misra, B. B., & Behera, H. S. (2016d). Fluctuation prediction of stock market index by adaptive evolutionary higher order neural networks. *International Journal of Swarm Intelligence*, 2(2-4), 229–253. doi:10.1504/IJSI.2016.081152

Nourani, V., Entezari, E., & Yousefi, P. (2013). ANN-RBF Hybrid model for Spatiotemporal Estimation of Monthly Precipitation Case Study: Ardabil Plain. *International Journal of Applied Metaheuristic Computing*, 4(2), 1–16. doi:10.4018/jamc.2013040101

Pai, G. V., & Michel, T. (2017). Metaheuristic Optimization of Constrained Large Portfolios using Hybrid Particle Swarm Optimization. *International Journal of Applied Metaheuristic Computing*, 8(1), 1–23. doi:10.4018/IJAMC.2017010101

Park, S., Smith, M. J. T., & Mersereau, R. M. (2000). Target recognition based on directional filter banks and higher-order neural networks. *Digital Signal Processing*, 10(4), 297–308. doi:10.1006/dspr.2000.0376

Romahi, Y., & Shen, Q. (2000). Dynamic Financial Forecasting with Automatically Induced Fuzzy Associations. *Proc. of the 9th International Conference on Fuzzy Systems*, 493-498.

Rout, M., Majhi, B., Majhi, R., & Panda, G. (2014). Forecasting of currency exchange rates using an adaptive ARMA model with differential evolution based training. *Journal of King Saud University-Computer and Information Sciences*, 26(1), 7–18. doi:10.1016/j.jksuci.2013.01.002

Sahu, K. K., Sahu, S. R., Nayak, S. C., & Behera, H. S. (2016). Forecasting foreign exchange rates using CRO based different variants of FLANN and performance analysis. *International Journal of Computational Systems Engineering*, 2(4), 190–208. doi:10.1504/IJCSYSE.2016.081380

Samantaa, S., Dey, N., Das, P., Acharjee, S., & Chaudhuri, S. S. (2013). *Multilevel threshold based gray scale image segmentation using cuckoo search*. arXiv preprint arXiv:1307.0277

Senthilnathan, C. R. (2016). Understanding Retail Consumer Shopping Behaviour Using Rough Set Approach. *International Journal of Rough Sets and Data Analysis*, 3(3), 38–50. doi:10.4018/IJRSDA.2016070103

Sermpinis, G., Theofilatos, K., Karathanasopoulos, A., Georgopoulos, E. F., & Dunis, C. L. (2013). Forecasting foreign exchange rates with adaptive neural networks using radial-basis functions and Particle Swarm Optimization. *European Journal of Operational Research*, *225*(3), 528–540. doi:10.1016/j.ejor.2012.10.020

Shin, Y., & Ghosh, J. (1995). Ridge Polynomial Networks. *IEEE Transactions on Neural Networks*, *6*(3), 610–622. doi:10.1109/72.377967 PMID:18263347

Venugopal Setty, D., Rangaswamy, T. M., & Subramanya, K. N. (2010). A review on data mining applications to the performance of stock marketing. *International Journal of Computers and Applications*, *1*(3), 33–43. doi:10.5120/88-187

Wang, Z., Fang, J., & Liu, X. (2006). *Global stability of stochastic high-order neural networks with discrete and distributed delays, Chaos, Solutions and Fractals.* doi:, 06.06310.1016/j.chaos.2006

White, H. (1998). Economic Prediction Using Neural Networks: The Case of IBM Daily Stock Returns. *Proceedings of the Second Annual IEEE Conference on Neural Networks, 1*(2), 451-458.

KEY TERMS AND DEFINITIONS

ANN: Artificial Neural Network.
ARCH: Auto-Regressive Heteroscedastic.
ARIMA: Auto-Regressive Integrated Moving Average.
ASONN-GA: Adaptive Second Order Neural Network with GA training.
BSE: Bombay Stock Exchange.
DE: Differential Evolution.
EA: Evolutionary Algorithm.
FLANN: Functional Link Artificial Neural Network.
GA: Genetic Algorithm.
GARCH: Generalized ARCH.
HONN: Higher Order Neural Network.
MAE: Mean Absolute Error.
MLP: Multilayer Perceptron.
MLR: Multi Linear Regression.
PSO: Particle Swarm Optimization.
RBF: Radial Basis Function.
RNN: Recurrent Neural Network.
SONN: Second Order Neural Network.

Chapter 11
Hybrid Non–Dominated Sorting Genetic Algorithm:
II–Neural Network Approach

Sankhadeep Chatterjee
University of Calcutta, India

Sarbartha Sarkar
Indian Institute of Technology Dhanbad, India

Nilanjan Dey
Techno India College of Technology, India

Amira S. Ashour
Tanta University, Egypt

Soumya Sen
University of Calcutta, India

ABSTRACT

Water pollution due to industrial and domestic reasons is highly affecting the water quality. In undeveloped and developed countries, it has become a major reason behind a number of water borne diseases. Poor public health is putting an extra economic liability in order to deploy precautionary measures against these diseases. Recent research works have been directed toward more sustainable solutions to this problem. It has been revealed that good quality of water supply can not only improve the public health, it also accelerates economic growth of a geographical location as well. Water quality prediction using machine learning methods is still at its primitive stage. Besides, most of the studies did not follow any national or international standard for water quality prediction. In the current work, both the problems have been addressed. First, advanced machine learning methods, namely Artificial Neural Networks (ANNs) supported by a well-known multi-objective

DOI: 10.4018/978-1-5225-4151-6.ch011

optimization algorithm called the Non-dominated Sorting Genetic Algorithm-II (NSGA-II) has been used to classify the water samples into two different classes. Secondly, Indian national standard for water quality (IS 10500:2012) has been utilized for this classification task. The hybrid NN-NSGA-II model is compared with another two well-known meta-heuristic supported ANN classifiers, namely ANN trained by Genetic Algorithm (NN-GA) and by Particle Swarm Optimization (NN-PSO). Apart from that, the support vector machine (SVM) has also been included in the comparative study. Besides analysing the performance based on several performance measuring methods, the statistical significance of the results obtained by NN-NSGA-II has been judged by performing Wilcoxon rank sum test with 5% confidence level. Results have indicated the ingenuity of the proposed NN-NSGA-II model over the other classifiers under current study.

INTRODUCTION

Water quality monitoring is a domineering process for maintaining safe and reliable water source. It is considered one of the serious problems that affect the individual's health. The furthermost death cause in Asia and Africa is the contaminated drinking water (Vasudevan, & Oturan, 2014). Deteriorated water quality originated widespread management labors in several countries to resolve and to predict water quality issue. Typically, several factors can affect the water quality, including i) the calcium level that exists in the natural water, and ii) the industrial wastes, rocks, sewage, which are another calcium source leading to lower water quality. Furthermore, the hard water is liable for the heart disease and many other serious and chronic diseases. Water contaminators are subsequently reached the ground water sources. Ultimately, water quality prediction techniques become urgent to evaluate and to test the water quality for addressing the specific water supply's problems. This ensures the water sources protection from prospective contamination toward achieving good quality water that preserves the overall public health (Edition, 2011). Water sources contamination is considered the major reason behind water pollution due to physical, chemical, and radioactive elements. In the urban areas, the municipal tap water is one of the main water sources for the domestic uses. Accordingly, in order to ensure the water supply quality, water quality analysis becomes obligatory.

Water quality prediction can efficiently achieved by using machine learning techniques, such as the NN that has been employed for water quality prediction process. In order to study the industrial waste effect on the water quality prediction, data is to be collected from a water treatment plant in terms of the water quality index. Machine learning, especially the NN has enormous applications in various aspects of environmental modeling and classification. Alongside, water quality predication magnetized the focus of several researchers. A recurrent NN has been employed to predict the water quality index, which compared to the results of the radial basis function NN based model. Reckhow and Kenneth (1999) carried out the Bayesian probability networks to study the eutrophication of the Neuse river estuary for determining the water quality. Wu *et al.* (2011) expected the chlorine residual in water distribution system using NNs using different flow features and water quality measurements. In addition, free ammonia content has been predicted. Furthermore, the NN has an extensive role in several applications (Hore *et al.*, 2016; Chatterjee *et al.*, 2016a; 2016b). Sheppard *et al.* demonstrated the remote sensing role as well as the global positioning systems to enrich the water quality detection in the Northern Alabama. The proposed system supervised, evaluated and predicted the non-point contamination sources. Jain *et al.* (2001) carried out the NN to model the short-term water demand. A comparative study has been carried out for six network prototypes, namely regression models and 2 time series models. El-Din *et al.* (2004) conducted the NN to model the process of wastewater treatment with conducted comparative study between the proposed ANNs approach and the conventional deterministic approach. The experimental results established that the NN contained huge extra information with respect to the modeled scheme. Wechmongkhonkon *et al.* (2012) grouped the water environment of Dusit District canals in Thailand using the NN through Levenberg-Marquardt algorithms with a high accuracy of 96.52%. Despite the effectiveness of the NN in various real life applications, the NN performance is highly dependent on the training strategy. In the intricate real life situations (Guesgen, & Marsland, 2016; Odella, 2017), the traditional back-propagation based algorithm (Paola, & Schowengerdt, 1995) is ineffectual due to the premature convergence of the training algorithms. Since water quality prediction is highly significant for public health, it demands more accurate and trustworthy model. Several analysis and optimization techniques have been employed in several applications for prediction and classification (Dey *et al.*, 2014; 2015a; 2015b; 2015c; Ashour *et al.*, 2015; Pal *et al.* 2015; 2015a; Mukherjee *et al.*, 2015; Araki *et al.*, 2015; Nandi *et al.*, 2015; Ghosh *et al.*, 2015; Maji *et al.*, 2015; Araki *et al.*, 2015; Ikeda, 2015; Kotyk *et al.*, 2015; Karaa *et al.*, 2016; Bureš *et al.*, 2016; Saba *et al.*, 2016; Virmani, 2016; Kausar *et al.*, 2016; Sharma, & Virmani, 2017; Manogaran, & Lopez, 2017; Boulmaiz *et al.*, 2017; Acharjya, & Anitha, 2017; Khachane, 2017; Juneja *et al*, 2017; Tyagi *et al.*, 2017; Ahmed *et al.*, 2017). Consequently, meta-heuristic algorithms can be conducted to train the NN using their ability to significantly improve the NN performance.

Consequently, in the current study three different models are engaged to predict the water quality. The water dataset is collected from different municipal areas on both sides of Hooghly river bank at West Bengal in India throughout one year (12 months). The water quality is classified into two classes, namely 'Safe' and 'Unsafe' water based on the IS 10500:2012 standard (Standard, 1991). First, the genetic algorithm (GA) as well as the PSO are engaged in to train the NN, which is referred as NN-GA and NN-PSO; respectively. Both models used the root mean squared error (RMSE) as their objective function. In addition, multi-objective GA based NN is employed using the RMSE and maximum error (ME) as its objective functions. Apart from these three NN models, the SVM also is engaged. All models are compared with each other with respect to the accuracy, precision, recall, F-measure, Matthews correlation coefficient (MCC) (Jurman *et al.*, 2012) and Fowlkes-Mallows index (FM index).

METHODOLOGY

Neural Network

The NN is neuron interaction inspired model that can be efficiently used to learn complex patterns. Understanding patterns lead to future prediction of certain value. The basic structure of a typical NN consists of several artificial neurons that are arranged into multiple layers. Neurons of a layer connect with the neurons of its preceding and succeeding layers. During the training phase, the data instances are fed to the ANN and the response is compared with the expected outcome. The difference between the expected outcome and response given by the NN is used as an error measure. This error quantity is utilized to adjust the weights associated with the NN to improve its performance. The same process is conducted for each data instance. At the last step of training phase, it is expected to have the optimal set of weights that used to minimize the misclassification probability. Throughout the testing stage, the NN is tested with a set of unknown data and its responses are checked to measure its performance. Figure 1 depicted a typical NN.

The traditional training algorithms (Møller, 1993) do not ensure the optimal training as they may trap in local optima while searching for the best solution. For ensuring that the NN obtains the optimal set of weights during the training phase ensures, the error is to be minimized, which can be considered as an optimization problem. In the current work, minimizing the error is used as the objective function to attain the optimal weights set. Thus, meta-heuristic algorithms can be employed to ensure convergence to the global optima. Consequently, meta-heuristic optimization methods, such as GA, PSO, and NSGA-II can be employed to train the NN.

Figure 1. One hidden layer NN structure

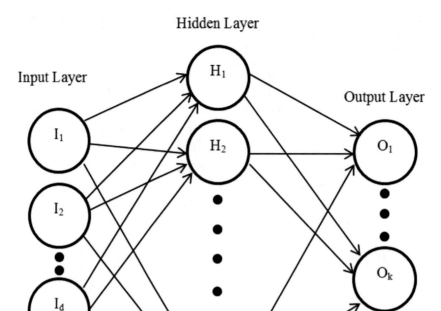

Genetic Algorithm

Genetic algorithm inspired by the evolutionary process is conducted to solve several problems (Gen, & Cheng, 2000). It includes a population that participates to find the solution, where each population's member denotes a potential solution of the considered problem. Furthermore, it is associated with a fitness function to define the superior solution. At every generation, the GA attempts to realize the best solution by propagating the superior solutions from the preceding generation. A multidimensional search involves an optimization of certain objective function. Initial random population is manipulated by using the definite genetic operators in order to produce new solutions. These operators are namely the selection, crossover, and mutation. Furthermore, the fitness values of the offspring are generally determined by the concerned objective function to be optimized. After calculating the fitness, some of the better solutions will participate in the next evolution level. It is expected that after certain number of generations, superior solution will be achieved. This process can be terminated after obtaining satisfactory fitness of the optimum solution in the population as illustrated in the following GA procedure (Algorithm 1).

Multi-Objective Genetic Algorithm

Generally, several problems comprise multiple objectives optimization at the same time to attain a potent solution. The multi-objective optimization (Coello, 1999) can properly be definite by finding the vector $\overrightarrow{x_p} = \left[x_1, x_2, ..., x_n \right]^T$ of n decision variables such that $\overrightarrow{f(x_p)} = \left[f_1\left(\vec{x}\right), f_2\left(\vec{x}\right), ..., f_n\left(\vec{x}\right) \right]^T$ satisfies some constraints. The vector $\overrightarrow{x_p}$ is considered Pareto optimal if only there is no $\vec{x}$ exist such that $\forall i \in \{1, 2, ..., n\}, f_i\left(\vec{x}\right) \leq f_i\left(\overrightarrow{x_p}\right)$ and there exist at least one i such that $f_i\left(\vec{x}\right) < f_i\left(\overrightarrow{x_p}\right)$. The set of solutions which is generated due to the Pareto optimality are generally addressed as non-dominated solutions. The working principle of multi-objective GA (NSGA-II) is analogous to the GA. However, the optimization process in the NSGA-II tries to optimize multiple objectives, which are sometimes contradictory to each other. A general NSGA-II algorithm has been depicted in Figure 2.

Algorithm 1. Genetic Algorithm

Begin

  Produce random *n* chromosomes population representing the suitable solutions

  Estimate the fitness of each chromosome

  Use the following iterative steps to create a new population:

    Choose from the population two parent chromosomes using their fitness

    Use the crossover probability to crossover the parents for new offspring formation

    Mutate new offspring

    Assign fresh offspring in a new population

  Utilize the new produced population for another iteration

   If the end constraint is achieved

    stop, and give the preeminent solution

   End if

  Repeat preceding steps

End

Figure 2. Flow chart of multi-objective GA

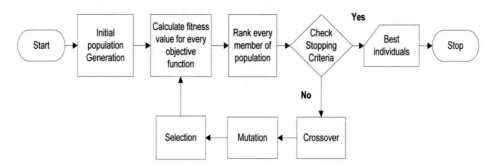

The selection process comes after a ranking of the current population, which is achieved in the current work by a non-dominated sorting (Deb, 2001) that used in the NSGA-II algorithm. For selection purpose a binary tournament method has been utilized. In NSGA-II (Li, & Zhang, 2009), the non-dominated sorting process is faster than the previous version. In addition, it also assures elitism of next generation, which is a key factor of successful and efficient convergence of the algorithm.

Particle Swarm Optimization

PSO algorithm is stimulated by the school of fishes or flock of birds' social interaction comportment, which can efficiently, engaged for single objective optimization problems. It can be carried out to determine the global minima of a real valued objective function $f(x)$, where $f(x) \in R$ at minima x_0, $f(x_0) \leq f(x) \forall x \in R^n$ is used. The PSO employs N number of search agents known as particles, which perform the searching operation over the domain (R^n). All search agents together are called the Swarm. During the searching for the minima, every i^{th} particle maintains its current position (x_i) with a velocity (v_i). Based on the gathered information, a solution (p_i or *pbest*) is maintained representing the best solution. The best of all particles (p_i s) is called the global best ($gbest$) at certain instance of time. The velocity and positions of particles are calculated using the following expressions:

$$v_i\left(t+1\right) = v_i\left(t\right) + a_1 * r_1 * (pbest_i\left(t\right) - x_i\left(t\right)) + a_2 * r_2 * (gbest_i\left(t\right) - x_i(t)) \quad (1)$$

$$x_i\left(t+1\right) = x_i\left(t\right) + v_i(t+1) \quad (2)$$

PROPOSED SYSTEM

In order to achieve efficient prediction and classification using the NN, a reasonable number of data instances of each class are required. Consequently, a dataset of 240 data samples collected from 10 different municipal areas on both sides of Hooghly river bank are involved in the current study. The water supply of those areas is highly dependent on the Hooghly river water source. This particular region is selected due to its high population density and presence of industrial sectors which reflects the population due to domestic as well as industrial sources.

Extracted Features

Different features are extracted in the present study from the water samples that collected from 10 different municipal areas of the Hooghly river side region by performing several laboratory based tests. Such features include the Chlorides, level of pH, total hardness, Turbidity, total alkalinity, and Residual Chlorine. The collected samples are investigated and are analyzed by different laboratory experiments to extract the following features that used to determine the water quality, which are namely i) the hydrogen ion concentration (pH) having the range limits of 6.50 to 8.50 maximum allowable limits given by the IS 10500:2012, ii) the chlorides, where a large chlorides concentration in the water indicates organic pollution that has maximum tolerable limit of 1000 mg/l as standardized by IS 10500:2012, iii) the total hardness that reflects the water quality having maximum allowable limit of 600 mg/l, iv) the calcium hardness having maximum tolerable limit of 200 mg/l, v) the total alkalinity of 600 mg/l maximum tolerable limit, vi) the turbidity having maximum tolerable limit of 5 N.T.U., and vii) the residual chlorine having maximum tolerable limit of 1 mg/l. Afterward, the water samples are labeled as 'Safe' and 'Unsafe' based on the Indian Standards (IS 10500:2012) using the meta-heuristic supported ANNs. The proposed system block diagram is illustrated in Figure 3.

Fitness Functions

In the present work, the root mean-squared error (RMSE) of the classifier to predict the water quality regarding the computed variable v_{i_k} is expressed as follows:

$$RMSE = \sqrt{\frac{\sum_{k=1}^{n} \left(v_{j_k} - v_{i_k}\right)^2}{n}} \tag{3}$$

Figure 3. A general flow of training phase of ANN using meta-heuristics

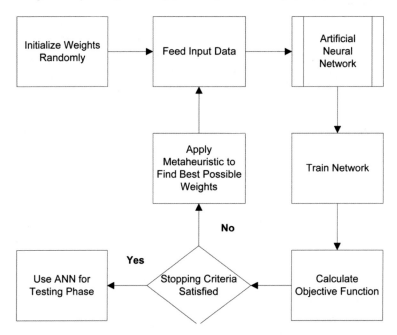

where, v_{j_k} represents the observed data instance k^{th} value, and v_{i_k} represents the forecasted value by the classifier. Apart from the RMSE, the NSGA-II is used simultaneously to optimize the ME, which is given by:

$$ME = Z_{\alpha/2}\frac{\sigma}{\sqrt{n}} \tag{4}$$

where, $Z_{\alpha/2}$ denotes the z-score having confidence level $(1-\alpha)$ and σ denotes the standard deviation of n many samples. The objective of the NSGA-II is to determine the Pareto optimal front from which no further improvement is possible without sacrificing one of the objectives. Additionally, in the current work, the LIBSVM (Chang, & Lin, 2011) is betrothed for predicting the water quality using the SVM.

Performance Metrics

In terms of different performance metrics, the optimization models are assessed using the confusion matrix (Powers, 2011), which are expressed by:

$$Accuracy = \frac{tp + tn}{tp + fp + fn + tn} \tag{5}$$

$$Precision = \frac{tp}{tp + fp} \tag{6}$$

$$Recall = \frac{tp}{tp + fn} \tag{7}$$

$$F - Measure = 2 * \frac{Precision * Recall}{Precision + Recall} \tag{8}$$

$$MCC = \frac{(tp * tn) - (fp * fn)}{\sqrt{(tp + fp) + (tp + fn) + (tn + fp) + (tn + fn)}}$$

$$\text{Matthews Correlation Coefficient} (MCC) = \frac{(tp*tn) - (fp*fn)}{\sqrt{(tp + fp) + (tp + fn) + (tn + fp) + (tn + fn)}} \tag{9}$$

$$FM - Index = \sqrt{Precision * Recall}$$

$$\text{Fowlkes} - \text{Mallows index} (FM\ index) = \sqrt{Precision*Recall} \tag{10}$$

SIMULATION RESULTS AND DISCUSSION

The proposed optimization model is simulated using MATLAB 2015a software. Each optimization method is run for 100 times, keeping the parameters same, where the GA parameters setup is used as reported in (Hore *et al.*, 2017). Objective function engaged in GA and PSO was the RMSE. Table 1 reports the performance of SVM, NN-GA, NN-PSO and NN-NSGA-II with respect to precision, F-measure, accuracy, recall, and MCC and FM-index.

Table 1 establishes that the SVM has poor performance with respect to the measured performance metrics where the precision, accuracy, recall, F-measure, MCC, and FM-index of 78.95%, 80.56%, 83.33%, 81.08%, 61.21%, and 81.11% values. The accuracy achieved by NN-GA is 86.11%, while it achieved 88.89% precision, 84.21% recall, 86.49% F-measure, 72.33% MCC, and 89.52% FM-index value. However, the NN-PSO achieved moderate performance, where 88.89% accuracy and 77.78% MCC are obtained. It is observed that the PSO supported NN model is slightly superior in predicting the water quality, but it is not a reasonable improvement. Multi-objective GA coupled NN model performed best among all. It reports 97.22% accuracy along with 94.74% precision, 100% recall, 97.3% F-measure, 94.59% MCC and 97.33% FM-index value. The NN-NSGA-II results reveal that the optimization models do not have a significant difference in terms of accuracy, recall, precision, and F-measure. However, the MCC and FM-index evidently designates the NN-NSGA-II superiority in predicting the water quality as illustrated in Figure 4.

Figure 4 depicts that the NN-NSGA-II is superior to the other models in predicting the water quality. This comparative study depicts the NN-NSGA-II model superiority. In the training phase, Figure 5 illustrates the convergence of GA. In addition, the objective function versus the iteration plot of PSO is shown in Figure 6.

Figures 5 and 6 reveal that the NN-PSO converges faster than NN-GA in the training phase. Figure 7 illustrates the plot of both objective functions employed in the training phase of NN-NSGA-II.

The Pareto front achieved by the NN-NSGA-II in Figure 7 demonstrates that both the objective functions are well minimized. The plot supports the results reported previously and further establishes its ingenuity over other models. In order to establish the statistical significance of the proposed NN-NSGA-II model,

Table 1. Comparative study of different models with NN-NSGA-II

	SVM	NN-GA	NN-PSO	NN-NSGA-II
Accuracy	80.56	86.11	88.89	**97.22**
Precision	78.95	88.89	88.89	**94.74**
Recall	83.33	84.21	88.89	**100**
F-Measure	81.08	86.49	88.89	**97.3**
MCC	61.21	72.33	77.78	**94.59**
FM-Index	81.11	86.52	88.89	**97.33**

Figure 4. Comparative study of NN-NSGA-II with NN-GA and NN-PSO

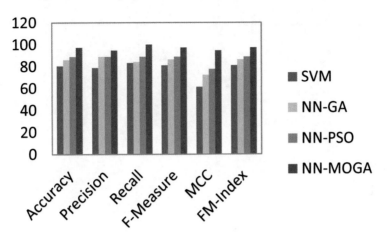

Figure 5. Convergence of GA during training the NN

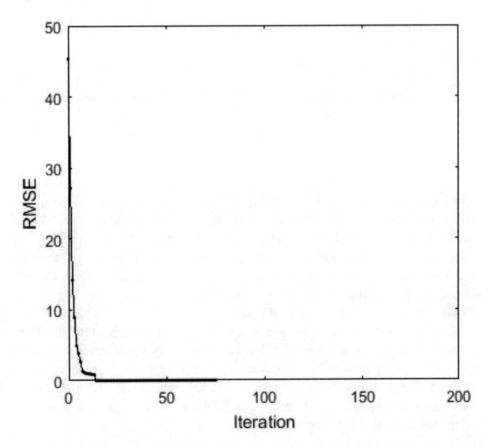

Figure 6. Convergence of PSO during training the NN

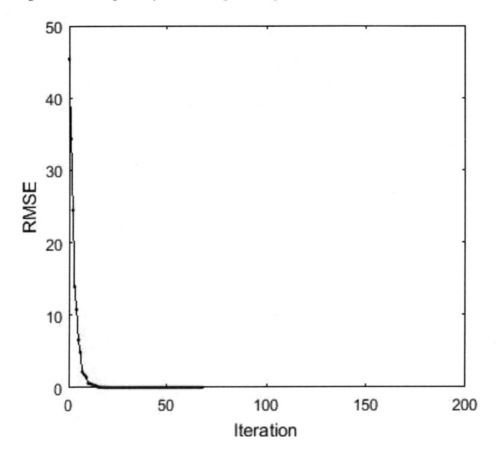

a well-known non-parametric statistical significance test called the Wilcoxon rank sum test (Wilcoxon *et al.*, 1970) is performed with 5% confidence level. As the meta-heuristic supported ANN models are highly probabilistic in nature, thus for a particular set up of weight vectors of ANN the models may perform differently. The optimization process is highly dependent on initialization of ANN parameters, meta-heuristic algorithmic set up etc. Consequently, Wilcoxon rank sum test is adopted to check the statistical significance.

The test is conducted using the performance values achieved in all 100 iterations for each model mentioned earlier. Table 2 reports the *P-values* achieved by each group (NN-NSGA-II vs. NN-PSO, NN-NSGA-II vs. NN-GA) for every performance measure. The null hypothesis is considered as there is no significant difference between the median values of two groups. The alternative hypothesis considers significant difference between median values.

Figure 7. Pareto front of the NSGA-II during training the NN

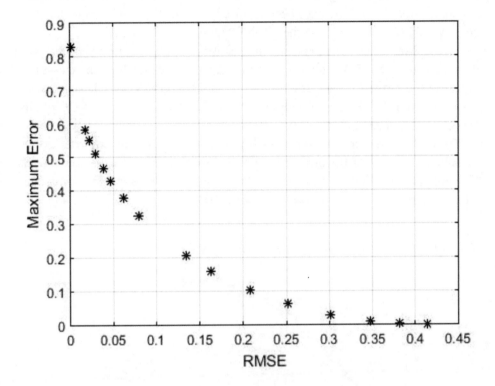

According to Bonferroni inequality, a threshold of 0.017 (0.05/3) is considered for achieving 5% level of significance. The *P-values* in Table 2 are smaller than the threshold, indicating a strong statistical significance of the achieved results. Hence, better performance metric values achieved by NN-NSGA-II (Table 1) has not been achieved by chance, the results are statistically significant.

Table 2. P-values of Wilcoxon rank sum test of NN-NSGA-II with other metaheuristic supported models

	SVM	NN-GA	NN-PSO
Accuracy	2.9E-03	3.2E-06	2.6E-09
Precision	2.7E-04	2.5E-07	2.4E-09
Recall	3.1E-03	2.2E-09	2.2E-08
F-Measure	2.6E-02	2.1E-08	2.5E-09

Further, the receiver operating characteristic (ROC) curves for meta-heuristic supported ANN classifiers have been reported. Figures 8 and 9 illustrate the ROC curve of NN-GA classifier and the NN-PSO classifier; respectively.

Figure 8 indicates moderate performance for both classes. However, in Figure 9 the ROC of NN-PSO depicts a better ROC the curves for both the classes are nearer to the top left corner of the plot than the NN-GA. This indicates that the performance of NN-PSO is slightly better than NN-GA. Finally, the ROC of NN-NSGA-II is depicted in Figure 10.

The ROC curves for both the classes are highly tending toward the top left corner. The plot reveals that the performance of NN-NSGA-II is better than previous models. However, all three ROC curves indicate that the results are statistically significance which is supporting the P-values reported in Table 2.

Figure 8. Receiver Operating Characteristic of NN-GA classifier

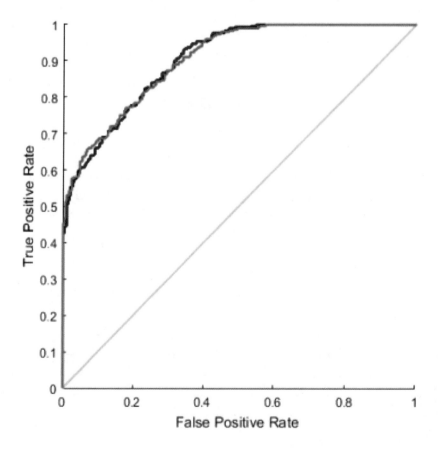

Figure 9. Receiver Operating Characteristic of NN-PSO classifier

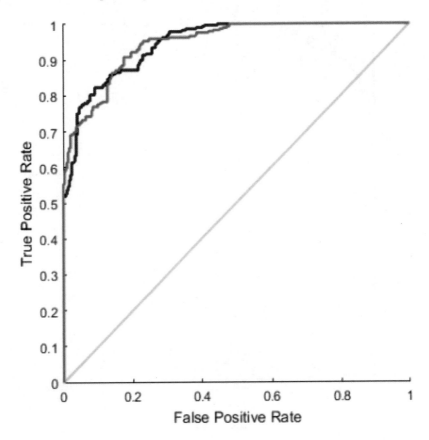

CONCLUSION

Water quality is a critical vital issue that directly affects the economy and health. It is extremely significant to guarantee safe drinking water supply for decent public health. Subsequently, accurate water quality prediction becomes a challenging issue. In the present work, an effective multi-objective GA supported the NN model has been conducted for predicting the drinking water quality. Water samples from different municipal areas in both sides of the Hooghly River (West Bengal, India) have been collected. The collected sample have been used in the present work to classify them into two different classes, namely 'Safe' and 'Unsafe' in accordance with the Indian standards (IS 10500:2012). The simulation results established

Figure 10. Receiver Operating Characteristic of NN-NSGA-II classifier

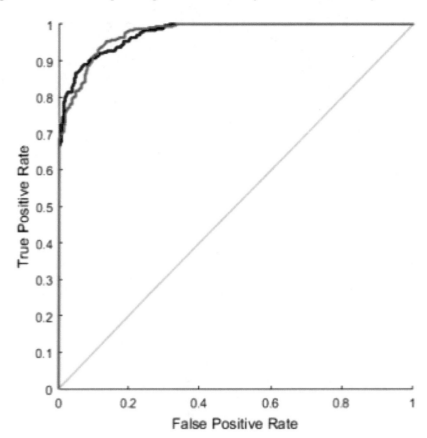

that meta-heuristic algorithms supported the NN modes for superior water quality prediction. Minimizing the multiple objective functions using NSGA-II during the training phase of the NN resulted in superior prediction. The NN-NSGA-II model realized superior accuracy of 97.22% compared to other optimization algorithms, such as NN-GA and NN-PSO.

REFERENCES

Acharjya, D., & Anitha, A. (2017). A Comparative Study of Statistical and Rough Computing Models in Predictive Data Analysis. *International Journal of Ambient Computing and Intelligence*, 8(2), 32–51. doi:10.4018/IJACI.2017040103

Ahmed, S. S., Dey, N., Ashour, A. S., Sifaki-Pistolla, D., Bălas-Timar, D., Balas, V. E., & Tavares, J. M. R. (2017). Effect of fuzzy partitioning in Crohns disease classification: A neuro-fuzzy-based approach. *Medical & Biological Engineering & Computing*, *55*(1), 101–115. doi:10.1007/s11517-016-1508-7 PMID:27106754

Araki, T., Ikeda, N., Dey, N., Acharjee, S., Molinari, F., Saba, L., & Suri, J. S. et al. (2015). Shape-Based Approach for Coronary Calcium Lesion Volume Measurement on Intravascular Ultrasound Imaging and Its Association With Carotid Intima-Media Thickness. *Journal of Ultrasound in Medicine*, *34*(3), 469–482. doi:10.7863/ultra.34.3.469 PMID:25715368

Araki, T., Ikeda, N., Dey, N., Chakraborty, S., Saba, L., Kumar, D., & Laird, J. R. et al. (2015). A comparative approach of four different image registration techniques for quantitative assessment of coronary artery calcium lesions using intravascular ultrasound. *Computer Methods and Programs in Biomedicine*, *118*(2), 158–172. doi:10.1016/j.cmpb.2014.11.006 PMID:25523233

Ashour, A. S., Samanta, S., Dey, N., Kausar, N., Abdessalemkaraa, W. B., & Hassanien, A. E. (2015). Computed tomography image enhancement using cuckoo search: A log transform based approach. *Journal of Signal and Information Processing*, *6*(03), 244–257. doi:10.4236/jsip.2015.63023

Boulmaiz, A., Messadeg, D., Doghmane, N., & Taleb-Ahmed, A. (2017). Design and Implementation of a Robust Acoustic Recognition System for Waterbird Species using TMS320C6713 DSK. *International Journal of Ambient Computing and Intelligence*, *8*(1), 98–118. doi:10.4018/IJACI.2017010105

Bureš, V., Tučník, P., Mikulecký, P., Mls, K., & Blecha, P. (2016). Application of ambient intelligence in educational institutions: Visions and architectures. *International Journal of Ambient Computing and Intelligence*, *7*(1), 94–120. doi:10.4018/IJACI.2016010105

Chang, C. C., & Lin, C. J. (2011). LIBSVM: A library for support vector machines. *ACM Transactions on Intelligent Systems and Technology*, *2*(3), 27. doi:10.1145/1961189.1961199

Chatterjee, S., Ghosh, S., Dawn, S., Hore, S., & Dey, N. (2016b). Forest Type Classification: A hybrid NN-GA model based approach. In Information Systems Design and Intelligent Applications (pp. 227-236). Springer India. doi:10.1007/978-81-322-2757-1_23

Chatterjee, S., Sarkar, S., Hore, S., Dey, N., Ashour, A. S., & Balas, V. E. (2016a). Particle swarm optimization trained neural network for structural failure prediction of multistoried RC buildings. *Neural Computing & Applications*, 1–12.

Coello, C. A. C. (1999). A comprehensive survey of evolutionary-based multiobjective optimization techniques. *Knowledge and Information Systems, 1*(3), 129–156.

Deb, K. (2001). Nonlinear goal programming using multi-objective genetic algorithms. *The Journal of the Operational Research Society, 52*(3), 291–302. doi:10.1057/palgrave.jors.2601089

Dey, N., Ashour, A. S., Ashour, A. S., & Singh, A. (2015b). Digital analysis of microscopic images in medicine. *Journal of Advanced Microscopy Research, 10*(1), 1–13. doi:10.1166/jamr.2015.1229

Dey, N., Ashour, A. S., Beagum, S., Pistola, D. S., Gospodinov, M., Gospodinova, E. P., & Tavares, J. M. R. (2015c). Parameter optimization for local polynomial approximation based intersection confidence interval filter using genetic algorithm: An application for brain MRI image de-noising. *Journal of Imaging, 1*(1), 60–84. doi:10.3390/jimaging1010060

Dey, N., Dey, M., Mahata, S. K., Das, A., & Chaudhuri, S. S. (2015a). Tamper detection of electrocardiographic signal using watermarked bio–hash code in wireless cardiology. *International Journal of Signal and Imaging Systems Engineering, 8*(1-2), 46–58. doi:10.1504/IJSISE.2015.067069

Dey, N., Samanta, S., Chakraborty, S., Das, A., Chaudhuri, S. S., & Suri, J. S. (2014). Firefly algorithm for optimization of scaling factors during embedding of manifold medical information: An application in ophthalmology imaging. *Journal of Medical Imaging and Health Informatics, 4*(3), 384–394. doi:10.1166/jmihi.2014.1265

Edition, F. (2011). Guidelines for drinking-water quality. *WHO Chronicle, 38*, 104–108. PMID:6485306

El-Din, A. G., Smith, D. W., & El-Din, M. G. (2004). Application of artificial neural networks in wastewater treatment. *Journal of Environmental Engineering and Science, 3*(S1), S81–S95. doi:10.1139/s03-067

Gen, M., & Cheng, R. (2000). *Genetic algorithms and engineering optimization* (Vol. 7). John Wiley & Sons.

Ghosh, A., Sarkar, A., Ashour, A. S., Balas-Timar, D., Dey, N., & Balas, V. E. (2015). Grid color moment features in glaucoma classification. *Int J Adv Comput Sci Appl, 6*(9), 1–14.

Guesgen, H. W., & Marsland, S. (2016). Using Contextual Information for Recognising Human Behaviour. *International Journal of Ambient Computing and Intelligence, 7*(1), 27–44. doi:10.4018/IJACI.2016010102

Hore, S., Chatterjee, S., Santhi, V., Dey, N., Ashour, A. S., Balas, V. E., & Shi, F. (2017). Indian Sign Language Recognition Using Optimized Neural Networks. In *Information Technology and Intelligent Transportation Systems* (pp. 553–563). Springer International Publishing. doi:10.1007/978-3-319-38771-0_54

Hore, S., Chatterjee, S., Sarkar, S., Dey, N., Ashour, A. S., Balas-Timar, D., & Balas, V. E. (2016). Neural-based prediction of structural failure of multistoried RC buildings. *Structural Engineering & Mechanics*, *58*(3), 459–473. doi:10.12989/sem.2016.58.3.459

Ikeda, N., Gupta, A., Dey, N., Bose, S., Shafique, S., Arak, T., & Suri, J. S. et al. (2015). Improved correlation between carotid and coronary atherosclerosis SYNTAX score using automated ultrasound carotid bulb plaque IMT measurement. *Ultrasound in Medicine & Biology*, *41*(5), 1247–1262. doi:10.1016/j.ultrasmedbio.2014.12.024 PMID:25638311

Jain, A., Kumar Varshney, A., & Chandra Joshi, U. (2001). Short-term water demand forecast modelling at IIT Kanpur using artificial neural networks. *Water Resources Management*, *15*(5), 299–321. doi:10.1023/A:1014415503476

Juneja, D., Singh, A., Singh, R., & Mukherjee, S. (2017). A thorough insight into theoretical and practical developments in multiagent systems. *International Journal of Ambient Computing and Intelligence*, *8*(1), 23–49. doi:10.4018/IJACI.2017010102

Jurman, G., Riccadonna, S., & Furlanello, C. (2012). A comparison of MCC and CEN error measures in multi-class prediction. *PLoS ONE*, *7*(8), e41882. doi:10.1371/journal.pone.0041882 PMID:22905111

Karaa, W. B. A., Ashour, A. S., Sassi, D. B., Roy, P., Kausar, N., & Dey, N. (2016). Medline text mining: an enhancement genetic algorithm based approach for document clustering. In *Applications of Intelligent Optimization in Biology and Medicine* (pp. 267–287). Springer International Publishing. doi:10.1007/978-3-319-21212-8_12

Kausar, N., Palaniappan, S., Samir, B. B., Abdullah, A., & Dey, N. (2016). Systematic analysis of applied data mining based optimization algorithms in clinical attribute extraction and classification for diagnosis of cardiac patients. In *Applications of intelligent optimization in biology and medicine* (pp. 217–231). Springer International Publishing. doi:10.1007/978-3-319-21212-8_9

Khachane, M. Y. (2017). Organ-Based Medical Image Classification Using Support Vector Machine. *International Journal of Synthetic Emotions*, *8*(1), 18–30. doi:10.4018/IJSE.2017010102

Kotyk, T., Ashour, A. S., Chakraborty, S., Dey, N., & Balas, V. E. (2015). Apoptosis analysis in classification paradigm: a neural network based approach. In *Healthy World conference* (pp. 17-22). Academic Press.

Li, H., & Zhang, Q. (2009). Multiobjective optimization problems with complicated Pareto sets, MOEA/D and NSGA-II. *IEEE Transactions on Evolutionary Computation*, *13*(2), 284–302. doi:10.1109/TEVC.2008.925798

Maji, P., Chatterjee, S., Chakraborty, S., Kausar, N., Samanta, S., & Dey, N. (2015, March). Effect of Euler number as a feature in gender recognition system from offline handwritten signature using neural networks. In *Computing for Sustainable Global Development (INDIACom), 2015 2nd International Conference on* (pp. 1869-1873). IEEE.

Manogaran, G., & Lopez, D. (2017). Disease surveillance system for big climate data processing and dengue transmission. *International Journal of Ambient Computing and Intelligence*, *8*(2), 88–105. doi:10.4018/IJACI.2017040106

Møller, M. F. (1993). A scaled conjugate gradient algorithm for fast supervised learning. *Neural Networks*, *6*(4), 525–533. doi:10.1016/S0893-6080(05)80056-5

Mukherjee, A., Dey, G., Dey, M., & Dey, N. (2015). Web-based intelligent EEG signal authentication and tamper detection system for secure telemonitoring. In *Brain-Computer Interfaces* (pp. 295–312). Springer International Publishing. doi:10.1007/978-3-319-10978-7_11

Nandi, D., Ashour, A. S., Samanta, S., Chakraborty, S., Salem, M. A., & Dey, N. (2015). Principal component analysis in medical image processing: A study. *International Journal of Image Mining*, *1*(1), 65–86. doi:10.1504/IJIM.2015.070024

Odella, F. (2017). Technology Studies and the Sociological Debate on Monitoring of Social Interactions. In Biometrics: Concepts, Methodologies, Tools, and Applications (pp. 529-558). IGI Global. doi:10.4018/978-1-5225-0983-7.ch022

Pal, G., Acharjee, S., Rudrapaul, D., Ashour, A. S., & Dey, N. (2015a). Video segmentation using minimum ratio similarity measurement. *International Journal of Image Mining, 1*(1), 87-110.

Pal, G., Rudrapaul, D., Acharjee, S., Ray, R., Chakraborty, S., & Dey, N. (2015). Video shot boundary detection: a review. In *Emerging ICT for Bridging the Future-Proceedings of the 49th Annual Convention of the Computer Society of India CSI* (vol. 2, pp. 119-127). Springer International Publishing. doi:10.1007/978-3-319-13731-5_14

Paola, J. D., & Schowengerdt, R. A. (1995). A review and analysis of backpropagation neural networks for classification of remotely-sensed multi-spectral imagery. *International Journal of Remote Sensing*, *16*(16), 3033–3058. doi:10.1080/01431169508954607

Powers, D. M. (2011). *Evaluation: from precision, recall and F-measure to ROC, informedness, markedness and correlation*. Academic Press.

Reckhow, K. H. (1999). Water quality prediction and probability network models. *Canadian Journal of Fisheries and Aquatic Sciences*, *56*(7), 1150–1158. doi:10.1139/f99-040

Saba, L., Dey, N., Ashour, A. S., Samanta, S., Nath, S. S., Chakraborty, S., & Suri, J. S. et al. (2016). Automated stratification of liver disease in ultrasound: An online accurate feature classification paradigm. *Computer Methods and Programs in Biomedicine*, *130*, 118–134. doi:10.1016/j.cmpb.2016.03.016 PMID:27208527

Sharma, K., & Virmani, J. (2017). A Decision Support System for Classification of Normal and Medical Renal Disease Using Ultrasound Images: A Decision Support System for Medical Renal Diseases. *International Journal of Ambient Computing and Intelligence*, *8*(2), 52–69. doi:10.4018/IJACI.2017040104

Sheppard, D., Tsegaye, T. D., Tadesse, W., McKay, D., & Coleman, T. L. (2001). The application of remote sensing, geographic information systems, and Global Positioning System technology to improve water quality in northern Alabama. In *Geoscience and Remote Sensing Symposium, 2001. IGARSS'01. IEEE 2001 International* (Vol. 3, pp. 1291-1293). IEEE. doi:10.1109/IGARSS.2001.976822

Standard, I. (1991). Drinking water-specification. 1st Revision, IS, 10500.

Tyagi, S., Som, S., & Rana, Q. P. (2017). Trust based dynamic multicast group routing ensuring reliability for ubiquitous environment in MANETs. *International Journal of Ambient Computing and Intelligence*, *8*(1), 70–97. doi:10.4018/IJACI.2017010104

Vasudevan, S., & Oturan, M. A. (2014). Electrochemistry: As cause and cure in water pollution—an overview. *Environmental Chemistry Letters*, *12*(1), 97–108. doi:10.1007/s10311-013-0434-2

Virmani, J., Dey, N., & Kumar, V. (2016). PCA-PNN and PCA-SVM based CAD systems for breast density classification. In *Applications of intelligent optimization in biology and medicine* (pp. 159–180). Springer International Publishing.

Wechmongkhonkon, S., Poomtong, N., & Areerachakul, S. (2012). Application of Artificial Neural Network to classification surface water quality. *World Academy of Science, Engineering and Technology, 6*.

Wilcoxon, F., Katti, S. K., & Wilcox, R. A. (1970). Critical values and probability levels for the Wilcoxon rank sum test and the Wilcoxon signed rank test. *Selected Tables in Mathematical Statistics, 1*, 171-259.

Wu, W., Dandy, G. C., & Maier, H. R. (2011). Application of artificial neural networks to forecasting water quality in a chloraminated water distribution system. *19th Int. Congr. Model. Simul. Modsim2011*, 1112-1118.

KEY TERMS AND DEFINITIONS

Classification: The sorting of certain case into one of two or several classes based on its extracted features vector.

Feature Extraction: The identification of the attributes that describe and characterize certain object or phenomena.

Neural Network: A machine learning computational model that used in several research disciplines and computer science applications. It is based on an assembly of connected artificial neurons at which a varying strength activation signal exist in the connection between these neurons.

Optimization Methods: Techniques that optimize a given problem by adjusting several parameters to attain suitable results. There are several optimization algorithms such as the particle swarm optimization, genetic algorithm, differential evolution, and ant colony optimization.

Compilation of References

Abdoun, O., & Abouchabaka, J. (2011). A Comparative Study of Adaptive Crossover Operators for Genetic Algorithms to Resolve the Traveling Salesman Problem. *International Journal of Computers and Applications*, *31*(11), 49–57.

Abinash, T., & Santanu Kumar, R. (2017). Classification of Sentiment of Reviews using Supervised Machine Learning Techniques. *International Journal of Rough Sets and Data Analysis*, *4*(1), 56–74. doi:10.4018/IJRSDA.2017010104

Abraham, A., Nath, B., & Mahanti, P. K. (2002). Hybrid Intelligent Systems for Stock Market Analysis. *Proceedings of the International Conference on Computational Science*, 337-345. doi:10.1109/FUZZY.2000.838709

Abu-Mahfouz, I. (2003). Drilling wear detection and classification using vibration signals and artificial neural network. *International Journal of Machine Tools & Manufacture*, *43*(7), 707–720. doi:10.1016/S0890-6955(03)00023-3

Acha, E., Fuerte-Esquivel, C., Ambriz-Perez, H., & Angeles, C. (2004). *FACTS: Modelling and Simulation in Power Networks*. John Wiley & Sons; doi:10.1002/0470020164

Acharjya, D., & Anitha, A. (2017). A Comparative Study of Statistical and Rough Computing Models in Predictive Data Analysis. *International Journal of Ambient Computing and Intelligence*, *8*(2), 32–51. doi:10.4018/IJACI.2017040103

Adler, A., & Guardo, R. (1994). A neural network image reconstruction technique for electrical impedance tomography. *IEEE Transactions on Medical Imaging*, *13*(4), 594–600. doi:10.1109/42.363109 PMID:18218537

Ahmad, H. A., Yu, H. J., & Miller, C. G. (2014). Medical imaging modalities. In *Medical Imaging in Clinical Trials* (pp. 3–26). Springer London. doi:10.1007/978-1-84882-710-3_1

Ahmadyfard, A., & Modares, H. (2008). Combining PSO and K-Means to enhance data clustering. *International Symposium on Telecommunication*, 688 - 691. doi:10.1109/ISTEL.2008.4651388

Ahmed Hamza, A., Ahmad Taher, A., & Aboul Ella, H. (2014). A New Heuristic Function of Ant Colony System for Retinal Vessel Segmentation. *International Journal of Rough Sets and Data Analysis*, *1*(2), 15–30. doi:10.4018/ijrsda.2014070102

Ahmed, R., Mahmoud, K., Mohammed, Y. D., & Aboul Ella, H. (2015). Forecasting Exchange Rates: A Chaos-Based Regression Approach. *International Journal of Rough Sets and Data Analysis*, 2(1), 38–57. doi:10.4018/ijrsda.2015010103

Ahmed, S. S., Dey, N., Ashour, A. S., Sifaki-Pistolla, D., Bălas-Timar, D., Balas, V. E., & Tavares, J. M. R. (2017). Effect of fuzzy partitioning in Crohns disease classification: A neuro-fuzzy-based approach. *Medical & Biological Engineering & Computing*, 55(1), 101–115. doi:10.1007/s11517-016-1508-7 PMID:27106754

Aja-Fern'andez, S., Jos'eEst'epar, R. S., Alberola-L'opez, C., & Westin, C. F. (2006). Image Quality Assessment based on Local Variance. *28th IEEE EMBS Annual International Conference*, 4815-4818.

Akashdeep, K., Kahlon, K. S., & Kumar, H. (2014). Survey of scheduling algorithms in IEEE 802.16 PMP networks. *Egyptian Informatics Journal*, 15(1), 25–36. doi:10.1016/j.eij.2013.12.001

Akyildiz, I. F., Wang, X., & Wang, W. (2005). Wireless mesh networks: A survey. *Computer Networks Journal (Elsevier)*, 47(4), 445–487. doi:10.1016/j.comnet.2004.12.001

Alba, E., Garcia-Nieto, J., Jourdan, L., & Talbi, E. G. (2007, September). Gene selection in cancer classification using PSO/SVM and GA/SVM hybrid algorithms. In *Evolutionary Computation, 2007. CEC 2007. IEEE Congress on* (pp. 284-290). IEEE.

Alexiei, D., Daniel, A., & Ruben, M. (2012). Turning Homes into Low-Cost Ambient Assisted Living Environments. *International Journal of Ambient Computing and Intelligence*, 4(2), 1–23. doi:10.4018/jaci.2012040101

Ali, E. S., & Abd-Elazim, S. M. (2011). Bacteria foraging optimization algorithm based load frequency controller for interconnected power system. *International Journal of Electrical Power & Energy Systems*, 33(3), 633–638. doi:10.1016/j.ijepes.2010.12.022

Ali, N. A., Dhrona, P., & Hassanein, H. (2009). A performance study of uplink scheduling algorithms in point-to-multipoint WiMAX networks. *Computer Communications*, 32(3), 511–521. doi:10.1016/j.comcom.2008.09.015

Al-Kadi, O. S., & Watson, D. (2008). Texture analysis of Aggressive and non-aggressive lung tumor CE CT images. *IEEE Transaction on Biomedical Engineering, 55*, 1822-1830.

Amal Mahmoud, A., & Sawsan, A. (2015). Hybridizing Artificial Bee Colony Algorithm with Multi-Parent Crossover Operator. *International Journal of Applied Metaheuristic Computing*, 6(2), 18–32. doi:10.4018/IJAMC.2015040102

Ambriz-Perez, Acha, Fuerte-Esquivel, & De la Torre. (1998). Incorporation of a UPFC model in an Optimal Power Flow Using Newton's method. *IEE Proc.-Generation Transmission Distribution, 145*(3).

Anand, B., & Jeyakumar, A. E. (2009). Load frequency control with fuzzy logic controller considering non-linearities and boiler dynamics. *ICGST-ACSE Journal*, 8(111), 15–20.

Anderson, J. A. (1972). A simple neural network generating an interactive memory. *Mathematical Biosciences*, *14*(3-4), 197–200. doi:10.1016/0025-5564(72)90075-2

Ang, L. M., Seng, K. P., & Heng, T. Z. (2016). Information Communication Assistive Technologies for Visually Impaired People. *International Journal of Ambient Computing and Intelligence*, *7*(1), 45–68. doi:10.4018/IJACI.2016010103

Aparna, R. R. (2016). Swarm Intelligence for Automatic Video Image Contrast Adjustment. *International Journal of Rough Sets and Data Analysis*, *3*(3), 21–37. doi:10.4018/IJRSDA.2016070102

Araki, T., Ikeda, N., Dey, N., Acharjee, S., Molinari, F., Saba, L., & Suri, J. S. et al. (2015). Shape-Based Approach for Coronary Calcium Lesion Volume Measurement on Intravascular Ultrasound Imaging and Its Association With Carotid Intima-Media Thickness. *Journal of Ultrasound in Medicine*, *34*(3), 469–482. doi:10.7863/ultra.34.3.469 PMID:25715368

Araki, T., Ikeda, N., Dey, N., Chakraborty, S., Saba, L., Kumar, D., & Laird, J. R. et al. (2015). A comparative approach of four different image registration techniques for quantitative assessment of coronary artery calcium lesions using intravascular ultrasound. *Computer Methods and Programs in Biomedicine*, *118*(2), 158–172. doi:10.1016/j.cmpb.2014.11.006 PMID:25523233

Ashizawa, K., Ishida, T., MacMahon, H., Vyborny, C. J., Katsuragawa, S., & Doi, K. (1999). Artificial neural networks in chest radiography: Application to the differential diagnosis of interstitial lung disease. *Academic Radiology*, *6*(1), 2–9. doi:10.1016/S1076-6332(99)80055-5 PMID:9891146

Ashour, A. S., Beagum, S., Dey, N., Ashour, A. S., Pistolla, D. S., Nguyen, G. N., & Shi, F. et al. (2016). Light microscopy image de-noising using optimized LPA-ICI filter. *Neural Computing & Applications*, 1–17.

Ashour, A. S., Samanta, S., Dey, N., Kausar, N., Abdessalemkaraa, W. B., & Hassanien, A. E. (2015). Computed tomography image enhancement using cuckoo search: A log transform based approach. *Journal of Signal and Information Processing*, *6*(03), 244–257. doi:10.4236/jsip.2015.63023

Atsalakis, G. S., & Valavanis, K. P. (2009). Surveying stock market forecasting techniques – part II: Soft computing methods. *Expert Systems with Applications*, *36*(3), 5932–5941. doi:10.1016/j.eswa.2008.07.006

Bag, V., & Kulkarni, U. V. (2017). Stock Price Trend Prediction and Recommendation using Cognitive Process. *International Journal of Rough Sets and Data Analysis*, *4*(2), 36–48. doi:10.4018/IJRSDA.2017040103

Bairoch, A., Bucher, P., & Hofmann, K. (1996). PROSITE: New developments. *Nucleic Acids Research*, 189-196.

Bakhshaii, A., & Stull, R. (2009). Deterministic ensemble forecasts using gene-expression programming. *Weather and Forecasting*, *24*(5), 1431–1451. doi:10.1175/2009WAF2222192.1

Bapuji Rao, B. K. (2017). An Approach to Clustering of Text Documents Using Graph Mining Techniques. *International Journal of Rough Sets and Data Analysis*, *4*(1).

Barik, M., Sheta, A., & Ayesh, A. (2007). Image Enhancement Using Particle Swarm Optimization. *Proceedings of the World Congress on Engineering*.

Bashiri, M., & Geranmayeh, A. F. (2011). Tuning the parameters of an artificial neural network using central composite design and genetic algorithm. *Scientia Iranica*, *18*(6), 1600–1608. doi:10.1016/j.scient.2011.08.031

Benala, T. R., Jampala, S. D., Villa, S. H., & Konathala, B. (2009). A novel Approach to Image Edge Enhancement Using Artificial Bee Colony Optimization Algorithm for Hybridized Smoothening Filters. *World Congress on Nature & Biologically Inspired Computing (NaBIC)*, 1071-1076. doi:10.1109/NABIC.2009.5393866

Benmounah, Z., Meshoul, S., & Batouche, M. (2017). *Scalable Differential Evolutionary Clustering Algorithm for Big Data Using Map-Reduce Paradigm. Int. Jr. Applied Metaheuristic Computing*, *8*(1).

Berkhin, P. (2002). *Survey of Clustering Data Mining Techniques*. Accrue Software.

Bhandaria, A. K., Sonia, V. A., Kumar, A., & Singh, G. K. (2014). Cuckoo search algorithm based satellite image contrast and brightness enhancement using DWT–SVD. *ISA Transactions*, *53*, 1286–1296.

Bhatt, P., Ghoshal, S. P., & Roy, R. (2010). Load frequency stabilization by coordinated control of Thyristor Controlled Phase Shifters and superconducting magnetic energy storage for three types of interconnected two-area power systems. *International Journal of Electrical Power & Energy Systems*, *32*(10), 1111–1124. doi:10.1016/j.ijepes.2010.06.009

Bill, C. H., & Chang, S. (2012). Protein Motif Extraction Using Neuro-Fuzzy optimization. *Bioinformatics (Oxford, England)*, *18*(8), 1084–1090. PMID:12176831

Binh, H. T. T., Hanh, N. T., & Dey, N. (n.d.). Improved Cuckoo Search and Chaotic Flower Pollination optimization algorithm for maximizing area coverage in Wireless Sensor Networks. *Neural Computing and Applications*, 1-13.

Binh, H. T. T., Hanh, N. T., & Dey, N. (2016). Improved Cuckoo Search and Chaotic Flower Pollination optimization algorithm for maximizing area coverage in Wireless Sensor Networks. *Neural Computing & Applications*, 1–13.

Bong, C. W., Lam, H. Y., Khader, A. T., & Kamarulzaman, H. (2012). Adaptive multi-objective archive-based hybrid scatter search for segmentation in lung computed tomography imaging. *Engineering Optimization*, *44*(3), 327–350. doi:10.1080/0305215X.2011.639369

Bontoux, B., Artigues, C., & Feillet, D. (2010). A Memetic Algorithm with a large neighborhood crossover operator for the Generalized Traveling Salesman Problem. *Computers & Operations Research*, *37*(11), 1844–1852. doi:10.1016/j.cor.2009.05.004

Boulmaiz, A., Messadeg, D., Doghmane, N., & Taleb-Ahmed, A. (2017). Design and Implementation of a Robust Acoustic Recognition System for Waterbird Species using TMS320C6713 DSK. *International Journal of Ambient Computing and Intelligence*, *8*(1), 98–118. doi:10.4018/IJACI.2017010105

Bouttier, C., Babando, O., Gadat, S., Gerchinovitz, S., Laporte, S., & Nicol, F. (2017). Adaptive Simulated Annealing with Homogenization for Aircraft Trajectory Optimization. In K. Doerner, I. Ljubic, G. Pflug, & G. Tragler (Eds.), *Operations Research Proceedings 2015: Selected Papers of the International Conference of the German, Austrian and Swiss Operations Research Societies (GOR, ÖGOR, SVOR/ASRO)* (pp. 569-574). Cham: Springer International Publishing. doi:10.1007/978-3-319-42902-1_77

Box, G. E. P., & Jenkins, G. M. (1976). *Time Series Analysis-Forecasting and Control*. San Francisco, CA: Holden-Day Inc.

Brezocnik, M., Kovacic, M., & Ficko, M. (2004). Prediction of surface roughness with genetic programming. *Journal of Materials Processing Technology*, *157*, 28–36. doi:10.1016/j.jmatprotec.2004.09.004

Bruyninckx, P., Loeckx, D., Vandermeulen, D., & Suetens, P. (2010, March). Segmentation of liver portal veins by global optimization. In *SPIE Medical Imaging* (pp. 76241Z–76241Z). International Society for Optics and Photonics. doi:10.1117/12.843995

Caponetto, R., Fortuna, L., Fazzino, S., & Xibilia, M. G. (2003). Chaotic Sequences to Improve the Performance of Evolutionary Algorithms. *IEEE Transactions on Evolutionary Computation*, *7*(3), 289–304. doi:10.1109/TEVC.2003.810069

Carpentier. (1979). Optimal Power Flows. *Electrical Power and Energy Systems, 1*, 959-972.

Carvalho, T., Junior, J. J., Valente, W., Natalino, C., Francês, R., & Dias, K. L. (2013). *A Mobile WiMAX Mesh Network with Routing Techniques and Quality of Service Mechanisms. In Selected Topics in WiMAX* (pp. 61–84). InTech.

Chaine, S., & Tripathy, M. (2015). Design of an optimal SMES for automatic generation control of two-area thermal power system using cuckoo search algorithm. *Journal of Electrical Systems and Information Technology*, *2*(1), 1–13. doi:10.1016/j.jesit.2015.03.001

Chakraborty, S., Chatterjee, S., Dey, N., Ashour, A. S., Ashour, A. S., Shi, F., & Mali, K. (2017). Modified cuckoo search algorithm in microscopic image segmentation of hippocampus. *Microscopy Research and Technique*. doi:10.1002/jemt.22900 PMID:28557041

Chang, C. C., & Lin, C. J. (2011). LIBSVM: A library for support vector machines. *ACM Transactions on Intelligent Systems and Technology*, *2*(3), 27. doi:10.1145/1961189.1961199

Chang, C. L., & Ching, Y. T. (2002). Fuzzy Hopfield neural network with fixed weight for medical image segmentation. *Optical Engineering (Redondo Beach, Calif.)*, *41*(2), 351–358. doi:10.1117/1.1428298

Chang, P.-C., Liu, C.-H., Lin, J.-L., Fan, C.-Y., & Ng, C. S. P. (2009). A neural network with a case based dynamic window for stock trading prediction. *Expert Systems with Applications*, *36*(3), 6889–6898. doi:10.1016/j.eswa.2008.08.077

Chan, H. P., Sahiner, B., Petrick, N., Helvie, M. A., Lam, K. L., Adler, D. D., & Goodsitt, M. M. (1997). Computerized classification of malignant and benign microcalcifications on mammograms: Texture analysis using an artificial neural network. *Physics in Medicine and Biology*, *42*(3), 549–567. doi:10.1088/0031-9155/42/3/008 PMID:9080535

Chan, T. F., & Shen, J. (2005). *Image processing and analysis: variational, PDE, wavelet, and stochastic methods*. Society for Industrial and Applied Mathematics. doi:10.1137/1.9780898717877

Chao, P. Y., & Hwang, Y. D. (1997). An improved neural network model for the prediction of cutting tool life. *Journal of Intelligent Manufacturing*, *8*(2), 107–115. doi:10.1023/A:1018552620196

Chatterjee, S., Ghosh, S., Dawn, S., Hore, S., & Dey, N. (2016b). Forest Type Classification: A hybrid NN-GA model based approach. In Information Systems Design and Intelligent Applications (pp. 227-236). Springer India. doi:10.1007/978-81-322-2757-1_23

Chatterjee, S., Hore, S., Dey, N., Chakraborty, S., & Ashour, A. S. (2017). Dengue Fever Classification Using Gene Expression Data: A PSO Based Artificial Neural Network Approach. In *Proceedings of the 5th International Conference on Frontiers in Intelligent Computing: Theory and Applications* (pp. 331-341). Springer. doi:10.1007/978-981-10-3156-4_34

Chatterjee, S., Nag, R., Sen, S., & Sarkar, A. (2017a, June). Towards Golden Rule of Capital Accumulation: A Genetic Algorithm Approach. In *IFIP International Conference on Computer Information Systems and Industrial Management* (pp. 481-491). Springer. doi:10.1007/978-3-319-59105-6_41

Chatterjee, S., Sarkar, S., Hore, S., Dey, N., Ashour, A. S., & Balas, V. E. (2016). Particle swarm optimization trained neural network for structural failure prediction of multistoried RC buildings. *Neural Computing & Applications*, 1–12.

Chen Yi-Cheng, K. Y.-W.-T.-F. (2011). Discovery of Protein Phosphorylation Motifs through Exploratory Data Analysis. *Discovery of Protein Phosphorylation Motifs (PLoS ONE)*, 6.

Chen, Pellicer, Tai, Harrison, & Pan. (2009). Novel efficient granular computing models for protein sequence motifs and structure information discovery. *International Journal of Computational Biology and Drug Design*.

Chen, S. D., & Ramli, A. R. (2003). *Contrast Enhancement using Recursive Mean Separated Histogram Equalization for Scalable Brightness Preservation*. Academic Press.

Chen, E. L., Chung, P. C., Chen, C. L., Tsai, H. M., & Chang, C. I. (1998). An automatic diagnostic system for CT liver image classification. *IEEE Transactions on Bio-Medical Engineering*, *45*(6), 783–794. doi:10.1109/10.678613 PMID:9609943

Cheng, B., Hudson, C., Kim, M., Crawford, A., Wright, J., & Che, D. (2011). Protein Sequence Motif Extraction using Decision Forest. *World Congress in Computer Science, Computer Engineering*.

Cheng, K. S., Lin, J. S., & Mao, C. W. (1996). The application of competitive Hopfield neural network to medical image segmentation. *IEEE Transactions on Medical Imaging, 15*(4), 560–567. doi:10.1109/42.511759 PMID:18215937

Chen, S. D., & Ramli, A. R. (2003). Minimum Mean Brightness Error Bi-Histogram Equalization in Contrast Enhancement. *IEEE Transactions on Consumer Electronics, 49*(4), 1310–1319. doi:10.1109/TCE.2003.1261234

Chen, S. D., & Ramli, A. R. (2004). Preserving Brightness in histogram equalization based contrast enhancement techniques. *Digital Signal Processing, 14*(5), 413–428. doi:10.1016/j.dsp.2004.04.001

Chen, Y., & Zhang, G. (2013). Exchange rates determination based on genetic algorithms using Mendels principles: Investigation and estimation under uncertainty. *Information Fusion, 14*(3), 327–333. doi:10.1016/j.inffus.2011.12.003

Chiang, W. C., Urban, T. L., & Baldridge, G. W. (1996). A Neural Network Approach to Mutual Fund Net Asset Value Forecasting. *Omega, 24*(2), 205–215. doi:10.1016/0305-0483(95)00059-3

Chidambaram, I. A., & Paramasivam, B. (2012). Control performance standards based load-frequency controller considering redox flow batteries coordinate with interline power flow controller. *Journal of Power Sources, 219*, 292–304. doi:10.1016/j.jpowsour.2012.06.048

Chien, C. L., & Tsai, W. H. (2014). Image Fusion with no Gamut Problem by Improved Nonlinear HIS Transforms for Remote Sensing. *IEEE Trans. on Geoscience and Remote Sensing, 52*, 651-663.

Chien, C. L., & Tseng, D. C. (2011). Color image enhancement with exact HIS color model. *Int. J. of Innovative Computing, Information and Control, 7*, 6691-6710.

Chung, T. S., & Li, Y. Z. (2001). A hybrid CA approach for OPF with consideration of FACTS devices. *IEEE Power Engineering Review, 21*(2), 47–50. doi:10.1109/39.896822

Cicconetti, C., Lenzini, L., Mingozzi, E., & Eklund, C. (2006). Quality of Service Support in IEEE 802.16 Networks. *IEEE Network, 20*(2), 50–55. doi:10.1109/MNET.2006.1607896

Cicirello, V. A., & Smith, S. F. (2000). *Modeling GA Performance for Control Parameter Optimization.* Paper presented at the GECCO.

Claas, A., Daniel, K., Michael, L., & Gerrit, K. (2011). IT-ASSIST: Towards Usable Applications for Elderly People. *International Journal of Ambient Computing and Intelligence, 3*(1), 33–41. doi:10.4018/jaci.2011010104

Coelho, L. D. S., Sauer, J. G., & Rudek, M. (2009). Differential evolution optimization combined with chaotic sequences for image contrast enhancement. *Chaos, Solitons, and Fractals, 42*(1), 522–529. doi:10.1016/j.chaos.2009.01.012

Coelho, L. S., & Mariani, V. C. (2008). Use of chaotic sequences in a biologically inspired algorithm for engineering design optimization. *Expert Systems with Applications, 34*(3), 1905–1913. doi:10.1016/j.eswa.2007.02.002

Coello, C. A. C. (1999). A comprehensive survey of evolutionary-based multiobjective optimization techniques. *Knowledge and Information Systems*, *1*(3), 129–156.

Cui Xiaohui, P. T. (2005). Document Clustering Analysis Based on Hybrid PSO K-means Algorithm. *Journal of Computer Sciences*, 27-33.

Dan, L., & Mathew, J. (1990). Tool wear and failure monitoring techniques for turning—a review. *International Journal of Machine Tools & Manufacture*, *30*(4), 579–598. doi:10.1016/0890-6955(90)90009-8

Das Shyama, I. S. (2010). Greedy Search-Binary PSO Hybrid for Biclustering Gene Expression Data. *International Journal of Computers and Applications*, *2*(3), 1–5. doi:10.5120/651-908

Das, A., & Bhattacharya, M. (2008, September). GA based neuro fuzzy techniques for breast cancer identification. In *Machine Vision and Image Processing Conference, 2008. IMVIP'08. International* (pp. 136-141). IEEE. doi:10.1109/IMVIP.2008.19

Das, D., Kothari, M. L., Kothari, D. P., & Nanda, P. J. (1991, November). Variable structure control strategy to automatic generation control of interconnected reheat thermal system. *IEE Proceedings. Control Theory and Applications*, *138*(6), 579–585. doi:10.1049/ip-d.1991.0080

Dash, Ch. S. K., Dash, A. P., Dehuri, S., & Cho, S. B. (2013). Feature Selection for Designing a Novel Differential Evolution Trained Radial Basis Function Network for Classification. *International Journal of Applied Metaheuristic Computing*, *4*(1), 32–49. doi:10.4018/jamc.2013010103

Dash, P., Saikia, L. C., & Sinha, N. (2014). Comparison of performances of several Cuckoo search algorithm based 2DOF controllers in AGC of multi-area thermal system. *International Journal of Electrical Power & Energy Systems*, *55*, 429–436. doi:10.1016/j.ijepes.2013.09.034

Davis, L. (1985). Applying Adaptive Algorithms to Epistatic Domains. San Francisco, CA: Academic Press.

Davis, L. D. (1991). Handbook Of Genetic Algorithms. Van Nostrand Reinhold.

Dawson, T. G., & Kurfess, T. R. (2005). Quantification of tool wear using white light interferometry and three-dimensional computational metrology. *International Journal of Machine Tools & Manufacture*, *45*(4), 591–596. doi:10.1016/j.ijmachtools.2004.08.022

De, G. (1989). Genetic Algorithms in Search, Optimization, and Machine Learning. Reading, MA: Addison-Wesley.

Debbarma, S., Saikia, L. C., & Sinha, N. (2013). AGC of a multi-area thermal system under deregulated environment using a non-integer controller. *Electric Power Systems Research*, *95*, 175–183. doi:10.1016/j.epsr.2012.09.008

Deb, K. (2001). Nonlinear goal programming using multi-objective genetic algorithms. *The Journal of the Operational Research Society*, *52*(3), 291–302. doi:10.1057/palgrave.jors.2601089

Deep, K., & Mebrahtu, H. (2011). New Variations of Order Crossover for Travelling Salesman Problem. *International Journal of Combinatorial Optimization Problems and Informatics, 2*(1), 2–13.

Deep, K., & Mebrahtu, H. (2012). Variant of partially mapped crossover for the Travelling Salesman problems. *International Journal of Combinatorial Optimization Problems and Informatics, 3*(1), 47–69.

Deng, S., Yue, D., Fu, X., & Zhou, A. (2015). Security risk assessment of cyber physical power system based on rough set and gene expression programming. *IEEE/CAA Journal of Automatica Sinica, 2*(4), 431-439.

Derrac, J., Garcia, S., Molina, D., & Herrera, F. (2011). A practical tutorial on the use of nonparametric statistical tests as a methodology for comparing evolutionary and swarm intelligence algorithms. *Swarm and Evolutionary Computation, 1*, 3-18.

Derrico, G. (1998). An adaptive system for turning process control based on tool temperature feedback. *Journal of Materials Processing Technology, 78*(1), 43–47. doi:10.1016/S0924-0136(97)00461-5

Devillez, A., Lesko, S., & Mozer, W. (2004). Cutting tool crater wear measurement with white light interferometry. *Wear, 256*(1), 56–65. doi:10.1016/S0043-1648(03)00384-3

Dey, N., & Ashour, A. S. (Eds.). (2016). *Classification and clustering in biomedical signal processing.* IGI Global. doi:10.4018/978-1-5225-0140-4

Dey, N., Ashour, A. S., & Althoupety, A. S. (2017a). Thermal Imaging in Medical Science. In *Recent Advances in Applied Thermal Imaging for Industrial Applications* (pp. 87–117). IGI Global. doi:10.4018/978-1-5225-2423-6.ch004

Dey, N., Ashour, A. S., Ashour, A. S., & Singh, A. (2015b). Digital analysis of microscopic images in medicine. *Journal of Advanced Microscopy Research, 10*(1), 1–13. doi:10.1166/jamr.2015.1229

Dey, N., Ashour, A. S., Beagum, S., Pistola, D. S., Gospodinov, M., Gospodinova, E. P., & Tavares, J. M. R. (2015). Parameter optimization for local polynomial approximation based intersection confidence interval filter using genetic algorithm: An application for brain MRI image de-noising. *Journal of Imaging, 1*(1), 60–84. doi:10.3390/jimaging1010060

Dey, N., Ashour, A. S., Chakraborty, S., Samanta, S., Sifaki-Pistola, D., Ashour, A. S., & Nguyen, G. N. et al. (2016). Healthy and unhealthy rat hippocampus cells classification: A neural based automated system for Alzheimer disease classification. *Journal of Advanced Microscopy Research, 11*(1), 1–10. doi:10.1166/jamr.2016.1282

Dey, N., Chakraborty, S., & Samanta, S. (2014). Optimization of watermarking in biomedical signal. *Heinrich-Böcking-Straße, 6*, 66121.

Dey, N., Chakraborty, S., & Samanta, S. (2014). Optimization of watermarking in biomedical signal. *Lambert Publication. Heinrich-Böcking-Straße, 6*, 66121.

Dey, N., Chakraborty, S., & Samanta, S. (2014). *Optimization of Watermarking in Biomedical Signal*: Lambert Publication. *Heinrich-Böcking-Straße, 6*, 66121.

Dey, N., Chakraborty, S., & Samanta, S. (2014b). Optimization of watermarking in biomedical signal.Lambert Publication. *Heinrich-Böcking-Straße, 6*, 66121.

Dey, N., Dey, M., Mahata, S. K., Das, A., & Chaudhuri, S. S. (2015a). Tamper detection of electrocardiographic signal using watermarked bio–hash code in wireless cardiology. *International Journal of Signal and Imaging Systems Engineering, 8*(1-2), 46–58. doi:10.1504/IJSISE.2015.067069

Dey, N., Samanta, S., Chakraborty, S., Das, A., Chaudhuri, S. S., & Suri, J. S. (2014). Firefly algorithm for optimization of scaling factors during embedding of manifold medical information: An application in ophthalmology imaging. *Journal of Medical Imaging and Health Informatics, 4*(3), 384–394. doi:10.1166/jmihi.2014.1265

Dey, N., Samanta, S., Yang, X. S., Das, A., & Chaudhuri, S. S. (2013). Optimisation of scaling factors in electrocardiogram signal watermarking using cuckoo search. *International Journal of Bio-inspired Computation, 5*(5), 315–326. doi:10.1504/IJBIC.2013.057193

Dhal, K. G., & Das, S. (2015). Diversity Conserved Chaotic Artificial Bee Colony Algorithm based Brightness Preserved Histogram Equalization and Contrast Stretching Method. *International Journal of Natural Computing Research, 5*, 45-73.

Dhal, K. G., & Das, S. (2017). Cuckoo search with search strategies. *Pattern Recognition and Image Analysis*. (accepted)

Dhal, K. G., Namtirtha, A., Quraishi, I. M., & Das, S. (n.d.). Gray level image enhancement using Particle Swarm Optimization with Lévy Flight: An Eagle Strategy Approach. *International Journal of Innovative Research in Science, Engineering and Technology, 5*, 79-86.

Dhal, K. G., Quraishi, I. M., & Das, S. (2015). Performance Analysis of Chaotic Lévy Bat Algorithm and Chaotic Cuckoo Search Algorithm for Gray Level Image Enhancement. *Information Systems Design and Intelligent Applications*, 233-244.

Dhal, K. G., Quraishi, I. M., & Das, S. (2017). An improved cuckoo search based optimal ranged brightness preserved histogram equalization and contrast stretching method. *Int. Jr. of Swarm intelligence Research, 8*, 1-29.

Dhal, K. G., Sen, M., & Das, S. (2017). Cuckoo search based modified Bi-Histogram Equalizationmethod to enhance the cancerous tissues in Mammography images. *Int. Journal of Medical Engineering and Informatics*. (accepted)

Dhal, K. G., Sen, S., Sarkar, K., Das, S. (2016). Entropy based Range Optimized Brightness Preserved Histogram-Equalization for Image Contrast Enhancement. *Int. Jr. of Computer Vision and Image Processing, 6*(1), 59-72.

Dhal, K.G, Quraishi, I. M., Das, S.(2015). Performance Enhancement of Differential Evolution by Incorporating Lévy Flight and Chaotic Sequence for the Cases of Satellite Images. *Int. J. of Applied Metaheuristic Computing, 6*, 69-81.

Dhal, K. G., & Das, S. (2017a). Combination of Histogram Segmentation and Modification to Preserve the Original Brightness of the Images. *Pattern Recognition and Image Analysis, 27*(2), 200–212. doi:10.1134/S1054661817020031

Dhal, K. G., Quraishi, I. M., & Das, S. (2015). *A Chaotic Lévy flight Approach in Bat and Firefly Algorithm for Gray level image Enhancement. I.J. Image, Graphics and Signal Processing,* 7, 69–76.

Dhal, K. G., Quraishi, I. M., & Das, S. (2015). *Development of firefly algorithm via chaotic sequence and population diversity to enhance the image contrast. Natural Computing* , 14, 1–12.

Dheeba, J., & Selvi, T. (2010, December). Bio inspired swarm algorithm for tumor detection in digital mammogram. In *International Conference on Swarm, Evolutionary, and Memetic Computing* (pp. 404-415). Springer Berlin Heidelberg. doi:10.1007/978-3-642-17563-3_49

Dimopoulos, C., & Zalzala, A. M. (2001). Investigating the use of genetic programming for a classic one-machine scheduling problem. *Advances in Engineering Software, 32*(6), 489–498. doi:10.1016/S0965-9978(00)00109-5

Doi, K. (2007). Computer-aided diagnosis in medical imaging: Historical review, current status and future potential. *Computerized Medical Imaging and Graphics,* 31(4), 198–211. doi:10.1016/j.compmedimag.2007.02.002 PMID:17349778

Dorigo, M., Birattari, M., & Stutzle, T. (2006). Ant colony optimization. *IEEE Computational Intelligence Magazine, 1*(4), 28–39. doi:10.1109/MCI.2006.329691

Duggirala Raja Kishor, N. V. (2016). A Novel Hybridization of Expectation-Maximization and K-Means Algorithms for Better Clustering Performance. *International Journal of Ambient Computing and Intelligence, 7*(2).

Dutta, S. (2016). Optimal Allocation of Static Synchronous. Academic Press.

Dutta, R., Paul, S., & Chattopadhyay, A. (2000). Applicability of the modified back-propagation algorithm in tool condition monitoring for faster convergence. *Journal of Materials Processing Technology, 98*(3), 299–309. doi:10.1016/S0924-0136(99)00295-2

Dutta, S., Roy, P. K., & Nandi, D. (2016). Series Compensator Controllers using Chemical Reaction Optimization for Reactive Power Dispatch. *International Journal of Energy Optimization and Engineering, 5*(3), 43–62. doi:10.4018/IJEOE.2016070103

Du–Yih, T. S. A. I. (1994). Automatic segmentation of liver structure in CT images using a neural network. *IEICE Transactions on Fundamentals of Electronics, Communications and Computer Science, 77*(11), 1892–1895.

Dwivedi, V., Chauhan, T., Saxena, S., & Agrawal, P. (2012). *Travelling Salesman Problem using Genetic Algorithm.* Paper presented at the National Conference on Development of Reliable Information Systems, Techniques and Related Issues.

Eberhart, R., & Kennedy, J. (1995, October). A new optimizer using particle swarm theory. In *Micro Machine and Human Science, 1995. MHS'95., Proceedings of the Sixth International Symposium on* (pp. 39-43). IEEE. doi:10.1109/MHS.1995.494215

Ebrahim, M. A., Mostafa, H. E., Gawish, S. A., & Bendary, F. M. (2009, November). Design of decentralized load frequency based-PID controller using stochastic particle swarm optimization technique. In *Electric Power and Energy Conversion Systems, 2009. EPECS'09. International Conference on* (pp. 1-6). IEEE.

Edition, F. (2011). Guidelines for drinking-water quality. *WHO Chronicle*, *38*, 104–108. PMID:6485306

Edris, A. (2000, March). FACTS Technology Development: An Update. *IEEE Power Engineering Review*.

Ee, K., Balaji, A., & Jawahir, I. (2003). Progressive tool-wear mechanisms and their effects on chip-curl/chip-form in machining with grooved tools: An extended application of the equivalent toolface (ET) model. *Wear*, *255*(7), 1404–1413. doi:10.1016/S0043-1648(03)00112-1

Eiben, A. E., Hinterding, R., & Michalewicz, Z. (1999). Parameter control in evolutionary algorithms. *IEEE Transactions on Evolutionary Computation*, *3*(2), 124–141. doi:10.1109/4235.771166

El Hassani, H., Benkachcha, S., & Benhra, J. (2017). New genetic operator (jump crossover) for the traveling salesman problem. In Nature-Inspired Computing: Concepts, Methodologies, Tools, and Applications (pp. 1739-1752). IGI Global.

Elayaraja, E., Thangavel, K., Chitralega, M., & Chandrasekhar, T. (2012). Extraction of Motif Patterns from Protein Sequences Using SVD with Rough K-Means Algorithm. *IJCSI International Journal of Computer Science Issues*, *9*(6), 350–356.

Elayaraja, E., Thangavel, K., Ramya, B., & Chitralegha, M. (2011). Extraction of Motif Patterns from Protein Sequence using Rough K-Means Algorithm. *Procedia Engineering*, *30*, 814–820. doi:10.1016/j.proeng.2012.01.932

El-Din, A. G., Smith, D. W., & El-Din, M. G. (2004). Application of artificial neural networks in wastewater treatment. *Journal of Environmental Engineering and Science*, *3*(S1), S81–S95. doi:10.1139/s03-067

Ercal, F., Chawla, A., Stoecker, W. V., Lee, H. C., & Moss, R. H. (1994). Neural network diagnosis of malignant melanoma from color images. *IEEE Transactions on Bio-Medical Engineering*, *41*(9), 837–845. doi:10.1109/10.312091 PMID:7959811

Eutamene, A., Kholladi, M. K., Gaceb, D., & Belhadef, H. (2017). *A Dual PSO-Adaptive Mean Shift for Preprocessing Optimization on Degraded Document Images. Int. Jr. Applied Metaheuristic Computing*, 8(1).

Fang, X., & Jawahir, I. (1993). The effects of progressive tool wear and tool restricted contact on chip breakability in machining. *Wear*, *160*(2), 243–252. doi:10.1016/0043-1648(93)90427-N

Farahani, R. Z., Rezapour, S., Drezner, T., & Fallah, S. (2014). Competitive supply chain network design: An overview of classifications, models, solution techniques and applications. *Omega*, *45*, 92–118. doi:10.1016/j.omega.2013.08.006

Ferreira, C. (2002). Gene Expression Programming: Mathematical Modeling by an Artificial Intelligence. Angra do Heroismo.

Ferreira, C. (2001). Gene Expression Programming: A New Adaptive Algorithm for Solving Problems. *Complex Systems*, *13*(2), 87–129.

Financial Forecast Center, LLC. (2017). *Why do the stock markets keep going up?*. Retrieved from www.forecasts.org

Forrest, S. (1993). Genetic algorithms: Principles of natural selection applied to Computation. *Science*, 872–878.

Freisleben, B., & Merz, P. (1996). *New genetic local search operators for the traveling salesman problem. In Parallel Problem Solving from Nature—PPSN IV* (pp. 890–899). Springer. doi:10.1007/3-540-61723-X_1052

Freixenet, J., Muñoz, X., Raba, D., Martí, J., & Cufí, X. (2002). Yet another survey on image segmentation: Region and boundary information integration. *Computer Vision—ECCV 2002*, 21-25.

Fujiwara & Konagaya. (2008). Protein Motif Extraction using Hidden Markov Model. *Genome Informatics*, 57-64.

Galeshchuk, S. (2016). Neural networks performance in exchange rate prediction. *Neurocomputing*, *172*, 446–452. doi:10.1016/j.neucom.2015.03.100

Gao, C., Panetta, K., & Agaian, S. (2013). No reference color image quality measures. *2013 Int. Conf. on Cybernetics*, 243-248.

Gatta, C., Rizzi, A., & Marini, D. (2002). ACE: An automatic color equalization algorithm. *Proceedings of the First European Conference on Color in Graphics Image and Vision (CGIV02)*.

Gen, M., & Cheng, R. (2000). *Genetic algorithms and engineering optimization* (Vol. 7). John Wiley & Sons.

Gerald, S. (2016). Gene Expression Analysis based on Ant Colony Optimisation Classification. *International Journal of Rough Sets and Data Analysis*, *3*(3), 51–59. doi:10.4018/IJRSDA.2016070104

Ghani, J. A., Rizal, M., Nuawi, M. Z., Ghazali, M. J., & Haron, C. H. C. (2011). Monitoring online cutting tool wear using low-cost technique and user-friendly GUI. *Wear*, *271*(9), 2619–2624. doi:10.1016/j.wear.2011.01.038

Ghazali, R., Hussain, A., & El-Deredy, V. (2006). Application of ridge polynomial neural networks to financial time series prediction. *2006 International Joint Conference on Neural Networks*, 913–20. doi:10.1109/IJCNN.2006.246783

Ghosh, A., Sarkar, A., Ashour, A. S., Balas-Timar, D., Dey, N., & Balas, V. E. (2015). Grid color moment features in glaucoma classification. *Int J Adv Comput Sci Appl*, *6*(9), 1–14.

Ghosh, N., Ravi, Y., Patra, A., Mukhopadhyay, S., Paul, S., Mohanty, A., & Chattopadhyay, A. (2007). Estimation of tool wear during CNC milling using neural network-based sensor fusion. *Mechanical Systems and Signal Processing*, *21*(1), 466–479. doi:10.1016/j.ymssp.2005.10.010

Girres, J.-F., & Touya, G. (2010). Quality Assessment of the French OpenStreetMap Dataset. *Transactions in GIS*, *14*(4), 435–459. doi:10.1111/j.1467-9671.2010.01203.x

Goel, S., Sharma, A., & Panchal, V. K. (2014). Multiobjective Cuckoo Search for Anticipating the Enemys Movements in the Battleground. *International Journal of Applied Metaheuristic Computing*, *5*(4), 26–46. doi:10.4018/ijamc.2014100102

Goel, S., & Wadhwa, V. (2013). A comparative analysis of PMX, POS and OX crossover operators for solving. *International Journal of Latest Research in Science and Technology*, *2*(2), 80–83.

Goldberg, D. E. (1989). Genetic Algorithms in Search, Optimization, and Machine Learning. Addison-Wesley Longman Publishing Co.

Goldberg, D. (1989). *Genetic Algorithms in Search, Optimization, and Machine Learning*. Addison Wesley.

Goldberg, D. E. (1989). *Genetic Algorithms in Search, Optimization and Machine Learning*. Addison-Wesley Publishing Company.

Goldberg, D. E., & Lingle, R. (1985). Alleles, loci, and the traveling salesman problem. *Proceedings of the First International Conference on Genetic Algorithms and Their Applications*, 154-159.

Golz, H., Schillo, E., Wolf, A., & Kaufeld, M. (1995). Bewertung von Werkzeugüberwachungssystemen aus Sicht der Anwender. *VDI-Berichte*, *1179*, 309–309.

Gonzalez, R. C., & Woods, R. E. (2002). *Digital Image Processing* (2nd ed.). New York: Prentice Hall.

Gopal, N. N., & Karnan, M. (2010, December). Diagnose brain tumor through MRI using image processing clustering algorithms such as Fuzzy C Means along with intelligent optimization techniques. In *Computational Intelligence and Computing Research (ICCIC), 2010 IEEE International Conference on* (pp. 1-4). IEEE. doi:10.1109/ICCIC.2010.5705890

Gorai, A., & Ghosh, A. (2009). Gray-level Image Enhancement By Particle Swarm Optimization. *Proceedings of World Congress on Nature & Biologically Inspired Computing*. doi:10.1109/NABIC.2009.5393603

Compilation of References

Gorai, A., & Ghosh, A. (2011). *Hue preserving color Image Enhancement by Particle Swarm Optimization*. IEEE. doi:10.1109/RAICS.2011.6069375

Gowri & Rathipriya. (2015). Extraction of Protein Sequence Motif Information using PSO K-Means. *Journal of Network and Information Security*.

Gowri & Rathipriya. (2015a). Biclustering using Venus Flytrap Optimization Algorithm. Computational Intelligence in Data Mining—Volume 1. *Advances in Intelligent Systems and Computing Series, 410*.

Gowri & Rathipriya. (2016a). Protein Motif Comparator using PSO K-Means. *International Journal of Applied Metaheuristic Computing, 7*(3), 56–68.

Gowri, R., & Rathipriya, R. (2015b). Venus Flytrap Optimization Algorithm. International Conference on Computational Intelligence, Cyber Security and Computational Models. *Advances in Intelligent Systems and Computing Series, 412*.

Gowri, R., & Rathipriya, R. (2016b). Extraction of Protein Sequence Motif Information using Bio-Inspired Computing. In *Handbook of Research on Computational Intelligence Applications in Bioinformatics* (pp. 240–262). IGI Global.

Gowri, R., & Rathipriya, R. (2016c). Quality based Clustering using MapReduce Framework. *International conference on Green Engineering and Technologies*. IEEE.

Gowri, R., & Rathipriya, R. (2016d). MR-GABiT: MapReduce based Genetic Algorithm for Biclustering Time Series Data. *International Conference on Advances in Computer Applications*. IEEE.

Gowri, R., & Rathipriya, R. (2017). Cohesive Sub-Network Mining in Protein Interaction Networks using Score Based Co-Clustering with MapReduce Model (MR-CoC). *International Conference on Big Data Analytics and Cloud Computing*. Springer.

Grefenstette, J., Gopal, R., Rosmaita, B., & Van Gucht, D. (1985). Genetic algorithms for the traveling salesman problem. *Proceedings of the first International Conference on Genetic Algorithms and their Applications*.

Grewal, V., & Sharma, A, K. (2010). On Performance Evaluation of Different QoS Mechanisms and AMC scheme for an IEEE 802.16 based WiMAX Network. *International Journal of Computer Applications, 6*(7), 12 – 17.

Guler, M., & Sahin, E. (1994). A new higher-order binary-input neural unit: Learning and generalizing effectively via using minimal number of monomials. *Third Turkish Symposium on Artificial Intelligence and Neural Networks Proceedings*. Middle East Technical University.

Gyugi, L. (1992, July). A Unified Power Control Concept for Flexible AC Transmission Systems. *IEE Procedings-C, 139*(4), 323–332.

Gyugyi, Schauder, Williams, Rictman, Torgerson, & Edris. (1995). The Unified Power Flow Controller: A New Approach to Power Transmission Control. *IEEE Trans. on Power Delivery, 10*(2), 1085-1097.

Hamdan, M., & Abderrazzaq, M. H. (2016). Optimization of Small Wind Turbines using Genetic Algorithms. *International Journal of Applied Metaheuristic Computing, 7*(4), 50–65. doi:10.4018/IJAMC.2016100104

Hamdaoui, F., Mtibaa, A., & Sakly, A. (2014, December). Comparison between MPSO and MSFLA metaheuristics for MR brain image segmentation. In *Sciences and Techniques of Automatic Control and Computer Engineering (STA), 2014 15th International Conference on* (pp. 164-168). IEEE. doi:10.1109/STA.2014.7086725

Hamou, R. M., Bouarara, H. A., & Amine, A. (2015). *Bio-Inspired Techniques in the Clustering of Texts: Synthesis and Comparative Study. Int. Jr. Applied Metaheuristic Computing, 6*(4).

Hans, W. G., & Stephen, M. (2016). Using Contextual Information for Recognising Human Behaviour. *International Journal of Ambient Computing and Intelligence, 7*(1), 27–44. doi:10.4018/IJACI.2016010102

Hasegawa, A., Lo, S. C. B., Lin, J. S., Freedman, M. T., & Mun, S. K. (1998). A shift-invariant neural network for the lung field segmentation in chest radiography. *The Journal of VLSI Signal Processing, 18*(3), 241–250. doi:10.1023/A:1007937214367

Hashemi, S., Kiani, S., Noroozi, N., & Moghaddam, M. E. (2010). An image contrast enhancement method based on genetic algorithm. *Pattern Recognition Letters, 31*(13), 1816–1824. doi:10.1016/j.patrec.2009.12.006

Heba, A., & Moustafa, Y. (2014). An Analysis of Device-Free and Device-Based WiFi-Localization Systems. *International Journal of Ambient Computing and Intelligence, 6*(1), 1–19. doi:10.4018/ijaci.2014010101

Heimann, T., Van Ginneken, B., Styner, M. A., Arzhaeva, Y., Aurich, V., Bauer, C., & Bello, F. et al. (2009). Comparison and evaluation of methods for liver segmentation from CT datasets. *IEEE Transactions on Medical Imaging, 28*(8), 1251–1265. doi:10.1109/TMI.2009.2013851 PMID:19211338

Hemanth, D. J., Vijila, C. K. S., & Anitha, J. (2010). Performance improved PSO based modified counter propagation neural network for abnormal MR brain image classification. *Int. J. Advance. Soft Comput. Appl, 2*(1), 65–84.

Hernández-Cisneros, R., & Terashima-Marín, H. (2006). Classification of individual and clustered microcalcifications in digital mammograms using evolutionary neural networks. *MICAI 2006. Advances in Artificial Intelligence*, 1200–1210.

Hicham El, H., Said, B., & Jamal, B. (2015). New Genetic Operator (Jump Crossover) for the Traveling Salesman Problem. *International Journal of Applied Metaheuristic Computing, 6*(2), 33–44. doi:10.4018/IJAMC.2015040103

Hingorani, N. G., & Gyugyi, L. (2000). *Understanding FACTS: Concepts and Technology of Flexible AC Transmission System*. IEEE Press.

Holland, J. (1975). *Adaptation in natural and artificial systems*. Ann Arbor, MI: The University of Michigan Press.

Holland, J. H. (1975). *Adaption in Natural and Artificial Systems*. The University of Michigan Press.

Holland, J. H. (n.d.). Genetic Algorithms and Adaptation. *Adaptive Control of Ill-Defined Systems, NATO Conference Series,* 16, 317-333.

Hong, J. H., & Cho, S. B. (2006). Efficient huge-scale feature selection with speciated genetic algorithm. *Pattern Recognition Letters, 27*(2), 143–150. doi:10.1016/j.patrec.2005.07.009

Hore, S., Chatterjee, S., Chakraborty, S., & Shaw, R. K. (2016b). Analysis of Different Feature Description Algorithm in object Recognition. *Feature Detectors and Motion Detection in Video Processing,* 66.

Hore, S., Chatterjee, S., Shaw, R., Dey, N., & Virmani, J. (2015a, November). Detection of chronic kidney disease: A NN-GA based approach. In *CSI—2015; 50th Golden Jubilee Annual Convention*.

Hore, S., Chakraborty, S., Chatterjee, S., Dey, N., Ashour, A. S., Van Chung, L., & Le, D. N. (2016a). An Integrated Interactive Technique for Image Segmentation using Stack based Seeded Region Growing and Thresholding. *Iranian Journal of Electrical and Computer Engineering, 6*(6), 2773–2780.

Hore, S., Chatterjee, S., Santhi, V., Dey, N., Ashour, A. S., Balas, V. E., & Shi, F. (2017). Indian Sign Language Recognition Using Optimized Neural Networks. In *Information Technology and Intelligent Transportation Systems* (pp. 553–563). Springer International Publishing. doi:10.1007/978-3-319-38771-0_54

Hore, S., Chatterjee, S., Sarkar, S., Dey, N., Ashour, A. S., Balas-Timar, D., & Balas, V. E. (2016). Neural-based prediction of structural failure of multistoried RC buildings. *Structural Engineering & Mechanics, 58*(3), 459–473. doi:10.12989/sem.2016.58.3.459

Hsiao, Y. T., Chuang, C. L., & Chien, C. C. (2004, September). Ant colony optimization for designing of PID controllers. In *Computer Aided Control Systems Design, 2004 IEEE International Symposium on* (pp. 321-326). IEEE.

Hsmmns, T. J., & Lim, S. K. (1997). Flexible AC Transmission System (FACTS). *Electric Machines & Power System, 25,* 73–85.

Hu, J. J., Tang, C. J., Duan, L., Zuo, J., Peng, J., & Yuan, C. A. (2007). The strategy for diversifying initial population of gene expression programming. *Chinese Journal of Computers-Chinese Edition, 30*(2), 305.

Ibrahim, S., Khalid, N. E. A., & Manaf, M. (2010, March). Empirical study of brain segmentation using particle swarm optimization. In *Information Retrieval & Knowledge Management,(CAMP), 2010 International Conference on* (pp. 235-239). IEEE. doi:10.1109/INFRKM.2010.5466910

Ikeda, N., Gupta, A., Dey, N., Bose, S., Shafique, S., Arak, T., & Suri, J. S. et al. (2015). Improved correlation between carotid and coronary atherosclerosis SYNTAX score using automated ultrasound carotid bulb plaque IMT measurement. *Ultrasound in Medicine & Biology, 41*(5), 1247–1262. doi:10.1016/j.ultrasmedbio.2014.12.024 PMID:25638311

Innocent, P. R., Barnes, M., & John, R. (1997). Application of the fuzzy ART/MAP and MinMax/MAP neural network models to radiographic image classification. *Artificial Intelligence in Medicine, 11*(3), 241–263. doi:10.1016/S0933-3657(97)00032-8 PMID:9413608

Iyad Abu, D., Faisal, A., Eslam Al, M., Mohammed Azmi, A.-B., & Basima Hani, F. H. (2013). Hybridizing Harmony Search Algorithm with Multi-Parent Crossover to Solve Real World Optimization Problems. *International Journal of Applied Metaheuristic Computing, 4*(3), 1–14. doi:10.4018/ijamc.2013070101

Jagatheesan, K., & Anand, B. (2012, December). Dynamic performance of multi-area hydro thermal power systems with integral controller considering various performance indices methods. In *Emerging Trends in Science, Engineering and Technology (INCOSET), 2012 International Conference on* (pp. 474-484). IEEE. doi:10.1109/INCOSET.2012.6513952

Jagatheesan, K., & Anand, B. (2014). Automatic generation control of three area hydro-thermal power systems considering electric and mechanical governor with conventional controller and ant colony optimization technique. *Advances in Natural and Applied Sciences, 8*(20), 25–34.

Jagatheesan, K., Anand, B., & Ebrahim, M. A. (2014). Stochastic particle swarm optimization for tuning of PID controller in load frequency control of single area reheat thermal power system. *International Journal of Electrical and Power Engineering, 8*(2), 33–40.

Jain, A., Kumar Varshney, A., & Chandra Joshi, U. (2001). Short-term water demand forecast modelling at IIT Kanpur using artificial neural networks. *Water Resources Management, 15*(5), 299–321. doi:10.1023/A:1014415503476

Jeffrey, G. A., Ghosh, A., & Muhamed, R. (2007). *Fundamentals of WiMAX: Understanding Broadband Wireless Networking*. Prentice-Hall.

Jena, P. R., Majhi, R., & Majhi, B. (2015). Development and performance evaluation of a novel knowledge guided artificial neural network (KGANN) model for exchange rate prediction. *Journal of King Saud University-Computer and Information Sciences, 27*(4), 450–457. doi:10.1016/j.jksuci.2015.01.002

Jennifer, H., Tom, L., & Paul Mc, K. (2011). AmbiLearn: Multimodal Assisted Learning. *International Journal of Ambient Computing and Intelligence, 3*(1), 53–59. doi:10.4018/jaci.2011010106

Jianfeng, L., Yongqing, Z., Fangrong, C., Zhiren, T., & Yao, W. (n.d.). *Wear and Breakage Monitoring of Cutting Tools By Optic Method (1st Part: Theory)*. Academic Press.

Jirapong, P. (2013, April-June). FACTS Devices Allocation for Power Transfer Capability Enhancement and Power System Losses Reduction. *International Journal of Energy Optimization and Engineering, 2*(2), 1–14. doi:10.4018/ijeoe.2013040101

Jog, P., Suh, J. Y., & Gucht, D. v. (1989). The effects of population size, heuristic crossover and local improvement on a genetic algorithm for the traveling salesman problem. *Proceedings of the Third International Conference on Genetic Algorithms.*

Johnson, D. S., & McGeoch, L. A. (2002). *Experimental analysis of heuristics for the STSP. In The traveling salesman problem and its variations* (pp. 369–443). Springer.

Joseph, R., Abraham, A., Das, D., & Patra, A. (2011). Damping oscillations in tie power and area frequencies in a thermal power system with SMES-TCPS combinations. *Journal of Electrical System, 1*(1), 71–80.

Juneja, D., Singh, A., Singh, R., & Mukherjee, S. (2017). A thorough insight into theoretical and practical developments in multiagent systems. *International Journal of Ambient Computing and Intelligence, 8*(1), 23–49. doi:10.4018/IJACI.2017010102

Jurkovic, J., Korosec, M., & Kopac, J. (2005). New approach in tool wear measuring technique using CCD vision system. *International Journal of Machine Tools & Manufacture, 45*(9), 1023–1030. doi:10.1016/j.ijmachtools.2004.11.030

Jurman, G., Riccadonna, S., & Furlanello, C. (2012). A comparison of MCC and CEN error measures in multi-class prediction. *PLoS ONE, 7*(8), e41882. doi:10.1371/journal.pone.0041882 PMID:22905111

Kadah, Y. M., Farag, A. A., Zurada, J. M., Badawi, A. M., & Youssef, A. B. (1996). Classification algorithms for quantitative tissue characterization of diffuse liver disease from ultrasound images. *IEEE Transactions on Medical Imaging, 15*(4), 466–478. doi:10.1109/42.511750 PMID:18215928

Kanungo, D. P., Janmenjoy, N., Bighnaraj, N., & Behera, H. S. (2016). Hybrid Clustering using Elitist Teaching Learning-Based Optimization: An Improved Hybrid Approach of TLBO. *International Journal of Rough Sets and Data Analysis, 3*(1), 1–19. doi:10.4018/IJRSDA.2016010101

Karaa, W. B. A., Ashour, A. S., Sassi, D. B., Roy, P., Kausar, N., & Dey, N. (2016). Medline text mining: an enhancement genetic algorithm based approach for document clustering. In *Applications of Intelligent Optimization in Biology and Medicine* (pp. 267–287). Springer International Publishing. doi:10.1007/978-3-319-21212-8_12

Karegowda & Kumari. (2013). Particle Swarm Optimization Algorithm Based K-Means and Fuzzy c-means clustering. *International Journal of Advanced Research in Computer Science and Software Engineering, 3*(7).

Karnan, M., & Logheshwari, T. (2010, December). Improved implementation of brain MRI image segmentation using ant colony system. In *Computational Intelligence and Computing Research (ICCIC), 2010 IEEE International Conference on* (pp. 1-4). IEEE. doi:10.1109/ICCIC.2010.5705897

Kas, M., Yargicoglu, B., Korpeoglu, I., & Karasan, E. (2010). A survey on scheduling in IEEE 802.16 mesh mode. *IEEE Communications Surveys and Tutorials, 12*(2), 205–221. doi:10.1109/SURV.2010.021110.00053

Kaur, P., & Kaur, T. (2014). A Comparative Study of Various Metaheuristic Algorithms. *International Journal of Computer Science and Information Technologies, 5*(5), 6701–6704.

Kausar, N., Palaniappan, S., Samir, B. B., Abdullah, A., & Dey, N. (2016). Systematic analysis of applied data mining based optimization algorithms in clinical attribute extraction and classification for diagnosis of cardiac patients. In *Applications of intelligent optimization in biology and medicine* (pp. 217–231). Springer International Publishing. doi:10.1007/978-3-319-21212-8_9

Khachane, M. Y. (2017). Organ-Based Medical Image Classification Using Support Vector Machine. *International Journal of Synthetic Emotions, 8*(1), 18–30. doi:10.4018/IJSE.2017010102

Kharrat, A., Gasmi, K., Messaoud, M. B., Benamrane, N., & Abid, M. (2010). A hybrid approach for automatic classification of brain MRI using genetic algorithm and support vector machine. *Leonardo Journal of Sciences, 17*(1), 71–82.

Khazaee, A., & Ebrahimzadeh, A. (2010). Classification of electrocardiogram signals with support vector machines and genetic algorithms using power spectral features. *Biomedical Signal Processing and Control, 5*(4), 252–263. doi:10.1016/j.bspc.2010.07.006

Kim, Y.T. (1997). Contrast enhancement using brightness preserving bi-histogram equalization. *IEEE Trans. Consum. Electron., 43*(1), 1–8.

Kishore, J. K., Patnaik, L. M., Mani, V., & Agrawal, V. K. (2000). Application of genetic programming for multicategory pattern classification. *IEEE Transactions on Evolutionary Computation, 4*(3), 242–258. doi:10.1109/4235.873235

Kong, N. S. P., & Ibrahim, H. (2008). Color image enhancement using brightness preserving dynamic histogram equalization. *IEEE Trans. on Consumer Electronics, 54*, 1962-1968.

Koss, J. E., Newman, F. D., Johnson, T. K., & Kirch, D. L. (1999). Abdominal organ segmentation using texture transforms and a hopfield neural network. *IEEE Transactions on Medical Imaging, 18*(7), 640–648. doi:10.1109/42.790463 PMID:10504097

Kotyk, T., Ashour, A. S., Chakraborty, S., Dey, N., & Balas, V. E. (2015). Apoptosis analysis in classification paradigm: a neural network based approach. In *Healthy World conference* (pp. 17-22). Academic Press.

Kotyk, T., Dey, N., Ashour, A. S., Balas-Timar, D., Chakraborty, S., Ashour, A. S., & Tavares, J. M. R. (2016). Measurement of glomerulus diameter and Bowmans space width of renal albino rats. *Computer Methods and Programs in Biomedicine, 126*, 143–153. doi:10.1016/j.cmpb.2015.10.023 PMID:26796351

Koza, J. R. (1992). *Genetic programming: on the programming of computers by means of natural selection* (Vol. 1). MIT Press.

Koza, J. R. (1994In press). *Genetic programming II: automatic discovery of reusable programs.* Cambridge, MA: MIT Press.

Kubusada, Y., Mohan, G., Manjappa, K., & Reddy, G. R. M. (2013). *A Gene Expression Based Quality of Service Aware Routing Protocol for Mobile Ad Hoc Networks. In Computer Networks & Communications* (pp. 283–290). NetCom.

Kumar Roy, P. (2013, July-September). Hybridization of Biogeography Based Optimization with Differential Evolution for solving Optimal Power Flow Problems. *International Journal of Energy Optimization and Engineering, 2*(3), 86–101. doi:10.4018/ijeoe.2013070106

Kumaran Kumar, J., Kailas, A., 2012. Prediction of future stock close price using proposed hybrid ANN model of functional link fuzzy logic neural model (FLFNM). *Int. J. Comput. Appl. Eng. Sci., 2*(1).

Kumar, N., Karambir, & Kumar, R. (2012). A Comparative Analysis of PMX, CX and OX Crossover operators for solving Travelling Salesman Problem. *International Journal of Latest Research in Science and Technology, 1*(2), 98–101.

Kumar, S. U., Inbarani, H. H., Azar, A. T., & Hassanien, A. E. (2014). Identification of heart valve disease using bijective soft sets theory. [IJRSDA]. *International Journal of Rough Sets and Data Analysis, 1*(2), 1–14. doi:10.4018/ijrsda.2014070101

Kundur, P. (1993). *Power System Stability and Control.* New York: McGraw-Hill, Inc.

Kunik, V., Solan, Z., Edelman, S., Ruppin, E., & Horn, D. (2005). Motif Extraction and Protein Classification: Computational Systems. *Proceedings of IEEE Computational Systems Bioinformatics / Life Sciences Society.*

Kuran, M. S., & Tugcu, T. (2007). A survey on emerging broadband wireless access technologies. *Computer Networks, 51*(11), 3013–3046. doi:10.1016/j.comnet.2006.12.009

Ladgham, A., Hamdaoui, F., Sakly, A., & Mtibaa, A. (2015). Fast MR brain image segmentation based on modified Shuffled Frog Leaping Algorithm. *Signal. Image and Video Processing, 9*(5), 1113–1120. doi:10.1007/s11760-013-0546-y

Lanzetta, M. (2001). A new flexible high-resolution vision sensor for tool condition monitoring. *Journal of Materials Processing Technology, 119*(1), 73–82. doi:10.1016/S0924-0136(01)00878-0

Laporte, G. (1992). The vehicle routing problem: An overview of exact and approximate algorithms. *European Journal of Operational Research, 59*(3), 345–358. doi:10.1016/0377-2217(92)90192-C

Larranaga, P., Kuijpers, C. M. H., Poza, M., & Murga, R. H. (1997). Decomposing Bayesian Networks: Triangulation of the Moral Graph with Genetic Algorithms. *Statistics and Computing, 7*(1), 19–34. doi:10.1023/A:1018553211613

Lashkar Ara, Kazemi, & Nabavi Niaki. (2012). Multi objective Optimal Location of FACTS Shunt-Series Controllers for Power System Operation Planning. *IEEE Transactions on Power Delivery, 27*(2), 481-490.

Leandro, C. (2009). A novel particle swarm optimization approach using Henon map and implicit filtering local search for economic load dispatch. *Chaos, Solitons, and Fractals, 39*(2), 510–518. doi:10.1016/j.chaos.2007.01.093

Le, D. A., & Vo, D. N. (2016, January-March). Cuckoo Search Algorithm for Minimization of Power Loss and Voltage Deviation. *International Journal of Energy Optimization and Engineering, 5*(1), 23–34. doi:10.4018/IJEOE.2016010102

Lee, C. C., & Chung, P. C. (2000). Recognizing abdominal organs in CT images using contextual neural network and fuzzy rules. In *Engineering in Medicine and Biology Society, 2000. Proceedings of the 22nd Annual International Conference of the IEEE* (*Vol. 3*, pp. 1745-1748). IEEE.

Lee, J. Y., Hwang, I. S., Liem, A. T., Lai, K. R., & Nikoukar, A. (2013). Genetic expression programming: A new approach for QoS traffic prediction in EPONs. *Photonic Network Communications, 25*(3), 156–165. doi:10.1007/s11107-013-0399-x

Leerink, L. R., Giles, C. L., Horne, B. G., & Jabri, M. A. (1995). Learning with product units. In G. Tesaro, D. Touretzky, & T. Leen (Eds.), Advances in Neural Information Processing Systems 7. Cambridge, MA: MIT Press.

Leung, Y. W., & Wang, Y. (2001). An orthogonal genetic algorithm with quantization for global numerical optimization. *IEEE Transactions on Evolutionary Computation, 5*(1), 41–53. doi:10.1109/4235.910464

Li, Y., Wen, P., Powers, D., & Clark, C. R. (1999). LSB neural network based segmentation of MR brain images. In *Systems, Man, and Cybernetics, 1999. IEEE SMC'99 Conference Proceedings. 1999 IEEE International Conference on* (Vol. 6, pp. 822-825). IEEE.

Li, B., Qin, Y., Low, C. P., & Gwee, C. L. (2007). Wireless Broadband Access: A survey on Mobile WiMAX. *IEEE Communications Magazine*, 70–75. doi:10.1109/MCOM.2007.4395368

Li, H., & Zhang, Q. (2009). Multiobjective optimization problems with complicated Pareto sets, MOEA/D and NSGA-II. *IEEE Transactions on Evolutionary Computation, 13*(2), 284–302. doi:10.1109/TEVC.2008.925798

Lin, S., & Kernighan, B. W. (1973). An effective heuristic algorithm for the traveling-salesman problem. *Operations Research, 21*(2), 498–516. doi:10.1287/opre.21.2.498

Lister, P., & Barrow, G. (1986). *Tool condition monitoring systems.* Paper presented at the Proceedings of the Twenty-sixth International Machine Tool Design and Research Conference. doi:10.1007/978-1-349-08114-1_36

Liu, Q., Wang, X., & Giannakis, G. B. (2006). A Cross-Layer Scheduling Algorithm with QoS Support in Wireless Networks. *IEEE Transactions on Vehicular Technology, 55*(3), 839–846. doi:10.1109/TVT.2006.873832

Li, X., & Nee, A. (1996). Monitoring cutting conditions for tool scheduling in CNC machining. *Manuf Syst, 25*(4), 377–383.

Li, Z., Shi, K., Dey, N., Ashour, A. S., Wang, D., Balas, V. E., & Shi, F. et al. (2017). Rule-based back propagation neural networks for various precision rough set presented KANSEI knowledge prediction: A case study on shoe product form features extraction. *Neural Computing & Applications*, 1–18.

Lu, M.-C., & Kannatey-Asibu, E. (2004). Flank wear and process characteristic effect on system dynamics in turning. *Transactions-American Society of Mechanical Engineers Journal of Manufacturing Science and Engineering*, *126*(1), 131–140. doi:10.1115/1.1643082

Maclin, P. S., & Dempsey, J. (1992). Using an artificial neural network to diagnose hepatic masses. *Journal of Medical Systems*, *16*(5), 215–225. doi:10.1007/BF01000274 PMID:1289469

Madeira, S. C., & Oliveira, A. L. (2004). Biclustering Algorithms for Biological Data Analysis. *Survey (London, England)*, 1–31. PMID:17048406

Maglaveras, N., Stamkopoulas, T., Pappas, C., & Strintzis, M. (1998). An Adaptive back-propagation neural network for real time ischemia episodes detection Development and performance using the European ST-T databases. *IEEE Trans., Biomed Engng.*, 805-813.

Maitra, M., & Chatterjee, A. (2008). A novel technique for multilevel optimal magnetic resonance brain image thresholding using bacterial foraging. *Measurement*, *41*(10), 1124–1134. doi:10.1016/j.measurement.2008.03.002

Maji, P., Chatterjee, S., Chakraborty, S., Kausar, N., Samanta, S., & Dey, N. (2015, March). Effect of Euler number as a feature in gender recognition system from offline handwritten signature using neural networks. In *Computing for Sustainable Global Development (INDIACom), 2015 2nd International Conference on* (pp. 1869-1873). IEEE.

Manogaran, G., & Lopez, D. (2017). Disease Surveillance System for Big Climate Data Processing and Dengue Transmission. *International Journal of Ambient Computing and Intelligence*, *8*(2), 88–105. doi:10.4018/IJACI.2017040106

Manthey, B., & Veenstra, R. (2013). *Smoothed analysis of the 2-Opt heuristic for the TSP: Polynomial bounds for Gaussian noise. In Algorithms and Computation* (pp. 579–589). Springer.

Marchant, J. A., & Onyango, C. M. (2003). Comparison of a Bayesian classifier with a multilayer feed-forward neural network using the example of plant/weed/soil discrimination. *Computers and Electronics in Agriculture*, *39*(1), 3–22. doi:10.1016/S0168-1699(02)00223-5

Marinakis, Y., & Magdalene, N. (2011). Discrete Artificial Bee Colony Optimization Algorithm for Financial Classification Problems. *International Journal of Applied Metaheuristic Computing*, *2*(1), 1–17. doi:10.4018/jamc.2011010101

Meryem, A., & Salim, C. (2016). Cooperative Parallel Metaheuristics based Penguin Optimization Search for Solving the Vehicle Routing Problem. *International Journal of Applied Metaheuristic Computing*, *7*(1), 1–18. doi:10.4018/IJAMC.2016010101

Meryem, B., & Abdelmadjid, B. (2015). Resolution of a Vehicle Routing Problem with Simultaneous Pickup and Delivery: A Cooperative Approach. *International Journal of Applied Metaheuristic Computing*, *6*(3), 53–68. doi:10.4018/ijamc.2015070103

Meryem, B., & Abdelmadjid, B. (2016). Quantum Inspired Algorithm for a VRP with Heterogeneous Fleet Mixed Backhauls and Time Windows. *International Journal of Applied Metaheuristic Computing*, *7*(4), 18–38. doi:10.4018/IJAMC.2016100102

Merz, P., & Freisleben, B. (1997). *Genetic local search for the TSP: New results.* Paper presented at the Evolutionary Computation, 1997., IEEE International Conference on. doi:10.1109/ICEC.1997.592288

Metenidis, M. F., Witczak, M., & Korbicz, J. (2004). A novel genetic programming approach to nonlinear system modelling: Application to the DAMADICS benchmark problem. *Engineering Applications of Artificial Intelligence*, *17*(4), 363–370. doi:10.1016/j.engappai.2004.04.009

Mhetre, N. A., Deshpande, A. V., & Mahalle, P. N. (2016). Trust Management Model based on Fuzzy Approach for Ubiquitous Computing. *International Journal of Ambient Computing and Intelligence*, *7*(2), 33–46. doi:10.4018/IJACI.2016070102

Michalewicz, Z. (1996). Genetic algorithms + data structures = evolution programs (3rd ed.). London: Springer-Verlag.

Middleton, I., & Damper, R. I. (2004). Segmentation of magnetic resonance images using a combination of neural networks and active contour models. *Medical Engineering & Physics*, *26*(1), 71–86. doi:10.1016/S1350-4533(03)00137-1 PMID:14644600

Milfelner, M., Kopac, J., Cus, F., & Zuperl, U. (2005). Genetic equation for the cutting force in ball-end milling. *Journal of Materials Processing Technology*, *164*, 1554–1560. doi:10.1016/j.jmatprotec.2005.02.147

Miller, A. S., Blott, B. H., & Hames, T. K. (1992). Review of neural network applications in medical imaging and signal processing. *Medical & Biological Engineering & Computing*, *30*(5), 449–464. doi:10.1007/BF02457822 PMID:1293435

Milton, C., & Shaw, M. (1984). *Metal cutting principles.* Oxford Science Publication.

Mohanpurkar, A. A., & Joshi, M. S. (2016). A Traitor Identification Technique for Numeric Relational Databases with Distortion Minimization and Collusion Avoidance. *International Journal of Ambient Computing and Intelligence*, *7*(2), 114–137. doi:10.4018/IJACI.2016070106

Møller, M. F. (1993). A scaled conjugate gradient algorithm for fast supervised learning. *Neural Networks*, *6*(4), 525–533. doi:10.1016/S0893-6080(05)80056-5

Moon, Y. H., Ryu, H. S., Kim, B., & Song, K. B. (2000). Optimal tracking approach to load frequency control in power systems. In *Power Engineering Society Winter Meeting, 2000. IEEE* (Vol. 2, pp. 1371-1376). IEEE.

Moscato, P., & Cotta, C. (2003). A gentle introduction to memetic algorithms. In Handbook of metaheuristics (pp. 105-144). Springer US. doi:10.1007/0-306-48056-5_5

Mostafa, A., Hassanien, A. E., & Hefny, H. A. (2017). Grey Wolf Optimization-Based Segmentation Approach for Abdomen CT Liver Images. In *Handbook of Research on Machine Learning Innovations and Trends* (pp. 562–581). IGI Global. doi:10.4018/978-1-5225-2229-4.ch024

Muhlenbein, H. (1989). *Parallel Genetic Algorithms, Population Genetics and Combinatorial Optimization*. Academic Press.

Mukherjee, A., Dey, G., Dey, M., & Dey, N. (2015). Web-based intelligent EEG signal authentication and tamper detection system for secure telemonitoring. In *Brain-Computer Interfaces* (pp. 295–312). Springer International Publishing. doi:10.1007/978-3-319-10978-7_11

Mukherjee, A., Paul, S., & Roy, P. K. (2015). Transient Stability Constrained Optimal Power Flow Using Teaching Learning Based Optimization. *International Journal of Energy Optimization and Engineering, 4*(1), 18–35. doi:10.4018/ijeoe.2015010102

Murata, T., & Itai, R. (2008). Enhancing Solution Similarity in Multi-Objective Vehicle Routing Problems with Different Demand Periods. In T. Caric & H. Gold (Eds.), *Vehicle Routing Problem*. InTech. doi:10.5772/5619

Naik, S. K., & Murthy, C. A. (2003). Hue Preserving Color Image Enhancement without Gamut Problem. *IEEE Trans. on Image Processing, 12*, 1591-1598.

Naik, A., Satapathy, S. C., Ashour, A. S., & Dey, N. (2016). Social group optimization for global optimization of multimodal functions and data clustering problems. *Neural Computing & Applications*, 1–17.

Nandi, D., Ashour, A. S., Samanta, S., Chakraborty, S., Salem, M. A., & Dey, N. (2015). Principal component analysis in medical image processing: A study. *International Journal of Image Mining, 1*(1), 65–86. doi:10.1504/IJIM.2015.070024

Nandi, R. J., Nandi, A. K., Rangayyan, R. M., & Scutt, D. (2006). Classification of breast masses in mammograms using genetic programming and feature selection. *Medical & Biological Engineering & Computing, 44*(8), 683–694. doi:10.1007/s11517-006-0077-6 PMID:16937210

Nayak, S. C., Misra, B. B., & Behera, H. S. (2012, October). Evaluation of normalization methods on neuro-genetic models for stock index forecasting. In *Information and Communication Technologies (WICT), 2012 World Congress on* (pp. 602-607). IEEE. doi:10.1109/WICT.2012.6409147

Nayak, S. C., Misra, B. B., & Behera, H. S. (2016a). Adaptive Hybrid Higher Order Neural Networks for Prediction of Stock Market Behavior. In Applied Artificial Higher Order Neural Networks for Control and Recognition (pp. 174-191). IGI Global. doi:10.4018/978-1-5225-0063-6.ch007

Nayak, S. C., Misra, B. B., & Behera, H. S. (2012). Stock Index Prediction With Neuro-Genetic Hybrid Techniques. *Intenational Journal of Computer Science and Informatics, IJCSI, 2*(3), 27–34.

Nayak, S. C., Misra, B. B., & Behera, H. S. (2014). Impact of data normalization on stock index forecasting. *Int. J. Comp. Inf. Syst. Ind. Manag. Appl, 6*, 357–369.

Nayak, S. C., Misra, B. B., & Behera, H. S. (2015a). A Pi-Sigma Higher Order Neural Network for Stock Index Forecasting. In *Computational Intelligence in Data Mining-Volume 2* (pp. 311–319). Springer India. doi:10.1007/978-81-322-2208-8_29

Nayak, S. C., Misra, B. B., & Behera, H. S. (2015b). Comparison of Performance of Different Functions in Functional Link Artificial Neural Network: A Case Study on Stock Index Forecasting. In *Computational Intelligence in Data Mining-Volume 1* (pp. 479–487). Springer India. doi:10.1007/978-81-322-2205-7_45

Nayak, S. C., Misra, B. B., & Behera, H. S. (2016). An Adaptive Second Order Neural Network with Genetic-Algorithm-based Training (ASONN-GA) to Forecast the Closing Prices of the Stock Market. *International Journal of Applied Metaheuristic Computing, 7*(2), 39–57. doi:10.4018/IJAMC.2016040103

Nayak, S. C., Misra, B. B., & Behera, H. S. (2016b). Improving Performance of Higher Order Neural Network using Artificial Chemical Reaction Optimization: A Case Study on Stock Market Forecasting. In *Applied Artificial Higher Order Neural Networks for Control and Recognition* (pp. 253–280). IGI Global. doi:10.4018/978-1-5225-0063-6.ch011

Nayak, S. C., Misra, B. B., & Behera, H. S. (2016d). Fluctuation prediction of stock market index by adaptive evolutionary higher order neural networks. *International Journal of Swarm Intelligence, 2*(2-4), 229–253. doi:10.1504/IJSI.2016.081152

Ni, Q., Vinel, A., Xiao, Y., Turlikov, A., & Jiang, T. (2007). Wireless Broadband Access: WiMax and Beyond - Investigation of bandwidth request mechanisms under point-to-multipoint mode of WiMax networks. *IEEE Communications Magazine, 45*(5), 132–138. doi:10.1109/MCOM.2007.358860

NizarBanu, P. K., & Andrews, S. (2015). Gene Clustering Using Metaheuristic Optimization Algorithms. *International Journal of Applied Metaheuristic Computing, 6*(4).

NizarBanu. (2015). Gene Clustering Using Metaheuristic Optimization Algorithms. *Int. Jr. Applied MetaheuristicComputing, 6*(4).

Nourani, V., Entezari, E., & Yousefi, P. (2013). ANN-RBF Hybrid model for Spatiotemporal Estimation of Monthly Precipitation Case Study: Ardabil Plain. *International Journal of Applied Metaheuristic Computing, 4*(2), 1–16. doi:10.4018/jamc.2013040101

Odella, F. (2017). Technology Studies and the Sociological Debate on Monitoring of Social Interactions. In Biometrics: Concepts, Methodologies, Tools, and Applications (pp. 529-558). IGI Global. doi:10.4018/978-1-5225-0983-7.ch022

Oliver, Smith, & Holland. (1987). *A Study of Permutation Crossover Operator on the TSP.* Academic Press.

Omkar, S. N., John, R. L., Choudhry, N., Kubusada, Y & Bhageshpur, G. (2013). *Crop Classification using Gene Expression Programming Technique.* Springer-Verlag Berlin Heidelberg.

Omkar, S. N., Ramaswamy, N., Senthilnath, J., Bharath, S., & Anuradha, N. S. (2012). Gene expression programming-fuzzy logic method for crop type classification. In *Genetic and Evolutionary Computing (ICGEC), 2012 Sixth International Conference on* (pp. 136-139). IEEE. doi:10.1109/ICGEC.2012.97

Omkar, S. N., Mudigere, D., Senthilnath, J., & Kumar, M. V. (2015). Identification of Helicopter Dynamics based on Flight Data using Nature Inspired Techniques. *International Journal of Applied Metaheuristic Computing*, *6*(3), 15. doi:10.4018/ijamc.2015070102

Omkar, S. N., Sivaranjani, V., Senthilnath, J., & Mukherjee, S. (2010). Dimensionality Reduction and Classification of Hyperspectral Data. *International Journal of Aerospace Innovations Multi-Science*, *2*(3), 157–163.

Onwubolu, G. C., & Babu, B. V. (2013). *New optimization techniques in engineering* (Vol. 141). Springer.

Osman, I. H., & Christofides, N. (1994). Capacitated clustering problems by hybrid simulated annealing and tabu search. *International Transactions in Operational Research*, *1*(3), 317–336. doi:10.1016/0969-6016(94)90032-9

Osman, I. H., & Kelly, J. P. (1996). *Meta-heuristics: an overview. In Meta-heuristics* (pp. 1–21). Springer. doi:10.1007/978-1-4613-1361-8

Ozkan, M., Dawant, B. M., & Maciunas, R. J. (1993). Neural-network-based segmentation of multi-modal medical images: A comparative and prospective study. *IEEE Transactions on Medical Imaging*, *12*(3), 534–544. doi:10.1109/42.241881 PMID:18218446

Padhan, S., Sahu, R. K., & Panda, S. (2014). Automatic generation control with thyristor controlled series compensator including superconducting magnetic energy storage units. *Ain Shams Engineering Journal*, *5*(3), 759–774. doi:10.1016/j.asej.2014.03.011

Padiyar & Uma Rao. (1999). Modeling and Control of Unified Power Flow Controller For Transient Stability. *Electrical Power and Energy Systems, 21*.

Padiyar, K. R., & Kulakarni, A. M. (1998). Control Design and Simulation of Unified Power Flow Controller. *IEEE Trans. on Power Delivery, 13*(4), 1348-1354.

Pai, G. V., & Michel, T. (2017). Metaheuristic Optimization of Constrained Large Portfolios using Hybrid Particle Swarm Optimization. *International Journal of Applied Metaheuristic Computing*, *8*(1), 1–23. doi:10.4018/IJAMC.2017010101

Pal, G., Acharjee, S., Rudrapaul, D., Ashour, A. S., & Dey, N. (2015a). Video segmentation using minimum ratio similarity measurement. *International Journal of Image Mining, 1*(1), 87-110.

Pal, G., Rudrapaul, D., Acharjee, S., Ray, R., Chakraborty, S., & Dey, N. (2015). Video shot boundary detection: a review. In *Emerging ICT for Bridging the Future-Proceedings of the 49th Annual Convention of the Computer Society of India CSI* (vol. 2, pp. 119-127). Springer International Publishing. doi:10.1007/978-3-319-13731-5_14

Pal, S. K., Bhandari, D., & Kundu, M. K. (1994). Genetic algorithms for optimal image enhancement. *Pattern Recognition Letters, 15*(3), 261–271. doi:10.1016/0167-8655(94)90058-2

Panetta, K., Gao, C., & Agaian, S. (2013). No reference color image contrast and quality measures. *IEEE Transactions on Consumer Electronics, 59,* 643-651.

Paola, J. D., & Schowengerdt, R. A. (1995). A review and analysis of backpropagation neural networks for classification of remotely-sensed multi-spectral imagery. *International Journal of Remote Sensing, 16*(16), 3033–3058. doi:10.1080/01431169508954607

Park, S., Smith, M. J. T., & Mersereau, R. M. (2000). Target recognition based on directional filter banks and higher-order neural networks. *Digital Signal Processing, 10*(4), 297–308. doi:10.1006/dspr.2000.0376

Parthiban, L., & Subramanian, R. (2008). Intelligent heart disease prediction system using CANFIS and genetic algorithm. *International Journal of Biological, Biomedical and Medical Sciences, 3*(3).

Pavlopoulos, S., Kyriacou, E., Koutsouris, D., Blekas, K., Stafylopatis, A., & Zoumpoulis, P. (2000). Fuzzy neural network-based texture analysis of ultrasonic images. *IEEE Engineering in Medicine and Biology Magazine, 19*(1), 39–47. doi:10.1109/51.816243 PMID:10659429

Pham, D. L., Xu, C., & Prince, J. L. (2000). Current methods in medical image segmentation 1. *Annual Review of Biomedical Engineering, 2*(1), 315–337. doi:10.1146/annurev.bioeng.2.1.315 PMID:11701515

Pietrokovski, S., Henikoff, J. G., & Henikoff, S. (1996). The BLOCKS database - a system for protein classification. *Nucleic Acids Research, 24*(1), 197–200. doi:10.1093/nar/24.1.197 PMID:8594578

Pitiot, A., Toga, A. W., Ayache, N., & Thompson, P. (2002). Texture based MRI segmentation with a two-stage hybrid neural classifier. In *Neural Networks, 2002. IJCNN'02. Proceedings of the 2002 International Joint Conference on* (*Vol. 3*, pp. 2053-2058). IEEE. doi:10.1109/IJCNN.2002.1007457

Ponomarenko, N., Silvestri, F., Egiazarian, K., Carli, M., Astola, J., & Lukin, V. (2007). On between-coefficient contrast masking of DCT basis functions. *Proc. of the Third Int. Workshop on Video Proc. and Quality Metrics.*

Pothiya, S., Ngamroo, I., & Kongprawechnon, W. (2007, December). Design of optimal fuzzy logic-based PID controller using Multiple Tabu Search algorithm for AGC including SMES units. In *Power Engineering Conference, 2007. IPEC 2007. International* (pp. 838-843). IEEE.

Powers, D. M. (2011). *Evaluation: from precision, recall and F-measure to ROC, informedness, markedness and correlation*. Academic Press.

Prasad, K. N., & Ramamoorthy, B. (2001). Tool wear evaluation by stereo vision and prediction by artificial neural network. *Journal of Materials Processing Technology*, *112*(1), 43–52. doi:10.1016/S0924-0136(00)00896-7

PriteshVora. (2013). A Survey on K-mean Clustering and Particle Swarm Optimization. *International Journal of Science and Modern Engineering*, *1*(3), 24–26.

Qin, A. K., Huang, V. L., & Suganthan, P. N. (2009). Differential evolution algorithm with strategy adaptation for global numerical optimization. *IEEE Transactions on Evolutionary Computation*, *13*(2), 398–417. doi:10.1109/TEVC.2008.927706

Quraishi, I. M., De, M., Dhal, K.G, Mondal, S., & Das, G. (2013). *Novel hybrid approach to restore historical degraded documents*. IEEE. DOI: 10.1109/ISSP.2013.6526899

Quraishi, I. M., Dhal, K. G., Paul Chowdhury, J., Pattanayak, K., & De, M. (2012). *A novel hybrid approach to enhance low resolution images using particle swarm optimization*. IEEE. DOI: 10.1109/PDGC.2012.6449941

Rahul Khandelwal, J. (2016). A Novel Multiobjective Optimization for Cement Stabilized Soft Soil based on Artificial Bee Colony. *International Journal of Applied Metaheuristic Computing*, *7*(4), 1–17. doi:10.4018/IJAMC.2016100101

Ramakrishnan, T., & Sankaragomathi, B. (2017). A professional estimate on the computed tomography brain tumor images using SVM-SMO for classification and MRG-GWO for segmentation. *Pattern Recognition Letters*, *94*, 163–171. doi:10.1016/j.patrec.2017.03.026

Rastgarpour, M., & Shanbehzadeh, J. (2013). The status quo of artificial intelligence methods in automatic medical image segmentation. *International Journal of Computer Theory and Engineering*, *5*(1), 5–8. doi:10.7763/IJCTE.2013.V5.636

Rathipriya, R., Thangavel, K., & Bagyamani, J. (2011). Binary Particle Swarm Optimization based Biclustering of Web usage Data. *International Journal of Computers and Applications*, *25*(2), 43–49. doi:10.5120/3001-4036

Reckhow, K. H. (1999). Water quality prediction and probability network models. *Canadian Journal of Fisheries and Aquatic Sciences*, *56*(7), 1150–1158. doi:10.1139/f99-040

Reinelt, G. (1991). TSPLIB—A Traveling Salesman Problem Library. *ORSA Journal of Computing*, *3*(4), 376–384. doi:10.1287/ijoc.3.4.376

Reza, B. (2016). Nephron Algorithm Optimization: Inspired of the Biologic Nephron Performance. *International Journal of Applied Metaheuristic Computing*, *7*(1), 38–64. doi:10.4018/IJAMC.2016010103

Riccardo, P., James, K., & Tim, B. (2007). Particle swarm optimization An Overview. *Swarm Intelligence*, 33–57.

Rocki, K., & Suda, R. (2012). *Accelerating 2-opt and 3-opt local search using GPU in the travelling salesman problem.* Paper presented at the High Performance Computing and Simulation (HPCS), 2012 International Conference on.

Romahi, Y., & Shen, Q. (2000). Dynamic Financial Forecasting with Automatically Induced Fuzzy Associations. *Proc. of the 9th International Conference on Fuzzy Systems*, 493-498.

Rout, M., Majhi, B., Majhi, R., & Panda, G. (2014). Forecasting of currency exchange rates using an adaptive ARMA model with differential evolution based training. *Journal of King Saud University-Computer and Information Sciences*, 26(1), 7–18. doi:10.1016/j.jksuci.2013.01.002

Roy, A., Dutta, S., & Roy, P. K. (2014, January). Automatic generation control by SMES-SMES controllers of two-area hydro-hydro system. In *Non Conventional Energy (ICONCE), 2014 1st International Conference on* (pp. 302-307). IEEE. doi:10.1109/ICONCE.2014.6808731

Roy, R., Bhatt, P., & Ghoshal, S. P. (2010). Evolutionary computation based three-area automatic generation control. *Expert Systems with Applications*, 37(8), 5913–5924. doi:10.1016/j.eswa.2010.02.014

Saba, L., Dey, N., Ashour, A. S., Samanta, S., Nath, S. S., Chakraborty, S., & Suri, J. S. et al. (2016). Automated stratification of liver disease in ultrasound: An online accurate feature classification paradigm. *Computer Methods and Programs in Biomedicine*, 130, 118–134. doi:10.1016/j.cmpb.2016.03.016 PMID:27208527

Sabar, N. R., Ayob, M., Kendall, G., & Qu, R. (2015). Automatic design of a hyper-heuristic framework with gene expression programming for combinatorial optimization problems. *IEEE Transactions on Evolutionary Computation*, 19(3), 309–325. doi:10.1109/TEVC.2014.2319051

Saha, S., & Bandyopadhyay, S. (2007, September). MRI brain image segmentation by fuzzy symmetry based genetic clustering technique. In *Evolutionary Computation, 2007. CEC 2007. IEEE Congress on* (pp. 4417-4424). IEEE. doi:10.1109/CEC.2007.4425049

Sahoo, A., & Chandra, S. (2013, August). L'evy-flight firefly algorithm based active contour model for medical image segmentation. In *Contemporary Computing (IC3), 2013 Sixth International Conference on* (pp. 159-162). IEEE. doi:10.1109/IC3.2013.6612181

Sahu, K. K., Sahu, S. R., Nayak, S. C., & Behera, H. S. (2016). Forecasting foreign exchange rates using CRO based different variants of FLANN and performance analysis. *International Journal of Computational Systems Engineering*, 2(4), 190–208. doi:10.1504/IJCSYSE.2016.081380

Salembier, P., & Marqués, F. (1999). Region-based representations of image and video: Segmentation tools for multimedia services. *IEEE Transactions on Circuits and Systems for Video Technology*, 9(8), 1147–1169. doi:10.1109/76.809153

Samanta, S., Acharjee, S., Mukherjee, A., Das, D., & Dey, N. (2013a, December). Ant weight lifting algorithm for image segmentation. In *Computational Intelligence and Computing Research (ICCIC), 2013 IEEE International Conference on* (pp. 1-5). doi:10.1109/ICCIC.2013.6724160

Samanta, S., Chakraborty, S., Acharjee, S., Mukherjee, A., & Dey, N. (2013b, December). Solving 0/1 knapsack problem using ant weight lifting algorithm. In *Computational Intelligence and Computing Research (ICCIC), 2013 IEEE International Conference on* (pp. 1-5). IEEE.

Samantaa, S., Dey, N., Das, P., Acharjee, S., & Chaudhuri, S. S. (2013). *Multilevel threshold based gray scale image segmentation using cuckoo search.* arXiv preprint arXiv:1307.0277

Samanta, S., Choudhury, A., Dey, N., Ashour, A. S., & Balas, V. E. (2016). *Quantum inspired evolutionary algorithm for scaling factors optimization during manifold medical information embedding. In Quantum Inspired Computational intelligence: Research and Applications.* Elsevier.

Sambyal, N., & Abrol, P. (2016). Feature based Text Extraction System using Connected Component Method. *International Journal of Synthetic Emotions, 7*(1), 41–57. doi:10.4018/IJSE.2016010104

Sangeetha, J., Nagaraj, K., Murthy, K. B., & Rustagi, R. P. (2016). A New Approach for Analyzing the Performance of the WiMAX Networks based on QoS Traffic Prediction Routing Protocol using Gene Expression Programming. *International Journal of Applied Metaheuristic Computing, 7*(2), 16–38. doi:10.4018/IJAMC.2016040102

Satapathy, S. C., Raja, N. S. M., Rajinikanth, V., Ashour, A. S., & Dey, N. (2017). Multi-level image thresholding using Otsu and chaotic bat algorithm. *Neural Computing & Applications*, 1–23.

Sean, C., & Kevin, C. (2014). An Active Low Cost Mesh Networking Indoor Tracking System. *International Journal of Ambient Computing and Intelligence, 6*(1), 45–79. doi:10.4018/ijaci.2014010104

Sekercioglu, Y. A., Ivanovich, M., & Yegin, A. (2009). A survey of MAC based QoS implementations for WiMAX networks. *Computer Networks, 53*(14), 2517–2536. doi:10.1016/j.comnet.2009.05.001

Senthilnathan, C. R. (2016). Understanding Retail Consumer Shopping Behaviour Using Rough Set Approach. *International Journal of Rough Sets and Data Analysis, 3*(3), 38–50. doi:10.4018/IJRSDA.2016070103

Senthilnath, J., Bajpai, S., Omkar, S. N., Diwakar, P. G., & Mani, V. (2012). An approach to multi-temporal MODIS image analysis using image classification and segmentation. *Advances in Space Research, Elsevier, 50*(9), 1274–1287. doi:10.1016/j.asr.2012.07.003

Senthilnath, J., Omkar, S. N., Mani, V., Vanjare, A., & Diwakar, P. G. (2014). Multi-Temporal Satellite Image Analysis Using Gene Expression Programming. *Proceedings of Second International Conference on Soft Computing for Problem Solving, 236*, 1039 – 1045. doi:10.1007/978-81-322-1602-5_109

Sermpinis, G., Theofilatos, K., Karathanasopoulos, A., Georgopoulos, E. F., & Dunis, C. L. (2013). Forecasting foreign exchange rates with adaptive neural networks using radial-basis functions and Particle Swarm Optimization. *European Journal of Operational Research, 225*(3), 528–540. doi:10.1016/j.ejor.2012.10.020

Setiawan, N. A. (2014). Fuzzy decision support system for coronary artery disease diagnosis based on Rough set theory. *International Journal of Rough Sets and Data Analysis*, *1*(1), 65–80. doi:10.4018/ijrsda.2014010105

Shanmugavadivu, P., Balasubramanian, K., & Muruganandam, A. (2014). Particle swarm optimized bi-histogram equalization for contrast enhancement and brightness preservation of images. *The Visual Computer*, *30*(4), 387–399. doi:10.1007/s00371-013-0863-8

Sharma, K., & Virmani, J. (2017). A Decision Support System for Classification of Normal and Medical Renal Disease Using Ultrasound Images: A Decision Support System for Medical Renal Diseases. *International Journal of Ambient Computing and Intelligence*, *8*(2), 52–69. doi:10.4018/IJACI.2017040104

Sharma, S., Kumar, S., & Singh, B. (2014). AntMeshNet: An ant colony optimization based routing approach to wireless mesh networks. *International Journal of Applied Metaheuristic Computing*, *5*(1), 20–45. doi:10.4018/ijamc.2014010102

Sharma, S., & Malik, A. (2017). Routing in Wireless Mesh Networks based on Termites Intelligence. *International Journal of Applied Metaheuristic Computing*, *8*(2), 1–21. doi:10.4018/IJAMC.2017040101

Sheikholeslami, R., & Kaveh, A. (2013). A Survey of Chaos Embedded Meta-Heuristic Algorithms. *Int. J. Optim. Civil. Eng.*, *3*(4), 617–633.

Sheppard, D., Tsegaye, T. D., Tadesse, W., McKay, D., & Coleman, T. L. (2001). The application of remote sensing, geographic information systems, and Global Positioning System technology to improve water quality in northern Alabama. In *Geoscience and Remote Sensing Symposium, 2001. IGARSS'01. IEEE 2001 International* (Vol. 3, pp. 1291-1293). IEEE. doi:10.1109/IGARSS.2001.976822

Shin, Y., & Ghosh, J. (1995). Ridge Polynomial Networks. *IEEE Transactions on Neural Networks*, *6*(3), 610–622. doi:10.1109/72.377967 PMID:18263347

Shweta, T., & Kamal, K. B. (2014). A Particle Swarm Optimization Approach to Fuzzy Case-based Reasoning in the Framework of Collaborative Filtering. *International Journal of Rough Sets and Data Analysis*, *1*(1), 48–64. doi:10.4018/ijrsda.2014010104

Sick, B. (2002). On-line and indirect tool wear monitoring in turning with artificial neural networks: A review of more than a decade of research. *Mechanical Systems and Signal Processing*, *16*(4), 487–546. doi:10.1006/mssp.2001.1460

Si, T., De, A., & Bhattacharjee, A. K. (2015). Brain MRI segmentation for tumor detection via entropy maximization using Grammatical Swarm. *International Journal of Wavelets, Multresolution, and Information Processing*, *13*(05), 1550039. doi:10.1142/S0219691315500393

Soleimani, H., & Kannan, G. (2015). A hybrid particle swarm optimization and genetic algorithm for closed-loop supply chain network design in large-scale networks. *Applied Mathematical Modelling*, *39*(14), 3990–4012. doi:10.1016/j.apm.2014.12.016

Song, D., Ru-Chuan, W., Xiong, F., & Le-Chan, Y. (2010). Gene expression programming for attribution reduction in rough set. *International Journal of Computers and Applications, 32*(2), 226–231. doi:10.2316/Journal.202.2010.2.202-2842

Sortino, M. (2003). Application of statistical filtering for optical detection of tool wear. *International Journal of Machine Tools & Manufacture, 43*(5), 493–497. doi:10.1016/S0890-6955(02)00266-3

Stagg, G. W., & El-Abid, A. H. (1968). *Computer Methods in Power System Analysis.* McGraw-Hill Book Co.

Standard, I. (1991). Drinking water-specification. 1st Revision, IS, 10500.

Structures of life. (2007). US Department of Health and Human Services.

Sun, D. I., Ashley, B., Brewer, B., Hughes, A., & Tinney, W. F. (1984). Optimal Power Flow by Newton Approach. *IEEE Transactions on Power Apparatus and Systems, 103*(10), pp2864–pp2880. doi:10.1109/TPAS.1984.318284

Sun, W., & Wang, Y. (2005). Segmentation method of MRI using fuzzy Gaussian basis neural network. *Neural Information Processing-Letters and Reviews, 8*(2), 19–24.

Surry, P. D., & Radcliffe, N. J. (1996). *Formal Algorithms + Formal Representations = Search Strategies.* Paper presented at the Parallel Problem Solving from Nature IV, London, UK.

Suzuki, K., Horiba, I., & Sugie, N. (2003). Neural edge enhancer for supervised edge enhancement from noisy images. *IEEE Transactions on Pattern Analysis and Machine Intelligence, 25*(12), 1582–1596. doi:10.1109/TPAMI.2003.1251151

Suzuki, K., Shiraishi, J., Abe, H., MacMahon, H., & Doi, K. (2005). False-positive reduction in computer-aided diagnostic scheme for detecting nodules in chest radiographs by means of massive training artificial neural network 1. *Academic Radiology, 12*(2), 191–201. doi:10.1016/j.acra.2004.11.017 PMID:15721596

Taher, S. A., Fini, M. H., & Aliabadi, S. F. (2014). Fractional order PID controller design for LFC in electric power systems using imperialist competitive algorithm. *Ain Shams Engineering Journal, 5*(1), 121–135. doi:10.1016/j.asej.2013.07.006

Tam, K. S., & Kumar, P. (1990). Application of superconductive magnetic energy storage in an asynchronous link between power systems. *IEEE Transactions on Energy Conversion, 5*(3), 436–444. doi:10.1109/60.105266

Tanner, R., & Loh, N. K. (1992). A toxonomy of multi-sensor fusion. *Journal of Manufacturing Systems, 11*(5), 314–325. doi:10.1016/0278-6125(92)90060-S

Tian, Z., Dey, N., Ashour, A. S., McCauley, P., & Shi, F. (2017). Morphological segmenting and neighborhood pixel-based locality preserving projection on brain fMRI dataset for semantic feature extraction: An affective computing study. *Neural Computing & Applications*, 1–16.

Tinney, W. F., & Hart, C. E. (1967, November). Power Flow-Solution by Newton's Method. *IEEE Transactions, 86,* 1449.

Tiwari, P. K., & Sood, Y. R. (2012). Efficient and optimal approach for location and parameter setting of multiple unified power flow controllers for a deregulated power sector. *IET Gener. Transm. Distrib, 6*(10), 958–967. doi:10.1049/iet-gtd.2011.0722

Tobias, O. J., & Seara, R. (2002). Image segmentation by histogram thresholding using fuzzy sets. *IEEE Transactions on Image Processing, 11*(12), 1457–1465. doi:10.1109/TIP.2002.806231 PMID:18249714

Tourassi, G. D., & Floyd, C. Jr. (1993). Artificial Neural Networks for Single Photon Emission Computed Tomography: A Study of Cold Lesion Detection and Localization. *Investigative Radiology, 28*(8), 671–677. doi:10.1097/00004424-199308000-00002 PMID:8375998

Tsai, A., Yezzi, A., Wells, W., Tempany, C., Tucker, D., Fan, A., & Willsky, A. et al. (2003). A shape-based approach to the segmentation of medical imagery using level sets. *IEEE Transactions on Medical Imaging, 22*(2), 137–154. doi:10.1109/TMI.2002.808355 PMID:12715991

Tsou, M.-H., & Smith, J. (2011). *Free and Open Source software for GIS education.* San Diego, CA: Academic Press.

Tyagi, S., Som, S., & Rana, Q. P. (2017). Trust based dynamic multicast group routing ensuring reliability for ubiquitous environment in MANETs. *International Journal of Ambient Computing and Intelligence, 8*(1), 70–97. doi:10.4018/IJACI.2017010104

Vasantha, M., Bharathi, D. V. S., & Dhamodharan, R. (2010). Medical image feature, extraction, selection and classification. *International Journal of Engineering Science and Technology, 1*(2), 2071–2076.

Vasudevan, S., & Oturan, M. A. (2014). Electrochemistry: As cause and cure in water pollution—an overview. *Environmental Chemistry Letters, 12*(1), 97–108. doi:10.1007/s10311-013-0434-2

Vavak, F., & Fogarty, T. C. T. C. (1996). *Comparison of Steady State and Generational Genetic Algorithms for Use in Nonstationary Environments.* Academic Press.

Venkateswara Rao, B., & Nagesh Kumar, G. V. (2014). Optimal Location of Thyristor Controlled Series Capacitor for reduction of Transmission Line losses using BAT Search Algorithm. *WSEAS Transactions on Power Systems, 9,* 459–470.

Venugopal Setty, D., Rangaswamy, T. M., & Subramanya, K. N. (2010). A review on data mining applications to the performance of stock marketing. *International Journal of Computers and Applications, 1*(3), 33–43. doi:10.5120/88-187

Verma, B., & Zakos, J. (2001). A computer-aided diagnosis system for digital mammograms based on fuzzy-neural and feature extraction techniques. *IEEE Transactions on Information Technology in Biomedicine, 5*(1), 46–54. doi:10.1109/4233.908389 PMID:11300216

VijayalakshmiPai, G. A., & Michel, T. (2017). Metaheuristic Optimization of Constrained Large Portfolios using Hybrid Particle Swarm Optimization. *Int. Jr. Applied Metaheuristic Computing, 8*(1).

Vincent, , & Bernard, , & Kockara. (n.d.). *Extraction of Protein Sequence Motifs Information by Bi-Clustering Algorithm. Academic Press.*

Virmani, J., Dey, N., & Kumar, V. (2016). PCA-PNN and PCA-SVM based CAD systems for breast density classification. In *Applications of intelligent optimization in biology and medicine* (pp. 159–180). Springer International Publishing.

Vladimír, B., Petr, T., Peter, M., Karel, M., & Petr, B. (2016). Application of Ambient Intelligence in Educational Institutions: Visions and Architectures. *International Journal of Ambient Computing and Intelligence, 7*(1), 94–120. doi:10.4018/IJACI.2016010105

Voß, S., Martello, S., Osman, I. H., & Roucairol, C. (Eds.). (2012). *Meta-heuristic: Advances and trends in local search paradigms for optimization.* Springer Science & Business Media.

Wall, M. (1996). *GAlib: A C ++ Library of Genetic Algorithm Components.* Academic Press.

Wang, Z., Fang, J., & Liu, X. (2006). *Global stability of stochastic high-order neural networks with discrete and distributed delays, Chaos, Solutions and Fractals.* doi:, 06.06310.1016/j.chaos.2006

Wang.G, & Dunbrack.R. (2003). PISCES: A protein sequence culling server. *Bioinformatics,* 1589-1591.

Wang, D., He, T., Li, Z., Cao, L., Dey, N., Ashour, A. S., & Shi, F. et al. (2016). Image feature-based affective retrieval employing improved parameter and structure identification of adaptive neuro-fuzzy inference system. *Neural Computing & Applications,* 1–16.

Wang, Y., Adali, T., Kung, S. Y., & Szabo, Z. (1998). Quantification and segmentation of brain tissues from MR images: A probabilistic neural network approach. *IEEE Transactions on Image Processing, 7*(8), 1165–1181. doi:10.1109/83.704309 PMID:18172510

Wang, Y., Heng, P. A., & Wahl, F. M. (2003). Image reconstructions from two orthogonal projections. *International Journal of Imaging Systems and Technology, 13*(2), 141–145. doi:10.1002/ima.10036

Wang, Y., Ma, X., Xu, M., Liu, Y., & Wang, Y. (2015). Two-echelon logistics distribution region partitioning problem based on a hybrid particle swarm optimization–genetic algorithm. *Expert Systems with Applications, 42*(12), 5019–5031. doi:10.1016/j.eswa.2015.02.058

Warsito, W., & Fan, L. S. (2001). Neural network based multi-criterion optimization image reconstruction technique for imaging two-and three-phase flow systems using electrical capacitance tomography. *Measurement Science & Technology, 12*(12), 2198–2210. doi:10.1088/0957-0233/12/12/323

Watson, J., Ross, C., Eisele, V., Denton, J., Bins, J., Guerra, C., . . . Howe, A. (1998). *The Traveling Salesrep Problem, Edge Assembly Crossover, and 2-opt. Academic Press.*

Watson, R. A., & Pollack, J. B. (2000). Recombination without respect: Schema combination and disruption in genetic algorithm crossover. *Proceedings of the 2000 Genetic and Evolutionary Computation Conference.*

Wechmongkhonkon, S., Poomtong, N., & Areerachakul, S. (2012). Application of Artificial Neural Network to classification surface water quality. World Academy of Science, Engineering and Technology, 6.

White, H. (1998). Economic Prediction Using Neural Networks: The Case of IBM Daily Stock Returns. *Proceedings of the Second Annual IEEE Conference on Neural Networks, 1*(2), 451-458.

Whitley, D., Starkweather, T., & Shaner, D. (1990). *The Traveling Salesman and Sequence Scheduling: Quality Solutions Using Genetic Edge Recombination.* Academic Press.

Whitley, L. D., Starkweather, T., & Fuquay, D. A. (1989). *Scheduling problems and traveling salesmen: The genetic edge recombination operator.* Paper presented at the ICGA.

Wilcoxon, F., Katti, S. K., & Wilcox, R. A. (1970). Critical values and probability levels for the Wilcoxon rank sum test and the Wilcoxon signed rank test. *Selected Tables in Mathematical Statistics, 1*, 171-259.

Wolberg, W. H., Street, W. N., & Mangasarian, O. L. (1995). Image analysis and machine learning applied to breast cancer diagnosis and prognosis. *Analytical and Quantitative Cytology and Histology, 17*(2), 77–87. PMID:7612134

Wu, W., Dandy, G. C., & Maier, H. R. (2011). Application of artificial neural networks to forecasting water quality in a chloraminated water distribution system. *19th Int. Congr. Model. Simul. Modsim2011*, 1112-1118.

Wu, Y., Giger, M. L., Doi, K., Vyborny, C. J., Schmidt, R. A., & Metz, C. E. (1993). Artificial neural networks in mammography: Application to decision making in the diagnosis of breast cancer. *Radiology, 187*(1), 81–87. doi:10.1148/radiology.187.1.8451441 PMID:8451441

Xu, L., Huang, Y., Shen, X., & Liu, Y. (2017). Parallelizing Gene Expression Programming Algorithm in Enabling Large-Scale Classification. *Scientific Programming, 2017.*

Xu, J., Hancock, K., & Southworth, F. (2003). Simulation of regional freight movement with trade and transportation multinetworks. *Transportation Research Record, 1854*, 152–161. doi:10.3141/1854-17

Yamamura, M., Ono, I., & Kobayashi, S. (1992). Character-preserving genetic algorithms for traveling salesman problem. *Journal of Japanese Society for Artificial Intelligence, 7*(6), 1049–1059.

Yang, X. S. (2010). A new metaheuristic bat-inspired algorithm. *Nature inspired cooperative strategies for optimization (NICSO 2010)*, 65-74.

Yang, X.-S. (2010). A new metaheuristic bat-inspired algorithm. In Nature Inspired Cooperative Strategies for Optimization. Springer Berlin. doi:10.1007/978-3-642-12538-6_6

Yang, X.-S. (2008). *Nature-Inspired Metaheuristic Algorithms*. Luniver Press.

Yeh, J. Y., & Fu, J. C. (2008). A hierarchical genetic algorithm for segmentation of multi-spectral human-brain MRI. *Expert Systems with Applications*, *34*(2), 1285–1295. doi:10.1016/j.eswa.2006.12.012

Yong, W. (2015). An Approximate Algorithm for Triangle TSP with a Four-Vertex-Three-Line Inequality. *International Journal of Applied Metaheuristic Computing*, *6*(1), 35–46. doi:10.4018/ijamc.2015010103

Youcheng, Nan, Majie, Kedi, Yuan, & Qu. (2012). K-means optimization clustering algorithm based on Particle swarm optimization and multiclass merging. *Advances in CSIE, 1*, 569-578.

Yuan, S., Skinner, B., Huang, S., & Liu, D. (2013). A new crossover approach for solving the multiple travelling salesmen problem using genetic algorithms. *European Journal of Operational Research*, *228*(1), 72–82. doi:10.1016/j.ejor.2013.01.043

Zadshakoyan, M., & Pourmostaghimi, V. (2013). Genetic equation for the prediction of tool–chip contact length in orthogonal cutting. *Engineering Applications of Artificial Intelligence*, *26*(7), 1725–1730. doi:10.1016/j.engappai.2012.10.016

Zadshakoyan, M., & Pourmostaghimi, V. (2015). Cutting tool crater wear measurement in turning using chip geometry and genetic programming. *International Journal of Applied Metaheuristic Computing*, *6*(1), 47–60. doi:10.4018/ijamc.2015010104

Zakaria, B., Souham, M., & Mohamed, B. (2017). Scalable Differential Evolutionary Clustering Algorithm for Big Data Using Map-Reduce Paradigm. *International Journal of Applied Metaheuristic Computing*, *8*(1), 45–60. doi:10.4018/IJAMC.2017010103

Zakir, H. A. (2010). Genetic algorithm for the traveling salesman problem using sequential constructive crossover operator. *International Journal of Biometrics & Bioinformatics*, *3*(6), 96–105.

Zangeneh, D., & Yazdi, M. (2016, May). Automatic segmentation of multiple sclerosis lesions in brain MRI using constrained GMM and genetic algorithm. In *Electrical Engineering (ICEE), 2016 24th Iranian Conference on* (pp. 832-837). IEEE. doi:10.1109/IranianCEE.2016.7585635

Zhaoa-Xing-Ming. (2005). A novel approach to extracting features from motif content and protein composition for protein sequence classification. *Neural Networks*, 1019–1028. PMID:16153801

Zheng & Tan. (2000). *Dynamic Character Study of UPFC Based on Detailed Simulation Model*. IEEE Power Conference 2000.

Zhou, Jiang, Yang, & Chen. (2002). Lung Cancer Cell Identification Based on Artificial Neural Network Ensembles. *Artificial Intelligence in Medicine, 24*, 25-36.

Zhu, W., Fang, J., Tang, Y., Zhang, W., & Du, W. (2012). Digital IIR Filters Design Using Differential Evolution Algorithm with a Controllable Probabilistic Population Size. *PLoS ONE, 7*(7), e40549–e40549. doi:10.1371/journal.pone.0040549 PMID:22808191

Zhu, Y., & Yan, Z. (1997). Computerized tumor boundary detection using a Hopfield neural network. *IEEE Transactions on Medical Imaging, 16*(1), 55–67. doi:10.1109/42.552055 PMID:9050408

Zuo, J., Tang, C., Li, C., Yuan, C., & Chen, A. (2002). Time series prediction based on gene expression programming. *International Conference on Advances in WebAge Information & Management, 3129*(1), 55–56.

About the Contributors

Nilanjan Dey is an assistant prof. at the Department of Information Technology, Techno India College of Technology, Kolkata, W.B., India. He holds an honorary position of Visiting Scientist at Global Biomedical Technologies Inc., CA, USA and Research Scientist of Laboratory of Applied Mathematical Modeling in Human Physiology, Territorial Organization of- Scientific and Engineering Unions, BULGARIA. Associate Researcher of Laboratoire RIADI, University of Manouba, TUNISIA. His research topic is Medical Imaging, Soft computing, Data mining, Machine learning, Rough set, Computer Aided Diagnosis, Atherosclerosis. He has 16 books and 300 international conferences and journal papers. He is the Editor-in-Chief of International Journal of Ambient Computing and Intelligence (IGI Global), US, International Journal of Rough Sets and Data Analysis (IGI Global), US, and the International Journal of Synthetic Emotions (IJSE), IGI Global, US. Series Editor of Advances in Geospatial Technologies (AGT) Book Series, (IGI Global), US, Executive Editor of International Journal of Image Mining (IJIM), Inderscience, and Associated Editor of IEEE Access and International Journal of Service Science, Management, Engineering and Technology, IGI Global. He is a life member of IE, UACEE, ISOC.

* * *

B. Anand received his B.E degree in Electrical and Electronics Engineering in 2001 from Government College of Engineering, Tirunelveli and M.E. degree in Power Systems Engineering from Annamalai University in 2002 and Ph.D. degree in Electrical Engineering from Anna University, Chennai in 2011. Since 2003, he has been with the department of Electrical and Electronics Engineering, Hindusthan College of Engineering and Technology, Coimbatore, Tamilnadu, INDIA. Currently, he is an Associate Professor. His research interests are Power System Control, Optimization, and application of computational intelligence to power system problems and he published more than 75 papers in National/International journals and conferences. He is IEEE member, SSI and ISTE.

Amira S. Ashour received the B.Eng. degree in Electrical Engineering from Faculty of Engineering, Tanta University, Egypt in 1997, M.Sc. in Image Processing in 2001 and Ph.D. in Smart Antenna in 2005 from Faculty of Engineering, Tanta University, Egypt. In 2005, she has appointed as a Lecturer in Electronics and Electrical Communications Engineering at Tanta University where she is now Assistant Professor and Head of Department-EEC. She has been the Vice Chair of Computer Engineering Department, Computers and Information Technology College, Taif University, KSA for one year from 2015. She has been the vice chair of CS department, CIT college, Taif University, KSA for 5 years. Her research interests are Smart antenna, Direction of arrival estimation, Targets tracking, Image processing, Medical imaging, Machine learning, Signal/image/video processing, Image analysis, Computer vision, and Optimization. She has 6 books and about 70 published journal papers. She is an Editor-in-Chief for the International Journal of Synthetic Emotions (IJSE), IGI Global, US. She is an Associate Editor for the IJRSDA, IGI Global, US as well as the IJACI, IGI Global, US. She is an Editorial Board Member of the International Journal of Image Mining (IJIM), Inderscience.

H. S. Behera has completed his ME (Computer Science & Engineering) from National Institute of Technology, Rourkela, India, and Ph.D. (Engineering) from Biju Pattanaik University of Technology. His area of interest includes data mining and soft- computing, software engineering, distributed system. Dr. Behera has more than 200 research publications in National and International journals and conferences. Currently he is working as Associate Professor, department of computer science engineering & information technology, VSS University of Technology, Burla, India. He has more than 20 years of experiences in teaching as well as research.

Jamal Benhra received his PhD in Automatic and Production Engineering from National Higher School of Electricity and Mechanics (ENSEM), Casablanca in 2007. He has his Habilitation to drive Researchs in Industrial Engineering from Science and Technology University, SETTAT in 2011. He is Professor and responsible of Industrial Engineering Department in National Higher School of Electricity and Mechanics (ENSEM), Hassan II University, Casablanca, Morocco. His current main research interests concern Modeling, Robot, Optimization, Meta-heuristic, and Supply Chain Management.

Said Benkachcha received his DESA in Laboratory of Mechanics of Structures and Materials, LMSM, of ENSEM – Casablanca in 2006. In 2011 He joined the Laboratory of Computer Systems and Renewable Energy (LISER) of the ENSEM Hassan II University, Casablanca, Morocco. His current research field is demand forecasting and collaborative warehouse management.

Shouvik Chakraborty currently pursuing Ph.D. in Computer Science and Engineering from the University of Kalyani. He completed his M.Tech in Computer Science and Engineering from the University of Kalyani, Nadia, West Bengal, India in 2016. He completed his B.Tech in Computer Science and Engineering from Hooghly Engineering & Technology College under Maulana Abul Kalam Azad University of Technology (Formerly known as West Bengal University of Technology), West Bengal, India in 2014. He has received AICTE National Fellowship during Master of Technology. He secured First class First position in Master of Technology. He is a member of International Association of Computer Science and Information Technology, Singapore, International Association of Engineers, Student Member, Institute of Research Engineers and Doctors (Universal Association of Computer and Electronics Engineers), USA, Governing body member, Chinsurah Computer Academy, India. His research interests include Soft and Evolutionary Computing, Digital Image Processing, Bio-medical Image Analysis, Pattern Recognition, Machine Learning and Optimization Techniques. He has published two book chapters and published and presented many research papers in different international and national journals and conferences.

Sankhadeep Chatterjee is currently pursuing M.Tech in Computer science & Engineering from University of Calcutta, Kolkata, West Bengal, India. He has completed his B.Tech in Computer science and Engineering from Maulana Abul Kalam Azad University of Technology (Formerly Known as West Bengal University of Technology) on 2015 and joined Calcutta University. He received National Fellowship during Master of Technology (2015 - 2017). His research interests include: Machine Learning, Pattern Recognition, Optimization Techniques and Image Processing. He has attended several International Conferences and has published his research works in several reputed International Journals. He has published 2 book chapters. He is a Student Member of Institute of Electrical and Electronic Engineers (IEEE), member of International Association of Engineers (IAENG), Hong Kong. He is a member of several International societies. He acted as a regular reviewer of IEEE *Access*, International Journal of Ambient Computing and Intelligence (IJACI), International Journal of Synthetic Emotions (IJSE), International Journal of Rough Sets and Data Analysis (IJRSDA) and several International Conferences.

D. Deepak Chowdary was born in Srikakulam, India in 1978. He received his Bachelor degree in Electrical and Electronics Engineering from College of Engineering, Gandhi Institute of Technology And Management (GITAM) Visakapatnam, Andhra Pradesh, India in 2000, the Master degree in Electrical Power Engineering from the College of Engineering, JNTU, Hyderabad in 2006 and He received his Doctoral degree from Jawaharlal Nehru Technological University, Hyderabad in

2014. He is presently working as Professor & Principal, Dr.L.Bullayya College of Engineering (for Women), Resapuvanipalem, Visakhapatnam. His research interests include gas insulated substations, FACTS devices, Power System Stability analysis, fuzzy logic and neural network applications, distributed generation, Partial Discharge Studies and Bearing less drives. He has published several research papers in national and international conferences and journals. He is a member of ISTE and IE.

Sanjoy Das completed his B.E. from Regional Engineering College, Durgapur, M.E. from Bengal Engineering College (Deemed Univ.), and Howrah, Ph.D. from Bengal Engineering and Science University, Shibpur. Currently he is working as Associate Professor in Dept. of Engineering and Technological Studies, University of Kalyani. His research interests are Tribology and Optimization Techniques.

Krishna Gopal Dhal completed his B.Tech and M. Tech from Kalyani Government Engineering College, Nadia, West Bengal, India. Currently he is working as Assistant Professor in Dept. of Computer Sc. & Application, Midnapore College (Autonomous), West Bengal, India. His research interests are image processing and Nature inspired Metaheuristics.

Hicham El Hassani received his engineer degree of Industrial Engineering in the National School of applied sciences in 2009. Since 2009, he works at the Hassania School of Public Works Casablanca. In 2011 He joined the Laboratory of Computer Systems and Renewable Energy (LISER) of the ENSEM Hassan II University Casablanca Morocco. He received his PhD thesis in 2016 in Industrial Engineering in ENSEM Casablanca Morocco. His current research field is Modeling Simulation and Optimization of global supply chain including environmental concerns and reverse logistic, Meta-heuristic, and Supply Chain Management.

R. Gowri, MCA, M.Phil, is pursuing full- time research in Department of Computer Science, Periyar University, Salem, India for the past 2 years. She is a UGC-NET JRF candidate doing research under guidance of Dr. R. Rathipriya, Assistant Professor, Department of Computer Science, Periyar University, Salem.

K. Jagatheesan received his B.E degree in Electrical and Electronics Engineering in 2009 from Hindusthan College of Engineering and Technology, Coimbatore and M.E. degree in Applied Electronics in 2012 from Paavai College of Engineering, Namakkal, and Ph.D. Degree in Information and Communication Engineering from Anna University Chennai in 2017.Currently, he is an Assistant Professor in Paavai college of Engineering with the department of Electrical and Electronic Engineering. His area of interest includes Advanced Control System, Electrical Machines and Power system modeling and control and he published more than 35 papers in National/International journals and conferences. He is an Associate Member of UACEE, Member of SCIEI, IACSIT, IAENG, ISRD and Graduate Student Member of IEEE.

G. V. Nagesh Kumar was born in Visakhapatnam, India in 1977. He graduated College of Engineering, Gandhi Institute of Technology and Management, Visakhapatnam, India, Masters Degree from the College of Engineering, Andhra University, Visakhapatnam. He received his Doctoral degree from Jawaharlal Nehru Technological University, Hyderabad. He is presently working as Professor in the Department of Electrical and Electronics Engineering, Vignans Institute of Information Technology, Visakhapatnam. His research interests include gas insulated substations, FACTS devices, Power System Stability analysis, fuzzy logic and neural network applications, distributed generation, Partial Discharge Studies and Bearing less drives. He has published more than 250 research papers in national and international conferences and journals. He received "Sastra Award", "Best Paper Award" and "Best Researcher Award". He is a member of various societies, ISTE, IEEE, IE and System Society of India. He is also a reviewer for IEEE Transactions on Dielectrics and Electrical Insulation, Power Systems and a member on Board of several conferences and journals.

Kalyani Mali is a full Professor at the Department of Computer Science and Engineering, University of Kalyani, Nadia. She was the Head of CSE department 4 times and recently during the period 2014 to 2016. She has more than 25 years of research experience and more than 23 years of teaching experience. She has completed her PhD on the topic Modeling of Heterogeneous Data in Data Mining. Her research interests include pattern recognition, data mining, bioinformatics, soft computing and multimedia.

B. B. Misra is currently working as Dean (Research) at Silicon Institute of Technology, Bhubaneswar, India. He received Bachelor degree from Kanpur University, India, Masters in Computer Science from Utkal University, Bhubaneswar, India and Ph.D. in Engineering from Biju Pattanaik University of Technology, Rourkela, India. He has done his Post Doctoral Research at AJOU University, South Korea. His areas of interests include Data Mining, Bioinformatics, Bio-inspired Computation and Computational Intelligence. He has published one book, three book chapters and more than 150 papers in different journals and conferences. He has been a key note speaker and session chair of different national and international conferences.

K. N. Balasubramanya Murthy received his Bachelor's degree from the Dept. of Electrical Power Engineering, University of Mysore, India, Masters in the Dept. of Electrical Engineering, Indian Institute of Science, Bangalore, India and Ph.D. in the Dept. of Computer Science & Engineering, Indian Institute of Technology, Chennai, India. He is currently the Vice-Chancellor of PES University, Bangalore and Director of PES Institute of Technology. He is currently serving as a member of a committee constituted by Karnataka Knowledge Council (KKC) for recommending mechanisms to enhance employability of engineering graduates. His research interest includes Networks & Security, Wireless Networks, Parallel Algorithms and Soft Computing.

Keerthiraj Nagaraj is currently pursuing PhD in the field of wireless and mobile networks from Electrical and Computer Engineering department at University of Florida, Gainesville, USA. He completed M.S from the department of Electrical and Computer Engineering at University of Florida, USA, and B.E from the department of Electronics and Communication Engineering at PES Institute of Technology, Bangalore, India. His research interests lie in the fields of Wireless and mobile networks, Mobile social networks, Social network analysis, Wireless localization and Nature inspired algorithms. You can reach him at keerthi (dot) n250 at gmail (dot) com.

Sarat Chandra Nayak holds a Ph.D. degree in Computer Engineering from VSSUT, Burla, India and M. Tech. in Computer Science from Utkal University, Bhubaneswar, India. His research interests are Data Mining, Soft Computing, Predictive Systems, Financial Time Series Forecasting, Computational Intelligence, Evolutionary Computation, and Classification. He has more than 30 research articles in reputed International journals and conferences, and 4 book chapters in his credit. He has 10 years of experience in teaching and research. Dr. Nayak currently associated with computer science and engineering department as a Professor at Kommuri Pratap Reddy Institute of Technology, Hyderabad, India.

Vahid Pourmostaghimi was born in Tabriz, Iran, in Jan 1982. He received the B.S. Degree in Manufacturing Engineering in 2006 and the M.Sc. Degree in Manufacturing Engineering in 2009 from the University of Tabriz, Iran. He is currently a Ph.D. student of Manufacturing Engineering at University of Tabriz, Faculty of Mechanical and Manufacturing Engineering. His focused area of research is adaptive control optimization, intelligent machining, predictive modelling in machining processes using metaheuristic methods.

R. Rathipriya, M.Sc, M.Phil, MCA, Ph.D, is an Assistant Professor in the Department of Computer Science, Periyar University, Salem for past 9 years. She has 11 years of teaching experience and 9 years of research experience. She has produced more than 50 research contributions in National and International Journals and Conferences.

Ram P. Rustagi received his M.Tech degree from the Indian Institute of Science, Bangalore, India. He received his PhD in the Department of Computer Science & Engineering, Indian Institute of Technology, Delhi, India. He is currently a Professor in the Department of Computer Science & Engineering, PES University, Bangalore, India. Previously he had served several industries like Kirusa Software Pvt Ltd, Pronto Networks Inc., Abeona Networks, Inc., Savera Systems Inc, and C-DoT. He has filed two patents. His areas of interest include Software Defined Networking, Vehicular Clouds, Web Archiving, Cyber security, Audio WiFi. He is a senior member of IEEE.

J. Sangeetha is pursuing her Ph.D. from Visvesvaraya Technological University, Belgaum, India. She is currently working as Associate Professor, in the Department of Computer Science & Engineering at PES University, Bangalore, India. She received her Master's in Information Technology from Bangalore University, India and Bachelor's degree from the Department of Computer Science & Engineering, from Bangalore University, India. Her research interest includes Mobile Computing, Wireless Networks, Networks and Security and Nature Inspired Algorithms.

Sarbartha Sarkar is currently pursuing M.Tech in Tunneling and Underground Space Technology in Indian Institute of Technology (Indian School of Mines), Dhanbad. He completed his B.Tech in Civil Engineering from Hooghly Engineering & Technology College. He has published his research works in peer reviewed International journals. His research interest is RC Structure, Environmental Engineering and Tunnel engineering.

Soumya Sen is an Assistant professor in A. K. Choudhury School of Information Technology under University of Calcutta since March, 2009. He has been awarded with Ph.D. (Tech) degree in 2016 from Department of Computer Science & Engineering, University of Calcutta. He obtained his M. Tech. Degree in Computer science & Engineering from University of Calcutta in 2007. Prior to this he completed his M.Sc in Computer & Information Science in the year 2005 also from University of Calcutta. Before joining A. K. Choudhury School of Information Technology Dr.

Sen also worked in IBM India Pvt. Ltd and RS Software. His industrial expertization includes ERP & Data Warehouse. Currently his research area interests are Data Warehouse & OLAP Tool, Big Data, Service Engineering, Distributed Database. He has around 25 research papers published in Peer reviewed journals and International Conferences. He has 3 patents registered in USA, Japan & South Korea. He has published also published a book with Springer, Germany. His research collaborations include Institutes like Ca' Foscari University, Italy; Winona State University, USA; National Institute of Technology, Duragapur, India etc.

Polamraju V. S. Sobhan was born in Ongole, A.P, India in 1977. He received his B.Tech. in Electrical and Electrical Engineering from SVH COE, Nagarjuna University, India in 1999 and M.E. degree in Control Systems from College of Engineering, Andhra University, India in 2002. He is pursuing Ph.D. from JNT University, Kakinada, India. Presently he is working as an Associate Professor in the Department of Electrical and Electrical Engineering, VFSTR University, Guntur, India since 2006. His research interests are Optimisation, Controller design, Active magnetic bearings and bearingless drives.

B. Venkateswararao was born in Ramabhadrapuram, India in 1978. He received his Bachelor degree in Electrical and Electronics Engineering from College of Engineering, Gandhi Institute of Technology And Management(GITAM) Visakapatnam, Andhra Pradesh, India in 2000, the Master degree in Electrical Power Engineering from the College of Engineering, JNTU, Hyderabad in 2007 and He received his Doctoral degree from Jawaharlal Nehru Technological University, Hyderabad in 2015. He is presently working as Associate Professor in the Department of Electrical and Electronics Engineering, V R Siddhartha Engineering College, Vijayawada. His research interests are Power system stability analysis, FACTS devices, Power system control and power system optimization. He has published several research papers in national and international conferences and journals. He is a member of ISTE and IE.

Mohammad Zadshakoyan was born in Maragheh, Iran, in May 1964. He received his B.S. Degree in Mechanical Engineering from University of Tabriz in 1987 and the M.Sc. Degree in Mechanical Engineering from the University of Bordeaux, France, in 1994. He received the Ph.D. Degree in Manufacturing Engineering from University of Bordeaux, France, in 1998. He is now Assistant Professor in the faculty of Mechanical and Manufacturing Engineering at University of Tabriz. His research interests include adaptive control, intelligent machining, mechatronic in manufacturing systems.

Index

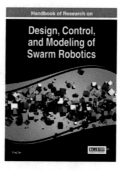

Stay Current on the Latest Emerging Research Developments

Become an IGI Global Reviewer for Authored Book Projects

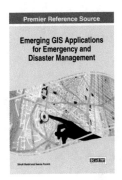

The overall success of an authored book project is dependent on quality and timely reviews.

In this competitive age of scholarly publishing, constructive and timely feedback significantly decreases the turnaround time of manuscripts from submission to acceptance, allowing the publication and discovery of progressive research at a much more expeditious rate. Several IGI Global authored book projects are currently seeking highly qualified experts in the field to fill vacancies on their respective editorial review boards:

Applications may be sent to:
development@igi-global.com

Applicants must have a doctorate (or an equivalent degree) as well as publishing and reviewing experience. Reviewers are asked to write reviews in a timely, collegial, and constructive manner. All reviewers will begin their role on an ad-hoc basis for a period of one year, and upon successful completion of this term can be considered for full editorial review board status, with the potential for a subsequent promotion to Associate Editor.

If you have a colleague that may be interested in this opportunity, we encourage you to share this information with them.

Information Resources Management Association

Advancing the Concepts & Practices of Information Resources
Management in Modern Organizations

Become an IRMA Member

Members of the **Information Resources Management Association (IRMA)** understand the importance
of community within their field of study. The Information Resources Management Association is an ideal
venue through which professionals, students, and academicians can convene and share the latest industry
innovations and scholarly research that is changing the field of information science and technology.
Become a member today and enjoy the benefits of membership as well as the opportunity to collaborate
and network with fellow experts in the field.

IRMA Membership Benefits:

- **One FREE Journal Subscription**

- **30% Off Additional
  Journal Subscriptions**

- **20% Off Book Purchases**

- Updates on the latest events and research on
  Information Resources Management through
  the IRMA-L listserv.

- Updates on new open access and downloadable
  content added to Research IRM.

- A copy of the Information Technology Management
  Newsletter twice a year.

- A certificate of membership.

IRMA Membership $195

Scan code or visit **irma-international.org** and begin by
selecting your free journal subscription.

Membership is good for one full year.

Printed in the United States
By Bookmasters